Democracy's Mountain

Public Lands History

GENERAL EDITORS

Ruth M. Alexander
Adrian Howkins
Jared Orsi
Sarah Payne

Democracy's Mountain

RUTH M. ALEXANDER

*Longs Peak and the
Unfulfilled Promises of
America's National Parks*

UNIVERSITY OF OKLAHOMA PRESS ː NORMAN

Publication of this book is made possible through the generous support of The Charles Redd Center for Western Studies at Brigham Young University, Colorado State University, and The Kerr Foundation, Inc.

Library of Congress Cataloging-in-Publication Data

Names: Alexander, Ruth M., 1954– author.
Title: Democracy's mountain : Longs Peak and the unfulfilled promises of America's national park / Ruth M. Alexander.
Other titles: Public lands history ; v. 5.
Description: Norman : University of Oklahoma Press [2023] | Series: Public lands history series ; volume 5 | Includes bibliographical references and index. | Summary: "Narrates the social and environmental history of Longs Peak in Rocky Mountain National Park with a focus on climbing and hiking the summit. It offers a greater historical understanding to help mitigate and overcome the harms to this natural treasure" Provided by publisher.
Identifiers: LCCN 2022059276 | ISBN 978-0-8061-9267-3 (hardcover) | ISBN 978-0-8061-9268-0 (paperback)
Subjects: LCSH: Rocky Mountain National Park (Agency : U.S.)—Management. | Longs Peak (Colo.)—History. | Longs Peak (Colo.)—Environmental conditions. | Rocky Mountain National Park (Colo.)
Classification: LCC F782.L83 A54 2023 | DDC 978.869—dc23/eng/20230223
LC record available at https://lccn.loc.gov/2022059276

Democracy's Mountain: Longs Peak and the Unfulfilled Promises of America's National Parks is Volume 5 in the Public Lands History series.

The paper in this book meets the guidelines for permanence and durability of the Committee on Production Guidelines for Book Longevity of the Council on Library Resources, Inc. ∞

For Kim

CONTENTS

ILLUSTRATIONS

MAPS

PREFACE AND ACKNOWLEDGMENTS

EVERY BOOK HAS AN ORIGIN STORY, and this one extends back to my youth. As a child growing up in East Harlem's public housing in the 1960s, I knew absolutely nothing about rock climbing or national parks. Sometimes, my siblings and I raced up and down the stairs of our twenty-story building for fun, and if we found the door to the roof unlocked, we'd head beyond the stairwell, delighting in expansive views of Manhattan. When the elevators at 425 East 105th Street were out of service and climbing the stairs to our tenth-floor apartment became mandatory, we did so with some disgruntlement. Occasionally I climbed trees in Central Park or across the 103rd Street footbridge on Wards Island, but vertical adventure in urban greenspace was not the norm. Rather, most of my time outdoors was spent in flat paved playgrounds, jumping rope, playing Ringo-levio, and roller-skating. Happily, for four consecutive summers, my father and mother (an actor and social worker from Egypt and Indiana, respectively) found affordable rental housing for their growing family (eventually seven kids in all) in the Catskill Mountains. I didn't know there were public lands in the area, including Catskill Park, nor did I learn about the Esopus peoples, a tribe of the Lenapes, who lived in the Catskills until they were displaced by European colonists in the seventeenth century. Nonetheless, during these summers from ages seven to ten I found great pleasure in exploring woods and streams, clambering over boulders, and riding a bicycle down deeply shaded dirt roads.

Summer sojourns to the Catskills became unaffordable the year I finished fifth grade. My adolescence and college years were filled, in all seasons, with exposure to the extraordinary creativity and ambition to be found in New York City as well as its striking disparities of wealth and opportunity. Even as a small child going to public school on 96th Street—the dividing line between East Harlem and the Upper East Side—I had been able to see that differences of race and class profoundly affected how people lived and what they were able to do, how children were perceived and treated by their teachers. By junior high, I was uncomfortably aware that gender mattered as well. The burgeoning civil rights, antipoverty, feminist, and gay rights movements offered critical insights into the complex social hierarchies operating in the United States, while the antiwar and environmental movements pushed me to think about the use and misuse of governmental power and humans' troubled relationship with the natural world. At City College of New York, I began to realize that history had extraordinary explanatory power, capable of illuminating the injustices *and* hopes that propelled contemporary women and men into the streets of New York to demand change.

Somehow, amid the intellectual excitement of discovering professors at City College—Joan Kelly Gadol, Barbara Engel, Eric Foner—who offered truly great courses in women's history and the history of United States during the Civil War and Reconstruction, I also learned about Outward Bound and won a scholarship for a month-long wilderness course in North Carolina. I loved the hiking and whitewater canoeing. The two or three days of rock climbing were exhilarating but scary. Outward Bound did not turn me into a rock climber, though it did my older sister Stephanie, who gradually helped me appreciate the problem-solving skills, mental discipline, strength, and agility of good climbers. Still, the Outward Bound experience propelled me toward lifelong athleticism and reawakened the interest in nature that I had begun to develop as a child summering in the Catskills.

More than a decade after that Outward Bound class, I moved to Fort Collins, Colorado, and took a faculty position teaching and researching American women's history and twentieth-century U.S. history at Colorado State University. In the early 2000s I added American environmental history to my teaching and research repertoire and became involved in the Public Lands History Center (PLHC) at CSU, an entity that does historical research and writing for the National Park Service, the U.S. Forest Service, and other state and local agencies. By this time, I was deeply engaged in thinking about how historical analyses of rights and freedom in the United States—who had them and who did not—could be strengthened by inquiries into humans' relationship to the natural and built environments around them. At about the same time, outdoor adventure became increasingly important to my sense of well-being. I took up long-distance road cycling in the foothills near Fort Collins and learned to backcountry ski at Montgomery Pass. I hiked frequently at Lory State Park and Horsetooth Mountain Park and occasionally at Rocky Mountain National Park and other national parks in the west. I hiked to the top of a few Colorado fourteeners, though not Longs Peak. I joined the Bicycle Racing Association of Colorado and began competing in bicycle races at the master's level. The annual Bob Cook Memorial Mt. Evans Hill Climb, in which cyclists race up the highest paved road in North America to a finish just 134 feet below the summit of the 14,264-foot peak, became my favorite event, and I competed in it year after year.

All this outdoor activity encouraged me to think about the values and resources that athletes—especially cyclists, backcountry skiers, and climbers—invest in sports that take them into stunning outdoor settings, often on public lands, where there is substantial risk to both human bodies and the natural environment. The cyclists, skiers, and climbers I knew worked hard to cultivate skills, ethics, and camaraderie suited to enjoying and protecting nature, but they also crashed and fell in hazardous terrain, and the vehicles they drove to races, snow-covered mountains, and rock faces spewed CO_2 and other pollutants into the air, adding to our deepening climate crisis. I saw, too, that all these outdoor sports required expensive equipment, and their participants, like me, were mostly White and middle-class. Moreover, the residents in the rural areas of Colorado where national parks and forests were located, and the employees who managed the public lands where people like me sought challenge and joy, were also White. Over time, these observations would inform the questions I asked about Longs Peak and its history.

In 2008, Cheri Yost, a research specialist at Rocky Mountain National Park's Continental Divide Research Learning Center, reached out to me at the PLHC and asked whether I might be interested in tackling a history project on Colorado's legendary Longs Peak. Cheri wanted a study that inquired into the history of climbers and climbing culture on the beloved fourteener *and* a history of the park's efforts to manage climbers and their environmental impact. I eagerly took on the project and attempted to summit Longs via the *Keyhole* route, turning back only when crowding and jostling on the exposed Narrows rattled my nerves. The setting was spectacular but the conditions were daunting, and I discovered my limits. My report, *People and Nature on a Mountaintop*, was completed in January 2010. I hoped to turn the study into a book, but other projects kept me from doing so for quite some time. In 2016 I was able to spend a semester-long sabbatical rethinking the book's goals, conducting more research, and doing a bit of writing. More time elapsed. In 2019 I decided to give the book something close to full attention. And with the book now ready for publication, I can finally acknowledge, on the printed page, all the people who have helped make it a reality. I am indebted to fellow scholars, archivists, students, park rangers, climbers, friends, and family members who have supported my project and cheered me along the way.

I want to begin by acknowledging that my place of work, Colorado State University, and the places my book studies, Longs Peak and Rocky Mountain National Park, are the traditional and ancestral homelands of the Arapaho, Cheyenne, and Ute nations and peoples. Other Native peoples also came to these places for trade and gatherings of many kinds. Native peoples were the original stewards of these lands. CSU is a great institution and Rocky is a wonderful park, but their founding and development came at a dire cost to indigenous peoples. All of us will benefit if Native connections to these places are renewed. Perhaps this book will make a small contribution toward that goal.

I remain grateful to Cheri Yost for asking me to conduct historical research on Longs in 2009, overseeing that project with great care, and encouraging me to work on a book once the report for the park was done. She read several draft chapters of *Democracy's Mountain* and offered thought-provoking comments. Many others at Rocky Mountain National Park also deserve acknowledgment. Ben Bobowski, Scott Esser, Chelsea Hernandez, Alexandra Hernandez, Sue Langdon, Kelly Dick, Michael Lukens, and Jeff Connor provided practical support, critical information about park management, and genuine encouragement. Mark Magnuson, Kevin Sturmer, and Jane Gordon sat for oral history interviews about professional assignments in the park relevant to Longs Peak. Tim Burchett provided access to the park's archives while I worked on the report. Kelly Cahill, curator of the park's museum collections and archives since 2013, has been an unwavering and enthusiastic guide to the park's hard-copy, digital, and visual collections, and she has answered my frequent queries for documentation with impressive efficiency. She has shown genuine interest in the complexities of my subject matter, and I offer her my profound thanks.

If Cheri Yost was critical to the success of the early report, my colleague Jared Orsi has been essential to the completion of the book. In fall 2019, Jared and I began meeting every two weeks to discuss our book projects, mine on Longs and Rocky, his on Quitobaquito in Organ Pipe Cactus National Monument. Our meetings continued as Covid-19 closed campus, moving online when it was cold and outside when the weather was warm. We helped one another develop conceptual frameworks, interpretive arguments, and narrative trajectories. We reviewed each other's chapters and discussed the contributions historical scholarship can make to public understanding, policy making, and a better future. We learned from one another's different approaches to writing. As writing buddies we produced better books than we would have done had we worked as solitary scholars.

Rocky Mountain National Park holds only some of the primary sources I needed to write this book. Katie Sauer provided friendly and expert assistance as I worked with the Colorado Mountain Club and Jim Detterline collections at the American Alpine Club Library in Golden, Colorado. Naomi Gerakios helped me identify materials related to the history of Longs Peak, climbers, and local tourism at the Estes Park Museum. Unnamed but wonderful archivists and librarians whom I will never meet made it possible for me to use digitized versions of archival sources held at the Boulder Public Library, the Denver Public Library, and the New York Public Library. The National Park Service has digitized an incredible array of historical reports on science and interpretation at national parks and moved the material online. The National Park Service History Electronic Library and Archive collects NPS publications, even the most obscure, allowing me to access sources almost impossible to find in hard copy. The digital Colorado Historic Newspapers Collection has also been vital to my work. I thank all the anonymous individuals who have contributed to creating these important digital research sites.

At CSU a wide circle of colleagues, students, and administrators supported and facilitated this project. Graduate student Catherine Moore and undergraduates Leslie McCutchen and Josh Weinberg provided research and mapping assistance for the early report on Longs. Subsequently, graduate student Mary

Swanson helped me gather and assess the scholarship related to the larger book project while Dillon Maxwell and Beth Hodgell organized some of my digitized primary sources. Graduate students Cori Knudten, Will Wright, and Mark Boxer shared research materials and insights from thesis projects on the history of automobility and energy use in Rocky Mountain National Park, and Ellen Blankers shared primary sources from her thesis research on the history of children's camps in the area around Rocky and Estes Park. Directing Ellen's thesis helped me gain important knowledge about summer camping and children's experience of climbing Longs and other peaks from the 1920s to the 1960s. Colleagues Tracy Brady, Michael Childers, Leisl Carr Childers, Mark Fiege, Adrian Howkins, Prakash Kumar, Jim Lindsay, Ann Little, Janet Ore, Sarah Payne, Doug Sheflin, and Adam Thomas offered thoughtful comments on presentations, conference papers, and drafts of a book proposal. Department chairs Diane Margolf, Doug Yarrington, and Robert Gudmestad supported requests for sabbatical release and funding to cover research travel, fees for oral history transcriptions, and map production. The College of Liberal Arts also provided research and conference funding at crucial stages of my work.

Program managers Maren Bzdek and Ariel Schnee at the PLHC offered administrative support and intellectual feedback on the park project and book. Kristi Ornelas, a PLHC graduate student intern, helped me arrange an extremely fruitful conversation with Steven Ochoa, the current Diversity Internship Cohort coordinator at the Rocky Mountain Conservancy. And while visiting the PLHC and CSU to give a presentation in fall 2021 on the repatriation of three Northern Arapaho children from the Carlisle Indian Industrial School, Yufna Soldier Wolf offered valuable perspective on the Arapaho Pack Trip at Rocky in 1914 and on contemporary efforts to empower Northern Arapaho women and promote understanding of traditional ecological knowledge. I thank her for her gracious and wise counsel.

Jill Baron, a senior research scientist at CSU's Natural Resource Ecology Lab, shared knowledge about ecological research at Rocky and allowed me to accompany her on field trips to the Loch Vale watershed, where she has been monitoring ecosystem processes, especially their response to atmospheric deposition and climate variability, since 1982. Gillian Bowser, an associate professor in the Department of Ecosystem Science and Sustainability at CSU, shared memories about traveling to national parks with her family as a child and becoming one of a tiny number of African American rangers employed in natural resource stewardship at iconic parks such as Yellowstone. Maricela DeMirjyn and Lindsey Schneider, faculty in ethnic studies at CSU, told me about scholars whose work on indigeneity and race might prove useful to my work on climbing and the NPS. Historians Paul Sutter and Thomas Andrews, at the University of Colorado Boulder, offered thoughtful commentary on this project at regional workshops, as did historian Katherine Morrisey at the University of Arizona. Kayann Short, also at UC Boulder, offered research tips on the history of Black families in

Boulder and shared her excellent article on the Blue Bird Club, an organization of White women from Chicago whose members traveled to Boulder each summer, for a period of more than twenty-five years in the early twentieth century, to enjoy independence, female friendship, and Colorado's stunning mountain landscapes. Brooke Neely, at UC Boulder's Center of the American West, told me about the work the center is doing to support Northern Ute, Cheyenne, and Northern Arapaho efforts to reconnect with Rocky and collaborate with park staff in creating exhibits that accurately portray the history and culture of indigenous peoples in the region and their troubled relations with the NPS. She told me, too, about her work on an edited volume that will illuminate contemporary efforts by tribal nations across the United States to redress national parks' colonial history through research, outreach, and careful collaboration.

I am indebted to climbers Dave Rearick, Mike Caldwell, Tommy Caldwell, Tom Hornbein, and Chris Reveley for allowing me to interview them about their climbing experiences on Longs and their views on outdoor recreation and environmental protection. Roger Briggs read the park report with a climber's sharp eye, pointing out errors of fact and interpretation. Bonnie Kamps allowed me to interview her by phone about her (deceased) husband Bob's experience climbing the Diamond with Dave Rearick in 1960. Walt and Marlene Borneman facilitated my efforts to reach out to Hornbein and Reveley and graciously hosted meetings and meals at their Estes Park home. As experienced hikers, climbers, and conservationists who have recreated in Rocky and lived in Estes Park for decades, Walt and Marlene had much to tell me about Longs Peak and Rocky in an interview of their own. They also introduced me to Dave Robertson and Janet Robertson, longtime members of the Colorado Mountain Club. Dave and Janet shared helpful information about change and continuity in the CMC over time, and Janet answered questions about her research on the history of women climbers in Colorado. More recently, Walt introduced me to Estee Rivera Murdock at the Rocky Mountain Conservancy, Erik Murdock at the Access Fund, and Jeffrey Boring at the Estes Valley Land Trust. All three shared critical knowledge about contemporary efforts to boost diversity and inclusion in visitation and interpretation at Rocky and in Estes Park. Erik also sharpened my understanding of current debates about pending regulations on fixed anchors at climbing sites on federal public lands. Phyllis Greenhill transcribed many of my oral history recordings with impressive speed and accuracy.

Sophia Linn, associate director of the Geospatial Centroid at CSU, oversaw the creation of maps by graduate student Amanda Hastings and the production of a photograph showing climbing routes on Longs by undergraduate Connor Siegfreid. Climber, author, and photographer Topher Donohue granted permission to use one of his beautiful photographs of Longs to show East Face and Diamond climbing routes, and he patiently reviewed our route placements for accuracy. I'm thrilled to feature his photo in my book, and I accept responsibility for any remaining errors in route placement.

Andrea Sanchez, Kim Kita, Olaf Morales Borrales, and Idalia Paz y Puente Fernandez applauded my progress on this book while commending my willingness to take breaks away from it to teach history and work with them at the CSU Todos Santos Center in Mexico. Antonio Diego, the zero waste coordinator at the center, often hiked with me in the hills behind the small campus, and I greatly enjoyed our conversations about environmental and societal challenges in both the United States and Mexico. As it turned out, teaching history and conducting oral history interviews in Todos Santos proved directly relevant to this book, as I discovered important parallels between the history of national parks, recreation, and tourism in the United States and the history of tourism and ecotourism in Baja California Sur.

Alessandra Jacobi Tamulevich, acquisitions editor at the University of Oklahoma Press, steered this book through the approval process with expertise and care. OUP's outside readers offered perceptive and helpful comments on the book proposal and completed manuscript. Having revealed her identity as a reader, Annie Gilbert Coleman met with me on Zoom for a fruitful discussion about my articulation of the NPS's evolving understanding of its multidimensional mission. I am indebted to my excellent copyeditor, Laurel Anderton, and to Amy Hernandez for spearheading the marketing of my book.

Throughout the writing of this book, my spirits have been buoyed by family and friends. My mother was in her nineties when she read my park report on Longs Peak and told me how much she liked it. She is now 101, and I'm grateful that I can thank her for her continued love and support. All my siblings, at various points in time, talked with me about my book and offered encouragement. Stephanie read a chapter and suggested ways to improve my descriptions of climbers, routes, and accidents and also answered innumerable questions about climbing techniques and gear. More importantly, Patrice, Stephanie, Mark, Nancy, Chip, and Matthew demanded my presence at family gatherings (whether in person on online during the pandemic) and made sure I remembered how to have fun. My nieces and nephews and their sweet offspring have generously shared their ebullience and laughter with me.

With Jane Reina, Pattie Cowell, Sherry Pomering, and Bruce Ronda I've enjoyed stimulating conversations about our varied projects and the events and trends shaping our troubled yet hopeful world. Renee Rondeau and Gordon Rodda have been close friends, fellow outdoor adventurers, and supporters of my work on Longs since its earliest days. As ecological scientists, they have influenced my framing of questions about national parks' environmental policies and challenges. Sandy North, Karin Budding, Robin Waterman, Erica Brann, and Lynne Anderson have been racing partners, hiking companions, and good friends for many years; all of them cheered me on as I wrote this book. When I was struggling with chapter 5, Sandy asked astute questions about the chapter's narrative arguments during a long hike in Rocky. Karin, a climber as well as a cyclist, offered helpful comments on chapter 6. Robin reminded me to measure progress in small steps when the size and scope of this project seemed overwhelming. On bikes, hikes, and at one another's homes, the six of us have amused and cared for one another.

Heidi von Nieda, Dave McComb, Bob Medlock, Marilyn Murphy, and Mary Davis have been excellent friends, especially during the pandemic. In 2020, when indoor social gatherings were proscribed and vaccines were nowhere in sight, we gathered outside for dinners on Heidi and Dave's patio, sometimes in winter jackets and hats, with members of each household bringing their own food, plates, utensils, and cups and sitting six feet from their friends. Everyone in this group has supported my book writing, in part by knowing when it was important to distract me from it. And we're still gathering for dinners, though we now have a greater choice of venues and can share food at a common table. So, too, since mid-2021, Steve and Karen Workman, my brother- and sister-in-law, have organized wonderful summer picnics in their backyard less than a mile from our home. With the pandemic still a meaningful threat, these outdoor gatherings have provided gratifying opportunities to socialize and catch up on family news.

Finally, I want to thank my husband, Kim Workman. He has lived with this book for more years than he wants to count and listened to me talk about Longs Peak day after day. He has attended my presentations about Longs and Rocky and pored over climbing maps and photos by my side. I'm lucky that Kim grew up in Fort Collins, climbed Longs' *Cable* route as a twelve- or thirteen-year-old, learned to ski at Rocky's Hidden Valley Ski Area, and as a teenager worked on a restoration crew at Hidden Valley one summer after a damaging windstorm. His firsthand accounts of playing and working in the park have enhanced my historical understanding of Rocky and its visitors.

Kim has watched this book come to completion while keeping my bikes and other outdoor gear in excellent repair. I think he knew I would be happier and would write a better book if I continued to ride and race as well as hike, camp, and ski. My solo rides around Fort Collins energized me, cleared my head, and allowed me to think through myriad writing challenges; they also afforded glorious views of Longs Peak across the seasons. Bike races filled me with excitement and offered lessons in how to face hard challenges and cultivate resilience. The multisport excursions Kim and I took together to national parks, county open spaces, wilderness areas, and state and national forests in Colorado, New Mexico, Wyoming, Idaho, Montana, Oklahoma, Tennessee, and North Carolina kept my spirits high and enriched my historical understanding of indigenous peoples and all Americans' relationship to their public lands. Kim and I cheered when one or the other of us won a spot on a race podium, and I suspect he'll shout with joy when *Democracy's Mountain* claims a spot on a table or shelf in our home. This book is dedicated to Kim and to adventuring in a world made more sustainable and democratic through shared joy and united effort.

ABBREVIATIONS

AAC	American Alpine Club
AAL	American Alpine Club Library
AIRFA	American Indian Religious Freedom Act of 1978
CDRLC	Continental Divide Research Learning Center
CMC	Colorado Mountain Club
CMCC	Colorado Mountain Club Collection
NAGPRA	Native American Graves Protection and Repatriation Act of 1990
NEPA	National Environmental Policy Act of 1969
NHPA	National Historic Preservation Act of 1966
NPS	National Park Service
ROMO	Rocky Mountain National Park
SAR	search and rescue
SAR	*Superintendent's Annual Report*
SMR	*Superintendent's Monthly Report*

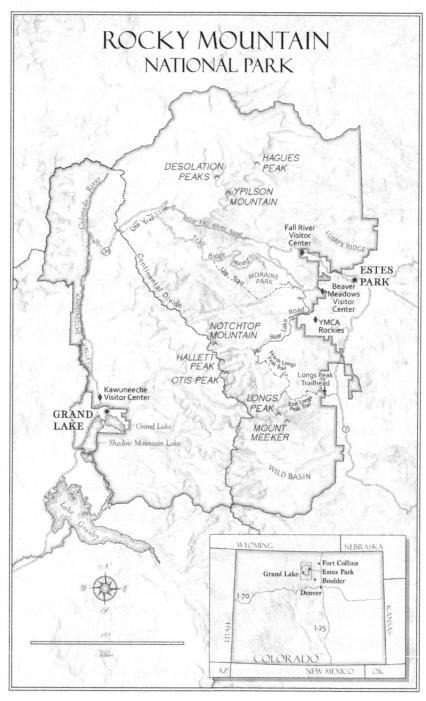

ROCKY MOUNTAIN
NATIONAL PARK

Colorado River

DESOLATION
PEAKS ˄

HAGUES
^ PEAK

˄ YPILSON
MOUNTAIN

Ute Trail

Old Fall River Road

Fall River
Visitor
Center

LUMPY RIDGE

Trail

Ridge *Road*

Ute Trail

MORAINE
PARK

**ESTES
PARK**

34

Continental Divide

Beaver
Meadows
Visitor
Center

KAWUNEECHE VALLEY

NOTCHTOP
MOUNTAIN
˄

Lake Road

YMCA
Rockies

Bear

HALLETT
PEAK ˄

*North Longs
Peak Trail*

OTIS PEAK ˄

Longs Peak
Trailhead

Kawuneeche
Visitor Center

LONGS
PEAK ^

*East Longs
Peak Trail*

**GRAND
LAKE**

Grand Lake

— *Shadow Mountain Lake*

MOUNT
MEEKER ^

7

WILD BASIN

*Lake
Granby*

N
W ⊕ E
S

WYOMING   NEBRASKA

• Fort Collins
Grand Lake   Estes Park
• Boulder

I-70   Denver

UTAH

I-25

KANSAS

10

Miles

COLORADO

AZ   NEW MEXICO   OK

Map 1. Rocky Mountain National Park. Cartography by Amanda Hastings.

Introduction

AT 14,259 FEET, Longs Peak towers over Colorado's northern Front Range and all the other summits in Rocky Mountain National Park. It captures the eye and imagination of residents and visitors alike in a "vacationland" state known for its stunning alpine landscapes and superlative recreational opportunities.[1] Indeed, Longs has been a prized site for mountaineering adventure since the 1870s, daring women, men, and children to test themselves against its bouldered slopes and steeply vertical granite faces. The peak provided inspiration for Rocky's founding in 1915, and since 1960 its Diamond Face has been a site of astonishing climbing achievements. In the second decade of the twenty-first century, Longs remains a highly popular destination, drawing over thirty-five thousand visitors annually, with ten thousand or so reaching its summit via more than 120 technical and nontechnical routes. The *Keyhole* route requires no ropes or protective gear, but climbers must scramble on hands and feet across unstable rock, along narrow, exposed ledges, and up a steeply pitched trough as they snake around Longs to its summit. Climber Mike Caldwell compares it to "a castle with defenses" that does not readily admit intruders.[2] The technical routes up Longs' East Face and nearly vertical Diamond wall present skilled rock climbers (most using protective ropes and gear, a few climbing "free solo" without protection) with some of the most challenging alpine ascents in North America. Precisely because of its difficulty of ascent, climbers revere Longs as a mountain of exhilarating challenge and grand reward.

Not surprisingly, the rewards of climbing on Longs have always been accompanied by risk and real harm. Fierce storms and lightning develop with little warning, even on sunny summer days. Seventy-one people have died on the peak since record keeping began in the 1880s, succumbing to falls, rockslides, and treacherous changes in weather. Many others have been seriously injured.[3] Other risks and harms are also present on Longs, though less obvious than threats to climber safety. By law, Rocky Mountain National Park must protect

1

and preserve the magnificent natural resources within its borders, but climbers' hands, feet, bolts, pitons, and trash have damaged Longs' fragile alpine plants, disrupted its wildlife, polluted its lakes, and marred its granite walls. Climate change and pollution—related in part to the vehicles, technical gear, and touristic infrastructure used by backcountry climbers—are also taking their toll on the mountain. Additionally, though Longs Peak sits in a national park established to exemplify the United States' commitment to the freedoms of a democratic people, both recreation and cultural interpretation on the peak reveal a repudiation and evasion of this obligation. Longs has been a nearly all-White site of outdoor adventure since the 1870s, continuing to mirror the nation's tenacious racial divides, even into the twenty-first century.[4]

The risks and harms on Longs deserve as much attention as climbers' pursuit of reward, and this book's goal is to bring reward and risk, along with the ethics and practices of care used to manage them, into simultaneous focus. In so doing, it asserts that Rocky and the National Park Service (NPS) have always contended with three fundamental obligations or promises of reward to Americans. The Organic Act, establishing the National Park Service in 1916, clearly identified two of the three obligations—to manage national parks as sites of visitor enjoyment and resource preservation.[5] Simultaneously, the Organic Act assumed that national parks would serve as sites of democratic freedom and equality. After all, national parks were, by definition, public lands owned by and for the people of the United States. Yet, until recently, the NPS, Rocky, and other national parks treated their pledge to democracy as something that could be taken for granted, rather than as an obligation requiring intentional practice and critique. Thus, while historians readily acknowledge the long-standing tension between visitor enjoyment and preservation in national parks, with the pleasure of visitors, including climbers, often taking precedence over environmental protection, they have barely begun to examine what democracy has meant and how it has been practiced—or neglected—in the National Park System. The history of Longs Peak and Rocky invite us to examine the interplay between visitor enjoyment, preservation, and democracy—and the risks of undermining them—over the span of more than a century.

The belief that national parks should embrace three fundamental obligations or promises of reward was first articulated by Frederick Law Olmsted Sr. (1822–1903) in 1865. A landscape architect best known for his design of urban parks, Olmsted also played a critical role in conceptualizing the purpose and value of national parks when he served briefly on the commission charged with managing Congress's grant of Yosemite Valley and the Mariposa Big Tree Grove to California as a public park. Drafting his *Preliminary Report* on the new park's value and proper management while the Union struggled to end the horrors of the Civil War, Olmsted assigned Yosemite a vital role in the nation's redemption of liberal values. He affirmed the federal government's decision to grant Yosemite Valley to California "upon the express conditions that the premises shall be held for the public's use, resort, and recreation . . . inalienable for all time" and declared it the "main duty" of the United States government, "the grounds of which rest on . . . the eternal base of equity and benevolence . . . to provide means of protection for all its citizens in the pursuit of happiness." In Olmsted's view, public parks were essential to the betterment of a democratic republic. The Almighty had "implanted in every human being" the "power of appreciating natural beauty," and science had shown that people were enlivened in body, mind, and spirit and moved to greater happiness when able to escape "ordinary cares" and experience the sublimity of nature. In fact, without "occasional recreation" and "release from business and household cares," men and women could not "proper[ly] exercise" their "intellectual and moral forces" or attend fully to their "important responsibilities." Wealthy Americans might purchase lovely places in nature for their exclusive gratification, but the government bore responsibility for making uplifting natural settings available to all the nation's people.[6]

Imagining public parks as places facilitating the rightful pursuit of happiness—indeed, the full humanity and dignity of a free people—Olmsted also conceived them as places dedicated to the preservation of nature. Like others of his generation, Olmsted lamented the environmental degradation of the Niagara Falls area produced by tawdry tourist concessions, grist and paper mills, and a stable operating near the stunning waterfalls. Knowing that "pecuniary advantage" would surely accrue to entrepreneurs and the state of California as visitation to Yosemite mounted, Olmsted urged those managing the park—a veritable "museum of natural science"—to resist the lure of touristic development and protect the park for the long term. Yosemite's commissioners must preserve its precious plant species and other natural resources against "artificial constructions . . . convenience . . . carelessness or wanton destructiveness."[7]

Olmsted's vision of public parks was profoundly aspirational, guided by the natural rights doctrine articulated in the Declaration of Independence and the U.S. Constitution, an aesthetic approach to the benefits of immersion in nature, a deep appreciation for America's rich natural resources, and emerging conservation values. As a key progenitor of the national park idea, Olmsted also reflected some of the prejudices and blind spots of social elites in his era. Olmsted was a staunch proponent of women's rights and spoke unambiguously in his *Preliminary Report* about wage-earning women's just demand for healthful recreation in nature, yet he neglected to speak of the legitimacy of African Americans' access to public parks. He was an opponent of slavery and overt racial oppression yet viewed Black Americans as people not yet fully civilized or Christian. So, too, Olmsted considered Native Americans savages and worried they would harm Yosemite by crossing its boundaries to hunt, camp, and light fires. He failed to recognize that Miwok peoples had called Yosemite home for generations and stewarded its resources. Olmsted similarly declined to acknowledge that English and European colonials grew in their understanding of natural rights, democracy, and federalism by observing the governing systems of Native Americans, with these observations informing the founding fathers' writing of the U.S. Constitution. Nor did he admit the illogic of the United States treating Native peoples as uncivilized dependents, deserving neither the individual rights of free citizens nor the collective rights of members of sovereign tribes.[8] Nonetheless, Olmsted conceptualized public parks as places of natural beauty essential to a free people's rightful pursuit of happiness and full humanity, establishing a principled standard against which national parks might be measured. And in declaring it a "duty" of government to preserve nature in Yosemite, he invited subsequent generations of Americans to evaluate national parks' care of their natural resources.[9]

Olmsted's vision subsequently inspired the founding of Yellowstone National Park in 1872 and, between 1890 and 1903, the creation of Sequoia National Park, Yosemite National Park, Mount Rainier National Park, Crater Lake National Park, and Wind Cave National Park. Theodore Roosevelt echoed Olmsted's sentiments when, in laying the cornerstone of the gateway to Yellowstone National Park in Gardiner, Montana, in 1903, he declared, "The creation and preservation of such a great natural playground . . . is noteworthy in its essential democracy. . . . This Park was created, and is now administered, for the benefit and enjoyment of the people."[10]

So, too, Olmsted's son, Fredrick Law Olmsted Jr., carried elements of his father's thinking forward. By 1916, however, when Olmsted Jr. penned the statement of purpose at the center of the Organic Act establishing the NPS, he articulated his father's ideas in a conceptual shorthand. The "fundamental purpose" of national parks, Olmsted Jr. wrote, "is to conserve the scenery and the natural and historic objects and the wildlife therein, and to provide for the enjoyment of the same in such manner and by such means as will leave them unimpaired for the enjoyment of future generations."[11] Olmsted Jr. did not bother to define the relationship of immersion in undeveloped nature to the rights and interests of a free people. Rather, "enjoyment" was shorn of the meaning Olmsted Sr. intended, detached from its relationship to human equality and Americans' just pursuit of happiness. In this regard, the founding of the NPS reflected the limits of the Progressive era from which it emerged—that is, the reform movement's disinclination to challenge the "scientific" racism, disenfranchisement, segregation, and violence that arose from the dismantling of Reconstruction and the conquest of the American West.[12] So, too, the Organic Act neglected to address the scientific value of preservation or explain how managers were to satisfy visitor interests and preserve park resources simultaneously. Indeed, as we'll see in chapter 1, advocates of national parks hoped the new "playgrounds" would stimulate commercial enterprise and the development of touristic infrastructure. They had forgotten Olmsted Sr.'s admonitions about tourism and ignored its capacity to harm park environments.

Over time, with so little spelled out in national parks' founding legislation, risk and harm, along with reward, became essential parts of the national park story. Indeed, as on Longs Peak, three forms of risk and harm became persistent and problematic across the entire National Park System. First and most obviously, visitors who pursued enjoyment in parks—especially those who ventured into rugged backcountry settings—risked exposure to the elements, even fatal injury, and imposed on parks a substantial burden of responsibility for education, protection, search, rescue, and recovery. Second, though national parks were tasked by their founding legislation with fostering both visitor enjoyment and preservation, over time touristic infrastructure and the heavy human imprint on national parks risked compromising both the quality of visitors' experience and parks' natural and historical environments. Finally, though owned by and for the American people, national parks risked (and quickly became) places of racial and class privilege. Many parks were established in places where predominantly White settler populations had recently expelled Native tribes, and people of color were not welcome in the new pleasure grounds, whether as park visitors, staff, or indigenous peoples attempting to sustain sovereign and sacred connections to their homelands. In design, amenities, and cultural interpretation, national parks appealed to middle- and upper-class White Americans with leisure time, money, and a fondness for park origin stories that began with Euro-American adventurers rather than with the Native peoples of North America.

Fine-grained historical study of a single emblematic peak in a famous national park gives us an opportunity to see how visitors and park managers have defined reward in one place and what they have perceived and experienced as risk and harm. It allows us to examine how, when, and why climbers and managers on Longs have thought it necessary to rebalance reward and risk by modifying their ethics and practices of care, and it permits us to see what their efforts have achieved. Each chapter in this book narrates and evaluates the handling of rewards and risks related to visitor enjoyment, preservation, and democracy on Longs and in Rocky Mountain National Park during a distinct period, moving from the nineteenth century to the present.

Democracy's Mountain offers a set of related arguments. I begin with the broad contention that we must recognize national parks' three fundamental obligations—to visitor enjoyment, preservation, and democracy—and challenge the presumption that the history of national parks can be told properly as a history of tension between the NPS's so-called dual missions—visitor enjoyment and the preservation of park resources. The tension between preservation and visitor enjoyment is certainly very real, and many valuable studies (discussed below) have shown that national park environments have been compromised by policies that prioritized the scenic pleasure and comfort of visitors over resource protection. Still, in lamenting national parks' halting investment in what conservationist Aldo Leopold called a "land ethic"—that is, an ethic dedicated to safeguarding the "integrity, stability, and beauty of the biotic community"—scholars have overlooked Leopold's keen recognition that humans' ill-conceived efforts to master the environment and use it for their pleasure overlapped historically with unjust efforts to master other humans. One did not occur without the other. Until recently, national park scholarship has neglected those people who have been removed or excluded from parks, overlooking contests about human freedom and justice that are at the core of U.S. history and the national park story. And it disregarded Olmsted Sr. and other Americans (whom we will encounter in the chapters that follow) who sought to remind the public that national parks are part of the United States' ongoing democratic project. This book gives democracy its deserved place in national park history. [13]

In a second and related argument, I argue that national park visitors should be understood as citizens, not just consumers of enjoyment, who have both rights and obligations related to public lands. Scholarship that focuses on the tension between enjoyment and preservation in national parks stereotypes the typical visitor as a modern consumer who travels through national parks in a gas-guzzling car, enjoys scenic views as commodities, and is oblivious to preservation imperatives. My historical examination of climbers on Longs has taught me to question and complicate this stereotype. On Longs Peak climbers have played critical roles in managing reward and risk. They have acted not simply as consumers of touristic and recreational reward but also as backcountry guides, educators in climbing skills and safety, skilled search and rescue operators, resource stewards, and vocal conservationists. Many have behaved, in other words, as responsible citizens helping to set standards for safe recreation and natural resource conservation in wilderness settings. Importantly, park superintendents have depended on climbers' civic investments in human safety and environmental preservation because inadequate budgets have always prompted them to prioritize care for Rocky's crowded "front country"—its busy roads, picnic areas, and wayside trails—over care for backcountry sites such as Longs. Certainly, carelessness and poor judgment among climbers have presented enduring problems on the celebrated peak, but this fact should not obscure many climbers' active partnership with park management or their willingness to endorse ethics of care encompassing human safety and environmental preservation. Indeed, climbers have sometimes taken stronger positions on environmental conservation than park officials. Park managers (along with historians) would be well advised to take seriously the multiple roles of climbers in the past and consider how their efforts to preserve both human life and nature on a site such as Longs might inform contemporary initiatives. In fact, as we will see in the epilogue, the NPS and its parks are presently heavily invested in "civic engagement"—that is, in treating visitors as essential partners in park management. The history of Longs has lessons to offer about the complexity of visitors' identities and their potential to act, not as consumers, but as collaborative citizens.

Third, this study shows that even in civic partnership, climbers and park staff have found safeguarding humans and the environment to be elusive goals, involving difficult choices, compromises, and circumstances beyond their immediate control. Though climbers and rangers have often partnered to promote safety and preservation, they have eschewed many forms of restriction and oversight, rejecting, for example, the idea of limiting access to Longs to those who meet strict criteria for mountaineering skills, appropriate equipment and clothing, and adequate food and water. They have proscribed behaviors obviously harmful to the environment, such as leaving trash on the mountain, but have rejected numeric limits on peak visitation that might reduce dangerous crowding among climbers or help mitigate their impact on alpine soils, water, rocks, plants, and animals. So, too, though standards of natural resource protection have risen appreciably over time, especially in response to the findings of ecological and climate science, the means to reach these standards remain insufficient. Many of those who play and work in national parks realize that place-specific "leave no trace" principles and practices developed and embraced in the 1970s, 1980s, and 1990s no longer suffice. Understanding climate change, they know that the most serious threats to natural park environments originate from human and industrial activities that occur well beyond park boundaries. Rangers and climbers are not in a position, however, to create policies or treaties that would compel national or global transitions to low-emission and renewable energy technologies, and they themselves remain dependent on products and industries that contribute to global climate change, loss of biodiversity, and the widespread pollution of water, soil, and air. Nonetheless, they can try to imagine and model both sustainable practices and civic engagement and thereby work for a better future.[14]

Finally, unlike the risk of harm to human bodies and the environment, the risk of harm to democracy itself—especially in the form of racial exclusion—has historically been overlooked by climbers and park staff on Longs. In behaving as citizens—not just as visiting pleasure seekers—and in elaborating an ethic of care, however imperfect, that encompassed human safety and the natural environment, White climbers seem not to have noticed that the grand rewards they enjoyed occurred in the context of loss to people of color. Longs Peak became a mountaineering prize just as Native Americans were expelled from nearly all of Colorado, including the area that would become Rocky Mountain National Park. Colorado's White majority subsequently adopted practices of racial segregation and discrimination that determined who was welcome in the gateway towns of Estes Park and Grand Lake and in Rocky Mountain National Park itself, who had the means to travel and could do so in safety and with dignity, and who had opportunities to participate in backcountry recreation. Practices and norms of racial exclusion persisted in the park and its gateway communities as people of color across the United States challenged barriers to racial equality in recreation and travel as well as in education, housing, employment, and policing. Indeed, these norms withstood the passage of the Civil Rights Act of 1964, which out-lawed discrimination and segregation on the basis of race, color, religion, and national origin in public places and accommodations. Though White women gained a significant place in mountaineering on Longs, albeit not one of full equality, people of color remained absent. Neither the park nor organizations such as the Colorado Mountain Club and Rocky Mountain Conservancy showed much interest in challenging long-standing patterns of racial exclusion or attract-ing a diverse demographic to the park or mountaineering. Efforts to recover the history and archaeological remains of Ute, Arapaho, Cheyenne, and other peoples in the park area and to engage actively with current members of tribes who still consider Estes Park and Rocky part of their homeland were similarly modest.

In the twenty-first century, important indicators of changes are broadly evident. Women are closing the gap with men in climbing ability and gaining acclaim for their stunning achievements. Young people of color are mobilizing to claim their rightful place in rock climbing and national parks, and they are com-mitting themselves to protecting parks' natural resources *and* their indigenous heritage. Organizations ranging from the (local) Colorado Mountain Club and Rocky Mountain Conservancy to the (national) Sierra Club and Access Fund are working to align long-standing commitments to visitor enjoyment and natural resource preservation with the still elusive goal of full democracy. So, too, NPS leaders and Native American tribes are increasingly invested in restoring indige-nous connections to national park land and telling honest stories of the nation's past. These promising developments are slowly encouraging managers at parks such as Rocky to consider innovations of scope and scale that might encourage more people of color to visit national parks, help Native communities rebuild ancestral ties to park lands, and democratize park history and experience. Still, institutionalizing new practices of care in the park system is difficult and often frustratingly slow.[15]

Longs Peak has not previously been the subject of scholarly inquiry, but it has been featured in numerous books about climbing history written for popular audiences. Some of these books focus entirely on Longs; others offer compelling stories about Longs while recounting the history of mountaineering throughout the Colorado Rockies. To varying degrees, these accounts offer guidance on climbing Longs while also describing heroic climbing achievements, some of the human tragedies on the peak, and the geology and wildlife of Longs and the Rockies. Careful readers will notice that these books do little to situate Longs in a national park (or park system) with multiple obligations and a dynamic history of management. Nor do they explore issues of environmental vulnerability and change in national park settings, though *100 Years Up High: Colorado Mountains and Mountaineers* lauds the Colorado Mountain Club's long-standing commit-ment to conservation. Only one, Janet Robertson's *The Magnificent Mountain Women: Adventures in the Colorado Rockies*, recognizes gender as a social category meaningful to the history of climbing. None of the popular accounts consider race and ethnicity in the history of climbing on Longs or in Colorado.[16] For all they do not do, these books speak to the values of mountain adventurers over more than a century. They offer insight into the culture of mountaineering on Longs and show us how climbers have invested meaning and identity in one place. They reveal climbers' athleticism, love of extreme challenge and adventure, commitment to camaraderie, reverence for nature, and varied investments in civic responsibility. They invite us to take climbers seriously as historical actors and to examine how they have shaped values and practices related to recreation, preservation, and democracy on Longs and in Rocky Mountain National Park.

Though there is no existing academic work on Longs, my work has benefited from, and engages with, scholarship in various subfields of American history, especially environmental histories of national parks; the history of Native Americans and national parks; histories of tourism, leisure, and recreation; and the history of African Americans and recreation. In working with this extensive historiography, I have learned from scholars' efforts to identify the multiple forces at play in national parks as human culture and nature have intersected over time. The general public is inclined to associate national parks with vacations and leaving behind everything except the impulse for fun, but this scholarship shows us that parks have been anything but trouble-free. The pursuit of fun in national parks has been bound up with histories of pain and harm and with ongoing dialogues about Americans' tolerance for physical endangerment, environmental degradation, and human—especially racial—injustice.

Recent scholarship on the environmental history of national parks has made an especially important contribution to knowledge about the NPS, doing much to reveal the deleterious impact of many park policies and practices on natural ecosystems. Implicitly and explicitly, work in this subfield acknowledges the tension between preservation and visitor enjoyment in national parks. Richard Sellars's book *Preserving Nature in the National Parks* has served as a foundational text, examining the problematic tension that emerged in national parks as administrators sought to fulfill the NPS's dual mission to protect park landscapes while fostering visitor enjoyment. Sellars traces the NPS's slow and halting movement toward managing national parks as complex natural ecosystems in the latter part of the twentieth century. He laments the NPS's long privileging of visitor enjoyment, thereby acknowledging the critical role of cultural assumptions in park history. Others build on Sellars and engage in more explicit analysis of the specific cultural values embedded in national parks. Thus, Alfred Runte shows for the entire park system, and Jerry Frank shows for Rocky Mountain National Park, the priority given by park administrators to landscape aesthetics and facade management. Frank shows, too, how Rocky Mountain National Park compromised ecosystem resilience as park managers turned the natural environment into a place for human spectatorship.[17]

Thomas Andrews is one of a small number of historians combining indigenous and environmental history, showing how indigenous peoples who had adapted over centuries to the difficult environment of northern Colorado were removed from their homeland in the Kawuneeche Valley as miners, homesteaders, tourists, and conservationists encroached on it. Once Rocky Mountain National Park opened as a scenic playground with the Kawuneeche Valley and gateway community of Grand Lake anchoring its west side, park managers had to grapple with competing claims from an array of nonnative stakeholders and an environment that was already fragmented. Andrews acknowledges environmental decision-making that was sometimes misguided, at other times wise. He sees signs of ecosystem resilience in the park while also noting the ominous scenarios predicted by climate modelers, and he urges greater use of the precautionary principle as park managers and visitors face the future. Andrews's work builds on scholarship that examines the expulsion of indigenous people across the United States from land that became national park land, highlighting parks' partnership with the tourism industry and their criminalization of activities such as hunting that had sustained Native peoples for centuries.[18] Importantly, an emerging group of scholars, mostly anthropologists and geographers, has also begun to produce narratives that explore on a global scale both past stories of exclusion from national parks and protected areas and the problematic recent efforts to honor roles and lifeways of indigenous people in these places.[19]

While historical scholarship has effectively traced indigenous expulsion and exclusion from national parks along with the NPS's persistent prioritizing of recreation and its slow investment in ecological management, it has done little to shed light on the experience, values, and choices of actual visitors. Environmental historians have tended to treat park visitors in superficial terms, assuming them to be a rather undifferentiated lot, pursuing recreation heedless of its impact on the environment.[20] Fortunately, a small group of historians has recently begun to produce scholarship that affords a deeper understanding of backcountry visitors to parks and other public lands. One cohort finds much to commend in the history of hikers and mountaineers, tracing how their love of mountains and nature led some to champion activism for protection of the wild.[21] Another cohort offers complex tales of paradox: thus, James Morton Turner shows how the move toward "leave no trace" wilderness practices in the late twentieth century was accompanied by a growing dependence on consumer goods manufactured by the wilderness recreation industry. And in his study of Yosemite climbers, Jay Taylor shows that fun-loving mountaineers who gradually embraced environmentalism also moved toward extreme masculinity and a devotion to high-tech consumerism. Silas Chamberlin traces American hikers' shift over time away from cooperative voluntarism toward an individualism that was, in fact, highly dependent on park policy makers and managers.[22] Like these authors, I find among climbers on Longs both devotion to natural resource conservation and enthusiastic consumerism. I am indebted to scholars who have examined the dynamic between these themes in other historical contexts and think it imperative that we do more to probe climbers' complex engagement over time with environmentalism and consumerism, in part by examining these issues against the backdrop of climbers' identity as citizens.

Though historians are beginning to examine visitors' complicated profiles, they have yet to study the issue of visitor safety in national park settings. There is a large social science literature on the subject, but it generally explores risks to human safety in national parks in isolation from other dynamics of reward and risk.[23] My work takes up this lacuna in the historical literature on national parks, recognizing that human safety is an essential piece of parks' commitment to fostering visitor enjoyment.

My book also draws on an emerging body of scholarship on people of color in the United States and their enduring struggle for safe, dignified, and equitable access to travel, leisure, and recreation. In recent decades sociologists, geographers, and other social scientists have examined the leisure behavior of racial and ethnic minorities and the obstacles to their recreation in various settings, including national parks. This scholarship has made important contributions to our understanding of differential patterns of leisure and attachment to place among racial and ethnic groups, noting the effects of overt discrimination on communities of color, the role of dominant cultural narratives in erasing people of color from the consideration of park managers, the process by which racial identity and difference become embedded in cultural landscapes, and, importantly, the values and adaptation strategies of communities of color.[24] Historians, too, are increasingly invested in examinations of race, travel, and leisure and have begun to analyze the racialized structures and cultural values that have operated in national parks and other outdoor settings, shaping the perceptions, experiences, and strategic resistance of communities of color. They are beginning to explore how parks that opened amid practices of indigenous exclusion subsequently kept multiple communities of color from enjoying park landscapes and recreational opportunities. Still, this work is at an early stage, and most of it focuses on metropolitan parks, beaches, and private resorts or on the experience of African Americans traveling by automobile within the United States. We have much to learn about the history of racialized values and practices in national parks, as well as the resistance to, and change in, such practices, and the recreational and leisure priorities of communities of color over time. So, too, we have a great deal to learn about the history of interpretive and educational offerings at national parks and the way these offerings have erased full understandings of the nation's history and affected the engagement of people of color, including Native Americans, with the National Park System.[25]

IN THE TWENTY-FIRST CENTURY the NPS has reasserted its goals for national parks in ways that resonate powerfully with the natural rights values found in Olmsted Sr.'s vision and in the Declaration of Independence and U.S. Constitution. In its

2001 report *Rethinking the National Parks for the 21st Century*, the NPS Advisory Board declared:

> The creation of a national park is an expression of faith in the future. It is a pact between generations, a promise from the past to the future. In 1916, Congress established the National Park Service to conserve the parks "unimpaired for the enjoyment of future generations." This act . . . echoes the promise of the Constitution "to secure the Blessings of Liberty for ourselves and our Posterity." We are that future, and we too must act on behalf of our successors. We must envision and ensure a system of parks and programs that benefits a new generation of citizens in a changing world.[26]

In making explicit the NPS's indissoluble connections to our nation's core democratic values, the Advisory Board offered numerous recommendations for reform and change. It urged the NPS to collaborate with "parks at state, regional, and local levels" to make sure that "people of all ages, races, and backgrounds can engage in a broad range of pursuits that enable them to 're-create' and find self-renewal." It recommended that the NPS "encourage public support of resource protection at a higher level of understanding" and put "greatly increased focus on the conservation of natural systems and the biodiversity they encompass." It urged the Park Service to "ensure that the American story is told faithfully, completely, and accurately. The story is often noble, but sometimes shameful and sad. In an age of growing cultural diversity, the Service must continually ask whether the way in which it tells these stories has meaning for all our citizens." Finally, the Advisory Board said, "The National Park Service should help conserve the irreplaceable connections that ancestral and indigenous people have with the parks. . . . Parks should become sanctuaries for expressing and reclaiming ancient feelings of place."[27]

The NPS has worked hard since 2001 to implement the Advisory Board's recommendations. In trying to address these challenges and fulfill the NPS's "multi-dimensional mission,"[28] the agency has committed resources and staff to expanding safe and enjoyable recreational opportunities to a diverse public while prioritizing the ecological management and conservation of natural and cultural resources. It has tried to attract people of color as employees, develop interpretive materials and commemorative sites that celebrate the diverse achievements of Americans, honor indigenous connections to park land, and tell honest histories of the nation's racial and ethnic divides.[29] Despite these efforts, injury among visitors, crowding and ecological degradation, lack of diversity among visitors and staff, and neglect of histories of difference and injustice remain critical challenges at many parks, including Rocky, one of the most heavily used "crown jewels" of the National Park System.[30] If these harms are to be mitigated or overcome, if the national parks are to devise value systems and modes of operation that successfully promote visitor enjoyment and safety as well as environmental sustainability and democratic freedom, we must gain greater historical understanding of the ways in which reward and risk have been navigated, by visitors and staff alike, in national park settings. In studying Longs Peak, this book seeks to illuminate the history of enduring challenges in the National Park System, thereby helping scholars, park managers, and a broad public audience identify future choices that might help our parks remedy past wrongs and fulfill the promises offered at their founding.

ONE | Becoming a Place for Outdoor Adventure
Longs Peak from the Indigenous Era to 1915

LONGS PEAK IS WIDELY KNOWN today as a spectacular site for high-altitude recreation, a mountain that offers adventuresome individuals the opportunity to experience great natural beauty and exhilaration as they clamber over boulders, climb steep rock faces, and contend with variable alpine weather. This place identity, however, is just a century and a half old. It developed in the second half of the nineteenth century as profound human turmoil transformed Colorado's cultural and physical landscapes.

Ute peoples had for centuries lived seasonally as hunter-gatherers in the area that would become Rocky Mountain National Park, as had small bands of Apaches. Over the eighteenth and nineteenth centuries other tribal groups, especially Arapahos, moved into the area after being displaced from the Midwest and Great Plains by Euro-American settlers. By this time all Native tribes in Colorado—whether old or new, dwelling in mountains or plains—were encountering U.S. government explorers and surveyors who had been sent to assess the geography and natural resources of the region and the disposition of its Native populations. White fur trappers, miners, farmers, ranchers, and business entrepreneurs quickly followed, altering the natural environment as they acquired land and developed industries, markets, towns, and transportation networks. As Colorado gained territorial status and its economy grew, White migrants made clear—through racist pronouncement, violence, political coercion, and economic pressure—their unwillingness to coexist with Native peoples. Indeed, by the time statehood was obtained in 1876, most Native Americans had been removed by U.S. Army troops from the mountains and plains of Colorado to reservations in southern Colorado and adjacent states. Only some Utes remained, and they were dispossessed of their land and removed to a Utah reservation by 1880.

Native American removal encouraged White settlers to embrace a nascent industry, mountain tourism, especially in and near Estes Park, a stunning area described by Milton Estes, son of its original White settler, as a "paradise" of mountains, valleys, streams, wild game, and mountain trout. The new settlers viewed the area as devoid of human history, a primitive and pristine place waiting to be shaped by their creative energies.[1] Estes Park's mountain topography was ill suited to large-scale urban development or to manufacturing, farming, and mining, but White settlers and their hardworking families saw its commercial potential and found modest success in operating inns, lodges, and summer resorts. Their customers were White middle-class Americans from Denver and other cities, both in and beyond the state. All sought relief in unspoiled nature from the clamor and stress of late nineteenth-century urban industrial life. Eventually, upper-class travelers from the United States and Europe also identified Estes Park as a desirable vacation destination. Inspired by nineteenth-century explorers, scientists, and adventurers whose published writings described invigorating mountain ascents in the American West, some of the visitors to Estes discovered that Longs Peak was a premier site for alpine mountaineering.

By the time Rocky Mountain National Park was founded in 1915, the entire region stretching from Estes Park to Grand Lake was considered a scenic "national playground," offering tremendous possibilities for recreation and the growth of tourism in Colorado.[2] Longs Peak, tucked within the new park's boundaries, had become the most popular mountaineering destination in the state, heralded for the demanding routes and splendid views it presented to climbers and its relative proximity to the nation's railway system and cities along the Front Range. The founding legislation of Rocky Mountain National Park obligated the park to promote the "freest use" of the park "for recreation purposes by the public" and "the preservation of the natural conditions and scenic beauties thereof."[3] It gave no guidance, however, on whether (or how) to promote visitation among members of "the public" who did not fit the profile of White moneyed tourists. It acknowledged neither the removal of Native Americans from the Rocky Mountain region nor the exclusion of African Americans and other minorities from Estes Park except as servants, cooks, and waiters. Nor did it offer advice on how to promote visitor enjoyment without compromising resource preservation. Indeed, advocates of the park and of the National Park Service, established in 1916, expressed naive faith in recreational tourism's compatibility with resource preservation, neglecting to consider emerging signs of tourism's harm to the natural world. Mountaineers were more rugged than the average recreational tourist and generally possessed a deep love for nature, but they were a subset of the larger group and were active participants in the tourism industry. When Longs became the emblem of the park in 1915, it represented the grand rewards of outdoor adventure in a "playground" from which people of color were excluded as well as the unacknowledged risks of promoting recreational tourism in unspoiled nature.

Explorers, Native Americans, and Recreational Climbers before 1900

Longs Peak was named for Major Stephen Harriman Long, a topographical engineer who noted the existence of the high peak in 1820 while leading an exploratory expedition for President James Monroe. The expedition had been ordered to explore the natural resources and Native tribes of the Great Plains and the Platte, Red, and Arkansas Rivers, but it met with one calamity after another. The major and his men suffered severe physical hardship and lost their way; they spent days following the Canadian River, having mistaken it for the Red. Three of Long's men deserted, never to be seen again, carrying the expedition's scientific notebooks with them. Encountering generally hostile Native tribes, Long signed no new treaties and made no discernible progress in asserting U.S. dominance in the West. The major's summary remarks about the expedition's findings matched his unfortunate experiences. Asked to consider the suitability of the Great Plains for settlement, Long confirmed the earlier opinion of explorer Zebulon Pike that the plains were "a Great American Desert," unfit for Euro-American habitation and development.[4]

The sighting of the Rocky Mountains and what came to be called Longs Peak was one of the few gratifying experiences of the entire expedition. According to Captain John Bell, the expedition's official journalist, Long and his men gained sight of the Rocky Mountains and a singularly high peak after enduring "the dull and uninteresting monotony of prairie country" for many weeks. "The whole range had a beautiful and sublime appearance," and "a high Peake was plainly to be distinguished towering above all the others as far as the sight extended." Long initially thought he was seeing Pikes Peak, named fourteen years earlier by Zebulon Pike. It was only after traveling farther south, where he found and then climbed Pikes, that Long realized his mistake. Eventually, the "high Peake" beyond the Platte was named for Major Long, though he and his men never ventured onto it.[5]

It would take nearly five decades for a Euro-American to record a successful summit on Longs, but in the intervening years the peak continued, as before, as a site of significance to Native peoples. Diverse Native groups living in the region as seasonally migratory hunter-gatherers hunted on Longs' slopes, used the peak for navigation, and made it part of their cosmology. Native cultures had been active throughout the area that became Rocky Mountain National Park for approximately eleven millennia; modern archaeologists have found the remains of their game drives, hunting and plant-processing camps, trails, battle sites, and sacred ritual sites in the park both east and west of the Continental Divide. Recent research has found sites west of Trail Ridge and on Longs Peak itself (in Jim's Grove and at Battle Mountain) that point to Longs' significance in shamanistic ritual and its use for seasonal camping, hunting, and food processing by prehistoric, protohistoric, and early historical Native Americans.[6]

Utes were the earliest tribal group of the historical period to live in the north-central Colorado Rockies, including the area that became Rocky Mountain National Park. Ute culture may have emerged from protohistoric Numic speakers who expanded away from the Great Basin sometime between AD 1100 and 1400; alternatively, Ute tribal culture may have developed in situ approximately five centuries ago from Paleo-Indian cultures already extant in the northern Colorado Plateau and southern Rockies. Ute bands probably resided in the area of Rocky Mountain National Park only in late spring and summer, hunting bighorn sheep, elk, and deer in the park's valleys and high tundra while also gathering food and medicinal plants. Winter took them to Colorado's Middle and North Parks or along the Colorado, Gunnison, and Yampa Rivers. The Kawuneeche Valley, on the future park's west side, became a particularly favored site during the warmer months, but Ute seasonal rounds extended as far as the eastern foothills of the Colorado Front Range. Longs Peak would have been a familiar sight as well as a place to hunt, camp, and process food. After acquiring horses from the Spanish sometime after the mid-seventeenth century, Utes extended their hunting territory at least one hundred miles eastward into the high plains, taking advantage of the bison herds.[7]

For more than a century the Apaches co-occupied with the Utes various areas of the Rocky Mountain National Park region. In the mid- to late eighteenth century, however, Utes and Comanches expanded the geographic range of their activities and pushed the Apaches south out of the mountains. Apaches may have continued to visit the area of the park until the mid-nineteenth century, though not without encountering hostility from competing tribes.[8]

Arapahos and Cheyennes were relative latecomers to the area of Rocky Mountain National Park, arriving in the early nineteenth century from points north and east as they were pushed out of territory claimed by westering Euro-Americans. By this time both tribes had acquired horses and firearms. Like the Utes, Apaches, Comanches, and the prehistoric bands that preceded them, the Arapahos and Cheyennes made use of abundant game animals, food, and medicinal plants in the Rocky Mountain National Park region. The Arapahos apparently viewed the Estes Park area as their own, regarding it as a huge game preserve. Relations between the newcomers and older tribes were often hostile, especially as they competed for land, food animals, and other resources in the face of Euro-American encroachment.[9]

The Arapahos knew Longs Peak, together with neighboring Mount Meeker, as Neníisótoyóú'u, or the "Two Guides." The two mountains served as landmarks for the entire region; "when viewed from the north or south" they presented "a very striking double peak."[10] Archaeologists of the Rocky Mountain region have discovered evidence of Native peoples trapping eagles from shallow pits on numerous Colorado mountain peaks, and Longs' summit probably served as one such site. In 1914 an elderly Arapaho man, Gun Griswold, explained to advocates of Rocky Mountain National Park that his father had hunted eagles from a pit on Longs Peak in the mid-nineteenth century. Speaking through an Arapaho translator, Griswold recounted not only the method by which his father hunted eagles on Longs but also why he chose such a high peak: "The reason that he had the trap up on top of the peak was because he had to have it some place where there weren't any trees around, for if there were trees the eagles would have lit on the trees instead of going straight to the tallow, and then the other eagles would have seen the first one caught and so would have been scared away. This way he caught them one by one as they came along."[11]

Of course, by the time Euro-Americans learned of native hunting on Longs in 1914, Gun Griswold no longer lived in the area that was soon to become a national park. The Arapahos had migrated from the area decades earlier, responding to the growing scarcity of bison in the Estes area and the horror of the Sand Creek Massacre in 1864, during which some 230 Arapahos and Cheyennes were brutally killed and mutilated by U.S. volunteer soldiers. Arapaho bands who had hunted in the Estes Valley moved to southern Wyoming in the late 1860s and were escorted by the U.S. Army to the Wind River Reservation in 1878, sharing the reservation uneasily with Shoshone peoples. By 1880, with the removal of White River and Uncompahgre Utes to the Uintah and Ouray Reservation in Utah, all Native Americans in Colorado had been dispossessed of their homelands, the consequence of two decades of intensive migration by Euro-Americans pursuing land, mining, farming, ranching, urban development, and commerce. Euro-American newcomers viewed Native peoples as inferior, primitive, strange, and violent. They could not imagine sharing the Colorado plains, foothills, or mountains with them and pursued Indian removal to reservations—by force or persuasion—as their only option. Giving voice to this sentiment, Massachusetts journalist Samuel Bowles said of Native Americans during his travels to the Colorado Territory in 1868: "We know they are not our equals . . . we know that our right to the soil, as a race capable of its superior improvement, is above theirs. . . . Let us say to him . . . you are our ward, our child, the victim of our destiny, ours to displace, ours to protect."[12] For Bowles, it did not matter that Native tribes viewed the Colorado Rockies as sacred and sovereign homeland. In his view, indigenous claims to land in Colorado simply did not exist.

As the newcomers constructed roads, buildings, and cities, cut trees and dug mines, moved cattle onto ranches and grew crops with the help of new irrigation ditches and reservoirs, they talked also of turning the mountains of Colorado into places for "amusement and adventure." With the help of railroads, tourism was already developing across the United States in locations as far-flung as New York's Catskills and Adirondacks, coastal Georgia, the lakes of Minnesota and Michigan, and Yosemite Valley and Mariposa Grove in California. White middle- and upper-class Americans sought pleasure, edification, diversion, and social status not simply in leisure at home but through travel to places of stirring natural beauty fitted out with comfortable lodges and resorts. White migrants imagined in Colorado a grand alpine version of the new tourism developing elsewhere.[13]

It was in the context of an emerging interest in high-altitude tourism that Longs Peak was first summited by a party of White men. Migrants to Colorado took excited note of Longs Peak, "lying like a smoky thunderhead in the far and indefinite horizon," and in 1864 William N. Byers, editor of the newly established *Rocky Mountain News*, attempted to climb the peak with three companions. The peak defied their strenuous efforts, causing Byers to opine that "no living creature, unless it had wings to fly, was ever upon its summit . . . and . . . no man ever will be." Disappointed though he may have been, Byers was not insensible to the merits of the area around Longs. He was particularly impressed by the beauty of Estes Park, still unnamed but recently inhabited by Joel Estes and his family. Estes had been a Missouri frontier farmer and slaveholder, then a gold miner in California and Colorado, before settling in the Rocky Mountain region. As Estes struggled to ranch cattle, Byers rightly predicted that the park would "eventually become a favorite pleasure resort."[14]

Just four years later, Byers found that Longs' summit was accessible after all. Major John Wesley Powell, a Civil War veteran and geology professor at Illinois Wesleyan University, had successfully climbed Pikes Peak in 1867 and was ready for another mountaineering challenge. He returned to Colorado in 1868 with thirty students and was joined by Byers. The party, calling itself the Colorado Scientific Exploring Expedition, traveled first to Middle Park and Grand Lake. From Grand Lake, the expedition headed for Longs on horseback, carrying ten days of rations. Moving southeast and across numerous ridges, the group had to abandon its horses as passage became increasingly difficult and despaired of reaching the top of Longs. Fortunately, a particularly intrepid student, L. W. Keplinger, scouted a route from Wild Basin, south of Longs, up a section of the peak (later known as Keplinger's Couloir) and thus made it possible for the entire party to summit the peak on August 23, 1868.[15]

Knowing of Powell's success, Ferdinand Hayden made the summit of Longs one of the many destinations of his government-sponsored survey. The Hayden survey (1871–73) was one of four army expeditions sent to the American West after the Civil War to study the region's geology, topography, and mineral, plant, and animal resources. By this time, the federal government realized that Zebulon Pike's and Stephen Long's dour prognostications were no longer relevant. Aggressive Indian removal policies along with new mining, farming, irrigation, and transportation technologies were making settlement in the Great Plains and Rocky Mountains both possible and profitable. The various survey teams were tasked with giving the government and settlers scientific and practical information to facilitate western development. The Hayden survey's exploration of Colorado resulted in publication of the *Atlas of Colorado* (1877), which mapped the topography, geology, drainage, and potential economic resources of the state. On Longs, the Hayden survey calculated the altitude of the peak at 14,255 feet and used what became known as the *Keyhole* route to reach the summit, winding around the west, north, and east sides of the peak. William Byers was again among the climbing party, which also included Anna Dickinson, a famous lecturer, feminist, and abolitionist. These two well-known figures added greatly to public interest in the survey. Simultaneously, Hayden's photographer, William H. Jackson, took images that encouraged Americans to consider Longs Peak in aesthetic and spiritual terms. Like his contemporaries, painters Thomas Moran and Albert Bierstadt, Jackson produced images that imbued the landscapes of Colorado with qualities of the sublime, the sacred, the nearly unfathomable. His stunning photographs showcased Longs Peak, the Mount of the Holy Cross, and the ancient ruins of the vanished peoples of Mesa Verde.[16]

Even as Hayden and Jackson explored the West, Longs was becoming a site of recreational climbing. Key to this development was the emergence of a cohort of rugged mountain guides willing to lead adventuresome tourists, both women and men, to daunting heights in wild natural settings. The sport of "alpinism," conceived by British and European elites, was gaining adherents in the United States, drawing mountain enthusiasts to the Rockies, Sierra Nevada, and Appalachians. Much as artists and geographers were teaching privileged Americans how to see and understand the aesthetic and spiritual dimensions of western landscapes, self-taught mountain guides showed them how to experience the mountains kinesthetically. Thus, the *Boulder County News* reported on August 26, 1871, that Estes Park guide Al Dunbar had recently assisted Addie Alexander and Harriet Goss in a climb on Longs, though Goss stopped short of the summit. Little is known about Dunbar or the two women he guided, though historian Janet Robertson thinks Alexander may have been a resident of the prosperous but short-lived Saint Louis Western Colony (in Evans, Colorado), drawn to the thrill and challenge of a Longs ascent.[17]

Isabella Bird, a popular writer admired for her audacity as a female world traveler, relied on another mountain guide, Jim Nugent, to reach the summit of Longs Peak in October 1873. Nugent was a hunter, fisherman, and mountaineer with a badly disfigured face and was known for telling wild tales about his past, none ever substantiated. While the early settlers of Estes Park tolerated Jim's inclination "to talk mostly to astonish his audience," Bird was fascinated, perhaps even attracted to the man, as he apparently was to her.[18] With Jim serving as guide and assisted by two other young men, Bird rode by horseback the first day of the expedition to about 11,000 feet, "all my intellect concentrated on avoiding being dragged off my horse by impending branches." The group sheltered that night in a "bower of pines." Still on horseback, Bird and her guides got to the peak's "Lava Beds" (Boulderfield) at 12,760 feet the next day; from there, traveling by foot and with Bird in a state of "extreme terror . . . slipping, faltering, gasping," the four climbers made their way across rock and precipice to the top of Longs. On the summit Bird and Jim put a slip of paper with their names and the date of the ascent in a small tin box "within a crevice." Atop "one of the mightiest of the vertebrae . . . of the North American continent," Bird felt "uplifted above love and hate and storms of passion, calm amidst the eternal silences." Time on the summit was short; from there Bird and her companions climbed back down to the Lava Beds, staying there overnight. A third full day was needed for the descent on horseback to Estes Park.

Writing about the climb in *A Lady's Life in the Rocky Mountains* (1877), Bird highlighted the rigors of the climb while also romanticizing her mountaineering guide in the person of "Rocky Mountain Jim." Bird made clear that her ascent was no mere pleasure jaunt in nature. It had nothing in common with the lei-surely strolls favored by many Americans of her day in pastoral settings or newly landscaped urban parks. Through Bird's eyes, readers learned that Longs was a mountain calling to those who sought a transformative experience in untamed nature. It presented to the world a "splintered grey crest . . . invested with a personality." The peak "generates and chains the strong winds, to let them loose in its fury. The thunder becomes its voice, and the lightnings do it homage. . . . The mark of fire is upon it; and though it had passed into a grim repose, it tells of fire and upheaval." Bird found it almost impossible to convey to readers the full character of Longs given "the glorious sublimity, the majestic solitude, and the unspeakable awfulness" of her three-day climb.[19]

Bird was not alone in finding both transcendent beauty and terrifying power, perhaps proof of God's hand, in wild nature. Indeed, her description of Longs echoed the views emerging among painters, photographers, and writers about the early national parks at Yosemite and Yellowstone. Upon seeing Yosemite for the first time, Samuel Bowles described feeling "the overpowering sense of the sub-lime, of awful desolation, of transcending marvelousness and unexpectedness. . . . It was the confrontal of God face to face, as in great danger, in solemn, sudden death." Similarly, visitors to Yellowstone experienced reverence for "that Almighty hand" as they viewed the sublimity of the Grand Canyon of the Yellowstone River yet were also transfixed by geothermal mud pots, geysers, and travertine terraces that were "startling" in appearance, "desolate," and "strange."[20] Isabella Bird's *A Lady's Life in the Rocky Mountains* remained in continuous print in the late nineteenth century and signaled the consolidation of critical modes of perception and ambition. With Bird's prompting, Longs Peak and the American West's other high mountains became recreational destinations for White middle-class women and men who, with the aid of skilled guides, sought witness to the natural world's beauty and overwhelming power, its extremes and unpredictability, both sacred and environmental.

The night before her climb, Bird had been happy to sleep in a rough cabin owned by Griff Evans, an early settler of Estes Valley who found that serving visitors added appreciably to the marginal income he and his family made in hunting and cattle ranching. Bird's accommodations with Evans and his wife were primitive, but she enjoyed a warm welcome, delicious food, and a clean bed.[21] Over the next decade the quality of tourist accommodations improved as Alexander MacGregor, Horace Ferguson, William James, Abner Sprague, and Elkanah Lamb all established comfortable resorts in Estes Park, aided by the unpaid labor of their wives and children and, eventually, by paid staff. The great majority of visitors to Estes were unpretentious Euro-Americans of middle-class standing, but the rich also found accommodations there. A wealthy Briton, the Earl of Dunraven, bought thousands of acres of land and opened the Estes Park Hotel, a pleasuring resort for the upper class, in 1877. The various resorts accommodated climbers as well as vacationers interested in fishing, sport hunting, horseback riding, and leisurely sightseeing. Most visitors were from Denver and other cities along Colorado's Front Range, but Estes Park also attracted travelers from other states and nations. By the 1880s and 1890s the region was likewise popular with tent campers who traveled in springboard wagons or four-wheeled surreys, viewing the splendid mountain scenery of Estes from the relative comfort of their horse-drawn vehicles. Some pitched their white canvas tents near the area resorts and took meals with lodgers; others brought food, kitchen, and dining supplies with them, including folding tables and chairs, cookstoves, portable sideboards, and chests full of dishes, cookery, and cutlery. Roadside campers enjoyed adapting to life in the scenic outdoors yet saw no virtue in privation and discomfort.[22]

Although it may have attracted some visitors interested in scenic roadside viewing, the Longs Peak House at the eastern base of the peak operated primarily as a facility for those with mountaineering ambitions. The inn was established by the Reverend Elkanah Lamb, who climbed Longs Peak and explored the Estes Park area after being transferred to Colorado by the United Brethren Church in 1871. Lamb's first climb on Longs Peak began in the company of other members of his church, though he was the only one who made it to the summit. There he saw a "grand panorama . . . presenting to nature's lover a scene compelling admiration and adoration of nature's God." Knowing little about the topography of the peak, Lamb started his descent down the east side, only to discover that his path was treacherous and allowed for no backtracking. Indeed, he soon came to a point where both grip and foothold failed, "and down I went with almost an arrow's rapidity," stopping only when he managed to catch "onto a bowlder that projected above the ice." His plunge through the permanent snowfield on the East Face of Longs Peak, memorialized as *Lamb's Slide*, was terrifying, yet the peak had captured Lamb's heart and soul. Moving his family to Estes Park in 1875, Lamb built the Longs Peak House, temporarily putting aside his vocation as a "fire and brimstone" preacher to pursue life's meaning on Longs, while managing the resort at its base. Lamb remodeled and enlarged the resort over the years, serving mountain tourists and climbers happy to enjoy comfortable beds and good food before and after their daring alpine exertions.[23]

In 1878 Lamb and his son Carlyle began offering their services as climbing guides to guests at the Longs Peak House and put in a "pony trail" on the peak; it subsequently became known as the East Longs Peak Trail. The new trail provided steep but safe passage on foot or horseback from the base of the peak to timberline, over Granite Pass, and into the Boulderfield. Horses went no farther.

Continuing on foot, most climbers took the *Keyhole* route to the summit, passing through a keyhole-like rock formation on the west side of the Boulderfield, then circling to the summit by following along the Ledges on the peak's west side, cutting sharply upward through the Trough, going out onto the exposed Narrows, and finally scrambling up the Homestretch to the peak's broad and nearly flat summit. The East trail and *Keyhole* route were used by the Lambs, the additional guides whom they hired, and other commercial guides in the area. They became the most popular means of accessing the summit, supplanting more primitive and arduous trails from Wild Basin and Glacier Gorge. A northern trail to the Boulderfield blazed in 1885 by Abner Sprague from his resort near Boulder Creek also gained many users.[24]

Lamb and the other lodge owners of Estes Park thus fitted nineteenth-century America's developing tourism industry to the specific needs and interests of mountain visitors and climbers. Urban Euro-Americans could not gain access to wild nature in the Rocky Mountains without a built environment supporting their travel, including a transportation infrastructure of railways, roads, and trails. All the Estes Park resorts relied on the nation's new coal-burning regional and transcontinental railroads to bring upper- and middle-class travelers as far as the cities and towns of the Front Range. From these locales, visitors relied on a variety of rough stage and toll roads to access the Estes area, some of them put in by the lodge owners themselves. Joel Estes built a very primitive road into the area from Lyons in 1858. Alexander MacGregor put in an improved toll road from Lyons in the 1870s that traced a somewhat different route along the North St. Vrain Creek, then crossed "over the intervening ridge to the Big Thompson River valley for the final approach to Estes Park." Simultaneously, Larimer County and private donors covered the costs of constructing a road from Namaqua to Estes, making the area accessible to visitors from Loveland, Fort Collins, and Greeley. And in 1876 Elkanah Lamb put in a twelve-mile-long toll road from Estes Park to his Tahosa Valley inn at the base of Longs Peak, following a route that became the basis for today's Highway 7. Road improvement and construction continued throughout the late nineteenth century. By the 1890s the roads to Estes Park were smooth enough to accommodate bicyclists, some of whom rode from Denver to Estes to climb Longs Peak, their final destination.[25]

Mountain tourism's built environment also encompassed resort kitchens, dining halls, local gardens, small herds of domestic cattle, and horses. Their upkeep and consistent operation required capital as well as labor inputs from resort proprietors and their wives, children, guides, cooks, waiters, maids, cattlemen, and stable keepers. A range of retail and wholesale commodities were also essential to mountain tourism's built environment and operation. Early mountain tourists and campers purchased most of their specialized clothing, shoes, packs, tents, and other equipment from retailers before they arrived in Estes. However, much of the food and drink tourists enjoyed in area resorts, the coal and oil used to cook their food or to warm and light their lodgings, and the furnishings and bedding that afforded them comfort, arrived from wholesalers who used rail and roadway to transport these goods to Estes Park.[26]

Mountain tourists and the larger tourist industry were also served by the numerous guidebooks published in the late nineteenth century containing detailed information about railroad schedules, stagecoach service, lodging, guiding, and Colorado's natural wonders.[27] Mountaineers carved out their own niche in the guidebook genre as they began publishing accounts of adventure that balanced striking descriptions of their experience in untamed alpine landscapes with commentary on the budding climbing community's need for improved trails, experienced guides, and comprehensive topographic information. For example, Frederick Chapin's *Mountaineering in Colorado: The Peaks about Estes Park*, published in 1889 under the auspices of the recently established Appalachian Mountain Club, described the Connecticut writer's stay at Ferguson's Ranch in Estes Park and his climbs on Longs and nearby peaks. Chapin found the view of the Mummy Range and the cliffs of Lily Lake from Ferguson's Ranch to be "indescribably beautiful." Of Longs, Chapin claimed it equivalent to the Swiss Matterhorn and "more difficult" of ascent than "any other peak in the range," retelling the story of a thrilling climb on Longs by Elkanah Lamb and Sylvester Dunham of Connecticut, during which they encountered "a whirling volley of ice and snow" in the Trough and an electric storm on the peak's summit. Describing his own climbs on Longs, Chapin emphasized the varied terrain—the mix of beautiful lakes and forbidding cliffs—as well as the relative accessibility of the peak. Though not insensible to the dangers of the Ledges, Trough, and Narrows, Chapin thought "the difficulties of the ascent of Long's Peak" were "frequently exaggerated." According to Chapin, a hundred people or more had been climbing the peak annually, most of them from towns in the foothills and along the Front Range, yet few went beyond the Keyhole. Chapin seemed to think that many more would try to reach Longs' summit if they had accurate information, greater access to commercial and club guides, and an improved mountain infrastructure. He urged alpine clubs to get to work on Longs and other peaks in the Rockies, as "paths are to be made, trails to be cut, detail maps to be laid out, before the grandest scenes among the mountains can be shown to the tourist."[28]

Enos Mills and Advocacy for Rocky Mountain National Park, 1900–1915

Enos Mills may never have met Chapin, but he took up his challenge, becoming an indefatigable champion of mountaineering tourism. Mills arrived in Estes Park, Colorado, as a rather sickly fourteen-year-old in 1884 and found work at the Elkhorn Lodge. The next summer he moved on to the Longs Peak House, helping care for guests whom Carlyle Lamb guided to the summit of Longs. Mills climbed Longs too, finding it an unforgettable experience. After his first ascent with companions, Mills climbed the peak another forty times by himself, wanting to become intimately familiar with the peak's challenging environment and granite features. Only then did he become one of the Lambs' commercial guides, successfully leading dozens of visitors along the circuitous and exposed *Keyhole* route to Longs' broad summit each summer. During the late 1880s and 1890s Mills moved to Butte, Montana, over the winter to work in the town's mines, but he returned to Estes every summer to serve as a guide on Longs Peak. Developing entrepreneurial interests along with his dedication to mountaineering, Mills purchased the Longs Peak House from the Lambs in 1902 and took on the operation of the resort as his primary responsibility. He hired local men with mountaineering experience as climbing guides and rebuilt the inn in a vernacular rustic style after it burned to the ground in August 1906.[29]

Renaming the lodge the Longs Peak Inn, Mills managed to balance the responsibilities of running a touristic business with passion for the natural world. Indeed, Mills continued mountaineering in all seasons and became a significant figure in the national Nature Study movement, lecturing and publishing magazine articles and books about his experience of nature on Longs Peak and in the surrounding region. Mills followed in the footsteps of Louis Agassiz, John Muir, Liberty Hyde Bailey, Mabel Osgood Wright, Anna Botsford Comstock, and other late nineteenth- and early twentieth-century advocates of nature study who worried about the enervating effects of urban industrial capitalism on Americans and recommended immersion in nature as a way to reverse this trend. Previous generations of Euro-Americans had worked to tame and subdue undeveloped nature, believing that wildness was the work of the devil's hand. The advocates of nature study rejected this view, seeing wild nature as a source of endless scientific wonder and inquiry, a fount of aesthetic beauty, a place where humans who suffered from the incessant demands, physical constraints, and corruption of modern industrial society might be reborn. Simultaneously, they subscribed to preservationist policies and ethics in a bid to save unsullied nature from industrial exploitation and development. As one of this cohort, Mills offered his readers dramatic tales of snow mountaineering and climbing, encounters with mountain wildlife, and timely escapes from thunder and lightning. He gave nature lectures to his guests at the Longs Peak Inn and ran an informal Trail School for visiting children, hoping to inspire in adults and youngsters alike a "poetic interpretation of the facts of nature" that acknowledged animals, plants, mountains, rivers, and weather patterns as players in "nature's storybook." Whether writing for the reading public or speaking to the guests at his lodge, he sought to awaken appreciation for the science and beauty, the danger and moral courage, the glorious satisfaction to be discovered in the Rocky Mountains' wild embrace.[30]

Mills also called for the creation of a national park, hoping to gain for Colorado's northern Rockies the protection already afforded other stunning landscapes, including Yellowstone, Yosemite, Sequoia, and Glacier National Parks. Much of the land surrounding Estes Park, including Longs Peak, had become part of the newly established Medicine Bow Forest Reserve in 1902 after farmers and other Coloradans sought federal protection of mountain watersheds that were endangered by cattle grazing and logging. Though an initial supporter of the reserve, Mills soon became a severe critic, believing it permitted grazing, logging, and sawmilling at levels damaging to the landscape's aesthetic splendor. The reserve and its successor, the Medicine Bow National Forest, might have been doing a reasonably good job of protecting the "practical" interests of farmers and city dwellers dependent on mountain runoff, but in Mills's view, reserve and Forest Service policies were inimical to the preservation of the mountains' "exceptional beauty and grandeur" and their value as "places of recreation."[31]

With the support of California's John Muir, the Estes Park Protective and Improvement Association, the Estes Park Woman's Club, the General Federation of Women's Clubs, the American Civic Association, the newly established Colorado Mountain Club, the Sierra Club, climbing clubs in other states, and local resort owners such as F. O. Stanley, Enos Mills worked tirelessly for nearly a decade to win support for a new national park. Uncompromising in temperament and doubting others' absolute dedication to the cause, Mills antagonized many park supporters. Still, his resolute efforts and lectures throughout the United States led to his being called the "father" of Rocky Mountain National Park. Despite the continued opposition of the Forest Service, Congress voted to establish the new park in 1915, with Longs Peak as its highest summit and centerpiece.[32]

In promoting Rocky Mountain National Park, Mills and other park advocates never questioned deepening patterns of racism in the United States that would likely prevent people of color from accessing the new park. After the Civil War and the abolition of slavery, White Americans grudgingly tried and then abandoned Reconstruction. They consolidated and reinvented the nation's race hierarchy, using cultural norms and science, racial segregation and miscegenation law, Indian removal and violence, immiseration and disenfranchisement as tools to keep African Americans, Native Americans, Mexican Americans, and a small population of Asian Americans in positions of subservient inferiority. Progressive reforms in the early twentieth century did little to weaken Whites' commitment to these practices.[33]

By this time, indigenous peoples had long since been removed from Colorado's mountain landscapes to reservations. Denver had a small African American community, but its members faced discrimination at home and rarely visited Estes Park for its recreational possibilities. As in other tourist towns across the United States, Estes Park's lodges and restaurants refused to welcome people of color as paying guests, assuming they lacked the refined sensibilities of those who sought aesthetic, scientific, and religious experiences in nature. That said, the White purveyors of touristic services were happy to take selective advantage of African Americans who challenged racist presumptions of inferiority through workplace excellence. Denver's Black community was thoroughly invested in education, racial uplift, and the politics of respectability, communicating their values and achievements through the *Statesman*, a local Black-owned newspaper. Those who ventured to Estes Park as servants, cooks, and waiters sought to demonstrate exemplary abilities—even leadership capacities—in these roles. In September 1909, for example, the *Statesman* reported that B. C. Curtis had returned to Denver after spending the summer season "in charge of the cuisine" at the Stanley Hotel in Estes Park, while J. W. Morris was "in charge" of the dining room and its waiters. "The colored help made such an impression on the guests and management that there will be little difficulty of their returning there next year if they wish." And, despite Whites' exclusionary practices and lack of faith in African Americans' capacity to appreciate wild nature, Denver's Black residents also sought access to alpine experiences. The *Statesman* and its successor, the *Denver Star*, reported on the sightseeing trips of members of the city's Black community to destinations such as Colorado Springs and Manitou Springs. The newspapers also advertised scenic round-trip railroad tours affording views of "Colorado's Grandest Scenery" in Durango, Ouray, and Silverton.[34]

At most, park advocates seem to have felt some historical curiosity about the legends and remembrances of Native Americans who had previously lived in what became Rocky Mountain National Park, perhaps seeing congruence between Native Americans' historical ability to live well in untamed nature and their own investment in witnessing the varied creations of the wild. Advocates for Rocky Mountain National Park did not go as far as park boosters and managers at Grand Canyon National Park and Glacier National Park who commodified Native cultures, hiring Native peoples to "display" primitive lifeways and the legitimacy of racial conquest.[35] Rather, advocates of Rocky, especially the Colorado Mountain Club, sought some exposure to Arapahos' historical presence in the region, hoping to discover and appropriate Native place names for landmarks in the new park.

Starting in mid-July 1914, Colorado Mountain Club member (and lawyer) Oliver Wolcott Toll, Longs Peak guide Shep Husted, and a young White student, David Hawkins, accompanied two elderly Arapaho men, Sherman Sage and Gun Griswold, and a young Arapaho translator, Tom Crispin, on a two-week pack trip through what was to become Rocky Mountain National Park. The instigator of the trip was Harriet Vaille, chair of the CMC's Nomenclature Committee, who was trying to assist the chief geographer of the U.S. Geological Survey in coming up with appropriate names for natural features in the area proposed for Rocky Mountain National Park. Vaille believed Native Americans' former use of the area should be acknowledged, and she traveled to the Wind River Reservation in Wyoming to solicit help from the Arapaho tribe, eventually persuading Sage (chief of police on the reservation), Griswold (a reservation judge), and Crispin (the reservation interpreter) to participate in the trip. The high tribal positions of the three suggest that the Wind River Arapahos attached genuine significance to the task of naming and remembering features and tribal lifeways within the proposed park, despite their removal from it and the surrounding region.[36]

The group traveled north from the Tahosa Valley at the base of Longs Peak to Estes Park, then moved west over Trail Ridge to Thunder Pass before heading south to Grand Lake and east over Flattop Mountain back to Estes Park. Oliver Toll was the official record keeper as the men traveled through the park area, collecting traditional place names, legends, and stories of past events and practices as they were related by the Arapaho men.

Surviving evidence of the pack trip, written almost entirely by Oliver Toll, suggests that the relationship between the White and Arapaho men ranged from racial tension and distrust to equivocality, respect, and mutual enjoyment. Oliver Toll thought some of the stories and names the Arapahos shared with him were quite possibly "manufactured for the occasion." In reporting on the trip, he resorted initially to simple racial stereotype, describing the Arapahos as a people "uncommunicative by disposition." Their language communicated the "practical use" of "things" but was not "adapted to abstract thoughts." Further interactions, however, tempered Toll's inclination to see only essential racial traits in the Arapaho men. While Toll noted that Gun Griswold, a seventy-three-year-old grieving the loss of a son, responded to questions "in a nearly inaudible whisper," he found Sage to be "as jolly as Griswold was quiet." Crispin interacted easily with Toll and the other Whites. And though Toll may have been inconvenienced by Griswold's taciturnity, he otherwise found little in the man to criticize, saying that "no one could help respecting him. He had a great deal of dignity and though he spoke little, was treated with consideration by the others." Of the other two Arapaho men, Sage "impressed one as particularly truthful and honest," with "a better sense of humor, by far, than the average white man." Crispin was "intelligent and accurate." Toll measured the Arapahos against a White standard, remarking that Crispin's "point of view is entirely that of the white man." Yet he also detected commonalities across White and Arapaho culture, commending the three Arapaho men for being "ideal camping companions; jolly and good natured."[37]

Toll also recognized that the Arapahos possessed collective knowledge about, and observational powers in, the park's landscape, though only Griswold had lived in the area for a portion of his youth. It was Griswold who told the story of his grandfather hunting eagles on Longs Peak. Toll also obtained from Griswold the Arapaho names for mountains, trails, creeks, and other natural features in Rocky Mountain National Park. All three Arapaho men helped Toll gain some understanding of Arapaho lifeways in the Rocky Mountain region, including the places and methods Arapahos used for hunting and preparing food, their spiritual practices and legends, warfare with other tribes, and how they built camps, marked trails, and cared for the ill. Toll could not help but admire the Arapahos' outdoor skills and careful use of nature's resources. Ultimately, however, Toll, the other Whites on the pack trip, and the CMC were engaged in the selective arrogation of Native knowledge and culture for the exclusive benefit of White visitors to Rocky Mountain National Park. Enos Mills met the Arapaho members of the pack trip during their journey through the park region and surely understood that their naming efforts would enhance White tourism in the new national park. Like other champions of the new pleasuring ground, Mills saw no reason to question Whites' privileged access to Rocky Mountain National Park.[38]

Disinclined to see anything wrong in Rocky's presumed racial exclusivity, Mills similarly saw no reason for pessimism about recreational tourism's impact on natural resource preservation. Testifying before the U.S. House Committee on Public Lands in December 1914, Mills reiterated his belief that the exceptional natural resources of the proposed park were threatened by Forest Service management "where the main idea is not the protection of scenery." He then moved to a confident appraisal of "the care which only park service can give" to protected lands open to tourism. "People will continue to visit it and enjoy it without in any way injuring its resources because whatever development would go on [would occur] with the idea that the resources there would be used for the people."[39]

Mills and others testifying in favor of the park made frequent mention of Longs Peak as the "king" of the Rockies, a "sentinel" lending "grandeur" to a wondrous landscape of mountain peaks, glaciers, gorges, chasms, lakes, and valleys. They did not mention developments in Estes that were increasing recreational tourism yet also disrupting the natural environment. The state of Colorado had recently begun to build the Fall River Road inside what would become the new park, hoping to cross the Continental Divide and connect the vacation towns of Estes Park and Grand Lake. Roadways to Estes Park were also undergoing continual improvement. The mountain town boasted a new road from Loveland and four automobile stage lines from the various cities to the east; residents also pointed with pride to newly constructed homes and a new church, school, and volunteer fire department, the town's first bank, a water company, a light and power company, and a local telephone exchange. The Stanley Hotel was the town's newest facility for wealthy tourists, numerous other lodges and resorts had been built, and the YMCA of the Rockies had opened its doors to large associational meetings and educational programs. The development of roads, resorts, utilities, schools, churches, and other services prompted increases in visitation and Estes Park's year-round population and boosted the area's economy. Many of those who visited Estes or built residences there must have had a genuine interest in nature. Simultaneously, however, the changes that facilitated visitation altered the local topography and disturbed native plant and animal habitats. Resort owners who kept domestic cattle, for example, sharpened interspecies competition among mammals for forage, especially for native grama grasses, which the cattle devoured. The nonnative oats and timothy that resort owners planted further upset native habitats. Sport hunting and fishing, much beloved by early tourists, also had a profoundly negative impact on native wildlife.[40]

Mills and his contemporaries would not have possessed enough scientific knowledge to understand all the ecosystem disturbances occurring around them. They did know, however, that resort owners and tourists in Estes Park had contributed to the extinction of local elk and mountain bison and to the near decimation of bighorn sheep and greenback cutthroat trout populations, all through excessive hunting and fishing. In the late nineteenth century, resort owners responded to these losses by working with county and state officials to stock local lakes, rivers, and streams with nonnative fish, and by the 1910s they were working with federal officials to import nonnative elk from Yellowstone National Park. Mills was undoubtedly aware of the declines in elk and fish populations, which were widely discussed by locals. Still, he was not yet prepared to acknowledge negative patterns in tourism's effects.[41] Mills was both an ambitious capitalist and a preservationist; for him tourists were people who spent freely while awaiting conversion in nature. The new roads, automobiles, and modern hotels in Estes Park were simply "beautiful and efficient improvements" that "harmonize[d] with the works of nature," permitting increased visitation to, and affection for, Rocky Mountain National Park.[42]

Testifying alongside Mills, Colorado governor Elias Ammons and governor-elect George Carlson also applauded the fusing of tourism with preservation. Both men described the boon to tourism that the new park would bring as an unequivocal good. The proposed park's "scenic value" and proximity to Denver and other cities would ensure that the new "national playground" had high visitation and would boost the state's economy. Affluent Americans who were usually drawn to Europe, currently mired in war, would gladly vacation in Colorado if a park were founded. With the completion of the Fall River Road linking Estes Park to Grand Lake, the park would become accessible from all directions and thus would be an even greater asset to the state as a recreational destination. Ammons and Carlson anticipated the number of tourists to the region around Estes jumping from its estimated 56,000 in 1914 to 125,000 or 150,000 in a single year "from the mere fact of calling it a national park."[43]

MILLS, AMMONS, AND CARLSON must have been persuasive, for when Congress wrote and approved legislation establishing Rocky Mountain National Park in 1915 it accepted the sanguine presumption that recreational tourism and preservation were altogether compatible. Congress "dedicated and set aside" the park "for the benefit and enjoyment of the people of the United States." The legislation stipulated that park rules and regulations had to aim "for the freest use of the said park for recreation by the public and for the preservation of the natural conditions and scenic beauties thereof."[44] Just one year later, in passing the Organic Act that created the National Park Service (NPS), Congress extended this line of thinking to all existing and future national parks. According to the Organic Act of 1916, national parks must "conserve the scenery and the natural and historical objects and the wild life therein" and must also "provide for the enjoyment of the same in such manner and by such means as will leave them unimpaired for the enjoyment of future generations." Automobile touring was one of the forms of enjoyment expected to grow in the parks. It had been endorsed in 1912 by the Department of the Interior and park superintendents, even though officials admitted concern about the accidents that cars might cause, their loud noise, "very obnoxious odors," and the oil and gasoline they dropped on roadways.[45]

In hindsight it is not hard to see that the legislation creating Rocky Mountain National Park and the NPS articulated a confident yet imprecise vision of park management, ignoring an already-emerging tension between resource protection and recreational tourism. So, too, the new legislation neglected to define the "public" for whom parks were intended and failed to consider how the "freest use of the said park for recreation by the public" was to be achieved in a nation sharply divided by race, ethnicity, gender, and class. Implying that parks should be democratic in spirit and widely accessible, the Rocky Mountain National Park Act and Organic Act never asked whether national parks would in fact be open to people with small pocketbooks or black and brown skin.

Indeed, the legislation establishing Rocky Mountain National Park and the NPS failed to address numerous issues that posed risks to park values and stewardship. The new laws ignored existing inequities that undermined American liberty and never considered the design of the "welcome mat" that park managers, visitors, and proprietors of tourism should weave for successive generations of the public. They did not try to establish how, in practice, park managers were to balance the scenic and recreational interests of tourists with the preservation of natural and historical resources. They made no mention of the role science ought to play in evaluating resource conditions, nor did they hint at the possibility that the tourism industry could be a source of harm to park resources. Finally, the legislation did not recognize the possibility that visitors might, in their enjoyment of nature, put their own lives at risk. Though ignored in 1915, all these issues would become salient, even urgent, at Longs Peak and Rocky Mountain National Park and at other national parks across the nation.

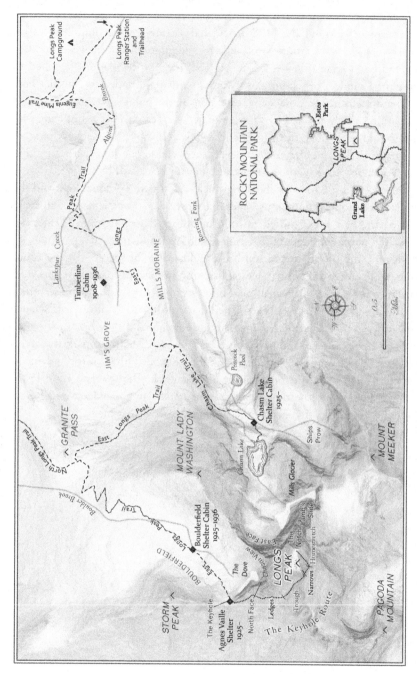

Map 2. Longs Peak. Cartography by Amanda Hastings.

TWO | The "King" of Rocky Mountain National Park, 1915–1925

BY THE TIME Rocky Mountain National Park was founded as a scenic "national playground" in 1915, hundreds of mountain adventurers were climbing Longs each year. Early park superintendents lauded Longs Peak as "a veritable King of Mountains" whose "stalwart, majestic" character invited exploration and discovery. They made some improvements to the trails used by climbers, but they were too understaffed and preoccupied with the needs of front-country tourists, nearly all of them sightseeing in automobiles, to manage recreation on the peak directly. Instead, the park turned to commercial guides and, more importantly, to the organized climbing community represented by the newly established Colorado Mountain Club, to offer instruction on how best to enjoy Longs' splendor, negotiate its alpine challenges, and avoid the perils it presented.[1]

The Colorado Mountain Club (CMC) emerged in 1912 as an advocate of the proposed Rocky Mountain National Park and a regional leader of mountaineers, offering guided outings to Longs and other peaks in the Rockies. Men and women participated in nearly equal numbers in these excursions, but the CMC was a Whites-only organization that declined to offer membership to African Americans or other people of color in Colorado's Front Range towns and cities. In this, it followed patterns of racial discrimination common throughout Colorado and the nation, and, as we will see, patterns acceptable to the early NPS. CMC members and their outing guests were also relatively affluent participants in America's consumer culture, using mountain tourism's infrastructure of roads and gasoline-powered automobiles and its array of specialized merchandise—climbing rope, boots, rain gear, sleeping bags, packs, sunglasses—to pursue the sport they loved. Still, it would be shortsighted to conclude that the CMC was about nothing more than privileged White individuals using consumer commodities to indulge in outdoor fun. Members of the CMC were educated professionals and civic leaders who tempered privilege with dedication to fostering safety and conservation in Colorado's mountain settings. Mountains were simultaneously places of splendor and adventure, danger and fragility, and the CMC balanced its pursuit of vertical pleasure with a keen sense of responsibility. Members sought to maximize the gratifications of climbing while endorsing conduct that limited risk to both humans and mountain environments.

Indeed, the CMC cultivated mountaineers' knowledge about, and appreciation for, the natural environments in which they climbed and developed standards of behavior in the outdoors that prioritized safety and teamwork. Moreover, the club championed natural resource preservation in the park, around Colorado, and in the National Park System, working at two levels. Through education and outreach the CMC took steps to limit mountaineers' damage to the wild landscapes that brought them exhilaration and joy. And in collaboration with other conservation groups, it countered state and federal policy initiatives that were likely to harm precious resources in Rocky and other national parks.

In effect, the early CMC attempted to mobilize a subculture of climbers devoted to an ethic of care in the wild that prioritized both safe adventure and "nature protection." This is not to say that the CMC discovered a fully sustainable balance between recreation and natural resource preservation. Still, the CMC was more deliberate than Rocky or other national parks in trying to identify and moderate the negative impact of mountain tourism and industrial development on protected land. By the 1920s park administrators in Rocky and other national parks were beginning to worry about tourism's harm to the environment, but unlike the CMC, they were not ready to act on these concerns. They could not see how to advance preservation within the small ranks of park staff or among visitors, pressured as they were to satisfy the touristic desires of the latter group, especially those relying on automobiles and roads for sightseeing.

Promoting Mountaineering on Longs Peak

In the first ten years of the park's existence, the permanent staff at Rocky Mountain National Park numbered fewer than ten people, and Longs Peak, though touted as the greatest of all the "lofty mountains" of the park, was not a managerial priority. The park's ethic of care, in an early stage of formation, prioritized the development of front-country amenities that would enhance the comfort and enjoyment of visitors sightseeing in automobiles and staying in private resorts within park boundaries or in Estes Park. There was only a single ranger responsible for the entire eastern portion of the park, including Longs, and he was frequently occupied with aiding motorists on Fall River Road, the steep, narrow, and dangerous gravel roadway still undergoing construction from east to west over the Continental Divide. Convict crews who cost the underfunded park nothing in wages and lived in extremely primitive cabins had been building the road since 1913, and they continued to extend its length during the 1920s.

Park personnel were much involved in supervising the convicts' work, even as they tended to the needs of visiting motorists.[2]

Auto tourism had become the focus of park management as the automobile industry of the 1910s captured the attention and pocketbooks of middle-class Americans (mostly White and native born) with its stylish designs, mass production, imaginative marketing, and moderate pricing. New roads were being built around the nation, and fuel distributors and retailers worked hard to increase travelers' access to gasoline. Though railroads remained a critical means of travel among tourists, growing numbers of vacationing Americans were turning to private cars to carry them into national parks and preserves and gain access to nature's grandeur. Printed guides and brochures from the National Park Service and U.S. Railroad Administration provided detailed information about train and automobile travel to the national parks and vivid descriptions of the scenic automobile tours and other forms of recreation awaiting visitors inside park boundaries. Photographs in park and railroad guides showed well-dressed White tourists observing breathtaking scenery as they stood near stylish automobiles. Additional photos showed visitors on horseback or camping and fishing at lovely alpine lakes. Young people climbed mountains. Women and children played tennis, golf, and croquet at private resorts in or near national parks. Automobile travel made all this possible. The material and cultural inducements to automobility were so pronounced that Stephen Mather, assistant secretary of the interior, remarked in 1916 about an "astonishing increase in motor travel in the parks."[3]

In fact, the number of visitors to Rocky Mountain National Park swelled rapidly after 1915, and virtually all arrived in private or rented automobiles: 31,000 visitors entered the park in 1915; visitation rose to 169,492 in 1919 and then to 233,912 in 1925. It rose yet higher to 274,408 in 1929, before dropping to 255,874 in 1930, the first full year of the Great Depression. Some of these visitors, especially those from out of state, probably took trains as far as Denver, then rented cars for the trip to Rocky Mountain National Park. Many in-state visitors probably relied entirely on private automobiles for their travel.[4]

As at other national parks, the large number of automobile visitors in Rocky put intense pressure on early superintendents to promote growth of a touristic infrastructure. Park superintendents actively encouraged the construction of new lodging facilities in Estes Park while working to acquire and absorb private inholdings within the park's boundaries. They also sought to improve roadways and wayside stops in the park, though this work was a colossal challenge. Roads in the park emerged not from a master plan but from a network of state, county, and private initiatives. The Fall River Road was constructed through the cooperative efforts of the state and Larimer and Grand Counties, but most roadways inside the park, especially in the popular Bear Lake area, had been built by private resort owners to widely varying personal standards. The private roads covered only short distances, and vast sections of the park had no roadways at all. Most important, there was no through-road going from the park's east to

west side. Park superintendents struggled to obtain funding for road improvements and to secure federal control over park roads that were still under private,
county, or state jurisdiction. It took until the end of the 1920s for Bear Lake
Road to be successfully reconstructed and resurfaced. Just as it was completed,
the park began seeking federal appropriations to replace the perilous Fall River
Road with a safe paved highway, Trail Ridge Road. Even as new roads were being
constructed, maintenance and snow removal were constant and arduous tasks.[5]

Though burdened by front-country responsibilities, the park's earliest administrators, C. R. Trowbridge (acting supervisor, 1915–1916) and L. Claude Way
(chief ranger in charge, 1915–1917, and then superintendent, 1917–1921),
expected Longs Peak to draw visitors to the area, as it had before the park was
established. Park bulletins written for the public highlighted the rewards of
Longs for both automobile sightseers and mountaineers. For those motoring in
Rocky, Longs was the centerpiece of a landscape breathtaking in its "nobility . . .
calm dignity, in the sheer glory of stalwart beauty." No other "mountain group"
excelled "the company of snow-capped veterans of all the ages which stands
at everlasting parade behind its grim, helmeted captain, Longs Peak." And for
alpinists Longs was the most "inspiring" and "strenuous" of climbs in the park.[6]

Going a step further, the bulletins included detailed first-person accounts by
climbers who had summitted Longs, trying both to inspire and to instill caution
in mountaineers. In one such account, Miss Edna Smith, a guest at the Longs Peak
Inn, recalled seeking Enos Mills's approval before undertaking a climb on Longs
on an August night shortly after a severe rainstorm. The climb from trailhead
to summit via the East Longs Peak Trail and *Keyhole* route proceeded without
difficulty, though Edna, her two women friends, and their commercial guide had
to climb through the Trough via steps cut into hard and slippery ice. The women
delighted in one scene of exquisite beauty after another, as the dense fog gave
way to a moonlit night sky and then, slowly, to a golden dawn. By comparison,
Mr. D. W. Roper admitted to climbing Longs Peak alone and "contrary to the
advice of those who knew its perils," immediately after a September snowstorm.
Mr. Roper enjoyed "magnificent views" but met with dangerous conditions, especially descending through the Trough, where "if one should start to slip . . . the
only certain place [to stop] appeared to be down near Glacier Lake, some 2,000
feet below." Mr. Roper lost the trail several times before getting back to the Keyhole from Longs' summit, thus enduring a far longer descent than anticipated.[7]

Accounts such as these must have worked to stimulate interest in Longs.
Indeed, the Colorado Mountain Club's *Trail and Timberline* magazine reported on
a "resistless urge" to climb the stalwart peak among CMC members and friends.
Climbing on Longs increased steadily in the decade after the park opened, though
climbing totals were small compared to the park's overall visitation figures. The
CMC made it possible to obtain a reasonably accurate count of the number of
individuals summiting Longs each year when it placed a "bronze weatherproof
cylinder on top of Longs Peak containing a small register book" in 1915.[8] That

year the register showed 260 signatures, dipping to 128 in 1916. By the 1920s, however, more than a thousand climbers summited the peak each year—for example, 1,060 in 1920, 1,247 in 1924, and 1,592 in 1925. Importantly, the register books did not account for climbers who did not summit Longs and thus undercounted the total number of mountaineers on the peak in any specific year.[9]

As climbers' numbers increased, so too did park superintendents' concerns about the inadequacies of the East Longs Peak Trail and *Keyhole* route, and they tried, as resources permitted, to fund trail improvements and construction. The park's entire trail system was woefully insufficient, but the trails and rocky routes on Longs were especially concerning, given the popularity and inherent risks of the peak.[10] In July 1918 Superintendent L. C. Way climbed the East trail and *Keyhole* route on Longs to gain firsthand knowledge of its shortcomings. He was most troubled about climbers becoming lost on the descent across the Ledges, where a feature known as the "false Keyhole" sometimes drew people onto a dangerous detour from the main route. Way's observations led him to instruct ranger Dean Babcock to place cairns and red flags on the route between the Keyhole and the summit. Three years later, Way ordered improvements to the section of trail leading from Jim's Grove to Granite Pass, reducing the grade of 30 and 40 percent to a more modest 15 percent. Mountaineers were thus able "to make quicker time and with much less fatigue." Probably knowing that funding shortfalls made durability in trail construction a must, the rangers and their work crews rebuilt the trail "to suffer the minimum damage from the rains and melting snows," locating it "to get the minimum of wash."[11]

Improvements to trail conditions on Longs continued under Superintendent Roger Wolcott Toll, Way's successor. In 1922 Toll ordered new painted dots (subsequently known as "bullseyes") on the route past the Keyhole, having concluded that the flags and cairns of his predecessor did not do enough to mitigate the dangers of becoming lost on the climb:

> The trail to the summit of Longs was marked by dots painted on the rocks. The trail above the Keyhole is often difficult to find or follow, since it is mostly over rocks and the traveled route is not plain. Over a thousand people make this climb in a season, and half or two-thirds of them go without licensed guides. A number of people have lost the trail and become confused, sometimes getting into dangerous places. It is hoped that the marking of the trail will help to prevent accidents on the peak. The dots are of two colors, a yellow background with a red center, so as to be readily visible, and placed close enough together so that even in times of storm or fog they will be of assistance to parties.[12]

Way and Toll applauded the growing numbers of people summiting Longs each year and hoped their improvements to the East Longs Peak Trail and *Keyhole* route would help keep them safe. There was little else they could do.

Rangers were preoccupied with surging automobile tourism in the park and had no time to advise or assist mountaineers, whether on Longs or other park peaks. Given these circumstances, it fell to the CMC and a relatively small number of licensed guides approved by the park to offer skilled assistance to climbers in Rocky Mountain National Park.

The Colorado Mountain Club began to lead groups of people on climbs to the summit of Longs and other mountains in the Rockies even before the founding of Rocky Mountain National Park and continued to do so after the park opened. Its role as the park's authority on mountaineering was broadly announced with the publication of *Mountaineering in the Rocky Mountain National Park* in 1919.[13] Based on CMC records, *Mountaineering* was published by the federal government as a supplement to the existing general bulletins on Rocky Mountain National Park. It was compiled by Toll, a founding member of the CMC and the son of a prominent Denver family. A civil engineer by profession, Toll was also an avid mountaineer with extensive experience climbing in the Colorado Rockies and the Swiss Alps. After serving in the military during World War I, Toll turned to publishing *Mountaineering*. He subsequently accepted employment with the National Park Service, superintending Mount Rainier National Park for two years before becoming superintendent of Rocky in November 1921.[14]

Meant to share both essential information and mountaineering ideals with backcountry visitors, Toll's guidebook urged readers to view Rocky Mountain National Park as a place dedicated to the enjoyment and preservation of nature. Since visitors could expect little interaction with rangers in the backcountry and scant park oversight, the information and commentary in *Mountaineering* were a substitute, "a compilation of the experiences of the Colorado Mountain Club which cover many years of climbing these very mountains. . . . If it will lessen the hardship of new climbers until experience shows them that there is no hardship, but in its stead vigorous nerves, bounding health, inspiration, and a rare communion with nature, its object and the hope of the club's members will be fulfilled."[15]

Certainly, Toll offered readers detailed guidance on how to engage in safe and pleasurable climbing. He provided information on appropriate clothing and equipment for mountaineering and camping, offered descriptions of climbing routes to mountain summits throughout the park, and included firsthand accounts of climbs on Longs and numerous other peaks. Toll encouraged climbers to assume responsibility for the quality of their mountaineering experience and urged them not to rush as they sought to reach mountain summits. On Longs, a peak that Toll encouraged all visiting mountaineers to climb, this might mean hiring a guide for an ascent that stretched over two days and staying overnight at the Timberline Cabin, a primitive hut at about eleven thousand feet in Jim's Grove, before climbing to the Keyhole and summit. The Timberline Cabin had been built by Enos Mills and his brother Joe in 1908 and was operated by the park as a rustic mountain concession offering cooked meals and heated shelter during the summer months. The small commercial cabin undoubtedly produced wood or coal soot as well as food and human waste, but in 1919 Toll was unaware of these potential problems, noting only its role in promoting climbers' well-being in an alpine setting.[16]

Though he lacked the ecological knowledge of later generations, Toll also intended *Mountaineering* to deepen climbers' understanding of nature in Rocky Mountain National Park and their own relationship to it. The guidebook offered scientific information about the weather, trees, birds, and small mammals in the park. It sought to instill in readers respect for the "hard battle for life at timberline" and encouraged them to appreciate the slow and stunted growth of trees at that elevation. Toll spoke of "your friend, the mountain," as a natural feature possessing a form of "solemn dignity" not generally found in human beings.[17]

Ultimately, Toll wanted readers to view mountaineering as a sport that oriented humans, though small, to the grandeur of mountains and the lessons they offered. "Mountaineering," he wrote, takes humans into "nature's workshop." It "creates in one a desire to know more about natural sciences" and to care about the well-being of the natural world. So, too, it "promotes the health and strength of the body, it teaches self-reliance, determination, presence of mind, necessity for individual thought and action, pride of accomplishment, fearlessness, endurance, helpful cooperation, loyalty, patriotism, the love of an unselfish freedom, and many other qualities that make for sturdy manhood and womanhood." Toll considered mountaineering a powerful route to the betterment of humans, their society, and the natural environment. Finding sacred qualities in mountaineering, Toll quoted fellow CMC member Emma Barnard, who lauded mountaineering as an activity that moved the soul in ways "man's temple" could not. "You can never be the same, since to Nature's vast cathedral you in silent worship came."[18]

Race and Gender in the Early Years of Mountaineering

Historians Susan Schrepfer and Peter Hansen argue that European and American mountaineering have deeply racialized and gendered histories, dominated by White men whose approach to climbing emphasized the masculine conquest of nature, the superiority of White imperial nations, and the exclusion or subordination of women climbers.[19] The early CMC complicates this interpretation. The organization's mission statement was notably democratic in spirit, stressing members' interest in making "readily accessible the alpine attractions of this region."[20] And there was little in Toll's language in *Mountaineering* to suggest a sweeping or declarative interest in dominion. Toll viewed mountains and mountaineering with reverence, finding that climbing on high peaks collapsed the distinctions between religion, sport, and science. In Toll's view, mountaineering strengthened individuals' resilience and judgment. Though "pride of accomplishment" was one benefit of mountaineering, the sport also encouraged "helpful cooperation." It stimulated interest in the natural sciences, respect for nature, and recognition of nature's connection to the divine. Toll's orientation toward mountaineering was shared by other Americans, who wrote about their experience of mountain landscapes in national parks in the late nineteenth and early twentieth centuries.[21] So, too, the first-person accounts by CMC members in *Mountaineering* offered careful descriptions of chosen routes and mountain geology, wildlife, and scenic views but said little suggestive of an interest in supremacy.

Moving from stated values to practice, the CMC appears to have both accommodated and avoided dominion in human relationships. As we saw in chapter 1, the CMC used Native history and culture in selecting Arapaho names for landmarks in Rocky Mountain National Park but never questioned the removal of Native Americans from the park region. And though the CMC's constitution urged its members to "stimulate public interest in our mountain area" and "render readily accessible the alpine attractions of this region," the club had an all-White membership (evident in published photos in *Trail and Timberline* and in the club's unpublished photos). The CMC's bylaws required that individuals be formally recommended for membership by two club members and then win the affirmative vote of the club's Board of Directors. This procedure assured the organization that new members would be like-minded individuals, enthusiastic about climbing and disposed to "helpful cooperation, loyalty, patriotism, [and] the love of an unselfish freedom." It also seemed to ensure that the club had an all-White membership not inclined to rebel against societal norms.[22]

Indeed, the CMC was persistently silent on matters of discrimination, though members surely knew something about racial, ethnic, and faith-based hierarchies in Colorado. After all, this was a club of well-educated and well-connected individuals, active in commerce, the professions, and civic affairs.[23] They must have known that all cities and towns in Colorado in the early twentieth century discriminated against Indians, Blacks, Mexican Americans, Chinese, Catholics, and Jews. Racism stretched from the segregation of parks, theaters, restaurants, stores, and swimming pools to White Protestants' exclusive access to leadership positions in government and to the best housing, schools, medical care, and employment.[24]

They must have known, as well, that the color line in Colorado was not altogether secure. Women and men in Denver's small African American community were using the political system as well as Black community organizations to improve Blacks' schooling and employment, access to recreation and health care, and political clout. African American women and men gained the right to vote in Colorado in 1893, allying with White women fighting for access to the ballot. They led efforts to elect Joseph Henry Stuart, Colorado's first Black elected official, to the state assembly in 1894 and successfully won passage of an 1895 state law that promised equal access to "public accommodation and amusement," regardless of race or color. Disappointingly, the law was not enforced, but that did not stop African Americans' continued mobilization for equality. Blacks in

Denver published the *Statesman* and the *Denver Star* to give voice to their community's civic and political concerns. So, too, relying on a "politics of respectability" and interracial collaboration, Denver's African Americans sought in 1915 to ban the showing of *Birth of a Nation* and founded the Colored Citizens' League and the Colored Protective League, the latter declaring that its goal was "to protect and advance the civil and political rights of the Negroes of Denver." Denver's organized Black community won generally supportive coverage from the *Rocky Mountain News* and *Denver Post* and established a local chapter of the NAACP in 1915, working with a few supportive Whites. Similarly, Denver's Catholic churches and the *Rocky Mountain News* regularly decried efforts by the American Protective Association to deepen anti-Catholic prejudices. And Denver's Jewish community published the *Jewish Outlook*, a newspaper that denounced acts of anti-Semitism, while also organizing a variety of self-help and charitable institutions. So, too, in southern Colorado coal miners from varied ethnic and racial backgrounds organized and went on strike to gain improved working conditions and pay in notoriously dangerous mines, winning rights to regular pay, unionization, improved workplace safety, and an eight-hour workday by the mid-1910s.[25]

Without explicit statements by the CMC about the color line, we cannot fully explain the club's inattention to the possibility of multiracial democracy, whether in Colorado's cities and towns or in mountaineering and the national parks. Some members of the club may have been sympathetic to Jewish, Black, and Catholic demands for rights, respect, and opportunity. Yet it is also probable that the CMC, in working closely with Rocky Mountain National Park, thought it best to adhere closely to park practice on matters of race, practices that were first made explicit in 1922. That year, one of the tasks of NPS administrators and park superintendents attending the NPS's annual summer conference was to draft and approve a statement discouraging African American park visitors. The NPS was only six years old, but its leaders were concerned about racial tension, perhaps responding to rising demands for civil rights and social freedoms among Black veterans of World War I and to horrific episodes throughout the United States of anti-Black violence and the reemergence of the Ku Klux Klan.[26] Eager to sidestep a racial tempest, the NPS pursued a policy of "polite" White exclusivity. As park leaders took in the stunning natural setting at Yosemite, they agreed that informal racial exclusion made sense in national parks. Black visitors were likely to offend Whites and disrupt racial hierarchies already in place in gateway towns and in the hotels and lodges that served national park guests. Their statement read: "One of the objections to colored people is that if they come in large groups they will be conspicuous, and will not only be objected to by other visitors, but will cause trouble among the hotel and camp help, and it will be impossible to serve them. Individual cases can be handled, although even this is awkward, but organized parties could not be taken care of. . . . While we cannot openly discriminate against them, they should be told that the parks have no facilities for taking care of them."[27]

The NPS statement sanctioned what was already the norm in Rocky Mountain National Park and its gateway communities. Estes Park business owners hired African American staff to help keep White park visitors and resort guests happy, but they did not accept African Americans as customers. CMC members occasionally availed themselves of lodgings and services in Estes Park and must have accepted their racial privilege as a given, just as they did in Denver, Fort Collins, Boulder, and Colorado Springs. Neither the CMC nor Rocky Mountain National Park signaled any public objection to the Ku Klux Klan's short-lived dominance of Colorado politics in the 1920s or its presence in Estes Park, Denver, Boulder, and other towns. Estes Park's local newspaper, the *Estes Park Trail*, portrayed the KKK as an active and generally well-regarded presence in town in the early and mid-1920s, reporting, for example, that it sent hooded members to a local church to present a Bible to a minister and wife departing for mission work in Africa and burned crosses at disreputable resorts that allowed dancing and the sale of bootlegged liquor. The town paper said little about the outright racism of the Klan, though it occasionally printed jokes about the Klan at the expense of African Americans, as when it asked, "Mose, what would you do if you received a letter from the Ku Klux Klan? a local negro was asked. 'Well, sah, I'd read it on a train,' replied Mose."[28] After 1925 the *Estes Park Trail* began to reprint overtly critical appraisals of the Klan from larger state and national newspapers, but the CMC and Rocky remained silent about the organization. By this time, Denver's African Americans were working hard to defeat the Klan in their city. As we will see in chapter 3, they were also building Lincoln Hills, a mountain resort in Gilpin County just forty-two miles from Rocky. In developing Lincoln Hills, Denver's African Americans signaled that they had given up on recreation in Rocky precisely because racist values and prohibitions were embedded in the park and surrounding community.[29]

Though the CMC never challenged racial privilege, it welcomed White women into the community of climbers, disavowing rigid gender conventions. Women had been among the earliest recreational climbers on Longs, and they were frequent participants in CMC climbing trips to Rocky Mountain National Park during its first years of existence. Drawing on club records for *Mountaineering*, Toll noted the presence of fifteen women in one group of twenty-seven climbers on Longs, seven women in a party of fourteen climbing Hagues Peak, and three of ten going to Otis Peak.[30] Other records from this period elaborate on women's active participation in the CMC, as both climbers and club leaders. In an era when Teddy Roosevelt and other White men promoted hypermasculinity, especially in the outdoors, the CMC actively encouraged White women's participation in climbing, on Longs and elsewhere.[31] The 1915 and 1916 summit registers show, for example, that approximately 20 percent of all those who summited Longs Peak were women. And trip reports reveal that when Colorado Mountain Club members and guests went on outings to Longs Peak in the early 1920s, it was not unusual for women to account for approximately half of all climbers on this strenuous ascent. Moreover, women served as outing leaders on Longs and on other CMC trips throughout the Rockies.[32]

So, too, while CMC presidents and vice presidents were always men, women in the organization served as committee chairs, section chiefs, and members of the organization's Board of Directors. They also wrote substantial copy for the club's *Trail and Timberline* magazine, choosing content and setting the tone of the publication. Overall, women played critical roles in developing the culture and priorities of the CMC. They brought to the club valuable skills in teaching, writing, science, business, and librarianship as well as true athleticism and tremendous interest in advancing the club's mission. Certainly, they helped to mold within the CMC a spirit of good-natured cooperation among women and men. Scholars Joseph Taylor, Silas Chamberlin, and Gordon Sayre have found similar gender camaraderie among climbers and hikers in California, Oregon, Washington, and the eastern and midwestern states during the early and mid-twentieth century.[33]

The relative equality of White men and women in the early CMC can be attributed to numerous factors. White women in Colorado won the right to vote in 1893, well ahead of other states, after forging strategic alliances with African Americans and Populists, the latter a burgeoning third party that sought to weaken Democrats and Republicans alike by supporting a variety of constituents and causes. White women who helped found the CMC came of age in an era of gradually broadening support, in Colorado and across the nation, for White women's higher education, participation in civic life, entry into the professions, and athletic endeavors. To be sure, local and national adversaries mounted vigorous opposition to gender equality, especially as the federal suffrage movement gained momentum in the 1910s. Still, the ill treatment White women endured was not as severe as that heaped on politically active Black women who faced rebuke by antisuffragists, violent opposition by White supremacists, and selective ostracism by White suffragists. Exercising race privilege while fighting gender oppression, significant numbers of White women managed to claim new rights and opportunities, including in mountaineering organizations such as the CMC.[34]

Interestingly, the women of the CMC may have encouraged appreciation of White women's skills not only in their own club but in Rocky Mountain National Park as well. The park was far more male-dominated than the CMC, being part of the National Park Service, a governmental agency with staffing and personnel policies that drew from an all-male military model of command. Still, the park took small steps in its early years to acknowledge White women's capabilities, perhaps impressed by the relative prominence and skill of women in the CMC and by initiatives taken in other parks to hire women "ranger-naturalists." Most notably, Rocky hired two sisters, Esther and Elizabeth Burnell, as "nature guides" in the summer of 1917, requiring them to prove by examination their knowledge of park wildlife, first aid, and geography. Esther was a graduate of the Pratt Art Institute of Brooklyn; Elizabeth had a master's degree in mathematics and physics from the University of Michigan and was chair of the Department of Mathematics and Physics at Lake Erie College in Ohio. Both women had vacationed at Longs Peak Inn and hiked extensively in the surrounding area, and Esther homesteaded briefly near Estes Park. As nature guides, the sisters were not permitted to take park visitors above timberline except in the company of a licensed guide, but they were considered invaluable teachers of "nature lore" among park visitors. The Burnell sisters and two additional women were hired as nature guides in 1918, and the park's hiring of women for its nature-guide program continued during the 1920s. By this time Anne and Isabel Pfifer had also made a name for themselves as climbing guides at the YMCA of the Rockies, leading hikers twenty-six miles from the Y to the summit of Longs and back again in a single day.[35]

"Nature Protection" and "Over Development" in Rocky Mountain National Park

Though its move away from hierarchical relations among humans was far from complete, the Colorado Mountain Club refused to condone human efforts to master nature, especially when such efforts despoiled wilderness environments. Established in 1912 to champion mountaineering and to support the founding of Rocky Mountain National Park, the CMC articulated five central goals in its mission statement:

1. To unite the energy, interest, and knowledge of the students, explorers, and lovers of the mountains of Colorado;
2. Collect and disseminate information regarding the Rocky Mountains on behalf of science, literature, art, and recreation;
3. Stimulate public interest in our mountain area;
4. Encourage the preservation of forests, flowers, fauna, and natural scenery; and
5. Render readily accessible the alpine attractions of this region.[36]

Like the Rocky Mountain National Park Act of 1915 and the Organic Act of 1916, the CMC's mission statement imagined compatibility between recreation and preservation. However, while the two pieces of national park legislation neglected to describe the conditions necessary for compatibility between these core goals, the CMC's mission statement pointed to a genuine love of mountains—born of immersive experience—and broad knowledge of natural environments as the basis for binding recreation to preservation. It also identified well-developed capabilities in leadership, science education, and public engagement as essential to forging harmony between the two goals. CMC members brought high levels of education and professional experience to the task of developing and articulating ideas about how backcountry recreation and preservation might coexist. Just as important, many CMC members identified as outdoor adventurers *and* civic leaders, ready to use mountain trails as well as the printed word and assembly-hall lecterns to promote complementarity between backcountry recreation and the preservation of natural resources.[37]

Early on, the CMC went beyond a verbal commitment to preservation, establishing a Nature Protection Committee to tackle emerging conflicts between recreational tourism and preservation. Even in its first decade, the CMC engaged in statewide efforts to educate hikers and climbers about low-impact backcountry practices, producing a "Good Woodsman" poster to communicate to backcountry visitors the importance of leaving nature intact, for its own sake and the enjoyment of future visitors. The "Good Woodsman" poster favored the burying of tin cans, surely an offense to twenty-first-century environmental sensibilities, but this measure reflected the best understanding of the time about minimizing harm to nature. Otherwise, the poster and the CMC's other educational activities actively discouraged sport hunting, tree cutting, and pulling up plants by their roots. In this, the club countered the widely circulated guidance of contemporary writers Horace Kephart, Elmer Krep, and Ernest Seton, who urged city-dwelling boys and men to recover their masculinity by camping in the wild, using a "woodsman's" skills to cut down trees and turn them into shelter and fuel, and killing wild animals for food.[38]

In addition, the CMC educated the public and worked successfully for the passage of a 1925 state law that criminalized the gathering of more than twenty-five columbines on public lands in a single day, as the state flower was being threatened by overzealous flower pickers. And at the national level, determined not to let the damming of Hetch Hetchy Valley in Yosemite National Park stand as precedent, the CMC lobbied successfully with other conservation organizations to amend the 1920 Federal Power Act, preventing the opening of national parks to the construction of dams, conduits, reservoirs, power houses, and power transmission lines for commercial purposes. These were significant measures, providing evidence of the CMC's recognition that both human recreation and industrial development could harm the natural resources in national parks. They also demonstrated the CMC's willingness to engage in outreach, among club members and the public at large, to promote preservationist ethics and activism. Indeed, the CMC's 1922 publication *The Colorado Mountain Club: Its History, Activities, and Purposes* reminded readers that "[The club] has taken an active and fighting part in the struggle that is continually being waged to keep our national parks free from the touch of those who would commercialize them for private ends." *Trail and Timberline*, the club's monthly magazine, sought consistently to communicate this message to members and to identify policy options and mountaineering practices that would minimize harm to natural resources.[39]

Roger Toll was a founding member of the CMC, yet as superintendent of Rocky Mountain National Park he had no option but to view front-country visitors' growing presence in the park as a positive good. Visitors were crucial to justifying the existence of national parks, and their presence required improved roads and other amenities. Still, Toll was not without concern about the potentially negative effects of touristic development in the national parks. At the Yosemite conference of 1922 where superintendents justified the informal exclusion of Blacks from national parks, Toll and his peers also discussed development, drafting a resolution that reaffirmed their commitment to development yet cautioned against "over-development." The resolution thus stated that "roads and trails should be improved and extended, ample accommodations should be provided for visitors, and other improvements carried out, so that the parks may better fulfill their mission of healthful recreation and education to a larger number of people." But it also asserted that "certain areas should be reserved in each park, with a minimum amount of development, in order that animals, forest, flowers and all native life shall be preserved under natural conditions."

Toll appended an explanatory letter to the resolution, wanting to stress national parks' importance to scientific understanding and public education, and to convey the difficulty of discerning the point at which development turned into overdevelopment. On a hopeful note, he pointed out that most parks developed no more than 10 percent of their land for automobile visitors. Unfortunately, he did not know whether these percentages would hold in the future: "There is no sharp line between necessary, proper development and harmful over-development. The best judgment and active work of all concerned must be focused together in order to secure the best results. At present the educational and economic value of the national parks to the nation, is restricted by insufficient development. Far-sighted men, however, are making plans for years ahead, and it is to guide future protection that the National Park Service announces its stand, 'For adequate development, but against over-development.'"[40]

As Toll struggled to identify in the abstract the line separating desirable park development from overdevelopment, he pressed ahead with improvements in Rocky Mountain National Park, determined to give the park's front-country visitors better roads, new campgrounds, and enhanced opportunities for scenic viewing and fishing. Thus, road improvements accrued by the year, with funding appropriated in 1929 for Trail Ridge Road, designed with sightseeing by automobile its primary purpose. On Bear Lake Road, park crews tried to improve travelers' views by replanting trees on sections of the old road that had been abandoned. The entire park had just one free public campground in 1920 but five by 1929 (including one at the base of Longs Peak), all with toilet facilities and running water. These served a minority of park visitors, as the majority stayed in privately owned resorts and inns operating within park boundaries or in an expanding array of lodges and resorts in Estes Park. Superintendent Toll also continued the predator control policies put in place by his predecessor: park rangers killed mountain lions, foxes, coyotes, and other predator species so the populations of elk and mountain sheep that visitors loved to see would increase. In addition, hoping to keep the park's forests perpetually verdant for the visiting public, Toll moved toward a policy of strict fire suppression and ordered the cutting and peeling of trees showing any sign of beetle infestation. Finally, park crews continued to stock the park's lakes with nonnative trout species to improve visitors' fishing experience.[41]

Though the vast majority of land in Rocky Mountain National Park remained undeveloped and inaccessible to all but the most rugged rangers and park visitors, policies calling for road and campground construction, predator control, fire suppression, and nonnative fish stocking had wide-ranging and harmful effects over time: wildlife habitat disturbance and fragmentation; ungulate overpopulation and overgrazing; hazardous fuel accumulations and massive pine beetle outbreaks; and disruption in aquatic habitats. Similar environmental harms were developing in other national parks, as the policies pursued at Rocky were commonplace across the National Park System.[42] Unfortunately, these harms were not yet well understood. Ecological science was a relatively new field and it gained virtually no traction in the early years of the NPS, especially after Stephen Mather, director of the National Park Service from 1916 to 1929, prioritized touristic development and pushed science to the margins of the agency. A preliminary critique of park programs in fire, wildlife, and fish management came in 1924 from one lone ecologist, Charles C. Adams, who urged his fellow scientists to "educate themselves, the public and the officials in learning how to perpetuate wilderness areas for scientific and educational purposes."[43] But Adams had no perceptible impact on the NPS or on individual parks. At Rocky, Toll was a strong proponent of the ranger-naturalist program, hiring highly educated scientists to lecture visitors on park geology and wildlife and thereby boost their appreciation of nature, but he had neither the knowledge nor the inclination to introduce ecological perspectives to park management.[44]

ROGER TOLL'S DETERMINATION to promote front-country visitation and park development—however underlain with disquiet—had important implications for Longs Peak and the mountaineers who sought its summit. Most obviously, park officials' preoccupation with front-country development prompted the Colorado Mountain Club to assume a leadership role in the backcountry. While the park accepted responsibility for maintaining and improving trails on Longs and in other wilderness locations as funding allowed, the CMC took seriously its obligation to provide authoritative guidance on backcountry recreation and nature protection, within and beyond the park. It used club outings, publications, educational outreach, and organized letter-writing campaigns to promote enjoyable, safe, and low-impact mountaineering on Longs and at other sites and to advocate for the long-term preservation of undeveloped public land. Still, the CMC could not possibly reach all climbers with its ethic of care. And though the organization pursued growth in membership, its outreach was aimed only at a White, educated middle class, primed by privilege to embrace mountaineering and the delights of unspoiled nature.

Nor could the CMC avoid a relationship of dependency on mountain tourism's infrastructure and market economy. CMC members were glad to leave commerce and urban environments behind as they set out for Longs or other peaks, but these park visitors, like others, relied on cars, gasoline, and decent roads to access the park. They also depended on specialized equipment for hikes, climbs, and ski outings, relied on well-maintained and clearly marked trails to reach Longs' summit and the summits of other peaks, and availed themselves of food and shelter at the Timberline Cabin, the small primitive concession near Longs' Boulderfield. Many sought accommodations in park campgrounds and private resorts just before or after returning from the backcountry. Mountain tourism and its extensive infrastructure enhanced CMC members' access to the outdoors, facilitating their deep attachment to nature and commitment to preservation.

The CMC recognized, early on, that mountain tourism came at some cost to both human safety and the environment, and it struggled to discern how best to protect humans and nature from harm while utilizing mountain tourism's goods, services, and infrastructure. It pursued this difficult balancing act while park officials fixed their attention on touristic development at Rocky Mountain National Park. In the latter half of the 1920s, as the next chapter shows, human tragedy on Longs Peak prompted park officials to become more actively involved in educating climbers and protecting them from potential harm, thereby forging a more active partnership with the climbing community. In effect, the park deepened its investment in an ethic of care on Longs. Paradoxically, in doing so, it promoted ever higher levels of visitation by inexperienced climbers and introduced new sources of environmental degradation on Rocky's loftiest peak.

THREE | The Agnes Vaille Tragedy and Its Aftermath

A CRISIS IN 1925 briefly diverted the park's attention from front-country development, though not toward natural resource preservation or multiracial access to Rocky and Longs. Rather, the preservation of human life on Longs Peak was at stake. In January 1925 Agnes Wolcott Vaille, a CMC leader and first cousin of Superintendent Roger Wolcott Toll, died of hypothermia after a fall on the North Face of Longs Peak. Herbert Sortland, one of the party trying to rescue Vaille, also died of exposure in the brutal winter weather. Three other climbers had died on the increasingly popular peak earlier in the decade, the first deaths on Longs since two were recorded in the 1880s. All three were inexperienced climbers: two fell and perished while climbing alone, and the third, though in the company of others, was hit fatally by lightning after reaching the summit via the *Keyhole* route. In contrast, Vaille was one of an emerging cohort of skilled technical climbers eager to ascend very challenging portions of the peak's North and East Faces, even in winter conditions. The five fatalities on Longs made manifest the perils associated with recreation on the beloved mountain, whatever climbers' level of expertise or exposure to the guidance of the CMC.[1]

Superintendent Toll might have responded to his cousin's tragic death and the other fatalities on Longs by restricting access to the peak. Instead, so strong was his belief in the virtues of mountaineering that he bolstered support for climbing on Longs, ordering trail improvements, the building of three new shelter cabins, and the placement of climbing cables on the peak's North Face. He also arranged for the installation of a telephone in the Boulderfield and increased rangers' presence on the peak. Toll acknowledged climbers' primary responsibility for their own safety, but he believed the park should try to save lives and reduce injuries by assigning rangers to Longs and making improvements to the peak's infrastructure. Through his leadership, Rocky Mountain National Park invested in a collaborative ethic of care with mountaineers, hoping that greater investments in human safety would sharply reduce serious accidents and deaths on Longs.

As it turned out, the park's improvements and enhanced oversight helped some expert and novice climbers avoid harm, but these innovations did not end human deaths on the peak. Nothing but an absolute ban on climbing could have done that. Rather, Toll's investments on Longs amplified the peak's appeal and prompted further increases in the number of visitors climbing it each year. Among them were children and adolescents attending summer camp in the area as well as growing numbers of inexperienced climbers, drawn to the peak by popular accounts of its beauty and news of its improved amenities. Nearly all climbers were Protestant, White, and middle-class, as racial, ethnic, and class barriers to mountain adventure in Rocky Mountain National Park remained firmly in place. The one small change to the social demographic on Longs was the inclusion among climbers of Catholic boys from eastern European immigrant homes. The boys attended Camp Saint Malo, a Catholic summer camp in Estes Park that prioritized mountaineering and made Longs the culminating destination of each summer's camp season.

The youngsters who climbed Longs were instructed by camp counselors with at least a modicum of training in nontechnical mountaineering. In contrast, most adult climbers in the late 1920s did not bother to seek the advice or direction of an experienced escort, whether CMC leader or commercial guide, and rangers' presence on the peak was still too slight to bring more than a small minority of climbers into direct contact with them. Thus, despite the park's protective measures, there were two more deaths on the peak before the 1920s ended, bringing the total for the decade to seven.

No one asked whether the seven fatalities were somehow acceptable, a reasonable price to be paid for the pleasure of the more than ten thousand climbers who had summited Longs successfully by 1930. Why should they? Six deaths occurred elsewhere in the park during the 1920s among front-country visitors who succumbed to heart attacks, hypothermia, falls, a sledding accident, even murder.[2] People were vulnerable to harm throughout the park, though the likelihood of harm was surely higher on Longs than at most other park sites. Park officials lamented the deaths on the peak, but the "monarch" of the Rockies was so central to the park's identity and so beloved by mountaineers that restricting access to it was never considered.

The improved infrastructure on Longs, especially the North Face cables and the Boulderfield Shelter Cabin—the latter run as a summer concession offering cooked meals, heated lodging, and commercial climbing guides—signaled the park's interest not simply in protecting climbers on Longs but in boosting their physical comfort and aesthetic gratification. Longs remained far from the front country, yet the Boulderfield Shelter Cabin, telephone, and *Cable* route brought touristic and recreational developments to the peak that were meant to moderate exposure to risk and enhance the peak's appeal to visitors. A few offended climbers denounced the Boulderfield Shelter Cabin's "commercialization" of the peak, but others delighted in the rustic hotel. No one asked whether the improvements, commercial activity, and heightened visitation on Longs might produce some level of environmental disturbance in the fragile alpine environment. In retrospect it seems certain that disturbances occurred.

Technical Climbers on Longs Peak

Park managers in the 1920s might have continued to pay little heed to climbers on Longs Peak had their numbers remained stable or had they been content to summit the mountain via the arduous but nontechnical *Keyhole* route during the summer months. As it turned out, however, more and more mountaineers appeared on Longs every year, among them a small cohort of technical climbers equipped with ropes, ice axes, and hobnail boots, who sought to establish new and more difficult routes, even in winter conditions. Climbers began to test themselves on the peak's North Face in the 1910s; by the 1920s particularly adventuresome climbers were tackling the nearly vertical East Face, leaving the East Longs Peak Trail before it reached Granite Pass and traversing Mills Moraine to Chasm Lake, then ascending the peak's East Face. The technical routes established during these years started on the lower portion of the East Face below the prominent horizontal ledge that became known as Broadway; once above Broadway, climbers used various couloirs, chimneys, and rock steps to reach the summit, almost always keeping to the left of the Diamond, the distinctive sheer wall that dominates the upper face. These early ascents on the East Face took place in the context of growing national interest in technical climbing, with routes being established on high peaks and vertical rock formations throughout the Colorado Rockies, in the Teton and Wind River Ranges of Wyoming, and in the Sierra Nevada, Cascade Range, and Appalachian Mountains. A few American climbers also ventured to Europe, wanting to climb in the Alps and learn about Swiss mountaineers' reliance on the belay and rappel and their masterful use of boots with edging nails as well as ice axes and crampons.[3]

Roger Toll was among the first to try a technical ascent on the North Face of Longs, climbing with two other members of the CMC in early September 1917 "to see if the north side of the peak could be made suitable for parties by placing ropes in the more difficult places." The North Face promised an unobstructed and breathtaking view of Chasm Lake, but Toll and his climbing companions found, to their disappointment, a "steep ice coated rock face," in which "the hand holds were filled with ice and each step had to be cut." The sparsely equipped group was forced to separate when Toll climbed too far above his companions for them to use either his short thirty-foot rope or the ice axe he carried. Carl Blaurock and William Ervin, two of Colorado's most skilled and ambitious climbers, backtracked and summited by the *Keyhole* route. Toll must have been discouraged by the trio's experience, for his CMC report on the climb did not bother to stress the importance of carrying appropriate technical gear. Rather, he stated simply, "This route would be less dangerous in July and August, but it should never be attempted when there is ice on the rocks."[4]

News of the three men's experience in 1917 seems to have slightly dampened climbers' interest in the North Face, even as the East Face beckoned. Over the next few years, a handful of individuals climbed and named routes on the East Face, though none ventured onto the Diamond. Werner Zimmerman, an accomplished alpinist and author from Switzerland, climbed alone to the top of Longs on August 23, 1919, leaving a somewhat cryptic note in the register: "Alone. Traverse east west by abyss chimney 20 yards south." Subsequent communication between Zimmerman and local climber and guide Paul Nesbit confirmed that a portion of Zimmerman's route followed what became known as *Alexander's Chimney*.[5] Dr. James Alexander, a math professor from Princeton, recorded the details of this route during a solo climb on September 7, 1922, the first carefully documented East Face climb. He and permanent ranger Jack Moomaw climbed the East Face again two days later using a somewhat varied route. It was on the second climb that Alexander gave the name "Broadway" to the traverse ledge across the East Face, with Moomaw capturing a photo of Alexander as he crossed it. The very next day Carl Blaurock, Hermann Buhl, Clara Buhl, and four other members of the Colorado Mountain Club climbed the East Face with the help of ice axes and seventy-five feet of rope, reaching the summit so late that they had to spend the night on Longs at the Timberline Cabin in Jim's Grove. Clara Buhl thus became the first woman to summit Longs via the East Face. Blaurock described the climb as "perfectly feasible" for experienced mountaineers carrying ice axes and a long rope, but he did not recommend it for "novices."[6] A couple of years later, Walter Kiener, a Swiss mountaineering guide living in Denver, put in *Kiener's* route on the East Face, possibly with the help of Carl Blaurock and Agnes Vaille. He climbed up *Lamb's Slide* to Broadway, then used the Notch chimney and negotiated steps, dihedrals, and ledges to reach the summit. Kiener may have intended to use the new route to guide relatively inexperienced climbers up the East Face.[7]

Other mountaineers followed the new technical routes, climbing in the summer, when sudden thunderstorms and lightning, rather than snow, presented the most significant threats. A few hardy souls attempted winter climbs, though avoiding both the East and North Faces. For example, Enos Mills climbed Longs one February sometime before 1920, mostly via the *Keyhole* route, encountering fierce winds the entire way. In one gully, "the wind sucked, dragged, pushed, and floated me ever upward." Near the top, Mills let the powerful wind push him across a slope that was steep and icy, knowing that if the wind lessened, "after I cast my lot in it, down the toboggan slope I would slide." And Ranger Jack Moomaw, like Mills an avid mountaineer in all seasons, successfully climbed Longs in January 1922, taking two days while off duty to complete the trip. He skied from Meeker Park, removed his skis to climb the saddle between Mount Meeker and Longs, and ascended to the summit along the Homestretch section of the *Keyhole* route.[8]

Park managers knew of Mills's and Moomaw's winter ascents and the East Face climbs by Alexander, Kiener, Blaurock, Buhl, and others. But the park did not assign rangers to oversee recreation on the peak, generally leaving the management of climbers to the CMC and local innkeepers and their commercial guides. The park sent rangers to Longs only to inspect and improve trail conditions or in response to a call from a park visitor or one of the hotel operators advising them of a problem. Over time, those problems became calamitous, as the much-publicized peak attracted the curiosity of precisely those "novices" who should have stayed away. Rangers were called on to search for Gregory Aubuchon and H. F. Targett, a teenager and middle-aged man who went missing in separate incidents on Longs in July and September 1921, yet they were unable to locate either of the men before they fell to their deaths, one on the East Face, the other at Peacock Pool below Chasm Lake. Then, in January 1925, skilled climber Agnes Vaille perished on Longs, as did Herbert Sortland, one of her would-be rescuers. Park staff reached a turning point, recognizing the need for new protective interventions on Longs.[9]

The Agnes Vaille and Herbert Sortland Tragedy

Agnes Wolcott Vaille was born to a prominent Denver family in 1890. Her father and uncle established Denver's first telephone exchange in 1881, eventually expanding telephone service to most of the state. Agnes was a first cousin of Roger Toll and grew up to embrace the identity of the well-educated and independent "New Woman" of the early twentieth century, adding a decidedly athletic twist. After graduating from Smith College, one of the nation's premier liberal arts colleges for women, Vaille served with the Red Cross in Europe during World War I. She never married, instead pursuing a professional career as the secretary of the Denver Chamber of Commerce. Vaille also became an avid skier and mountaineer, serving as the outing chair of the CMC and leading numerous CMC nontechnical climbs on Longs, often in harsh conditions. An August 1920 CMC climb via the *Keyhole* route encountered high winds, cold temperatures, and "swirling mists," yet under Vaille's careful guidance twenty of the thirty-two climbers in the party reached the summit and everyone completed the trip safely. The following year Vaille led a group of thirty-three men and twenty-three women on the *Keyhole* route. Fortunately, rain did not become heavy until midafternoon, long after the slowest members of the "fine, game party" made it to the summit.[10]

Over time, Vaille attempted increasingly difficult climbs and made a name for herself as one of Colorado's rising technical climbers. In the early fall of 1924, Vaille and Walter Kiener resolved to climb the East Face of Longs while looking at the mountain wall from atop Mount Evans, nearly fifty miles to the south. Vaille had never attempted a technical climb of such difficulty, but she was apparently confident that Kiener, a veteran of snow and ice climbing in the Swiss Alps, was well qualified to lead the ascent. Agnes's friend Elinor

Eppich Kingery later recalled that Vaille was a firm proponent of the CMC dictum "Let the leader lead." Once having placed her faith in Kiener, she would have been disinclined to question his judgment. Indeed, according to Kingery, "nothing but complete physical exhaustion could have persuaded Agnes to object or renege on the leader's course." As it turns out, Vaille's trust in Kiener may have been misplaced. Vaille and Kiener's ill-fated climb in January 1925 was their fourth summit attempt that winter. Carl Blaurock accompanied Vaille and Kiener on their failed second attempt and tried on numerous occasions to dissuade them from making the climb again before spring, as did other members of the Colorado climbing community. Pressure on Vaille from anxious friends and associates was intense, yet she and Kiener refused to abandon their plan.[11]

After spending the night at the Timberline Cabin, on the morning of January 11 Kiener and Vaille began their ascent of Longs' East Face, staying south of the Diamond and following *Kiener's* route. The climb was far more difficult than anticipated, and by four in the afternoon, Kiener later recalled, "I was greatly perturbed and grieved to note that my companion's strength was about spent." Still far from the summit, "for close to twelve hours I had to cut the steps alone, handle the rope, and pull, lift and assist her until we finally reached the summit about 4 a.m." By then Kiener's thermometer registered fourteen degrees below zero, and wind and snow were gusting powerfully.[12] Given the difficulty of the climb, the lateness of the hour, and the worsening weather, Kiener and Vaille decided on a descent via the North Face, thinking it would be faster than going down the route they had just climbed. Vaille must have been aware of Toll's assessment of the dangers of North Face winter climbing, as she had stayed with his wife in Estes Park while he, Blaurock, and Ervin attempted their 1917 ascent.[13] Toll had concluded that mountaineers should avoid going up *or* down the North Face whenever icy conditions prevailed, as it was simply too dangerous a place for climbers. Still, attempting an East Face descent on *Kiener's* would have been even more perilous for the climbers, especially in their dire circumstances.

Tragically, it was on the North Face that Vaille lost her life. The descent was very slow "on account of their continued exertion for 24 hours," and "when they came to the most difficult part of the north side route," Agnes lost her footing. With her face showing "the most appalling lines of suffering and anguish," Agnes slipped as she tried to climb over a large rock. She fell "a long ways down the smooth snowy slope" and then lay unmoving in the bitter cold while Kiener struggled to reach her. Vaille sustained only slight injuries in the fall, but Kiener knew she was utterly exhausted and close to death even before he started across the Boulderfield for help.[14]

While Kiener was trying to descend the mountain, Herbert Sortland, the caretaker of the Longs Peak Inn, was on his way up with three local men, having been told by Elinor Eppich, waiting at the inn, that Vaille and Kiener were overdue from their summit attempt. Eppich also called park headquarters about the missing climbers. A second search party, which included Rangers Jack Moomaw and Walter Finn, Superintendent Roger Toll, Assistant Superintendent Thomas Allen, local citizens, and Denver CMC members, headed for the mountain in a heavy snowstorm to search for the missing climbers. By the time Moomaw and Finn arrived at the Timberline Cabin, Kiener had been there and returned to the base of the North Face with one of the local men, where they discovered Vaille, dead from hypothermia. It was three more days before rangers could retrieve her body because of the severity of the storm. Kiener suffered terrible frostbite during the ill-fated expedition and subsequently lost parts of numerous fingers and toes and a portion of his left foot. He spent several months recovering in a Denver hospital.[15]

Superintendent Toll noted in his monthly report that the park staff, hotel operator, and local citizens had made extraordinary efforts to rescue Vaille. Indeed, Herbert Sortland died in the attempt, after losing his way in the blinding snow on Longs Peak, stumbling into a ravine, and breaking a hip. Yet no one, Toll said, should be blamed for the pair of tragedies.[16] The superintendent wanted to move forward, eschewing blame or regret. The question was how. The hazards on Longs Peak, especially for those wishing to climb the East and North Faces, might have induced Toll to place strict limits on climbers' access to the peak, or at least deliberately discourage climbing in winter. Toll had previously subscribed to the latter view, and the local newspaper, the *Estes Park Trail*, held to this position, declaring, "Climbing the peak in winter, however, should never be attempted—the risk is too great for the glory attached."[17] This was no longer Toll's inclination, however. Perhaps because he had lost his cousin and did not want to believe she had died in vain, Toll embraced more fervently than ever the values and ambitions of dedicated mountaineers, insisting that humans' best qualities and capacities were improved by direct experience of wild nature and a willingness to face risk. He declared admiration for Vaille's "mountaineering ability, strength, endurance, and courage. . . . She knew the dangers and faced them willingly, without fear or dread of death." He must have appreciated *Trail and Timberline*'s memorial for Vaille, which described her as having "strength and courage above that of most men. . . . Kindly, unselfish, self-reliant, resourceful, she was gloriously full of life." Toll realized, too, that Longs was Rocky's most well-known backcountry destination, drawing novices and experienced mountaineers to its steep and rocky slopes from far and near. Instead of rolling out prohibitions on Longs, Toll opted for a system of physical interventions, improvements, and oversight that would preserve climbers' access to "one of the wildest and most impressive spots in the Colorado Mountains."[18] Toll sought to manage climbers' risk of harm on Longs while facilitating their daring alpine adventure.

Improving Access and Safety on Longs Peak

In supporting continued recreational access to Longs, Toll acknowledged that it was not in the power of Rocky Mountain National Park to eliminate poor judgment, bad luck, or accidents among climbers. The park might, however, encourage climbers to weigh their options carefully and lessen their exposure to unnecessary risk and harm. Toll thus decided to increase rangers' presence on Longs, improve the East Longs Peak Trail, and enhance climbing routes, communication systems, and shelter facilities on the upper reaches of the mountain. These improvements were meant to provide indirect and nonrestrictive forms of management and oversight that would allow climbers to find enjoyment on the peak while increasing their odds of survival in times of duress or crisis.

During the 1925 summer season, Chief Ranger Jack Moomaw and two workers installed the first of the new improvements, the *Cable* route on the North Face of Longs Peak. Using single jack sledgehammers and short rock drills, Moomaw and his workers created holes in the granite rock, fixed large eyebolts into the holes, and threaded two separate sections of steel cable, one 160 feet long, the other 30 feet, through the bolts.[19] A later generation of rangers and climbers would conclude that the human-made cables were an artifice that detracted from the "wilderness values" of the peak, but this way of thinking did not exist in 1925. Rather, Toll was trying to match safety measures to climbers' ambitions. He had previously insisted that the North Face should never be climbed when icy but knew that alpinists were ignoring his admonitions, and he simply wanted to lessen the risks of the climb. Moderating his earlier views, Toll explained why the new cables made sense: "An increasing number of visitors have recently climbed the peak by this route, which is often dangerous, on account of weather conditions. The placing of this cable greatly increases the safety of this route, and makes it possible for good climbers, or those with guides, to go up the peak from the north, and then descend by the usual [*Keyhole*] route. This adds considerably to the interest of the climb, and shortens the time of ascent by an hour."[20]

Moomaw and his trail crew also built a spur trail from Mills Moraine on the East Longs Peak Trail to Chasm Meadows, giving climbers more direct access to the East Face, and rerouted the upper portion of the East Longs Peak Trail from timberline to the Boulderfield. The 1925 trail relocation reduced the grade, extended the trail half a mile into the Boulderfield, and made it possible for horses to carry climbers the additional distance. Even more so than the *Cable* route, the trail relocation relied on methods that disturbed the mountain environment. A crew of about five men used two tons of dynamite to blast the way for the rerouted trail and then moved enormous amounts of rock and gravel to fill it in, creating pits wherever they removed material.[21]

The park also replaced the telephone line to the Timberline Cabin, previously connected to the Longs Peak Inn by a private cable, with one that was connected to the public exchange in Estes Park. Park crews then extended the telephone line, now connected to town, from the Hewes-Kirkwood Inn near the Longs Peak trailhead to the Timberline Cabin and on to the terminus of the trail at the Boulderfield. The new telephone and other improvements were intended to mitigate a host of dangers on Longs. In combination, they moderated the steep trail from timberline that tired climbers even before they reached the East Face or Boulderfield, eased the difficulty of the treacherous North Face ascent, and reduced delays in calling for help.[22]

Toll's official monthly and annual reports described these improvements in some detail yet made scant reference to the tragedies prompting them. He had no inclination to question Longs' suitability as a destination for visitors eager to experience the beauty and wildness of an alpine environment. Rather, in speaking of the rerouting of the East Longs Peak Trail into the Boulderfield, Toll emphasized the "three spectacular viewpoints" within half a mile of the trail's new terminus, and the ease with which horseback riders could walk to them after dismounting. Toll also noted that rangers' "special trip above timberline, for the purpose of repairing the Boulder Field telephone line" meant that the phone line could be "kept in use during the winter months," thereby helping to safeguard winter climbers.[23]

Toll also ordered the construction of new shelter cabins for climbers. Several existed in other areas of the park, and in past years Enos Mills had operated the Timberline Cabin in Jim's Grove near the East Longs Peak Trail under a concession license with Rocky Mountain National Park. After his death in 1922, Enos's widow continued to keep the rustic cabin stocked with food and supplies during the summer climbing season, and climbers could use it for a fee. But in the aftermath of the Vaille tragedy, Mrs. Mills chose not to continue the concession, and park managers decided not to staff the cabin or seek a new concessionaire to take over the license. Located at the eastern side of Jim's Grove, and two miles by trail from the Boulderfield and the East Face, the Timberline Cabin was a long distance from where accidents were likely to occur.[24] The Timberline Cabin continued to be used, even as it fell into disrepair, but the park wanted to build more conveniently located shelters. Mindful not only of Vaille's and Sortland's deaths but also of the experience of Hermann Buhl, an expert climber injured in a storm-related fall on Longs Peak in May 1926, Toll remarked, "Such accidents emphasize the need for shelter at Boulder Field and other points on the Longs Peak Trail."[25] Toll may also have been thinking of the potential for harm among some of the resolute but aging individuals who enjoyed climbing the *Keyhole* route. Civil War veteran William Butler of Longmont climbed Longs for the fourth time on his eighty-fifth birthday in September 1926, setting the pace for two young friends. According to a report on this remarkable achievement in the *New York Times*, Butler was determined "to spend at least one more birthday on the mountain top."[26]

Contractor M. L. Larsen built the Boulderfield's stone shelter cabin and horse barn at an altitude of 12,700 feet between August 1926 and June 1927 in extraordinarily challenging conditions. Describing the cabin and its construction, National Park Service historian Merrill J. Mattes noted: "Its principal features were concrete foundations on a bed of boulders leveled by dynamite, massive corner-buttressed walls of boulders from the immediate vicinity, and a timbered roof held down by more boulders, all of them wired together. The structure was further strengthened by interior tie rods. . . . The work was hampered by transportation problems (everything but the boulders had to be brought up by horses), ice storms, and winds of hurricane force that tore off the first three roofs before one of sufficient strength was finally devised."[27]

The park arranged with Robert Collier Jr., a Denver teacher, Colorado Mountain Club member, and frequent Longs Peak guide, to operate the Boulderfield cabin under a concession as a primitive hotel during the summer months. The stone building was small, "fourteen by eighteen feet inside dimension—and walls two feet thick at the base and eighteen inches at the top," with bunks for about ten visitors. Collier and his wife, Dorothy (who was paid by the park to be a fire lookout), provided food and overnight lodging for a fee, and commercial guides were available at the cabin to lead climbers to the summit. The cabin opened in mid-June each season and closed on Labor Day. In the winter, though it was not staffed, the unlocked cabin was open to alpinists seeking shelter from storms or bitter nighttime temperatures.[28]

Longs gained a second new cabin when Agnes Vaille's father funded the construction of a small cone-shaped emergency shelter built of granite (which still stands) at the far side of the Boulderfield. Suggested by the friends who retrieved Agnes's body from Longs, the shelter was intended to memorialize Vaille, "who had sacrificed her life to the love of adventure and the thrill of mountaineering." So, too, it was meant to protect the lives of other intrepid alpinists. It was built deliberately at the Keyhole on Longs, a "strategic point" at the far west side of the Boulderfield at an altitude of thirteen thousand feet. At this location climbers often encountered sudden and tempestuous changes in weather. After scrambling through the Keyhole, they faced "a wilderness of rock, devoid of protection." The shelter was imagined not only as a place that might have saved Vaille and Sortland from death but one that might offer "temporary protection" to future climbers facing "urgent" circumstances.[29]

The park built a third stone cabin near Chasm Lake in 1931. It contained rescue supplies and was available for climbers (particularly those attempting technical ascents of the East Face) to use as an emergency shelter. It was not staffed and had no telephone until 1970. Finally, in the late 1920s park trail crews improved the North Longs Peak Trail and made another round of modifications to the East Longs Peak Trail, rerouting the lower portion to the south of the historical route, which began at Longs Peak Inn, to the Longs Peak Ranger Station and campground, both constructed in 1929, just above the Hewes-Kirkwood Inn. When finished, the improved trail was 7.5 miles long from the trailhead through the Keyhole to the summit, with an elevation gain of just under five thousand feet. Some of these modifications were completed under the direction of Acting Superintendent Thomas Allen and Superintendent Edmund Rogers after Roger Toll moved to Yellowstone National Park in 1929. At Yellowstone Toll became park superintendent and field assistant to NPS director Stephen Mather.[30]

The Advantages of Improvement

The dramatic and much-publicized story of Vaille's and Sortland's deaths did little to discourage climbing on Longs. Rather, climbers took advantage of the improvements Toll ordered. The East Longs Peak Trail, substantially rerouted, eased the rigors of the nontechnical portions of the peak for both horses and climbers, and the spur trail to Chasm Lake, built in 1926, made the difficult East Face routes more accessible to skilled climbers. The *Cable* route quickly became a more popular means of nontechnical ascent than the *Keyhole* route, affording fantastic views and cutting the time needed to reach the peak's summit. Often, it was used for the descent as well. During the summer months, the Boulderfield cabin, advertised in local papers, offered climbers inexpensive lodging and meals in an extraordinary location as well as commercial guiding services. And throughout the year the Boulderfield cabin, along with the Chasm Lake and Keyhole shelters, offered emergency protection to climbers who got caught in storms or needed unanticipated overnight refuge. Finally, climbers benefited from the increased presence of rangers on the peak who were prepared to offer informed guidance, protection, and rescue.[31]

In combination, the various changes on Longs contributed to rising visitation. Summit registers showed the number of climbers moving generally upward over the course of the 1920s, from 623 in 1923 to 1,592 in 1925, 1,701 in 1927, and 1,644 in 1930.[32] The Vaille tragedy had not diminished interest in the peak; rather, the park's deliberate improvements and continued efforts to highlight Longs in local newspapers and other visitor publications supported growing popular interest in the peak as a superb climbing destination for recreationists of varying ability. Indeed, Longs was the site of an occasional wedding. Lucyle Goodman of Sterling, Colorado, and Burl Stephens of Fort Collins took their vows on the summit on June 14, 1927. "Weather conditions were very bad, but the wedding took place as scheduled."[33]

Children and counselors from summer camps in Estes Park were also among those climbing Longs in the mid- and late 1920s. Camps in Estes Park emerged in response to an international movement popularizing the idea that boys and girls from White middle-class urban homes needed an escape from the artifice and moral taint of city life and opportunities for supervised summer recreation in beautiful natural settings.[34] Frank Cheley became the most successful operator of summer camps near Estes Park and Rocky Mountain National Park, opening Bear Lake Trail School for boys in 1921 and extending camping opportunities to girls with the opening of Camp Chipeta in 1926. The Bear Lake Trail School (later Camp Hiayaha) was initially located inside Rocky Mountain National Park; by the end of the 1920s, the Cheley camps operated from facilities outside the park but took extensive advantage of the nearby "national playground." Mountaineering was one of the campers' principal pursuits. For boys and girls at the Cheley camps, Rocky Mountain National Park offered unlimited opportunity for adventure. Climbing Longs Peak was the culminating exploit of the summer season, "the hardest hike of the year," and one that signaled real achievement in mountaineering. Cheley camp literature suggests that boys and girls prepared diligently for the difficult climb and were carefully guided by counselors up Longs' steep ascent.[35]

By this time, schoolchildren in Estes Park and adult visitors to the YMCA of the Rockies, a conference center for religious educators just beyond the east-central boundary of Rocky Mountain National Park, were also among the growing number of visitors to Longs Peak. Sisters Anne and Isabel Pfifer were key figures in these climbs. The two young women were intrepid mountaineers, having been introduced to the joys of mountain adventure while visiting the YMCA of the Rockies with their parents in 1920. They became teachers in the Estes Park school system, occasionally leading their young students on hikes to Longs. Additionally, they led numerous groups of adults to Longs Peak while working in the summer as hike masters for the YMCA of the Rockies. Anne and Isabel wanted others to discover the joys of mountain climbing. They tried to make sure that all those who attempted to summit Longs Peak were adapted to the altitude and properly attired, though many in their climbing parties, whether schoolchildren or adults, were inexperienced hikers and climbers.[36]

With Longs' appeal growing, both novice and expert climbers encountered the post-Vaille changes on the peak. The park intended the *Cable* route to become the preferred nontechnical means of ascending to Longs' summit, with the *Keyhole* route serving for the descent, and most nontechnical climbers probably made this intended switch. Certainly, the Boulderfield cabin guides made the North Face cables their principal means of reaching the summit.[37]

Anecdotal evidence points to differences, large and small, that Toll's improvements made to the experiences of climbers on Longs. For example, Joe and Paul Stettner, German brothers who had considerable climbing experience in the European Alps and had recently immigrated to Chicago, noted how they benefited from the new measures on Longs during their 1927 attempt to establish a new route on the peak's East Face, south of the Diamond. On the September afternoon they set out for the peak, a chance encounter with a ranger showed them the benefits of increased interaction between park staff and visitors, one of Toll's "improvements" after the Vaille tragedy. The ranger found them putting up their small tent and suggested they go to the abandoned Timberline Cabin, where they would have "decent quarters." The hike to the Timberline Cabin from their campsite was three and a half miles long (though not as far as the Boulderfield cabin), and the building itself was "in a powerful state of disorder," with shattered windows and a leaking roof. Still, the Stettners soon realized they were lucky to have followed the ranger's advice. A violent storm broke overhead shortly after their arrival and raged all night, with winds so strong the brothers feared the cabin might "be blown off its foundation." They did not sleep well, but the two men—and the cabin—survived the night.[38] A night in their pup tent would not have ended as happily.

The Stettners' lucky encounters with the recent innovations on Longs continued the next day, as they concluded their grueling first ascent up the full vertical length of the East Face and discovered, fortuitously, the cables on the peak's North Face. Joe and Paul were exceptional climbers, not only in their level of skill but in their use of specialized equipment. On Longs, they used the belay maneuver to arrest falls, a technique still virtually unknown among Americans, and relied on the felt-soled climbing shoes and iron pitons familiar to European climbers. The piton was a malleable iron spike with an eye at one end; hammered into a crack in the rock, it molded to the rock's contours, providing a firm anchor for the safety rope looped through the eye. They had expected to use a specialized climbing rope as well, of the sort used by alpinists in Europe, but there was none for sale in Estes Park, and the staff at the Longs Peak Inn refused to loan their climbing rope to the brothers, believing it was too late in the season to make the climb. Despite having to settle for a length of sisal livestock rope, the Stettners put in a new route on the lower East Face to Broadway and then climbed *Kiener's* to the summit in less than seven hours. Still, they found the ascent hard almost to the point of impossibility and knew they could not have succeeded without the pitons they hammered into the rock and the rope that connected them. Joe fell once in an overhanging section, but "Paul had a good belay place and was able to hold me well." By the time they finished their ascent the brothers were very fatigued, and it was snowing, nearly dark, and freezing cold. As they began to descend Longs via the North Face, they discovered the *Cable* route entirely "by chance." Joe and Paul had not known of its existence; now, the steel cables allowed the brothers to descend rapidly and without incident.[39] Their route on the East Face, *Stettner's Ledges*, was considered the most difficult climb in the United States for the next twenty years, and there was only one other successful ascent on the route before Joe Stettner climbed it again in 1942.

Less experienced climbers who encountered the improvements on Longs found them helpful and, sometimes, lifesaving. In 1926 a group of girls and their counselor from Camp Chipeta used the Boulderfield's new phone to inform camp staff of their location and the likely timing of their ascent to the summit. The young campers were not in danger and simply wanted to make good use of the mountain's communication technologies. In contrast, forty-six young people from the University of Colorado Boulder descended on the Boulderfield Shelter Cabin one summer night, trying to escape an "advancing cloudburst." Bob Collier packed the entire group into the tiny structure, where they spent the night "trying to dry their clothes." More serious still, three students from the Colorado Agricultural and Mechanical College in Fort Collins were in dire need of shelter when they found their way to the Boulderfield cabin during a winter outing in 1928. The three had made a successful East Face ascent of Longs Peak on December 31, 1928, but "extremely stormy weather necessitated their spending three nights at the shelter cabin on the Boulderfield." Park staff considered the students' winter climb dangerous and unwise, yet they were grateful the shelter cabin had protected them from potentially fatal weather conditions.[40]

Importantly, Rocky's improvements on Longs were put in place just as Colorado's climbing community was beginning to publicize, through a new genre of guidebooks and articles in climbing journals and the local press, a budding interest in what would come to be known as "peak bagging." The Colorado Mountain Club celebrated the distinctiveness of the state's highest peaks in a 1914 leaflet listing all those above fourteen thousand feet.[41] By 1923 CMC members Carl Blaurock and Bill Ervin had summited all the known "fourteeners" in Colorado.[42] Other climbers, including Agnes Vaille and her close friend Mary Cronin, were engaged in the same pursuit, climbing the state's highest peaks as quickly as time, weather, and skill allowed. That same year, Roger Toll published *The Mountain Peaks of Colorado* as a supplement to the CMC's *Trail and Timberline* magazine. The booklet identified forty-six peaks above fourteen thousand feet high and established the relative order of height among all the named peaks in the state.[43]

Not surprisingly, the new guidebooks gave special attention to Longs Peak. In 1925, John Hart published *Fourteen Thousand Feet: A History of the Naming and Early Ascents of the High Colorado Peaks* with the CMC. *Fourteen Thousand Feet* categorized the highest peaks by geographic region, offered data from various geographic surveys, and provided accounts of notable climbs. Hart singled out Longs as the state's "best known peak," and one that required climbing, not just hiking. Importantly, as Hart and others noted, though Longs was not easy to climb it was highly accessible, located near Colorado's Front Range cities and towns and inside a national park. A second edition of Hart's book appeared in 1931, with updated information and a new section, "A Climber's Guide to the High Colorado Peaks," by Elinor Eppich Kingery, another CMC member and close friend of Agnes Vaille. In this edition, Hart described Longs Peak as "an ideal mountain for trying new ways." Its rock was "a fine, firm granite with good holds." Though noting the recent fatalities on Longs' North Face and cautioning inexperienced climbers away from technical routes for which they were ill prepared, Hart recommended the peak as a site for pleasurable alpine exploration. He made a special point that alpinists could stay at any of several "splendid" hotels at nine thousand feet near Estes Park before and after climbing Longs, thus making "comfort" a part of their excursion to Rocky's highest peak. With Longs as representative icon, a popular quest to scale every fourteener in Colorado had begun.[44] Indeed, Mary Cronin refused to be discouraged by Vaille's death, and in 1934 she became the first woman to scale all the state's peaks over fourteen thousand feet.[45]

Exclusion from Rocky's Most Popular Peak

Though Longs grew in popularity after Toll ordered improvements to the peak, the mountain continued to be off-limits to people of color. The Ku Klux Klan's overt presence in Estes Park and the discriminatory practices in local lodges, restaurants, and the park itself kept Blacks and other people of color from visiting Rocky Mountain National Park and its famous peak. The Cheley and YMCA camps were open only to White children and families, as racial segregation remained firmly embedded in recreational programs in Colorado and the nation. Other children's camps in Estes Park were also White and middle class, though George W. Olinger ran a Christian military-style encampment in Rocky for boys from the Highlands, a Denver neighborhood of working-class Italian and German immigrants.[46]

Camp Saint Malo also slightly revised the demographic norm. The camp was Catholic, and in addition to accepting fee-paying boys from affluent families, it accepted without payment altar and choir boys from Denver's Cathedral of the Immaculate Conception. These boys were the "tough sons of hardy Irish and Italian, Spanish and Greek immigrants who had little time or energy to cultivate the art of parenting. The families . . . beginning to taste prosperity hardly needed reminding of the 'physical and moral dangers' along East Colfax," the main thoroughfare running through their neighborhood. In the 1920s those dangers included anti-Catholic sentiment, fueled by growth of the KKK in Denver. Somehow, Camp Saint Malo's founder, Father Joseph Bosetti, managed not to attract overt hostility from the KKK in Estes Park, perhaps because his camp was funded by a wealthy and well-connected Catholic family. Bosetti envisioned a mountain camp for boys that would inspire love of nature and the maturation of body and soul. Far less interested in structured leisure and close supervision than Frank Cheley and other local camp directors, Bosetti was a true devotee of mountaineering. For Bosetti, there was "no such thing as too much mountaineering." It allowed campers "to realize our smallness in the presence of God's power and magnificence, to emancipate ourselves from the muddy and slimy and stifling vicissitudes of city life and exchange it for a few breaths of pure oxygen that alone can add immeasurably to health of body and soul." Hikes were the "core of the camp experience," and an ascent of Longs was the "climax" of the summer season.[47]

People of color who were denied opportunities to ramble in Rocky Mountain National Park or attempt a climb to the summit of Longs were nonetheless creating openings for pleasure and recreation in mountain settings. By the 1920s the African American community in Denver had grown to nearly five thousand, with nearly all Black residents clustered in the Five Points district. According to historian Candacy Taylor, Five Points had more Black-owned businesses than any urban neighborhood outside New York's Harlem, and it was known as the "Harlem of the West." Doctors, lawyers, musicians, and entrepreneur Madam C. J. Walker called it home. Five Points also attracted Black travelers from across the nation to its stores, movie theaters, restaurants, jazz clubs, and hotels. In addition to creating places of leisure in urban settings, the district's ambitious and innovative residents and visitors sought access to ease and recreation in Colorado's mountain landscapes.

Undeterred by Whites who presumed them incapable (or unworthy) of witnessing the sublime in nature, African Americans from Denver and other cities purchased 640 acres near Nederland, Colorado, just forty-two miles from Rocky Mountain National Park, and opened an all-Black resort, Lincoln Hills. The resort's initial brochure in 1925 advertised the property as "A Wonder Spot In Nature's Vast Expanse Of The Rocky Mountains. In Many Ways Equaling And Excelling Estes Park Or Any Other Summer Play Ground In Colorado And Far Surpassing All In Accessibility." Endorsing the planned resort, J. H. P. Westbrook, an African American physician in Denver, noted that Lincoln Hills offered African Americans a critical opportunity to resist racial segregation in mountain tourism and recreation. "I have lived in Colorado for twenty years and have seen Bear Creek Canyon, Estes Park, Daniels Park and other territory adjacent to Denver built up by white people. . . . This is the last opportunity for colored people to get such a location. . . . In a few years it will be impossible for our group to get anything one half as desirable for Summer camping." The Lincoln Hills Company sold lots to private owners who built small cabins for annual summer vacations, and the resort quickly became a beloved haven for hiking, fishing, and horseback riding. Opening in 1928, Winks Lodge was Lincoln Hills's full-service hotel and cultural venue, attracting prominent African American musicians, singers, and writers to the mountain enclave for short visits. Lincoln Hills was one of only eighteen African American resorts in the United States, and the only one in the Rocky Mountain West. In addition to serving adults and families, the resort also hosted Camp Nizhoni, a summer facility operated by the African American Phyllis Wheatley Branch of the YWCA. Barred from attending the YWCA's Camp Lookout near Idaho Springs, African American girls at Camp Nizhoni delighted in swimming, hiking, fishing, and horseback riding, developing a lifelong appreciation for mountain recreation.[48]

Improvement's Unintended Consequences

The improvements on Longs and continued popularity of the peak even after Vaille's death proved gratifying to park managers who had dedicated themselves to facilitating human enjoyment in unspoiled nature. Still comfortable with the racial hierarchy present in Estes Park and Rocky, they did not consider or regret the absence of people of color from Longs Peak. The improvements and growing popularity of the peak were not, however, without unintended consequences and complications. By the late 1920s approximately 75 percent of those climbing the peak were doing so without the assistance of commercial guides (or camp instructors), thus forsaking formal instruction and guidance. The *Cable* route had become far more popular than the *Keyhole* route and was reputed to be readily accessible and safe, making hired guides seem like an unnecessary luxury. Nor was the CMC much involved in leading climbers on Longs. For all its interest in the peak before and after Vaille's death, the Denver chapter of the CMC led no more than one trip to the summit in any given year in the late 1920s, as its members were eager to climb high peaks throughout the Colorado Rockies and in Wyoming's Tetons. Other chapters of the CMC probably led climbs to Longs even less often than the Denver group.[49]

The great majority of those who climbed Longs without guides did so without serious incident, probably having made reasonable and judicious use of the improvements on Longs. Still, the shift away from commercial guides and club-led mountaineering on Longs may have increased the likelihood of foolish and potentially dangerous conduct on the peak, especially since the park assigned only a single ranger to Longs. Indeed, Bob Collier, operator of the Boulderfield cabin, found himself having to aid climbers who tried to summit Longs without guides but became desperate for help after becoming injured or stranded on the mountain. Collier described one such rescue involving three boys from Iowa in August 1927. Admonished by a ranger not to attempt an ascent by the formidable East Face, the inexperienced boys made their way to the summit, probably by the *Cable* route. Having reached the top, they began to descend the East Face but soon found themselves stranded on a three-foot ledge two hundred feet below the summit. "They got to hollering for help. So, we . . . took up ropes" and got above them onto an overhang. "We had to swing the thing—a pendulum—back and forth—and dropped the rope—landed on this—place where these [boys] were. They'd taken their shoes off and were fixing to head on down the way—we recovered the shoes about seven years later." Collier and his helpers pulled the boys up with their rope, took them down to the cabin, fed them, and let them sleep. After waking up, the boys went off down the trail "and didn't say thank you for saving their lives."[50] Collier did not mention what the boys wore on their feet on the hike down the mountain.

Even worse, a number of inexperienced climbers who declined commercial, camp, or club instruction met calamity on Longs, despite the park's new provisions for protection and rescue. In July 1927 Forrest Ketring died while trying to climb the East Face of Longs with a friend. The two young men had climbed the peak previously by the *Keyhole* route and returned to Longs to climb the far more challenging East Face, using the route established by James Alexander in 1922. Neither of the men, however, had technical climbing experience, nor did they carry a rope. When Ketring encountered poor footing in the Notch Couloir and slipped on the steep rock face, his companion was without means to arrest his fall or prevent his death. Ketring's friend managed to climb down off the East Face and find assistance, but the park's recovery and removal of Ketring's body was onerous, involving Ranger Jack Moomaw, Superintendent Toll, and a trail crew that had been working near Chasm Lake. Two years later, in September 1929, Charles Thiemeyer perished on Longs' East Face while climbing with Dr. and Mrs. Arthur Stacher. All three were members of the Denver Swiss Alpine Club and had extensive climbing experience, but they had never climbed the East Face. Thiemeyer ignored the admonitions of his friends not to climb onto a section of rock that looked especially dangerous and failed to properly secure the party's belay rope; he fell 1,500 feet from the Notch Couloir to his death, taking the rope with him. According to Moomaw, Thiemeyer's friends were for a time "paralyzed by fright" but were eventually able to move to a "wet rocky shelf" near the head of the couloir. There, they were stranded overnight, even after shouting for help and attracting the attention of the Colliers in the Boulderfield cabin. The Colliers used the cabin's telephone to call for assistance; it took rangers until the next morning to rescue the pair and send them down the East Longs Peak Trail on horseback. Having learned from the Stachers of Thiemeyer's terrible fall, the rangers then worked with a search party of twelve to locate the young man's badly battered body and remove it from the peak. Attempting to climb the daunting expanse of the East Face without appropriate guidance or experience, Ketring and Thiemeyer were beyond help when they most needed it and far beyond their own capabilities of survival.[51]

Finally, the new improvements on Longs brought the technologies, fuels, and pollutants of development to the alpine peak. These included dynamite for trail excavation, July 4 fireworks for entertainment, coal for heating the Boulderfield Shelter Cabin (transported daily by burro), horse, burro, and human waste, and perhaps food waste as well. Compared to the industrial, urban, and touristic developments occurring along the Front Range, in Estes Park, and in Rocky's front country, the developments on Longs were minuscule in scale. They were meant to facilitate human enjoyment and safety rather than to modify the environment substantially for permanent human habitat. Still, the improvements increased traffic by humans and pack animals and heightened ecological disruption and pollution in the fragile alpine environment. No studies of environmental harm on the peak were done at the time, but Moomaw's dynamite explosions must have harmed and unsettled plant and animal life. The powerful fireworks that Bob Collier set off from the Boulderfield on July 4, hoping they would be seen in Longmont, must have perturbed birds and animals for miles around. The coal used for heating and cooking in the Boulderfield Shelter Cabin released carbon dioxide and other pollutants into the thin mountain air. There was a latrine on-site, but it is doubtful that Bob or Dorothy Collier, the cabin's proprietors, carefully managed the disposal or transport of human waste, much less waste from horses or burros. All of this detritus had the potential to pollute water sources, spread harmful pathogens, and disturb the local ecology.[52] Modest though they were, the recreational developments and improvements on Longs after Agnes Vaille's death brought increased risk to the peak's alpine environment.

THE IOWA BOYS whom the Colliers rescued in 1927 were both imprudent and ungrateful but far luckier than Forrest Ketring or Charles Thiemeyer. Perhaps the boys' rescuers and park officials held out hope that they would learn a lesson or two from their misadventures. Ranger Jack Moomaw was less sanguine. He later wrote that he somewhat regretted the opening of the East Face "because for quite a time thereafter many climbers were killed attempting the feat." More-over, whenever there was an accident on the East Face, Moomaw was assigned to it, causing him "a lot of hard work."[53]

Moomaw recognized that the post-Vaille dynamic between climbers and park management, imagined as a system of collaborative shared responsibility, was imperfect. The park's improvements were drawing more people to the peak, offering them promise of safe alpine adventure, but rangers faced an uphill battle in protecting climbers from unpredictable conditions and their own bad judgment. Search, rescue, and recovery operations were infrequent, but when they became necessary they were dangerous, labor intensive, and costly.

Moomaw was not the only skeptic about the post-Vaille "improvements" on Longs. Albert R. Ellingwood, a technical climber renowned for his extraordinarily difficult first ascents in the Colorado and Wyoming mountains, bemoaned the increased accessibility of the peak to inexperienced climbers. Though he believed that "the beauties and the benefits of the mountains [could] and should be generously opened up to the multitude who need them so badly," Ellingwood wanted the Rockies' highest and most difficult peaks to be left in some "seclusion, to be reached by those who know what they want, and want it badly enough to make the effort necessary to attain it." He thought Longs had been severely compromised and could only hope that the sacrifice of the peak to the masses would save others from desecration: "Noble Longs Peak is fatally near the beaten track, and already has its guides and its tariffs, and the inevitable steel cable. May it be a sufficient sop to Cerberus!"[54]

Ironically, Helen Donahue, one of the "masses" on Longs whose presence Ellingwood deplored, expressed concerns that aligned with his, at least in part. Recounting a climb on Longs in 1927 at age sixteen with her parents and younger sisters, Donahue described her father's disparagement of the Boulderfield hotel and its keepers:

> Sitting in the vast bowl strewn with huge boulders was "Colliers Hotel." Papa was visibly disgruntled by the presence of such a commercial concession in this untamed primordial place at the base of the towering peak, so we quickly bypassed the structure on our way to the Keyhole. I remember stories about the Boulderfield Inn—like the outrageous price of one dollar for a cup of coffee in the day of $.05 per cup! And about Mrs. Collier who had a chronic heart problem. Several times every summer she would collapse and the telephone wires we had stepped over would sizzle with the call of help. Park rangers always hurried up to carry her out. Within a few days she would stubbornly return to her high summer chalet, only to repeat the scenario. At the end of each summer huge rocks were hoisted to the roof of the hotel in an effort to save it from the ravaging winter winds. It was a fruitless effort, however, for each summer the roof had to be replaced.

The qualms expressed by Moomaw, Ellingwood, and the Donahues seem not to have been widely shared. Certainly, the young men who served as climbing guides at the Boulderfield Shelter Cabin thoroughly enjoyed the excitement of living and working on Longs Peak, leading climbers to the summit via the North Face cables, and occasionally saving them from peril. None were experienced climbers before being hired as guides. Rather, Collier took the men under his wing and taught them to be mountaineers. Sometimes, "when business was dull," the guides would "scramble up and down the North Face by ourselves . . . to see who could make the round trip by that route in the fastest time." Bob Collier, his wife, Dorothy, and their daughter "Tiny" also loved the challenge of living at 11,760 feet amid rock, snow, and extraordinarily changeable weather and trying to provide their guests comfortable but rudimentary accommodations. Though Mrs. Collier may have had heart trouble, many knew her as a robust and enthusiastic mountaineer, climbing when she could spare time from care of the cabin and its guests.[55]

Guests at the Boulderfield cabin also enjoyed their visits, finding the unique setting fine recompense for the risks and inconveniences they experienced on Longs and in the shelter cabin. Guests squeezed into the tiny rock cabin, shared in good-natured camaraderie, anticipated and recounted their climbs to the summit, and eagerly consumed the Colliers' home cooking. At night and when weather conditions were bad, guests, hosts, and guides listened to records on a "wheezy wind-up phonograph" including the songs of Rudy Vallee and the marching tunes of John Philip Sousa.[56]

And even as new fatalities occurred on Longs, Rocky's superintendents continued to express confidence in the value of improvements on the peak and the general trustworthiness of its climbers. Superintendent Rogers's report on Thiemeyer's death in 1929 placed positive emphasis on the resourcefulness of the Stachers in calling for the Colliers' help and obtaining rescue. Rogers also reminded officials in Washington of the importance of Longs to the park, highlighting the value of the Boulderfield cabin: "The ascent of Longs Peak continues to be one of the most popular climbs in the park. The shelter cabin on the Boulderfield has proven a boon to climbers who wish to make the climb in installments."[57] Rogers wanted Longs Peak to remain a major backcountry destination in the park, despite the occasional tragedy on its slopes. In 1929 he could not foresee how events in the following decade would intensify the appeal of the peak while amplifying concerns about risks to humans and the environment. Nor could he foresee that the 1930s and 1940s would raise, and then foreclose, questions about race and democracy in national park settings.

FOUR | Climbing and Vacationing in Economic Crisis and War

EVEN DURING THE GRINDING HARDSHIP of the Great Depression, Americans visited their national parks. President Franklin Roosevelt encouraged them to do so, hailing the parks as lands of extraordinary natural beauty that evoked the "fundamental idea . . . that the country belongs to the people. . . . The parks stand as the outward symbol of this great human principle. . . . I express to you the hope that each and every one of you who can possibly find the means and opportunity . . . will visit our national parks."[1] While lauding national parks as places where dispirited Americans might delight in nature and renew their faith in democracy, FDR and his New Deal administration also envisioned the parks as instruments of economic recovery. The parks were to become sites of meaningful work for young men rescued from unemployment by the Civilian Conservation Corps (CCC); in turn, CCC workers and park visitors would reinvigorate depressed local economies by spending their hard-earned dollars on goods and services in gateway communities.[2]

Rocky diligently followed the basic contours of FDR's regenerative script, adding detail and nuance suited to the locale. Like the president, Rocky's managers conveyed a democratic message of public ownership to Americans, declaring in visitor guides, "Rocky Mountain National Park, like all the National Parks, is yours."[3] In park guides and the tourist media, park staff extolled the mountain vistas to be observed while driving the newly opened Trail Ridge Road. Wanting to safeguard Rocky's reputation as a paradise for hikers and climbers, they also made sure visitor guides described the park's matchless opportunities for alpine recreation and the exceptional experience to be had on Longs Peak. So, too, the park's superintendents and rangers put CCC crews to work improving Rocky's campgrounds, roadways, and other visitor amenities, while urging CCC workers and park visitors to patronize the shops, restaurants, and lodges in the gateway communities of Estes Park and Grand Lake.

Though the nation's economic crisis in the 1930s provoked novel interventions from the federal government, national parks collaborating with the New Deal employed a familiar ethic of care, prioritizing the enjoyment of White visitors, improvements to visitor services and facilities, and parks' synergistic relationship with the tourist industry. Yet, perhaps because Americans were urged to deepen their appreciation for national parks, the decade also opened a window for reassessing extant rewards and risks. NPS field biologists George Wright, Ben Thompson, and Joseph Dixon used nascent ecological methods to evaluate national parks' preservation of wildlife and found in their system-wide survey that common park practices—such as reducing predators to encourage increase in the ungulate species dear to visitors—badly disrupted local habitats. At Rocky, managers saw that the killing of coyotes and other predators was leading to overlarge elk herds that damaged their habitats in searching for food. So, too, in visitor safety, Rocky noted that many inexperienced climbers failed to consider the risks of alpine mountaineering. Tragically, amid a host of serious accidents on Longs, there were five fatalities on the mountain in the 1930s. Four of the five who died had attempted climbs far beyond their experience and skills. Finally, Roosevelt's invocation of parks as places of democracy, and efforts by the secretary of the interior to end formal segregation in southern parks suggested that Rocky and other national parks might need to evaluate patterns of racial access and exclusion.[4]

These varied provocations for reform led, at best, to modest changes in Rocky's ethics and practices of care. Wildlife biologists' calls for ecological management across the NPS were rejected because they sounded radical, truly at odds with current policy. At Rocky managers balked at reducing the size of the park's elk population through culling, not wanting to lessen visitors' pleasure in sighting large elk herds. In contrast, when it came to mountaineering safety on Longs and other high peaks, park rangers deemed incremental improvements in their existing ethics and management practices appropriate to the challenges at hand. Rocky did not stop promoting climbing as an activity suitable for those of little experience, but it did augment its precautionary practices, embarking on a new educational campaign, in partnership with the CMC, that stressed "safe and sane" alpine adventure.

Rocky made no moves to welcome a more diverse public, as it perceived no risk or harm in its current practices. FDR's democratic messaging about the parks, Rocky's own echoing of that message, and Secretary of the Interior Harold Ickes's efforts to end racial segregation in Shenandoah National Park and Great Smoky Mountains National Park failed to elicit introspection about exclusionary practices at Rocky. Rather, Rocky Mountain National Park commissioned a study of visitor attitudes and backgrounds that confirmed the status quo, concluding that visitation by a relatively well-educated and moneyed Euro-American elite aligned well with the park's interests.[5]

The U.S. entry into World War II thrust Americans into yet another momentous crisis, but again NPS ethics of care shifted hesitantly, slightly, and sometimes not at all. As the nation mobilized for war, parks lost funding, CCC units disbanded, and visitation plunged. Park managers across the country looked forward to peacetime and the return of vacationing Americans to national parks, yet they also worried about how to address a growing backlog of maintenance projects and still-unresolved problems in natural resource management. At Rocky, managers took tentative steps to address known ecological problems, wary of admitting that their focus on visitor enjoyment sometimes put the well-being of natural resources at risk. In its management of mountaineering, the park retained faith in the educability of climbers, making incremental improvements in mountaineering education and rescue, even as it saw troubling instances of misbehavior and vandalism in the backcountry. Rocky faced the future with some uncertainty, realizing that in resource preservation and mountaineering its ethics and practices of care might need further change. In democratic access, the park simply continued its facile denial of risk, disregarding African Americans' "Double V" campaign against racial discrimination and sustaining practices that favored visitation by White middle-class Americans.

Enjoyment for a Dispirited Nation: *Automobile Travelers and Mountaineers*

President Roosevelt's New Deal was capacious, treating parks along with cities, factories, and farms as places vital to national recovery and the evolution of a "moral capitalism" committed to the well-being of all Americans. FDR intended urban jobs programs, collective bargaining, farm subsidies, unemployment insurance, and Social Security to put more purchasing power in Americans' pockets and revive their faith in the nation's economy and government; so, too, he imagined the NPS and its parks rekindling confidence in the nation's integrity and worth. National parks were to propel the nation forward by uplifting visitors in body and spirit, giving idle and dispirited youth healthful and remunerative employment in public works, and stimulating consumer spending in local economies.[6] Rocky Mountain National Park worked to fulfill each element of this vision, with messaging that emphasized Americans' public ownership of the park and right to enjoy it freely: "You, its owners, are free to see it and enjoy it in your own way. You may live in the hotels or lodges or camp out with your own equipment and supplies. You are free to climb to its alpine meadows, ascend its mountains, explore its canyons and its countless lakes, study its wild life, and fish in its streams."[7]

Trail Ridge Road became the primary emblem of a park committed to public enjoyment and revitalization. Construction of the transmountain route began in 1929, and it opened to automobile travel in 1932, though it took many more years of work by CCC crews to complete landscaping and surfacing wayside viewing areas and parking lots. The road extended from Estes Park across the Continental Divide to Grand Lake, opening a new alpine corridor to automobile tourists and replacing the dangerously steep Fall River Road as the park's principal roadway. Trail Ridge Road had a modest grade, never exceeding 7 percent, and was twenty-four feet wide, giving motorists ample room to pass one another and maneuver safely. While much easier to drive than Fall River Road, Trail Ridge also afforded motorists more spectacular views of the Rockies than the old road, as ten miles of the roadway were above tree line and at an altitude of more than eleven thousand feet. On Rocky's sweeping new road visitors could enjoy seeing mile after mile of snow-covered peaks, alpine lakes, canyons, magnificent wildlife, and beautiful wildflowers, all while seated comfortably in fast-moving automobiles. The park publicized the roadway in local and national print media and was pleased to see that it quickly boosted visitation: 292,000 people traveled to the park in 83,000 automobiles in 1933; by 1938, 660,000 visitors traveled through the park in 200,000 cars. Aldo Leopold, Robert Sterling Yard, and other members of the Wilderness Society were beginning to argue that automobile travel in national parks jeopardized wilderness preservation, but their criticism did nothing to distract from the allure of Trail Ridge Road. Representing a feat in facade management, Rocky's new roadway offered the public a wilderness mountain aesthetic that obscured evidence of environmental engineering and landscape manipulation. In design and use, the road affirmed the idea that national parks could foster love of country by offering aesthetic experiences of inspiring landscapes on a monumental scale.[8]

Still, Longs Peak and alpine recreation remained central to the park's identity. Automobile visitors in the 1930s probably observed Longs Peak as but one high point in a vast mountain vista seen from Trail Ridge Road, but each annual edition of the Rocky Mountain National Park visitor guide included photos of the singular fourteener, and some editions gave Longs pride of place on the brochure cover. In language that persisted from one year to the next, the visitor guides described Rocky Mountain National Park as a "land of lofty mountains" and "stalwart beauty," with Longs Peak "the greatest of all the mountains in the park."[9] National and international print media also carried news and photographs of the national park and its famed peak, offering what the *Estes Park Trail* considered "wonderful advertising for the region."[10] Park visitor guides provided information about the trailhead location, length, and difficulty of numerous backcountry trails in Rocky but always highlighted Longs, describing the climb to its summit as strenuous but inspiring, a marvelous endeavor for anyone of adventurous disposition:

> Of the many fascinating and delightful mountain climbs, the ascent of Longs Peak is the most inspiring, and it is one of the most strenuous. The great altitude of the mountain, 14,255 feet above sea level and more than 5,000 feet above the valley floor, and its position well east of the Continental Divide, affording a magnificent view back upon the range, make it much the most spectacular viewpoint in the park. The difficulty of the

ascent also has its attractiveness. Longs Peak is the big climb of the Rocky Mountain National Park. And yet the ascent is by no means forbidding. One may go more than half-way by horseback. Over a thousand men and women, and occasionally children, climb the peak each season. Those making the Longs Peak trip should have strong, comfortable shoes, stout warm clothing, and remember that cold or stormy weather is sometimes encountered.[11]

And summit the mountain visitors did, throughout the 1930s. A total of 2,132 climbers reached the summit of Longs Peak in 1931, perhaps because they had been motivated by the park's promotional literature and by coverage in travel media. This was the greatest number of summits thus far recorded in a single year, not surpassed until 1954. Climbers came from around the world and across the United States. Examining Longs' summit registers for 1934 up to August 3, Dorothy Collier found that climbers hailed from Switzerland, Holland, England, Siberia, Egypt, and Germany as well as thirty-three of the forty-eight U.S. states. All climbers benefited from improvements made by park management after the Vaille tragedy: the East Longs Peak Trail, substantially rerouted in the late 1920s and early 1930s, eased the rigors of the climb to the Boulderfield for both horses and hikers. The spur trail to Chasm Lake, built in 1926, made the difficult East Face routes more accessible to experienced rock climbers. The installation of cables along the steepest section of the North Face gave inexpert climbers a nontechnical route to the peak's summit that afforded spectacular views of Chasm Lake and was significantly shorter than the *Keyhole* route. In the summer, the Boulderfield cabin provided both skilled and novice climbers with guiding services, lodging, and meals, albeit in very rustic style. Throughout the year, the Boulderfield, Chasm Lake, and Keyhole shelters offered emergency protection to climbers who were caught in sudden storms or found themselves in unanticipated need of overnight refuge.[12]

Adults climbing Longs' nontechnical routes without benefit of commercial guides or a night at the Boulderfield cabin sometimes completed the entire trip from trailhead to summit and back in one long day; others made a two-day trip, camping overnight in Jim's Grove to get an early start on the summit leg of the trip. Some of these groups were quite large, as when "thirty-five members of the Washington Park Community Church, Denver, climbed Longs Peak under the leadership of their pastor, Dr. Albertson."[13] Since lightning storms were frequent on summer afternoons, prudent climbers tried to be off the summit by noon, though it was not unusual for climbers to misjudge the time required for the descent and encounter rain, thunder, and lightning on their way down the mountain.

Park rangers with mountaineering expertise occasionally led nontechnical climbs. Ranger Jack Moomaw, for example, led Helene Wentzel of Cheyenne, Wyoming, on an ascent to Longs' summit in June 1934, going up the *Keyhole* route on the peak's west side and down "the icy North Face." "The day was far from perfect for the climb, but it failed to daunt Miss Wentzel who didn't mind the cold. Of course, the ranger was in his element." More often, inexpert climbers hired guides employed at the Boulderfield Shelter Cabin. Though guides working for the Colliers escorted only a fraction of all climbers in the 1930s, they were busy nonetheless, often making two or three summit climbs a day during the summer season via the *Cable* route.[14] As in the 1920s, the Boulderfield cabin tended to attract people who enjoyed mixing conviviality with the challenges of climbing. Some had probably learned of the cabin from national news publications, such as Hearst's *American Weekly*, which described the "hotel" as "one of the finest in the world" for "those who find mountain scenery eye-filling and soul stirring."[15] When storms materialized quickly, the cabin often became crowded as climbers seeking shelter pressed in among already-registered guests. In these circumstances, those gathered inside dispensed with formality and, sometimes, their usual standards of modesty. Hull Cook, one of the guides, remembered:

> After the brief but heavy afternoon rain showers that are frequent in the mountains, we would often reach the cabin drenched, and wish to change into dry clothes, only to find the place crowded with tourists seeking shelter. My wife believes that this is where I lost my modesty, because we boys changed to dry clothes, crowds or not. We would step to a corner of the room, and while facing away from the people . . . peel down to the bare facts and dry off. Women showed surprise, shock, and embarrassment until, seemingly reassured by our confident composure, their discomfort was usually converted to amusement.[16]

Children attending summer camp or climbing with adult family members also sought Longs' summit. The summit registers for the 1930s show that groups of youth campers and counselors reached the top of Longs nearly every day of July and August. "Baker Armstrong of Camp Audubon near Brainard Lake led a party of 50 boys to the summit . . . and got them all back without mishap." Probably climbing in a family group, a five-year-old girl, the youngest climber yet, made it to the top of the peak in 1930, and a five-year-old boy reached the summit in 1933.[17]

Children and adolescents who climbed Longs as part of the summer camp experience undoubtedly felt many emotions as they ascended the peak, ranging from fear to elation. At the same time, they were encouraged by their elders to attach specific cultural meanings to the peak. At camps around the United States and in Canada, venturing into nature was considered an opportunity for critical lessons about oneself and one's place in the world. And though summer camps generally anchored young people's class, gender, and racial identity, counselors expected mountain climbing to push children toward personal introspection and growth. Children attempted to summit Longs not merely because it was revered as a spectacular destination, but because camp staff urged them to view the climb as an activity that built physical strength, encouraged powers of observation in nature, and aided campers' emotional, spiritual, and moral development. Girls and boys attending summer camp near Rocky came from White, relatively well-off homes, but their families had few guarantees of security in the Great Depression, and camp staff may have wanted to build young people's resilience and ability to thrive amid uncertainty and adversity.[18]

At Allsebrook Camp for Girls, established near Estes Park in 1930, counselors sought to create a camp experience that offered "an aura of aspiration, of growth, of seeking to be the best one could be."[19] The Christian nondenominational camp expected girls to engage in daily morning reflection, and for this purpose it used "Sunrise Meditations" written by counselors about lessons and insights to be found amid the nearby mountains. Over the course of the summer, girls at Allsebrook also climbed many of the local mountains and reflected on what they had learned from each one. In the "Sunrise Meditations," Otis Peak represented the girls' quest for "quiet strength," their "need for loving, friendly union with every member of our charmed circle in beautiful Allsebrook." Hallett was "stately, graceful, upward-lifting," inspiring each girl to have faith in herself. It urged each girl to declare: "I let my spirit soar. . . . From my inmost being, loving, joyous LIFE pours out . . . in a hundred ways. . . . I AM. I CAN. I WILL." Green Mountain taught girls that even disappointments in life "may be a real value." And Longs stirred each Allsebrook girl to identify her life's ideal and act on it. Sometimes it demanded "endurance and stick-to-itiveness." At other times, the mountain called for "great effort and the utmost skill." Always Longs asked those who observed and climbed its slopes whether they could "face a failure and not be crushed," could eliminate "the petty things in your life—worry, jealousy, selfishness, fear." Having gained the summit of Longs, girls were ready "to commune with the highest and the best." As their eyes took in the "form, color, and beauty" below, each girl could say, "Here is my reward!" Yet, the peak also cautioned against overconfidence and pride. As one girl recorded in the camp newspaper, reaching Longs' summit initially stimulated "the feeling of intense success." Within minutes, however, Betty Lou Bolce realized "how very tiny and insignificant I was. . . . I was subdued, and the impression of the power of the mountains will never leave me."[20] Longs Peak had taught this girl that personal confidence needed always to be tempered by consciousness of one's small place in the whole of nature.

The peak also held distinctive meaning for experienced climbers, immersed in a culture that prized athletic achievement and the ability to persevere in the most challenging of alpine environments. Longs continued to be sought out by ambitious mountaineers wanting to "bag" fourteeners in Colorado, California, Oregon, and Washington. It also appealed to climbers wanting to try routes on difficult rock faces. The Stettner brothers returned to Longs twice in the 1930s, using belay maneuvers and pitons to ascend the peak. Other climbers on the challenging East Face routes still relied on little more than climbing ropes, ice axes, and hobnailed boots to aid their ascents to the summit. As in previous decades, climbers pursued new firsts: Dorothy Collier and three Boulderfield Shelter Cabin guides made the first all-night ascent of Longs' East Face in August 1931. In 1932 Clerin Zumwalt, one of the Boulderfield cabin guides, set the record for fifty-three climbs in a single year, using multiple routes. That same year, Everett Long, another of the Boulderfield cabin guides, became the first person to have climbed all fifteen of the then-known routes on Longs. George Greeley climbed to Longs' summit by four different routes on a single day in August 1935. And in 1939 a twenty-three-year-old man from Denver, Edwin Watson, became the first person to climb the East Face alone in winter in what was described as "the most remarkable feat of solo climbing in the country's history." Hailing Watson's courage and remarkable performance, the *New York Times* reported that Watson "battled his way through deep snowdrifts covering crevices and precipices, crawled over glaciers and clung to rocky ledges in his ascent to the wind-whipped summit of the peak in Rocky Mountain National Park." The ascent was "an entirely different matter from the trek up the tourist [*Keyhole*] trail," which, "although a stiff test of wind and muscle, has been made by 8-year-old children." Incredibly, Watson's "Winter conquest" had required climbing "vertically more than 2,800 feet from the edge of one of the numerous black glacial lakes which dot the region, with hardly a crevice or a ledge to break its surface and provide a handhold." The young man used no unusual equipment but "gave much credit to the homemade spikes he wore on his shoes."[21]

Whether visitors to Rocky Mountain National Park climbed Longs Peak or traveled through the park by automobile on Trail Ridge Road, men hired by New Deal public works programs were in the background, undertaking tasks that facilitated their enjoyment. Park managers hired men through the New Deal's Emergency Conservation Work (ECW) program and through the larger Civilian Conservation Corps. Crews in both programs lived in CCC camps scattered around the park. Landscaping and the construction of wayside parking areas on Trail Ridge Road was a CCC priority, as the completion of these projects allowed automobile visitors to stop for scenic viewing and take short strolls on roadside trails. CCC crews also improved the park's campgrounds and constructed an amphitheater and museum at Moraine Park for visitors' enjoyment and edification. They built reservoirs and fishponds, put in sewer treatment plants and sewer collection lines, repaired and improved telephone, water, and utility lines, and engaged in routine maintenance.[22] In addition, CCC and ECW crews worked on backcountry assignments that included controlling insect infestations in the park's splendid stands of ponderosa and lodgepole pine, firefighting, and improving backcountry trails and facilities. CCC workers performed trail work on Longs Peak and rebuilt the approach road to the trailhead campground in 1934. They were probably the workers assigned to install new poles for the Longs Peak telephone line in 1934 and 1935.[23]

Rocky Mountain National Park's efforts to promote the enjoyment of both front-country and backcountry visitors had decidedly positive effects on the local economy, just as FDR and his New Deal officials had hoped. The financial hardships of the Great Depression may have required visitors to watch their spending carefully, but local businesses in the gateway communities of Estes Park and Grand Lake nonetheless "reaped a harvest of tourist dollars" and began to create new job openings for the region's unemployed. The *Estes Park Trail* reported that CCC workers also spent money locally, injecting some $2,000 into the local economy each month. According to Superintendent David Canfield, goodwill between the park and the gateway communities soared: "In the villages of Estes Park and Grand Lake . . . national park interests are as close to the villages as their own interests, and local suspicions of this government bureau are being replaced by a spirit of cooperation."[24]

The Calculus of Reward and Risk

Visitor enjoyment was clearly the principal goal of park officials at Rocky in the 1930s, yet the decade also provoked at least some disquiet about the park's calculus of reward and risk. The Dust Bowl may have been a contributing factor, as it offered shocking proof that modern Americans had abused rather than stewarded nature while seeking financial gain and consumer reward. Certainly, FDR and leading agronomists agreed that American farmers had overplanted their land year after year, causing calamitous soil erosion and the destitution of farm families. Farmers needed to embrace soil conservation practices that included revegetation, the building of check dams, and reliance on terracing and contour planting. CCC crews became key to the restoration of farmland, working under the guidance of the New Deal Soil Conservation Service to reverse erosion and restore the soil on private farms.[25]

America's magnificent national parks probably seemed a world apart from its exhausted farmlands, but a small number of field biologists in the NPS recognized signs of ecological disturbance in the national parks and sounded an alarm about the NPS's shortsighted management of natural resources, especially park wildlife. George Wright, Ben Thompson, and Joseph Dixon conducted a system-wide analysis of the effects of NPS wildlife management practices, relying on ecological principles and methods that stressed the interrelationship of life forms in the natural world. Their 1933 and 1935 published reports, *Fauna of the National Parks of the United States*, Fauna Series No. 1 and No. 2, were an urgent call for change. Fauna Series No. 1 recognized the fundamental "anomaly" confronting park managers who were obliged "to restore and perpetuate the fauna in its pristine state" while accommodating large numbers of visitors eager to see and enjoy park wildlife. As the authors pointed out, "The national parks owe much of their unique charm to the unusual opportunities they afford for observing animals amid the intimacies of wild settings in which even the observers feel themselves a part. It is one of the causes contributing to their constantly increasing popularity. The thrill of being in the same meadow with an elk, no fence or bar between, reaches everyone, young or old." Yet, the parks had not handled the challenge well: "mushrooming growth in park travel" had resulted in "an alarming depletion of wildlife resources."

In fact, the report found that parks systematically harmed and destabilized wildlife while trying to enhance the experience of the visiting public. National parks that deliberately extirpated predator species saw the populations of elk, deer, and reindeer beloved by visitors become "unnaturally abundant"; these animals both overgrazed their habitats and became dangerously malnourished. Parks with damaged and depleted habitats also witnessed the invasion of exotic plants and animals that competed with native species and exposed them to disease. So, too, when parks relied on alien stock to replenish native herds of elk or reindeer, they hybridized local populations and risked the introduction of foreign diseases and pests. None of the parks were large enough to provide "year-round sanctuary for adequate populations of all resident species," and very few were trying to adjust their boundaries so that fauna might "become self-sustaining and independent." Fauna Series No. 1 and No. 2 urged the parks to restore depleted habitats and reestablish extirpated species, reduce the numbers of overpopulated fauna, try to eliminate or control exotics, and alter their boundaries to better suit the yearlong needs of faunal species. They embraced continued scientific research and called upon the NPS to adopt ecological approaches to resource management.[26]

Coincidental with the publication of these reports, wilderness advocates such as Bob Marshall lamented the CCC's emphasis on recreational construction projects in national parks rather than on the preservation of pristine wilderness sites. So, too, wildlife ecologist Aldo Leopold and botanist Merritt L. Fernald argued that CCC tree-planting, fish stocking, and fire-prevention work in national parks harmed rather than preserved natural resources. In the view of these critics, the labor of CCC employees was exacerbating the worst tendencies in park management, rather than preserving parks for the future.[27]

Fauna Series No. 1 identified Rocky Mountain National Park as a place with particularly worrisome indicators of overpopulation and malnourishment among its elk. The park had deliberately killed predator species and now had insufficient winter habitat for its growing elk herd. Rocky's smaller mountain valleys—Moraine, Beaver, and Horseshoe Parks and Black Canyon—were the best sites for winter grazing, but these valleys were crowded with private lodges and cabins, many built before the park was established. The domestic stock (especially horses) that belonged to these properties heavily grazed the valley grasses, leaving little for elk. Fauna Series No. 1 found that "during the winter of 1930 aspen was extensively barked by the elk. This was the first indication that the elk herd was reaching the limit of its food supply and that range abuse and starvation were in the offing." More problematic still, when the park's hungry elk moved beyond park boundaries in winter to look for food sources in Estes Park, property owners there complained bitterly that the animals destroyed fences, gardens, and other assets. Rangers did not want the elk to be a "nuisance to the countryside" but were only beginning to address the park's inadequate carrying capacity for the animals.[28]

Much of Fauna Series No. 1's evaluation of elk at Rocky came from data supplied by the park, and over the remainder of the 1930s concern about elk in the park increased among its rangers and superintendents.[29] The condition of the park's elk, however, was not the only concern among those tasked with the preservation of Rocky's natural resources. Park officials considered how best to respond to growing pressure from skiers and the Estes Park Chamber of Commerce to allow championship ski racing in the park and the development of an ice rink, ski runs, and a commercial ski resort. Even more worrisome was pressure from the Bureau of Reclamation, farmers, and municipal leaders to allow construction of a transmountain water tunnel from Grand Lake all the way through the park to the east slope. Tunnel advocates hoped to satisfy the irrigation demands of east slope farmers and supply hydroelectric power to burgeoning communities on the Front Range. The park already contained within its boundaries some eighteen ditches and reservoirs, all built before the park was established, diverting water from west to east, but park officials thought the massive scale of the proposed transmountain tunnel made it altogether different from the earlier water projects. Superintendent Thomas Allen, new to Rocky in 1936, called it the "greatest problem facing this park." He and numerous conservation organizations argued that the tunnel project would badly deface the park, open it to still more commercial and environmental exploitation, and violate its commitment to "perpetual preservation." Their adversaries, however, were persistent and politically well connected.[30]

Disquiet about risks to human safety, especially in the backcountry, grew alongside concerns about wildlife and development. Although Rocky's front-country visitors were sometimes hurt in car accidents or on roadside trails, the vast majority enjoyed a park experience free of injury. Superintendent Edmund Rogers thought it "remarkable" that only eleven minor car accidents and one fatal car accident occurred in fiscal year 1935, though more than 109,000 automobiles drove through the park. The likelihood of injury to any single individual was more pronounced, however, in the park's rugged backcountry. There, someone traveling by foot (or horseback) entered an environment of inherent and varied risk, regardless of the time of year, including rocky and sometimes wet or icy trails and climbing routes, rapid drops in temperature, dangerous storms and lightning strikes, hypothermia and altitude sickness, falling rocks, and avalanches. These risks were magnified on Longs Peak, where the climb to the summit involved not only sudden changes in weather and scrambling across unstable rock and ice, but also dangerous drop-offs along steep and unprotected rock surfaces, even on nontechnical routes.[31]

Indeed, park staff and the Boulderfield shelter guides contended with frequent accidents on Longs, some requiring long and difficult rescues, as the popularity of the peak continued to grow. Eight months after his successful solo climb on the East Face, Edwin Watson was involved in another East Face climb with two other experienced alpinists, during which the lead climber, Gerald Clark, died of exposure to freezing temperatures. The three men were attempting a new route, and thirty-year-old Clark had been hammering a piton into the rock face when the head of his hammer flew off. Unable to secure protection and perched on a small ledge in Fields Chimney "with water and spray running around him," Clark lowered the rope to Watson and the third climber so they could descend safely and go for help. Ranger Ernie Field and four CMC members responded to the call for rescue, but according to Field, "the elements seemed to be against all of us that night . . . and our climbing was retarded by darkness, rain, and fog." At dawn, the rescuers reached Fields Chimney, but "Mr. Clark was so hidden by the storm and trough" that the rescuers had difficulty finding him. When they finally reached him, Clark was hypothermic and terribly weakened. The rescue took an additional five hours as Field and his helpers lowered Clark down the rock face, with snow and sleet hampering their efforts. Clark died minutes after his unconscious body was placed on the ground at the base of the East Face.[32]

Climbers far less skilled than Clark accounted for the four other fatalities on Longs in the 1930s. R. B. Key, an inexperienced climber from Mississippi, was climbing alone on September 13, 1931, when he fell to his death from some-where above Mills Glacier. Key's body was discovered by other hikers and was transported from the park in a two-day recovery operation involving the park's assistant superintendent and five rangers. Robert Smith, the forty-one-year-old general manager of a publishing company in Indianapolis, was killed instantly by falling rock on July 18, 1932, at Chasm View, just below the North Face *Cable* route. Smith, his wife, and four companions had traveled by horseback to the Boulderfield and were about to begin a guided climb up the North Face *Cable* route. Gary Secor, a sixteen-year-old from Longmont, fell to his death on August 8, 1932, when, against the advice of his teenage climbing partner, he took a shortcut while descending the *Keyhole* route. And John Fuller, a young man who had climbed to Longs' summit thirteen times by its nontechnical routes, fell to his death after deciding to try out new climbing shoes on the rocky terrain to the right of the *Cable* route. Fuller was climbing alone, and it is not known whether he slipped and fell or was killed by falling rock.[33]

In addition to these tragic fatalities, numerous other climbers were hurt on Longs each year, some very badly. Ralph Bittelheim was climbing the peak in 1939 when he encountered a rockslide and "was struck in the back by a heavy boulder." "The blow paralyzed his arms and legs. Rangers lowered him by a rope and transported him to a hospital." The brief write-up of the incident that appeared in Bittelheim's hometown newspaper, the *New York Times*, barely began to account for the many hours rangers spent rescuing him or the difficulties they must have faced trying to move him down Longs' rocky surfaces and trails without causing further trauma.[34]

CMC members were sometimes on hand to assist rangers with rescue and recovery, as in the case of Gerald Clark. CCC workers also occasionally assisted park rangers with rescues on Longs Peak. Reporting on one such rescue in August 1934, the park superintendent noted, "It is no mean job to move a person nine miles over a rough mountain trail on a stretcher. However, Rangers Moomaw and Ratcliff and eighteen C.C.C. men did a splendid piece of work when they carried Mr. Thomas to the Long's Peak Campground on August 16." Mr. Thomas had fallen on the East Face of Longs Peak, suffering bruises and shock.[35]

Often, however, no rangers, CMC members, or CCC men were nearby, and it fell to Robert Collier and his guides to rescue injured, lost, or stranded climbers on Longs. In one such incident, Collier helped save teenagers lost in a lightning storm in the middle of the night as they tried to reach the *Cable* route for a North Face descent; in another he was called on to aid a young woman who, during a midnight climb, lost all the fingers on one hand when her male companion inadvertently shoved a large rock over her extended arm. By the 1930s the phone in the Boulderfield worked very intermittently, so it could not have been easy for the Colliers to call for additional help.[36]

Especially when injuries were serious or life threatening, park rangers, the Colliers, and others involved in search, rescue, and recovery acted under very substantial strain, and it did not help that the Boulderfield cabin, touted as a place of shelter, turned out to be ill suited to the demands placed on it. Built to accommodate only ten individuals, the cabin was frequently overcrowded, with more than twenty people at a time. Robert Collier estimated that the cabin served as a place of refuge for 1,500 people each summer. The high number reflected the Colliers' obligation to shelter climbers who turned up suddenly because they were cold, wet, hungry, fatigued, or injured, while also caring for registered guests. But because the cabin had been built on a shifting glacial field, it was fundamentally unstable. Less than ten years after its construction, the cabin's walls showed signs of cracking and the walls and roof began to separate. Robert Collier tried to limit the movement of the building by weighing down its roof with rocks, but this hardly resolved the cabin's inadequacies as a place of shelter from dangerous alpine conditions. Neither the Keyhole shelter nor the Chasm Lake shelter cabin were good alternatives, as their locations and even smaller size made them less useful than the Boulderfield cabin.[37]

Responding to Risk and Harm

Despite incentives to reevaluate risks to both natural resources and the safety of backcountry climbers, the park largely upheld its existing ethics and practices of care. National parks' role in economic revitalization surely played a role in precluding change, as officials across the park system continued to see high levels of visitor use, enjoyment, and spending as crucial to the economic revitalization of national parks and their gateway communities. In this context, Wright, Thompson, and Dixon's call for the ecological management of wildlife gained little traction anywhere in the NPS, although the men laid the groundwork for ecologically informed policy in subsequent decades. Simply put, they were asking for too dramatic a shift in orientation. At Rocky, park rangers had clear proof that its elk were both malnourished and destructive; desperately hungry elk were eating the shoots, leaves, bark, and cambium of aspen, killing trees throughout the park, especially in Beaver Meadows. Still, a recommendation from the park superintendent in 1935 to cull the growing herd by lethal force went unheeded, as it competed with the conviction, held by resource managers and the superintendent himself, that Rocky must satisfy visitors' desire to see large herds of magnificent elk. The park tried to expand its available elk forage by purchasing some 12,500 acres of land from private owners, but this modest enlargement barely improved grazing conditions.[38]

In a related matter, Rocky's managers were disappointed to lose their fight against the water-diverting Colorado–Big Thompson Project, though they vowed to protect the park's view-scape for visitors. And despite some misgivings about development inside the park, Rocky moved to improve winter visitor amenities. By the late 1930s the park was keeping Trail Ridge Road open to Hidden Valley, accommodating visitors who wanted to drive to the area most popular with skiers. At Hidden Valley the park cleared and maintained a pond for ice skaters, widened the existing informal ski runs and sledding trails, built two warming shelters and toilet facilities for winter recreators, and gave permission for a ski school to offer lessons. Winter use of parks was growing across the NPS, and administrators at Rocky continued to hear from skiers throughout the country who wanted a full-service ski resort in the park with rope tows and concessions.[39]

In managing mountaineering, Rocky did not deny or delay action in response to harsh realities as it did in managing wildlife. Rather, the park maintained that it was reasonable to keep Longs and other peaks open to both novice and experienced climbers as long as it tried to reduce accidents and fatalities among both groups. Facing an imbalance between reward and risk less daunting than the one facing wildlife managers, rangers renewed their partnership with the CMC and fine-tuned the ethic of care elaborated in the 1920s, focusing on education as the best way to promote both enjoyment and safety in climbing.

This work amounted to a campaign for "safe and sane" climbing. Using the CMC's *Trail and Timberline* magazine as a primary means of communication, skilled climbers and park rangers stressed the importance of careful planning for alpine adventures, diligent training, and communication with guides and rangers. In 1932 and 1933 *Trail and Timberline* published several articles on rock and ice climbing methods, targeting somewhat experienced climbers eager to try mountaineering techniques developed in the Alps. Excitement about these techniques was promoting a "true mountaineering spirit" in Colorado, and the CMC hoped that printed discussions of how to rope and belay, use pitons and carabiners, friction climb, and rappel would help climbers appreciate the technical skills required to reach "more exhilarating heights with less wasted effort and fewer misadventures." Rock climbing was no longer a sport of haphazard or "catch-as-catch-can" methods. The "engineering methods of modern rock climbing technique" made previously "impossible" routes attainable, yet the adoption of these methods also demanded that climbers make "SAFETY . . . the foremost consideration."[40]

Reaching out to Colorado's more numerous inexperienced climbers, Boulderfield cabin guide Clerin Zumwalt contributed an article to *Trail and Timberline* in May 1933 that described rock climbing as a "thrilling, healthy sport," but one that required "conscientious training" in balance and movement on rock as well as careful appraisal of weather and route conditions. In his view accidents occurred primarily because inexperienced climbers "were trying to climb rocks which the experienced would never think of climbing." Other articles in *Trail and Timberline* offered climbers, both technical and nontechnical, opportunities to hear directly from park rangers. Sharing "a ranger's side of the story," Ranger John S. McLaughlin urged climbers to practice "sane mountain climbing" by informing rangers of their plans and expected time of return and by turning around if they discovered that "time was running short." He tried to impress on climbers the need to consider the well-being of frantic family members when a climber went missing, and he asked them to contemplate the hazards rangers faced when attempting rescues and recoveries in dangerous terrain and adverse conditions.[41]

As the "safe and sane" climbing campaign moved forward, managers at Rocky also ordered the demolition of the Boulderfield Shelter Cabin in 1936. The cabin had come to the end of its possible use as a place of refuge because it stood on a rock glacier, and, as Robert Collier recalled, "The constant melting and the freezing of the . . . ice would move the rocks and spread the walls and . . . the Park Service felt [it was] better to tear it down before something fell down and hurt somebody." Concerned that the building put human safety at risk, park managers did not acknowledge that the haphazard disposal of human and (domestic) animal waste near the cabin polluted water on Longs or that the cabin's coal smoke polluted the mountain air. Nor did they seem to notice that the large numbers of humans and pack animals who congregated at the cabin in the summer months were disturbing wildlife on Longs. The Colliers recalled seeing only marmots and pikas on Longs Peak, though deer, mountain lions, black bears, elk, porcupines, and golden-mantled ground squirrels were all indigenous to the subalpine and alpine zones on the mountain. Still, with the cabin's demolition in 1936, a source of environmental harm was removed.[42]

The CMC and Rocky Mountain National Park pursued further innovations in the campaign for "safe and sane" climbing between 1938 and 1940. Perhaps because the Colliers and their guides were no longer on hand in the Boulderfield to guide and rescue climbers, the park appointed Ernie Field to the new position of seasonal (summer) Longs Peak ranger in 1938. His regular presence on the peak improved climbers' access to expert guidance and rescue. Field also enhanced climbers' knowledge of Longs by contributing articles about the peak to *Trail and Timberline*. His June 1939 article, "Rock Work on Long's Peak," identified (on maps) the twenty different routes put in on Longs by then. Even more important, he shared with climbers a new scheme classifying the routes, "coincident with the degree of danger" from "easy" to "moderate," "difficult," and "severe." Urging technical and nontechnical climbers to choose routes suited to their ability and experience, Ranger Field also warned everyone, regardless of competence, to be wary of Longs' falling rocks and on the alert for its frequent lightning storms. Also in 1939, *Trail and Timberline* announced that the CMC's annual Summer Outing would become a "school of mountaineering," with instruction in rock and ice climbing techniques as well as "pace setting" and group dynamics. And in 1940 Field revealed in *Trail and Timberline* the creation of a poster telling mountain climbers how to "play safe." Since some climbers might not read or remember the advice communicated in *Trail and Timberline*, the poster would take the principles of "safe and sane" climbing into the field. It "was to be mounted . . . at strategic points by the National Forest and Park Services. We hope it will do for safe and sane climbing what the Good Woodsman [poster] has done for nature protection and help adventurous but inexperienced climbers to get the greatest possible enjoyment out of their Colorado mountain vacations." The poster placed great emphasis on climbers' interaction with park personnel, urging them to discuss their routes with local rangers and ask for advice regarding weather, natural hazards, and the adequacy of their equipment and clothing. All these measures could help alpinists avoid needless risk of serious harm.[43]

Some individuals in the climbing community thought it important to go beyond "safe and sane" climbing practices and convey the message that mountaineering was more than mere sport. Father Joseph Bosetti, the director of Camp Saint Malo, wrote a piece for *Trail and Timberline* on the "philosophy of mountaineering" that sought to help mountain enthusiasts understand that "alpinism" was not about "dangers and risks for their inherent thrills." Rather, authentic alpinism involved "pragmatic curiosity for a palpable reality." Alpinists climbed so that the reality of mountains would be revealed to them. They tested their own capacities for initiative, alertness, and good judgment. Alpinism also offered spiritual insight and inspiration. And though alpinists sometimes competed against one another, mountaineering "obliterated" differences of culture and class and brought people together, relieved of the "hypocrisy of conventionalities," on the mountaintops.[44]

Importantly, alongside articles on climber safety and mountaineering values, *Trail and Timberline* published articles that asked climbers who loved the outdoors to consider what humans' thoughtless degradation of the natural environment meant to their own well-being. At a moment in time when the NPS still resisted ecological thinking, the CMC embraced it. For example, M. Walter Pesman asked readers to ponder how humans' economic actions had caused soil erosion and dust storms, overgrazing, the loss of fish and wildlife, deforestation, and the proliferation of invasive weeds. "Man, the Troublemaker," was "the only animal that can reason and won't," Pesman opined, and humans could not continue their "thoughtless spoils system" indefinitely. They were destined to find that nature "is a pitiless avenger if we try to beat her at her own game." Pesman pursued a similar line of thinking in condemning the killing of predators on public and private lands. Meanwhile, Francis Ramaley, professor of biology at the University of Colorado, asked local climbers to support the setting aside of new preservation areas at the local, state, and national levels. And Earl Davis urged the Colorado Mountain Club to use education and lobbying to lessen the destructiveness of "economic progress" and promote the preservation of "unspoiled" nature. The CMC intentionally communicated support for an ecological ethic of care on public lands, but it had no authority to change policy, whether in the NPS or other government agencies.[45]

Complacency about Racial Exclusion at Rocky Mountain National Park

Rocky Mountain National Park's admission of problems in mountaineering safety and wildlife management in the 1930s produced disparate responses, as the park took more constructive and deliberate steps to reduce climber accidents than it did to restore the health of elk and aspen. Since the park never admitted the existence of practices barring free access to the park, it took no steps to attract visitors representing the nation's full diversity. Rocky may have readily echoed FDR's invocation of national parks as sites of democratic freedom and public ownership, but it felt no incentive to welcome Americans of color to the park. The park was far removed from the South, where Secretary of the Interior Harold Ickes was attempting, without great success, to move racially segregated parks such as Shenandoah National Park toward integration, and its managers probably saw the racial dynamics unfolding there as irrelevant to a park in Colorado.[46]

Yet, had Rocky paid closer attention, there were many signs of interest among people of color in the kinds of outdoor experiences available in national parks, along with clear evidence of discrimination against them. Lincoln Hills continued to operate just forty-two miles from Rocky Mountain National Park. The resort proved mountain recreation's ongoing appeal to African Americans living in Colorado and other states as well as their necessary accommodation with segregation to gain access to the outdoors. Though Lincoln Hills sustained losses in membership because of the Great Depression, many Black families returned to the resort year after year. The resort also continued to host Camp Nizhoni, affording African American girls excluded from the YWCA's Camp Lookout treasured opportunities to hike, swim, observe wildlife, and delight in "God's Wonderland."[47]

Elsewhere in Colorado, Denver's African Americans sustained an ongoing campaign to end racial discrimination through a local chapter of the NAACP, the Denver Interracial Committee, and the Cosmopolitan Club. While these organizations focused on discriminatory practices in housing and education, Denver's African American community also decried Blacks' exclusion from restaurants, hotels, parks, campgrounds, and swimming pools. In this, they were far from alone. Across the nation African Americans evinced growing interest in long-distance vacationing, camping, and access to the outdoors. Family-owned automobiles facilitated their quest for freedom. So, too, Latinx people in Colorado and other states embraced automobility, and in towns such as Boulder, Mexican American families and teenagers took up hiking and camping. *The Negro Motorist Green Book* began publication in 1936, offering African Americans information on how and where to find safe and courteous access to food, lodging, car services, and outdoor recreation while on the road. Initially focusing on travel to state parks and points of interest in and near New York City, by 1937 the *Green Book* was national in scope and included coverage of Colorado.[48] Finally, leading African Americans in the Interior Department, including Mary McLeod Bethune and William J. Trent, were calling not simply for an end to formal segregation in Great Smoky Mountains National Park and Shenandoah National Park but for an end to informal practices of exclusion and discrimination against African Americans across the National Park System.[49]

None of these developments seemed to register with park officials at Rocky Mountain National Park. They may have been influenced by the knowledge that NPS planners in Washington who had been assigned to guide the nationwide expansion of state park facilities were encouraging southern states to build so-called "Negro parks." They may have heard that park superintendents during their annual conference in 1939 confirmed continued reliance on segregation in national parks situated in areas where it was required by law in the surrounding area, stating, "It is recommended that, in providing accommodation for Negroes in National Park Service areas, the control, type and extent of accommodation conform to existing State laws, established customs of adjacent communities, and Negro travel demands." So, too, park officials may have realized that FDR's New Deal jobs and farm subsidy programs generally accommodated existing racial hierarchies, as the president believed he could not afford to lose the support of conservative Democrats, especially those in the South.[50]

Certainly, the park was under no pressure from the CMC to embrace more inclusive practices. To the contrary. A letter from the Membership Committee of the CMC's Denver branch to the CMC's Board of Directors in 1938 expressed regret that "two members in good standing" had sponsored Isadore Karl Silverman for CMC membership. Mr. Silverman wanted to participate in the club's ski outings and climbs to high peaks, but he was a Jewish man of German heritage, employed as a hydraulics engineer for the Bureau of Reclamation in Denver. Learning that there was "some hesitation" among CMC members about accepting his application "because of his race," the CMC Membership Committee deliberated about the matter. It concluded that turning down the application would be an act of "bad faith" that would put "the applicant and his sponsors in an embarrassing position." Still, the committee did not want Mr. Silverman's admission to the CMC to establish a precedent. The committee wrote: "We should like to request herewith that the above applicant be accepted at once with the understanding that this be an exception to the unwritten rule regarding admittance of certain races." The committee's request was accepted by the board. Mr. Silverman remained in the CMC for only two years, resigning in 1941.[51]

Rocky's managers also disregarded the racism experienced by the small number of CCC workers in the park who were of African American, Mexican, and Mexican American background. Rocky's CCC camp newspapers, written by enrollees, habitually ridiculed Black CCC workers and African American life-ways. White camp enrollees hurled racial slurs at anyone with skin darker than their own. The Colorado State Department of Public Welfare noted numerous desertions among Spanish-speaking men from the park's CCC camps but did not fault park administrators. And though Rocky acknowledged the region's indigenous heritage by adding a display on Ute and Arapaho culture to the new museum at Moraine Park, the exhibits were designed with White visitors in mind, interpreting Native Americans as primitive people whose lifeways were incompatible with modern progress.[52]

Neither Rocky Mountain National Park nor a single business in Estes Park or Grand Lake was listed in the *Green Book* before the end of the decade, indicating their persistent unwillingness to host visitors of color. African Americans trying to further discern racial attitudes in Estes Park by reading its local newspaper would have found much to confirm its reputation for intolerance. The *Estes Park Trail* mentioned "Negros" every so often in the 1930s, but usually in the context of stereotypic jokes told at their expense or in presuming a Black man to be the perpetrator of a local crime. Even announcements of performances by Blacks highlighted racial difference: "NEGRO SINGERS COMING . . . the McWilliams Choral Club, made up of forty of the best negro voices of Denver, will give a free recital at our Community church. No one can sing those dear old spirituals quite like the negro voice." One church in Estes Park hosted a discussion for youth on the question "Is Race Prejudice Inevitable?" in July 1934 but said nothing about how it might frame the discussion.[53]

Rather than consider more open access to the park, Rocky seems to have renewed its support for the status quo, funding a study by Associate Professor John V. K. Wagar, head of the Forestry Division at Colorado State College, which sought "to find possible correlations between the outdoor abilities and interests of visitors to Rocky Mountain National Park and their educational, occupational, avocational, family, and residential backgrounds."[54] The national parks had become a symbol of the nation's greatness, and the study hoped to provide future rangers with information about park visitors' attitudes regarding conservation and "to find in what respects people need teaching to increase their appreciation of and profit from the richness of outdoor America."[55] Wagar did not directly address democratic access; instead, his study validated park officials' disregard for multiracial democracy.

Members of Wagar's research team talked with 583 adult visitors from more than thirty states in locations throughout Rocky Mountain National Park, including trails, fishing spots, parking lots, campgrounds, and hotels. Analyzing the visitors' responses, Wagar found a striking correlation between occupation and visitation, noting that teachers had the greatest presence among visitors to the park, followed by students, farmers from Colorado and neighboring states, engineers, mechanics, and clergy. Presumably, Wagar realized that teachers were advantaged by a school-year schedule that left them freer than most working adults to travel in the summer. More than 60.7 percent of the respondents were in college, college graduates, or married to college graduates. "Well educated and generally intelligent people predominate among those who use the park."[56]

Wagar noted that "hiking interested most park visitors, and a great number claimed skill in this activity, no matter from what region they came." His research team also found that "when asked concerning the proper distribution of roads, trails, and wild areas, 90 percent thought the diversified arrangement in Rocky Mountain National Park ideal." A few of the visitors who interacted with researchers were observed "thoughtlessly disregarding" park regulations that forbade "collecting specimens or bursting rocks with geology hammers," but most park visitors seemed to behave responsibly and spoke in favor of preservation. Seventy-eight percent of respondents rated "Preservation of Scenic Wonders" as the most important purpose for the national parks; 94 percent "favored the preservation of primeval forests," and 92 percent "favored setting aside wilderness areas to be used for primitive means of travel."[57]

Wagar's study investigated the values of park visitors at a time of increased visitation, mounting ecological disturbance, and renewed emphasis on the park system as a source of pride in national identity. The visitors whom Wagar interviewed appeared to understand that they bore some responsibility for supporting the preservation of nature, though Wagar did not ask how visitors to national parks might, by their presence or behavior, adversely affect the environment. Rather, Wagar concluded that the education and racial identity of those he interviewed constituted positive criteria for visitation. He was impressed by the "general intelligence" of park visitors and the fact that 77 percent "were from families in which one or all ancestors had migrated to the United States before 1860" (that is, well before the surge in immigration from eastern and southern Europe and Asia between 1880 and 1914). "Most of the visitors were from pioneer families associated with opening American wilderness. . . . Whatever the meaning may be, most of the visitors were Nordics or folks long associated with wild lands through tradition or ingrained liking." The fact that people of "pioneer" heritage appreciated the national parks could be attributed to their having become "professional men rather than laborers," he said, "or some may wish to see in it what they believe to be racial tendencies." Wagar found his "audit" of visitors "most heartening. . . . We need not turn back, nor retrace our steps into another way. We need only to continue this good thing."[58]

Enduring War and Looking to the Postwar Future

The U.S. entry into World War II in December 1941 brought new hardships and challenges to the NPS and Rocky Mountain National Park. The entire National Park System lost funding, staff, and visitors. The military gained access to park lands, using them for training and maneuvers and for the rest and relaxation of military personnel, and often damaged park resources. Some parks, though not Rocky, came under intense pressure to allow cattle grazing and timber cutting.[59] Rocky Mountain National Park's operating budget was slashed nearly in half, and it operated with a skeleton crew. Several of the permanent staff, including Superintendent David Canfield, enlisted in the armed forces. The CCC camps were dismantled in 1942, with heavy equipment, vehicles, and buildings loaned or transferred to the army, navy, and Civil Aeronautics Authority. Annual visitation to the park went from its highest ever, 681,845 in 1941, to a low of 124,353 in 1943, before moving upward to 211,953 in 1944 and 356,793 in 1945. Mountaineering also declined, with only 644 recorded climbs on Longs Peak in 1944, the lowest since 1920.[60]

Rocky's managers viewed the war years as a period of retrenchment, and the park accumulated a sizable backlog of maintenance projects. Reduced staff and funding made it difficult to innovate or approach risk in new ways. Superintendent John Doerr claimed that the park "advanced in the field of wildlife management" when it began an intensive elk culling campaign in 1943 in response to extensive range degradation, yet the campaign was called off in 1946 when the park learned that "the [NPS] Director's office had a 'strong dislike' for reduction programs either inside or adjacent to NPS units." Doerr and some park staff were edging toward the ecological management of natural resources, but neither they nor national park leaders were able to figure out how to align the desperately needed culling of elk with a continued commitment to visitors' visual enjoyment of majestic wildlife species.[61]

Meanwhile, climbers and backcountry rangers continued to adapt their mountaineering ethic of care to changing circumstances, buoyed by the nation's growing appreciation for mountaineering in wartime. Mountaineers in the army's Tenth Mountain Division made critical contributions to Allied victories in the Italian Alps, gaining the attention and approbation of state and national media.[62] On the domestic front, the Colorado Mountain Club pronounced mountaineering an antidote to the pessimism and hardship of war, an activity that boosted "civilian morale" in a fighting nation. Civilians needed to work harder and more efficiently in wartime, but they could do so only if they had "periods of relaxation and recreation." Mountaineering strengthened the body, "and in the mountains one finds it hard to worry, which is excellent for the mind." In this context, it is not surprising that Longs Peak remained a highly esteemed destination for local climbers, despite the decline in the number of annual summits. For children attending summer camps near Rocky Mountain National Park, climbing on Longs and other peaks continued as a favorite activity. Though the CMC saw a decline in membership during the war, local chapters of the club led climbs to Longs Peak for juniors as well as adults throughout the war, with *Trail and Timberline* reporting on their adventures. Wartime rationing of gasoline and tires made it imperative that the CMC sponsor trips and help mountaineers share precious resources.[63]

Longs Peak also gained the attention of the movie industry and national news media. The Fox Movietone Company filmed German-born Joe Stettner climbing various routes on the East Face of Longs in 1942. On *Stettner's Ledges*, he was accompanied by Robert Ormes, a nationally known climber from Colorado Springs. On one of the other routes, Stettner's partners were two women, fellow members from his Chicago Mountaineering Club. According to the *Estes Park Trail*, "Misses Alma Grimmich and Edith Reidl . . . had never attempted such an ambitious climb," but the two discovered "they were 'quite at home' on narrow six inch ledges with drops of hundreds of feet below them, feeling safe in their confidence to make the climb." The *Trail* expected the movie to be seen "for the next three years in practically every city, town, and hamlet in the country," reaching "over 50 million people [and] arousing interest in mountain climbing as a vacation sport in this region." The Associated Press also produced news and images of Longs Peak for popular audiences, creating a feature with "pictures and story, describing an east face ascent of Longs Peak by Ranger Ernest K. Field" that was released in 1943.[64] As climbers' daring exploits came to the attention of the public, the publisher of *Webster's Dictionary* wrote to Rocky Mountain National Park, requesting help in defining several terms "hitherto not recognized by lexicographers" but "in common usage by alpinists," including "crampon," "piton," and "rappel."[65]

Rather than discourage attentiveness to the risks of climbing, appreciation for the rewards of climbing during wartime helped sustain the campaign for "safe and sane" climbing. Ernie Field published a lengthy article describing safe rock-climbing techniques, with an accompanying photo of an ice axe, rock pitons, carabiners, crampons, and piton hammer in the *Estes Park Trail* in April 1941. And he improved the likely success of rescue operations on Longs by placing caches of critical emergency equipment in the park's utility area and at the base of Longs and by preparing additional caches for placement in the Boulderfield and at Chasm Lake. Acknowledging rangers' and climbers' need for telephone service in emergencies, the park reconstructed the Longs Peak telephone line in 1942.[66]

Building on Field's work, the CMC continued its "school of mountaineering" as part of the club's annual Summer Outing. The CMC also published an annotated list of its most "fundamental policies and practices" for the backcountry, highlighting the importance of leaders, safety in numbers, communication, and proper equipment, experience, and fitness. So, too, *Trail and Timberline* published "hints for beginners" contemplating nontechnical climbs on Longs Peak as well as advice to mountaineers wanting to learn rock-climbing techniques.[67] The park reported no serious accidents or fatalities on Longs during the war years, no doubt cheering those who were behind the campaign for "safe and sane" climbing.

As the nation moved, however, with growing confidence toward victory in war, Superintendent Doerr anticipated a sharp and worrisome rise in visitation. Already in 1945, the park was seeing a "heavy increase in travel and visitor use . . . [that] brought forward with force the importance of establishing and maintaining good public relations." The park's trails, roads, buildings, campground tables, and fireplaces were in poor condition, and increased visitation could easily produce "overuse that [might] result in the permanent impairment of park values." Doerr feared a loss of public confidence and respect if visitors enjoyed the park less than in prewar years. Indeed, a recent instance of bad conduct suggested that disrespect was already at hand: "Vandalizing of the emergency mountain climbing and rescue caches at the Boulder Field and Chasm Lake shelter cabins resulted in the loss of much valuable equipment, such as rope, pitons, blankets, heating pads, food and clothing, or their later destruction by rodents to which they were exposed."[68]

Complicating matters further, Doerr acknowledged "problems of wildlife protection and forest management" that extended to bears, beavers, aspen, insects, fire, deer, and elk. He believed deer and elk management would have to be addressed with more "emphasis upon the ecology" than in the past but did not specify what that meant or how the park might move beyond its assumption that ecological management and visitor enjoyment were somehow at odds. Primarily, Doerr was listing problems, worrying that in the years immediately after the war Rocky Mountain National Park would face daunting challenges in preserving resources, satisfying visitors, and keeping them safe.[69]

All the challenges he identified became quite real indeed in the postwar era, demanding adaptability, initiative, and resilience on the part of park managers, front-country travelers, and climbers on Longs, as we will see in the next chapter. Importantly, Doerr was not thinking (or worrying) about potential changes in race relations and visitor demographics. The nation was concluding a war against fascistic governments and their brutally racist practices, yet it tolerated racism domestically and forced more than 110,000 people of Japanese ancestry into internment camps after the attack on Pearl Harbor. Near at hand, the residents of Estes Park pushed Ryoji Kato, a Japanese-born art shop owner, to depart Colorado for California in 1943. Civilian and military men and women from African American, Japanese American, Latinx, and Native American communities attempted to use the messages of America's war against racism abroad to fight racism at home, campaigning for "Double Victory." Yet Doerr and the NPS took little notice. Secretary of the Interior Ickes pressured Shenandoah National Park to end formal segregation, but real integration did not become the new norm; rather, because Blacks were no longer assured of access to specific facilities and were wary of interacting with hostile Whites, their visitation to the park dropped.[70]

The CMC also appeared uninterested in questions of democratic access. Long-standing and prominent club member M. Walter Pesman complained to the board in 1945 that the CMC was "snobbish" and "undemocratic," holding votes on amendments to the club's constitution at expensive annual banquets that most members could not afford to attend. Member Anna Timm similarly complained of votes on amendments to club bylaws that were rushed through without discussion. Moreover, in Pesman's view, the club was "very close to being anti-semitic, which was all the worse when some of our members were being investigated for pro-Nazi tendencies by the F.B.I." Pesman's letter earned only a dismissive rebuke from CMC leaders: "It may save you some embarrassment to know that the club has Jewish members." And Timm's complaint does not appear to have been answered.[71] Did the CMC board address its members' questions about voting procedure? Had the CMC moderated its policies on "certain races" since the board's discussion of Mr. Silverman's membership in 1938? Were Pesman's contentions of anti-Semitism irrelevant, as the club's response to him implied? Club records are frustratingly opaque on these matters, but it does seem that both the CMC and Rocky Mountain National Park entered the postwar era ill prepared to contend with demands for open and just democracy.

Climbers on the Summit of Longs Peak, circa 1890

By the late nineteenth century, the summit of Longs Peak had become a destination of choice for White tourists seeking adventure and inspiration in dramatic wilderness settings. Tourists in Colorado liked to think of themselves as the true discoverers of the state's Rocky Mountains. They were not inclined to acknowledge that their exhilaration on mountains such as Longs came at the expense of Native peoples, who by 1880 had been entirely removed from their homelands in the northern Colorado Rockies to reservations in Wyoming and Utah. White Americans recreating in Colorado took cues from governmental and journalistic reports that portrayed indigenous peoples as primitive, inferior, and incapable of appreciating or making good use of the American West's rich natural and aesthetic resources. Image courtesy of Rocky Mountain National Park.

Longs Peak House, Late Nineteenth Century, with Longs Peak in the Background
Elkanah Lamb opened Longs Peak House as a tourist lodge in 1878, catering to guests who
were eager to climb the majestic fourteener directly behind the rustic inn. Lamb and the guides
he employed typically led visitors up the East Longs Peak Trail, across the vast Boulderfield,
and then on to Longs' summit via the *Keyhole* route. Lamb built the East Longs Peak Trail
during the mid-1870s; the Hayden survey identified the *Keyhole* route while mapping
Colorado for the federal government in 1873. The East Longs Peak Trail and *Keyhole* route are
still the most popular means of gaining Longs' summit. Accessible roads, trails, climbing routes,
guiding services, and lodging were all essential to the popularization of mountaineering. Over
time, rustic lodges such as Longs Peak House became well-appointed resorts offering middle-
class amenities, as well as guiding services, to mountain tourists. Image courtesy of Rocky
Mountain National Park.

Timberline Cabin at Jim's Grove on Longs Peak

Enos Mills was Elkanah Lamb's nephew, and he became the owner of Longs Peak House in
1902, remodeling, expanding, and renaming it over the years. A passionate mountaineer and
climbing guide, Enos and his brother, Joe, built the Timberline Cabin in Jim's Grove on Longs,
a couple of miles from the Boulderfield, in 1908. Climbers on Longs Peak were vulnerable to
altitude sickness, injury, and dangerous changes in alpine weather, and the Timberline Cabin,
located at 10,920 feet, provided a primitive but safe haven for outdoor adventurers in all
seasons. During the summer months the cabin ran as a concession, providing simple lodging
and meals to mountaineers for a modest fee. It was in operation until 1925 and remained
standing until 1936. Image courtesy of Rocky Mountain National Park.

In the Trough on the *Keyhole* Route, 1909
From the late nineteenth century to the present, climbers have most often ascended to the summit of Longs via the *Keyhole* route, which begins at a keyhole-like granite formation on the western edge of the Boulderfield. Though it does not require ropes or technical gear, the *Keyhole* route takes climbers across exposed ledges, along steep cliffs, and through a very steep trough, pictured here. Loose rock has always endangered climbers in the Trough, especially when multiple people are climbing at the same time. Those high in the Trough can easily, albeit unintentionally, send loose rock cascading down toward climbers in the Trough's lower section. Image courtesy of Rocky Mountain National Park.

Enos Mills in His Role as Nature Guide, 1910s
Mills (third from right) was a nature writer and public speaker as well as a passionate mountaineer and successful resort operator. He became a prominent figure in the Nature Study movement in the 1910s as well as a tireless promoter of Rocky Mountain National Park, which opened in 1915. Image courtesy of Rocky Mountain National Park.

Arapaho Pack Trip, 1914

People of the Northern Ute, Northern Arapaho, and Cheyenne nations were removed from the region that would become Rocky Mountain National Park by 1880, but individuals and organizations advocating the founding of a new national park in the 1910s nonetheless thought it appropriate to assign Native place names to locations and landmarks that tourists would explore in Rocky. The Colorado Mountain Club's Harriet Vaille spearheaded this effort and sought assistance from the Northern Arapahos on the Wind River Reservation in Wyoming. The result was a two-week pack trip through the proposed park in July 1914 by three Arapaho men and three White men. Shown in this photo are the members of the pack trip. Standing from left to right are Longs Peak climbing guide Shep Husted; Sherman Sage, the chief of police at Wind River; Gun Griswold, a Wind River judge; Tom Crispin, the Wind River Reservation translator; and Colorado Mountain Club member (and lawyer) Oliver Wolcott Toll. David Hawkins, a student, is seated. The high tribal positions of the three indigenous men suggest that the Wind River Arapahos attached genuine significance to the task of naming and remembering physical features and tribal lifeways within the proposed park, despite their compulsory removal from it. While on the pack trip, Gun Griswold recalled stories of men, including his father, hunting eagles on Longs Peak. Though the Northern Arapahos have found it exceedingly difficult to sustain or renew tribal connections to their homeland in Rocky, in 2014 tribal members returned to Estes Park and Rocky, with the support of park personnel and Larimer County officials, to celebrate the one hundredth anniversary of the 1914 expedition. Image courtesy of Rocky Mountain National Park.

Climbers in the Boulderfield on Longs Peak, 1921
Members of Boulder's Rocky Mountain Climbers Club posing for a photograph with the
East Face of Longs Peak and the Diamond behind them. Image courtesy of Rocky Mountain
National Park.

Climbers at the Keyhole on Longs Peak, 1921

The opening of Rocky Mountain National Park stimulated an uptick in climbing on Longs Peak. Here, members of Boulder's Rocky Mountain Climbers Club gathered for photos in the Boulderfield and at the Keyhole during an excursion to Longs. The RMCC was eventually eclipsed by the Colorado Mountain Club, as the CMC engaged in energetic public outreach, established chapters all along Colorado's Front Range, regularly led climbing excursions to Longs and other Rocky Mountain peaks, published an attractive magazine, and instructed members in mountaineering safety and natural resource conservation. The towns and cities of Colorado's Front Range had small populations of African Americans, Mexican Americans, Jews, and Asian Americans, some of whom evinced keen interest in mountain recreation, but climbing organizations excluded members of these groups from membership, though they welcomed White women. Racial exclusion and anti-Semitic practices were common across the nation, even when not mandated by law, and NPS superintendents determined, in a meeting in 1922, not to encourage Black visitation in national parks. Within a year of the climb photographed here, African Americans from Denver were working to establish Lincoln Hills, a mountain resort for the Black community near Nederland, just forty-two miles from Rocky Mountain National Park. Image courtesy of Rocky Mountain National Park.

Fall River Road, 1924

Fall River Road was the main thoroughfare in Rocky Mountain National Park during the park's early years. Rocky had a tiny staff, with only one ranger overseeing the park's entire east side (including Longs Peak), and the east side ranger was often at Fall River Road aiding motorists who found themselves unable to negotiate its steep twists and turns. Climbers rarely encountered a ranger on Longs or Rocky's other peaks during the park's first decade. Rather, the CMC assumed primary responsibility for guiding climbers, promoting safe mountaineering practices, and enhancing climbers' understanding of the park's natural history. Image courtesy of Rocky Mountain National Park.

Professor James Alexander on the East Face's Broadway Ledge, 1922
Not content with the rigors of the *Keyhole* route, climbers began to test themselves on Longs' North Face in the 1910s; by the 1920s adventuresome climbers with hobnail boots and ropes were tackling the nearly vertical East Face of Longs. James Alexander made the first recorded ascent on the East Face of Longs Peak in 1922. His success on *Alexander's Chimney* inspired other mountaineers to attempt ascents of their own on the East Face, though some were inexperienced or ill prepared. Seven people died on Longs in the 1920s, the first recorded deaths on the peak since the 1880s. Image courtesy of Rocky Mountain National Park.

Ranger Jack Moomaw
Moomaw was the ranger responsible for Longs Peak and large portions of the east side of Rocky from the 1920s to the 1940s. An enthusiastic mountaineer in his own right, Moomaw accompanied James Alexander during the latter's second successful ascent of *Alexander's Chimney* in 1922. He was subsequently involved in the rescue and recovery of numerous climbers involved in terrible accidents on the East Face. Image courtesy of Rocky Mountain National Park.

AGNES VAILLE DIES IN STORM
AFTER CLIMBING LONGS PEAK

Body of Chamber of Commerce Secretary Found Frozen in Snow.

(Continued From Page One.)

Oscar Brown; Jacob Christy and Herbert Sortland, all employed at the inn.

Sortland became exhausted after going about a mile from the house and, suffering from a frozen face and frozen ears, left the party and started back to the shelter. That was the last any of the party saw of the man and it is feared that he fell exhausted in the deep snow and froze to death. Thermometers carried by Kiener showed a temperature of 50 degrees below zero. The heavy snow storm, virtually a blizzard, which raged on the peak yesterday, was accompanied by a strong wind.

Body Found Frozen in Snow.

When the party of men reached the spot where Kiener had left his companion, they found her lying in the snow, dead from the cold and exposure. She had evidently succumbed to her desire for sleep, natural to one slowly freezing to death, and had died but a short time before her rescuers reached her. She had been alone on the mountain saddle from 11 o'clock yesterday morning to 4 o'clock yesterday afternoon, when the men found her body, Kiener's journey to the shelter house and the return trip of the party consuming this amount of time because of the severity of the storm.

AGNES W. VAILLE.

Newspaper Article about Agnes Vaille's Death on Longs Peak, 1925
Agnes Vaille, the daughter of a prominent Denver family and a college-educated "New Woman" of the early twentieth century, was an avid mountaineer and prominent member of the Colorado Mountain Club. She was also a cousin of Roger Toll, Rocky Mountain National Park's superintendent in the 1920s. Vaille's tragic death—while descending Longs' North Face after a brutally difficult East Face ascent in January 1925—prompted the park to assume greater oversight of climbers on Longs and construct new shelters and other safety features on the peak. Image courtesy of Rocky Mountain National Park.

Walter Kiener Serving as a Fire Lookout on Twin Sisters Peak, circa 1925
Walter Kiener, a Swiss alpinist, was Agnes Vaille's companion during her ill-
fated climb on Longs in January 1925. Family and friends had urged the two
mountaineers not to attempt the January climb because of dangerous winter
conditions, but Kiener and Vaille refused to abandon their plans. Kiener
suffered severe frostbite during his climb with Vaille, spending months in the
hospital recovering from the amputation of numerous fingers and toes and a
portion of his left foot. Subsequently, he worked as a fire lookout for the park
on Twin Sisters. Eventually Kiener earned a PhD in botany, studying the alpine
vegetation of Longs Peak, and joined the faculty at the University of Nebraska.
Image courtesy of Rocky Mountain National Park.

Climbers on the *Cable* Route, 1927
In the aftermath of the Vaille tragedy, Superintendent Roger Toll ordered the installation of cables on the North Face of Longs Peak, hoping they would lessen the inherent dangers of the climb. Using single jack sledgehammers and short rock drills, Jack Moomaw and two workers created holes in the granite rock, fixed large eyebolts into the holes, and threaded two separate sections of steel cable, one 160 feet long, the other 30 feet in length, through the bolts. Though Toll assumed the *Cable* route would be used primarily by skilled mountaineers, it came to be the preferred route for nontechnical climbers who had previously used the longer *Keyhole* route to reach Longs' summit. Image courtesy of Rocky Mountain National Park.

Boulderfield Shelter Cabin and Colorado Mountain Club Members, circa 1927

The Vaille tragedy also prompted Superintendent Toll to order the construction of a shelter cabin in the Boulderfield on Longs Peak and to extend a telephone line to the cabin. The cabin operated as a park concession during the summer season, offering meals, lodging, and guided climbs to Longs' summit via the *Cable* route. It remained open for emergency shelter (with no services) during the winter months. The cabin's summertime climbing guides were boisterous young men, and guests at the cabin enjoyed hot meals, clean accommodations, music played on a wind-up phonograph, and annual Fourth of July fireworks set off by concessionaires Robert and Dorothy Collier. Some climbers condemned the presence of this commercial operation on Longs, believing it defiled the alpine setting. The park also built an emergency shelter cabin at Chasm Lake, and Vaille's family paid for the construction of a memorial emergency shelter at the Keyhole. The Boulderfield cabin was dismantled because of structural instability in 1936, but the Agnes Vaille memorial shelter remains at the Keyhole, and a shelter cabin (though not the original) still stands at Chasm Lake. Image courtesy of Rocky Mountain National Park.

Joe Stettner during the First Ascent of *Stettner's Ledges*, 1927

Joe and Paul Stettner were skilled German American alpinists who used felt-soled shoes, pitons, and belay maneuvers during their climb, the first to extend the entire vertical length of the East Face on Longs Peak. After climbing *Stettner's Ledges* on the lower East Face, the brothers traversed Broadway and climbed *Kiener's* to the summit. The Stettners may not have made it to the East Face at all had they not encountered a ranger who advised them to seek shelter from a severe storm at the derelict Timberline Cabin the night before their daring ascent. After summiting, the exhausted men discovered the *Cable* route by chance and thus avoided descent via the longer *Keyhole* route. Image courtesy of Rocky Mountain National Park.

Finding the *Cable* Route, circa 1935

By the 1930s nearly two thousand visitors were climbing Longs Peak annually. Many of them were girls and boys attending summer camps in the Estes Park area. Though the Great Depression depleted Americans' economic resources, many eagerly traveled to national parks for backcountry adventure or sightseeing by automobile. They were encouraged to do so by President Franklin D. Roosevelt, who praised the parks for representing the "fundamental idea . . . that the country belongs to the people." He thought "each and every" American who could "possibly find the means and opportunity" should visit a national park. Climbers' growing presence on Longs caught the attention of park managers. This photograph, produced and distributed by the park, was intended to help orient climbers as the East Longs Peak Trail reached the Boulderfield. Points A, B, and C mark sections of the *Cable* route; point D marks the location of the Keyhole. The park encouraged climbers to ascend the *Cable* route and descend via the *Keyhole* route along Longs' West Face. Image courtesy of Rocky Mountain National Park.

Girls at Camp Nizhoni, circa 1935

Regardless of FDR's inclusive language about national park visitation, African Americans found no welcome at Rocky or in Estes Park in the 1930s, and Black children were barred from the area's numerous summer camps. Camp Nizhoni, a summer facility operated by the African American Phyllis Wheatley Branch of the YWCA, was hosted at Lincoln Hills, the Black resort near Nederland, Colorado. The young girls in this photo, mostly from Denver, were living proof that the Centennial State's African American population enjoyed outdoor recreation, despite the efforts of Whites to keep parks, mountains, and forests to themselves. Girls at Camp Nizhoni eagerly participated in hiking, fishing, swimming, and horseback riding, and many of them developed a lifelong appreciation for mountain environments. Image courtesy of Denver Public Library Special Collections.

Rescue Party on North Longs Peak Trail, 1935

The growing popularity of Longs Peak in the 1930s was not without
problems. Climbing accidents and fatalities occurred with troubling frequency
on Longs and other peaks in Rocky, requiring rangers and enrollees in the
park's Civilian Conservation Corps (CCC) to carry out difficult search and
rescue (SAR) missions. A small number of African American and Mexican
American men served in the CCC at Rocky, and some of these young men
of color may have participated in SAR operations like the one pictured here.
Unfortunately, they also experienced hostility and derision from White
members of the corps. Climbing accidents in the 1930s also prompted the
CMC and Rocky's park rangers to collaborate in a "safe and sane" climbing
campaign via articles in the CMC's *Trail and Timberline* magazine and
placards posted in popular climbing areas. Image courtesy of Rocky Mountain
National Park.

Horses in the Boulderfield, circa 1935

Visitors have traveled by horseback through Rocky's backcountry since the park was founded in 1915. Over the decades many visitors hoping to summit Longs have ridden horses to the Boulderfield and then climbed on foot to the top of the peak via the *Keyhole* or *Cable* route. When the park built the Boulderfield Shelter Cabin after the Vaille tragedy, it constructed a stone barn with multiple stalls alongside it. This photo probably dates from the shelter cabin era, though the horse barn is not visible. Decades later, in the 1970s and 1980s, long strings of horses were frequent on both the East Longs Peak Trail and North Longs Peak Trail to Granite Pass, where the trails converged for 1.7 miles to the hitching racks at the Boulderfield. Hikers often had to step off the trail and wait for horses to pass. As hikers became aware of environmental problems such as trail erosion and deteriorating water quality, the presence of horses—and the manure, dust, and insects associated with them—became sources of bitter contention. The park's 1982 Trails Management Plan recommended a new trail for horses from the East Longs Peak trailhead to Eugenia Mine to relieve horse-hiker conflicts, but funding constraints kept the park from building the new trail. Horses are currently still allowed on the East Longs Peak Trail and North Longs Peak Trail but not in Jim's Grove. Image courtesy of Rocky Mountain National Park.

First Ascent, *Chasm View Cutoff*, 1950

In the 1950s, Longs Peak attracted increasingly adept technical climbers to its East Face. Bill Eubanks, Brad Van Diver, and Tom Hornbein successfully made the first ascent of *Chasm View Cutoff* in 1950, dealing with exposed rotten rock on the traverse. The men probably paid little attention to the plant life visible on the ledge traverse; it was not until the 1970s that some in the climbing community began to complain about climbers who thoughtlessly trampled on or removed fragile alpine flora. Image courtesy of Rocky Mountain National Park.

Visitors at Rock Cut, Trail Ridge Road, July 1960

Trail Ridge Road, which opened in the 1930s, consolidated Rocky's commitment to automobile tourism. The carefully engineered thoroughfare provided safe and comfortable travel and afforded spectacular views of the park's mountains, alpine lakes, and valleys. With the nation's return to prosperity following World War II, young White middle-class families made automobile travel through national parks a favorite vacation pastime. The family in this photo had stepped a few feet from their car to enjoy a panoramic view of Rocky Mountain National Park, but the rough sign provided no information about the peaks, lakes, and valleys in front of them. Inadequate signage was just one of many problems confronting Rocky and other national parks. Overuse resulted in crowded roadways, degraded campgrounds, and eroded trails. The NPS's response, Mission 66, resulted in a ten-year program of park upgrades and improvements in visitor services at Rocky, including new roadway signage and interpretive programming and a new visitor center at Beaver Meadows. Image courtesy of Rocky Mountain National Park.

The Diamond Wall, East Face of Longs Peak, undated
By the mid-1950s some technical climbers believed they had the
skills and experience necessary to climb the Diamond wall, which
had previously been considered an impossible ascent. Dale Johnson
was particularly persistent in requesting access to the Diamond. Park
officials refused to grant Johnson or anyone else permission to tackle
the Diamond, thinking they were unrealistic about the perils of the
climb and too eager for publicity. In 1959, however, with Mission 66
in full swing and the NPS having renewed its commitment to "visitor
enjoyment," officials in Washington made it clear to managers at Rocky
that the Diamond could not remain off-limits to climbers with the
skills, equipment, and support crew necessary for such a demanding
ascent. Image courtesy of Rocky Mountain National Park.

Bob Kamps and Dave Rearick, Check Equipment before the First Ascent of the Diamond, July 1960

By 1960 the park was ready to open the Diamond. Bob Kamps (left) and Dave Rearick were the first climbers to gain permission to ascend the steep rock face. The men's route, *D1*, went up the center of the Diamond but required the climbers to negotiate blocks, overhangs, and ice-filled chimneys. Two years later Layton Kor and Charlie Roskosz made the second successful ascent of the Diamond on the *Yellow Wall*, a route 150 feet to the left of *D1*. Over the next decade, as technical climbers' presence on the Diamond grew, park rangers enhanced programs to educate and monitor the climbers and provide search, rescue, and recovery services when serious accidents occurred. Importantly, having far less privilege than young White male climbers who opened the Diamond, African Americans across the United States mobilized grassroots communities during the same period to end the racist practices that constrained free access to transportation, schooling, employment, voting, recreation, service, and public accommodation. Resistance to their demands was intense and often violent, yet communities of color and their leaders persevered. The *Brown v. Board of Education* decision, Civil Rights Act of 1964, and Voting Rights Act of 1965 were important victories, even as they failed to produce the full range of freedoms and opportunities sought by courageous activists. Certainly, the gains made by African Americans in the 1950s and 1960s were not enough to break down racial barriers to travel and recreation in national parks or to participation in historically White sports such as rock climbing. Image courtesy of Rocky Mountain National Park.

Technical Mountain Rescue Training, 1963

The opening of the Diamond to technical climbers required park authorities to prepare for rescue operations on sheer rock faces. Dave Rearick, one of the men who made the first successful ascent of the Diamond in 1960, was hired as a summer ranger in 1962 to help the park prepare for difficult rescues on the steep wall. Image courtesy of Rocky Mountain National Park.

Beaver Meadows Visitor Center, 1967

The Beaver Meadows Visitor Center was the centerpiece of Mission 66 improvements to Rocky Mountain National Park, and it was meant to demonstrate the park's commitment to visitor enjoyment and edification. The center offered park visitors a comfortable setting in which to enjoy stunning views of Rocky's mountains, professionally curated exhibits and films, and dynamic presentations by interpretive rangers. Mission 66 did not, however, resolve all the important challenges faced by national parks. By the 1960s NPS scientists were increasingly vocal about threats to natural resource preservation across the park system, yet superintendents at Rocky and other parks remained reluctant to address environmental problems, worried that environmental remediation might inconvenience visitors. Moreover, national parks and their gateway communities remained wary of visitors and park employees from communities of color. As readers will discover in chapter 6, in 1965 residents of Estes Park reacted with hostility to plans for a Job Corps center in Rocky that would have brought two hundred young men from inner-city neighborhoods, some of them Black and Brown, to the park for two-year assignments in park conservation. Local opposition persuaded park officials to abandon the proposal. Image courtesy of Rocky Mountain National Park.

Climbing the *Cable* Route on the North Face of Longs Peak, circa 1968
In the late 1960s park rangers became concerned about accidents and fatalities on the *Cable* route. Many nontechnical climbers were using the route for descent as well as ascent, and the route was sometimes very crowded. Climbers got in one another's way and movement was slow. When storms materialized suddenly, climbers were vulnerable to lightning strikes and dangerous drops in temperature. Rangers also began to suggest that the cables were an artificial installation that compromised the wilderness values of the peak. Despite growing concern, Rocky kept the popular cables in place until 1973. Rangers removed the *Cable* route in July 1973, having determined that the installation violated the standards of the 1964 Wilderness Act. Image courtesy of Rocky Mountain National Park.

Broadway Traverse, East Face of Longs Peak, 1981

Climber and independent ecologist Chip Salaun studied the flora of Longs Peak in the mid-1970s, just a few years before this photo was taken, identifying rare and fragile plants on the Broadway traverse and in niches all over the East Face. He was among an emerging cohort of climbers concerned about reducing climbers' harm to rock, alpine flora, and wildlife. After discovering many rare species of flowering plants on the East Face, Salaun tried to convince climbers not to remove flora and soil from rock walls as they placed protection and sought hand and footholds. He also urged them not to leave any trash on rock walls or ledges, even something as apparently benign as an orange peel, as the misplaced bit of organic matter might block sun from reaching a delicate native plant. Salaun published articles in climbing magazines and spoke about protecting alpine flora at meetings with local climbers and park rangers. Image courtesy of Rocky Mountain National Park.

Solar Toilet at the Boulderfield, Longs Peak, 1985

Human waste on Longs Peak was a serious problem by the 1970s. Rocky installed vault toilets on the peak, but the helicopters used to remove the vaults for emptying were noisy and sometimes spilled large amounts of waste. Park rangers replaced the vault toilets at Chasm Junction and the Boulderfield with dehydrating solar toilets in the mid-1980s. The toilets needed special reinforcement to withstand high wind, but maintenance and cleaning was relatively easy. With the volume of human waste greatly reduced by dehydration, the park could use llamas to carry waste off the peak. Solar toilets remain in use on Longs and at other backcountry locations in Rocky in the twenty-first century. They have not, however, resolved the problem of backcountry visitors who relieve themselves without bothering to use either toilets or "wag" bags that can be packed out of the park. Image courtesy of Rocky Mountain National Park.

Climber Drilling a Bolt by Hand, 1991

In the 1980s rangers at Rocky became concerned about climbers' use of motorized drills to place bolts and anchors on rock faces. Following the recommendation of its Climbing Task Force, Rocky Mountain National Park prohibited the use of motorized drills for the placement of bolts in 1990 and tried to encourage technical climbers to limit their use of hand-drilled bolts. The new prohibition reflected the park's interest in applying leave-no-trace principles to technical rock climbing. In the 1990s the newly organized Access Fund and other climbing organizations began working hard to reduce climbers' impact on the environment, hoping to prevent the closure of popular climbing areas because of overuse and environmental harm. In recent years the Access Fund and American Alpine Club have also attempted to inform the writing and implementation of new NPS regulations at climbing sites in wilderness areas, especially regulations on the use of fixed anchors. This work is ongoing and is a testament to climbers' investment in using the tools of civil society and fair governance to protect both the environment and their beloved sport. Image courtesy of Rocky Mountain National Park.

View of Chasm Lake and Twin Sisters from the Summit of Longs Peak, 1982

In the twenty-first century, Longs Peak remains a stunning place, offering views much like this one captured in 1982. The National Park Service has acknowledged, however, that urban development, loss of biodiversity, pollution, climate change, and habitat fragmentation pose grave challenges to Longs and other treasured sites across the park system. Visitor congestion surely contributes to these problems. Rocky has greatly increased its reliance on ecological monitoring and adaptive management to protect its natural resources; it has also introduced a new timed-entry reservation system to lessen the impact of visitors on natural resources and is weighing how to use timed entry at Longs. As the park attempts to limit visitors' environmental impact, it is also trying to respond effectively to demands that it welcome Northern Arapahos, Utes, and Cheyennes as sovereign tribes returning to their homelands and other people of color as citizens, visitors, and employees. The Access Fund and American Alpine Club have become vocal proponents of diversity and inclusivity in national parks and climbing. So, too, new organizations run by and for people of color, including Brown Girls Climb and Natives Outdoors, are demanding that national parks embrace a multidimensional mission that encompasses inclusivity, environmental sustainability, and recognition of parks' indigenous heritage. Image courtesy of Rocky Mountain National Park.

Selected Routes, East Face and Diamond Wall on Longs Peak, 1871 to 2020

1   Lamb's Slide, FD 1871
2   Alexander's Chimney, FA 1922
3   Notch Couloir, FA 1922
4   Kiener's, FA 1924
5   Stettner's Ledges, FA 1927
6   The Diagonal, FA 1959
7   D1, FA 1960
8   The Yellow Wall, FA 1962
9   Eclipse, FA 1963
10 D7, FA 1966
11 Forrest Finish, FA 1970
12 Dunn-Westbay, FA 1972
13 Perverical Sanctuary, FA 1974
14 Casual Route, FA 1978
15 King of Swords, FA 1987
16 Honeymoon Is Over, FA 1995
17 Hearts and Arrows, FA 2010
18 Gambler's Fallacy, FA 2020

FA = First Ascent
FD = First Descent

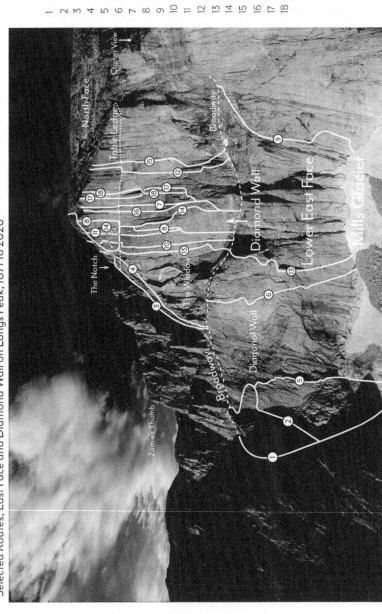

Map 3. Selected routes, East Face and Diamond Wall on Longs Peak, 1871 to 2020. Photo courtesy of Topher Donahue. Route mapping by Connor Siegfreid.

FIVE | Ambition and Access on Longs Peak, 1945–1960

SUPERINTENDENT DOERR WAS RIGHT. Travel to Rocky and other national parks soared after World War II ended, with the number of visitors to all parks rising from 21,772,000 in 1946 to 50,000,000 in 1955. The United States had become a global superpower, and its booming economy fueled an expansion of the middle class and a sharp upsurge in consumer spending on leisure goods and activities, including outdoor travel and recreation. National parks were a huge draw, especially for young White middle-class families, many of them headed by male veterans whose schooling, jobs, and single-family homes had been acquired with the help of GI benefits largely denied to men of color. Men in this privileged cohort married early and quickly started families with their young brides, settling into the nation's burgeoning Whites-only suburbs. Happy to leave behind the hardships of the Depression and World War II, White middle-class couples embraced an ideal of "family togetherness" that included vacation travel with children. For millions of parents and youngsters, this meant loading camping gear into the family automobile and taking to the road each summer, with national parks a favored destination. A new interstate highway system greatly facilitated families' travel ambitions.[1]

In each of the national parks they visited, motoring White families expected to find inspirational scenery and wholesome outdoor fun, good roads, spacious campgrounds, readily accessible trails, and friendly, informative rangers. Too often, they were disappointed by park realities: traffic jams and rutted roads, congested wayside attractions and eroded trails, overcrowded campgrounds and noisome toilets, overworked rangers and scant informational signage. Parents and children were left to navigate national park settings on their own, with little practical or interpretive guidance. NPS leaders could not ignore the chorus of visitor complaints that landed on park superintendents' desks and knew the parks were facing a veritable crisis. "Immensely increased use" meant that the

National Park System was "no longer capable of giving its users the degree of enjoyment and satisfaction intended." As visitation mounted, NPS director Conrad L. Wirth declared the parks in danger of being "loved to Death" and called for funding that would allow their comprehensive renovation.[2]

As if the pressure of millions of motoring families on park roads, campgrounds, and trails was not enough, rangers in western national parks such as Yosemite, Rocky, and Mount Rainier had to contend with a new generation of highly ambitious climbers. Interest in mountaineering grew substantially after 1945, and the number of climbers on already-popular peaks, including Longs, steadily increased. Most climbers used nontechnical routes to reach awe-inspiring mountain summits, but some had developed exceptional technical abilities and were eager to attempt challenging first ascents on walls never previously climbed. In Rocky Mountain National Park, technical climbers announced their readiness to tackle the Diamond, the nearly vertical upper wall on Longs' East Face. For park rangers, this was a deeply unsettling development. Fatalities and serious injuries on Longs and other peaks in Rocky remained a vexing problem, and now the long-standing consensus among climbers and rangers that the Diamond was too difficult and dangerous to climb was breaking down. Much as rangers wanted to sustain their support of mountaineering on Longs, interest in the Diamond provoked doubts about technical climbers' good judgment while amplifying worries about serious injury, the park's search and rescue capabilities, and the resiliency of Rocky's collaborative relationship with the climbing community.[3]

Families driving through national parks' front country and climbers ascending parks' highest peaks were hardly interchangeable, as one group favored scenic viewing in comfortable automobiles while the other pursued daring alpine adventure. Still, both groups prioritized visitor satisfaction and resisted any loss of gratification. Most NPS leaders emphatically shared this mindset, believing that increased visitation of all kinds in the postwar era required parks to redouble their commitment to human enjoyment. Speaking for the entire agency, Director Wirth opined, "The primary justification for a National Park System lies in its capacity to provide enjoyment in its best sense, now and in the future." Though Wirth agreed that "protection" of parks' natural and historic resources was an "absolute requirement" of the NPS, for him "protection" was "but a means to an end—it is requisite to the kind and quality of enjoyment contemplated in the establishment and perpetuation of parks."[4]

Under Wirth's leadership, Mission 66 emerged in 1956 as the NPS's system-wide response to the loss of enjoyment that came with mounting visitation and overuse. Mission 66 was a ten-year program of park upgrades, mandating the improvement of roads, campgrounds, close-in trails, visitor centers, and ranger services. Rocky's park-specific Mission 66 plan followed the national model, producing notable improvements in the facilities and services encountered by visitors in the spectacular mountain landscape.[5] Importantly, while Rocky actively pursued front-country development, dedication to visitor enjoyment in the Mission 66 era also shaped its response to climbers' interest in "opening" the Diamond. True, the park refused to allow climbers on the sheer wall for a number of years, but Mission 66 priorities wore away at this resistance. In 1959 new NPS-wide rules on mountaineering endorsed Mission 66 values and made it clear that Rocky would need to accommodate the daring ambitions of the postwar generation.

In privileging visitor enjoyment in both backcountry and front-country settings, Mission 66 renewed the NPS's commitment to an ethic and system of care that had been in place since the early twentieth century. Rather than stretch the contours of that care to encompass emerging environmental harms, Mission 66 pushed mounting evidence of ecological disruption to the sidelines, to the dismay of wildlife biologists and wilderness advocates. These critics worried that Mission 66 would further compromise park ecosystems and wilderness values, but NPS leaders claimed they were fulfilling their obligation to preserve park resources "unimpaired for the enjoyment of future generations" simply by keeping most visitors in the front country and encouraging their transit through the park in one or two days. In truth, park managers were not yet ready to tackle existing forms of ecological degradation, such as that caused by elk overpopulation in Rocky. Nor were they ready to evaluate the impact of mounting numbers of visitors and gasoline-powered automobiles on the well-being of natural resources in either front-country or backcountry settings.

Park managers' evasion of ecological harms occurred alongside their ducking of another obligation, namely the promotion of democratic access and equality. Across the American South and in cities as widespread as Los Angeles, Denver, Chicago, and New York, adults and children in African American communities campaigned for freedom from racism in education, employment, transportation, public accommodation, housing, and recreation. Mexican Americans, Jewish Americans, and indigenous peoples similarly engaged in demands for reform and equal rights.[6] Vacation travel continued as one manifestation of marginalized Americans' quest for equality, as it had before World War II, and magazines produced by and for African Americans deliberately encouraged Black readers to consider visiting stunning national parks such as Yosemite, Yellowstone, and Rocky. Importantly, Mission 66 proclaimed national parks to be places open to all, regardless of race. Still, the program made little effort to match reality to promise. Park managers at Rocky overlooked evidence of racial bias in the park and its gateway communities and were disinclined to see that national parks functioned as spaces set aside for the exclusive enjoyment of Whites. The park embraced its obligation to facilitate visitor access and enjoyment, even preparing to open the perilous Diamond to a new generation of audacious climbers, but it was not prepared to admit that African American aspirations to travel and enjoy the outdoors echoed values professed by Mission 66.[7]

A "Greatly Overtaxed" Park: *Motorists and Climbers at Rocky Mountain National Park*

Once World War II ended, it did not take long for Rocky Mountain National Park to become a much-loved and overused site of open-air enjoyment. Colorado claimed standing as "the top vacation state of the nation"—a place for grand adventure and conviviality in stunning outdoor settings—and the state's Department of Public Relations produced travel guides showcasing Colorado's frontier heritage, spectacular mountains, and splendid opportunities for scenic driving and outdoor recreation. Rocky Mountain National Park appeared as one of Colorado's greatest attractions, offering fantastic venues for sightseeing, skiing, fishing, horseback riding, hiking, and climbing. Its gateway cities offered an appealing array of choices for lodging, dining, and shopping.[8]

Not content with the state's campaign, Rocky produced brochures of its own that highlighted the park's magnificent scenery and accessibility: "The region is famous for its rugged gorges, broad valleys, spectacular peaks, alpine lakes, flowered meadows, abundant wildlife, and plunging streams. . . . Easily accessible by overnight travel from midwestern States, the park is only 68 miles northwest of Denver, which is served by the principal air, rail, and bus lines. Three high-standard approach highways, one of which is Transcontinental Route US 34, make the park equally attractive as an objective or as a stop-over for motorists." Purposeful outreach paid off, and travelers flocked to Rocky in the years following World War II. Yearly visitation to the park had been 31,000 in 1915, 240,966 in 1920, 255,874 in 1930, and 627,847 in 1940. In 1950, 1,265,988 visitors entered the park, and in 1960 Rocky welcomed 1,532,500 annual visitors.[9]

Like visitors in earlier decades, the great majority of those entering the park in the postwar era planned to spend most of their time in Rocky's front country, enjoying the park's wildlife and scenic vistas while staying close to paved roadways. They differed from earlier generations, however, in the brevity of their park visits and their unceasing demands on park amenities and staff. During the 1910s and 1920s most visitors to Rocky Mountain National Park had been affluent White middle-class Americans who vacationed for several weeks at a time at private lodgings in Estes Park or at privately owned resorts in the park itself. Resort owners accepted significant responsibility for guests' enjoyment and often guided their recreation in the park. During the Depression years and World War II, the park continued to attract visitors able to afford lengthy vacations in comfortable resorts, but it also appealed to people of modest means willing to stay for a week or more in its front-country campgrounds. By the postwar era, the great majority of visitors were White middle-class suburban families who intended to make the most of their mobility. Private automobiles had become reliable and powerful, comfortable and capacious. Parents and children expected to stay just a day or two in Rocky before driving to another national park or some other vacation destination via improved toll roads, state highways, and interstate freeways. Families expected to see thrilling vistas and outstanding natural and historic assets during their brief driving tours and short wayside hikes in Rocky. When overnight accommodations were needed, many hoped to stay in the park's campgrounds rather than in local resorts or lodges. Well-maintained campsites, roads, and roadside trails were crucial to the success of family vacations, as were helpful rangers and informative signs and displays.[10]

Unfortunately, Rocky Mountain National Park was ill prepared to meet these expectations. The park's vistas were indeed spectacular, but front-country facilities, mostly unchanged since the 1930s, were wholly inadequate to meet the needs of the postwar visiting public. Visiting families waited in long lines just to enter the park, especially at the Fall River entrance, and Trail Ridge Road was often terribly congested, with cars backed up for many miles. Most of the park's roads were badly in need of resurfacing, and there were few parking areas along Trail Ridge where visitors could stop for scenic viewing. The park's superintendent readily admitted that Rocky's six front-country campgrounds were "greatly overtaxed," having roads, water systems, sewers, tables, and fireplaces "far below appropriate standards." None of the campgrounds were big enough to accommodate organized groups, which meant that people in these parties had "to scatter among individual campsites," causing "inconvenience to the groups and considerable disturbance to other campers." Of equal concern, most park visitors had no opportunity to learn about the landscape through which they motored. They might be awed by scenic views and magnificent wildlife but were given no assistance in understanding what was before them. The majority of "visitors had no contact with the interpretive field trips . . . and scarcely any contact with the balance of the [park's interpretive] program." The park was unable to serve its auto tourists well, lacking adequate staff for "roadside information duty . . . [a] central museum at a strategic point on the main highways . . . and orientation stations near the park entrances."[11]

Though Rocky's motoring visitors did little more than gaze at Longs Peak from afar, the vast mountain was hardly ignored by the postwar public. Indeed, it attracted a swelling number of climbers drawn to the peak by its storied reputation. Park brochures vividly described the extraordinary reward awaiting those who reached its summit: Longs Peak was "the highest summit in northern Colorado, and one of the world's most popular climbs." Its "two favored [nontechnical] routes . . . offer the mountain climber access to its summit from which remarkable panoramas spread in every direction." Brochures, advertisements, and tourist guides produced by Estes Park businesses also touted the splendor and accessibility of the peak, even for inexperienced backcountry travelers. The Colorado Mountain Club characterized Longs as a destination for seasoned mountaineers and probably thought Estes Park businesses oversold Longs to novice climbers, yet the organization surely contributed to the growing numbers on Longs. Some of its local chapters led nontechnical climbs to the summit on a regular (often annual) basis. By the 1950s Longs had decades of history as a climbing destination, was centrally featured in climbers' guidebooks and accounts of Colorado mountaineering, and beckoned powerfully to those with interest in a true alpine experience. The park's annual reports for the years 1950–1953 show that 1,300–1,850 climbers obtained the summit of Longs Peak each season, most via the nontechnical *Cable* and *Keyhole* routes. Thousands more climbed partway to the summit each year. In 1954, 2,189 people reached Longs' summit, surpassing the annual record set in 1931.[12]

Predictably, as their numbers grew, climbers on Longs overtaxed the mountain's modest infrastructure and visitor resources, mirroring what was happening in the front country. Rocky's superintendent conceded that the road to Longs' East trailhead, the trailhead campground, the trail itself, and the mountain's emergency shelters were all in "a poor state of repair."[13] While climbers of all skill levels lodged complaints about these deficiencies, nontechnical climbers also complained about inadequate access to professional climbing guides. The park awarded concessions to only two or three professional guides each year, and the guides devoted their attention to technical rock climbers. Since most of the park's field rangers were assigned to front-country sites and visitors, nontechnical climbers were left entirely on their own to navigate the rigors and considerable exposure of the *Cable* and *Keyhole* routes.[14] Degraded conditions and scarce access to expert guidance undermined the enjoyment and safety of nontechnical climbers and added to the worries of park staff.

Technical climbers on Longs were few, but they too overtaxed the park, specifically its capacities for oversight and rescue in high-altitude settings. The postwar era was producing a new generation of American rock climbers notable for their highly developed skills and boundless ambition. Primarily young, White, male, and single, many in this cohort were deliberately countercultural, embracing a lifestyle that gave primacy to climbing while sidelining marriage, family, and regular employment. As Yosemite climber and historian Steve Roper recalled, many climbers of the 1950s and 1960s rejected the "materialism and complacence" of the era and, as "rebellious eccentrics," became "the most gifted rockclimbers in the world." The "brotherhood of the rope" sought to establish multipitch routes on big rock walls in California, Oregon, Colorado, and other states, and Longs was one of the peaks that captured their imagination. Female climbers, though present in this ambitious group, were never equal members in a "brotherhood" of highly driven young men.[15]

Improved equipment and technique helped these climbers turn imagined first ascents into reality. The postwar generation had ready access to equipment simply unavailable to earlier climbers. The U.S. Army's mountaineering expeditions in Italy during World War II required the mass production of nylon rope, iron pitons, and carabiners; after the war, these products became available to civilian climbers through army surplus outlets. Nylon rope was stronger and more flexible than rope made of natural fibers, and innovations in the mid-1950s increased its durability. Moreover, climbers quickly improved on some of the army's climbing hardware. In California, Yosemite climber John Salathé developed a high-strength carbon steel alternative to the army's soft iron pitons, while Raffi Bedayn designed and produced new lightweight aluminum carabiners. Roy Holubar of Boulder, Colorado, employed a local blacksmith to manufacture steel pitons stronger than those available from army sources or European imports and, with his wife, Alice, opened Holubar Mountaineering to equip avid climbers. Alice's business acumen and native German language abilities made it possible for the retail outlet to gain exclusive rights to top-quality German, Swiss, and Austrian climbing gear as well as the best American-made equipment.[16]

With nylon rope, pitons, bolts, and carabiners, postwar climbers adapted belaying techniques to the demands of difficult multipitch ascents. In employing the belay, one climber remained at the bottom of a rock face or pitch as the "anchor" and prevented the rope from developing slack, while the lead climber, with the rope securely attached to his or her body, moved up the rock, hammered pitons and drilled bolts into cracks, affixed carabiners and rope to pitons and bolts for protection, and sometimes stood on the pitons and bolts or attached slings to their ropes for footholds. If a climber slipped or lost a hand or foothold, the belayer limited the distance and danger of the fall by increasing friction on the rope and allowing it to absorb the energy of the fall. When climbers used pitons, bolts, or slings for direct hand or foot support, they were "aid climbing"; when they used equipment only for protection in the event of a fall and otherwise ascended using the rock's natural hand and footholds, climbers were "free climbing." On most of the difficult new routes of the 1950s, climbers used both free climbing and direct aid techniques, moving up a rock face one pitch at a time. That is, the lead climber would ascend what seemed a manageable distance, stop after finding a place for a secure stance, and then belay the second climber to the top of the pitch. The second climber removed at least some hardware as he or she climbed, so it could be used in subsequent pitches.[17]

In Colorado, Bill Eubanks and Brad Van Diver put improved equipment and technique to the test when they established *The Window* on Longs' East Face in 1950. Tracing a route that went through a hole in a K-shaped formation in the buttress on the south edge of the Diamond, some portions of the new route involved delicate slab climbing and terrific exposure; other portions required Eubanks and Van Diver to work their way up chimneys and around unstable chockstones. Tom Hornbein, a young climber who first summited Longs as a boy at a Cheley camp, put up a route on Zumie's Thumb, a large, detached spire at the top upper left of Longs' East Face, with two friends in 1951. And in 1953 Hornbein led a first ascent of the *Hornbein Crack* below Chasm View, described by climbing historian Jeff Achey as "one of the hardest crack pitches in the state at the time, and poorly protected to boot."[18]

As the very best technical climbers in Colorado put up new routes on the East Face, lesser climbers repeated their ascents, some assisted by commercial guides. Commercial guides had been losing clients since the 1930s, but their fortunes revived in the 1950s, thanks to postwar interest in technical climbing. Whether assisted by guides or climbing on their own, between 70 and 150 alpinists reached the summit of Longs by way of an East Face technical ascent each year during the early 1950s.[19]

For climbers searching out difficult technical routes, the nearly vertical Diamond on the upper East Face of Longs Peak beckoned. It had previously been considered a rock face that was impossible to climb, but postwar improvements in equipment, method, and skill led ambitious climbers to believe the Diamond was within reach. Climbers were already scaling vast multipitch rock walls in other national parks, especially Yosemite, and Colorado climbers who had been putting up difficult multipitch climbs in the Flatirons near Boulder were impatient to test themselves on Longs' Diamond. Though only a third the size of some of the big walls in Yosemite, the Diamond was uniquely challenging because of its long approach, high altitude, and variable alpine weather.

On July 26, 1954, "after three months of intensive preparation," Boulder climbers Dale Johnson and Bob Sutton thought themselves ready to attempt the Diamond. They drove to Rocky and told the rangers at park headquarters what they had in mind. No existing regulation prohibited their climb or required them to inform the rangers of their plans, yet, to the climbers' dismay, the park's rangers sought to rebuff them. Claiming that Johnson and Sutton's planned use of drills and expansion bolts would deface the rock and constitute "unlawful" harm to protected resources, rangers dissuaded them from making the ascent.[20] In truth, the rangers were far more concerned about human safety than rock defacement, but they had no regulatory means of turning the men back on safety grounds. Rocky was struggling with serious mountaineering accidents and fatalities, some involving harrowing search, rescue, and recovery missions, and the last thing they wanted was a grave injury or fatality on the "extra hazardous" Diamond.

Indeed, tragedy shadowed Longs' growing attraction. During World War II both climbing and fatalities on the peak declined, but as Longs' appeal rebounded following the war, accidents and fatalities also increased. Fatalities occurred on other mountains in Rocky as they, too, attracted postwar mountaineers. Charles Grant, a nineteen-year-old from Chicago, fell six hundred feet to his death in September 1946 while climbing *Stettner's Ledges* on the East Face with two companions. And Dale Devitt and Bruce Gerling, two students from Colorado A&M, became lost on October 9, 1949, probably on Flattop Mountain, after ignoring the advice of experienced mountaineers who advised them to return to Grand Lake because of adverse weather. Assistant Chief Ranger Ernie Field coordinated the work of rescue teams during a seven-day search in blizzard conditions, but the boys were never found. John Tallmadge, a novice climber attempting a solo ascent of Hallett Peak, died in a fall on July 11, 1952: it took rangers four months to discover his body. Kathryn Rees and Sandra Miller, ages fifteen and seventeen, died while climbing the Little Matterhorn with a Cheley camp group on July 31, 1953. Rees fell to her death after slipping on the ridge-line leading to the summit. Witnessing Rees's fall, Miller rushed to seek rangers' assistance but fell to her own death from a hundred-foot cliff nearby. Each of these climbing deaths was tragic, involving some combination of inexperience, poor judgment, and bad luck.[21]

Earl Harvey's death on Longs on June 5, 1954, was especially fresh in the minds of the rangers who turned Johnson and Sutton away. Against the advice of park staff, twenty-year-old Harvey and a friend ascended the *Cable* route while there was heavy snow on Longs. Neither was an experienced climber. Rather than descend the North Face cables or use the alternate *Keyhole* route, the two young men tried to improvise a descent on the precipitous East Face. Before long, Harvey "slipped on a steep snowbank and was unable to regain his footing," falling down Zumie's Chimney and the Left Dove. "He plunged approximately 1,100 feet and was killed instantly." Park staff recovered his body the following day.[22]

Even when cases of injured or lost climbers ended well, families, friends, and rangers endured the anxieties and grueling labor of search and rescue missions. In the two months between Harvey's deadly fall and Johnson and Sutton's thwarted ascent of the Diamond, park rangers at Rocky were called out for multiple rescues. They were deployed to rescue seventeen-year-old Richard Platt after he badly bruised his leg and was washed over Alberta Falls. And they spent days looking for John Dalie, a nontechnical climber who became lost on Longs after summiting via the *Cable* route. Dalie was a guest on a CMC trip and apparently became impatient with the pace set by the leader. He and six others deliberately broke away from the main group, though they were warned they would be on their own. All in the breakaway group except Dalie made the trip successfully. He got lost on the descent during a sudden violent snowstorm and could not be found despite a five-day search. Miraculously, Dalie wandered into a Forest Service campground six days after going missing, unhurt but exhausted and hungry. Leahdell Dick, climbing alone on Hallett Peak, slipped and fell down a snowbank, losing consciousness and suffering lacerations, contusions, and abrasions. The young woman was able to walk to assistance after regaining consciousness, but this was another close call.[23]

All these incidents weighed on park staff. Indeed, Harvey's death was something of a "last straw," prompting park staff to talk about devising a new regulation that would require climbers to register before attempting Longs and give rangers the authority to deny permission when bad weather, inexperience, or poor judgment endangered climber safety. Interest in such a regulation only intensified as Johnson and Sutton sought access to the Diamond. These were obviously climbers with advanced skills and experience, yet park staff doubted their judgment and motivation. Acting Superintendent Peterson considered the men too intent on the "glory of achievement" and the "distinction of making [a] first ascent." In his view, the climbers downplayed the extreme danger the Diamond posed to both themselves and the rangers who might be summoned to their rescue. The proposed climb was "probably more difficult than anything of its kind ever done in America—and possibly the world. . . . So far as we know, human physical endurance has not been tested to [the] extent believed necessary in this climb." In rejecting Johnson and Sutton's planned ascent on the grounds that their expansion bolts would deface the rock face, Peterson used an existing regulation in an admittedly "picayunish" way, but at that time it was the only regulation he had at hand.[24]

Johnson and Sutton deeply resented the park's thwarting of their ambitions and guessed that the argument about expansion bolts was a ruse. The park soon proved them right. By 1955 the one-time reliance on rules against defacement had been replaced by an outright ban on "public use" of the Diamond "in the interest of visitor safety." Rocky's superintendent was determined to protect climbers and park rangers from serious harm, and he initiated the ban shortly after turning down another request to climb the Diamond, this one by Bill Dunaway and Dick Pownall. Yet as it turned out, the park's denial of access to climbers and subsequent closure of the Diamond were stopgap measures, gradually giving way to persistent pressure to open the sheer rock face to daring climbers.[25] Much as evidence of disgruntled visitors on crowded roads and campgrounds prompted Rocky to redouble its commitment to visitor enjoyment in the front country, so, too, discontented elite climbers would prod the park to open the Diamond in the name of "visitor enjoyment."

Protecting Visitor Enjoyment: *Mission 66 at Rocky Mountain National Park and on Longs Peak*

As we have seen, climbers and front-country visitors of the postwar era experienced a range of impediments to pleasure in Rocky Mountain National Park. Comparable barriers to visitor enjoyment existed across the National Park System. In all regions of the country, national parks were overcrowded and overused. Rocky was the only park that closed a hazardous rock face to climbers, though rangers struggled with climber oversight and accidents at numerous national parks.[26] And nowhere were parks' problems easy to resolve. Between 1945 and 1955 the National Park Service offered no centralized guidance on the issues at hand. The agency was hampered by an annual budgeting process in Congress that made it difficult to pursue long-range innovations or tackle systemic challenges that carried over from one year to the next. And it was impossible for individual parks to attempt ambitious improvements on their own.[27]

By 1955, however, the NPS had devised a response to greatly increased visitation and overuse, at least in the front country. Director Conrad Wirth identified wholesale improvements to park infrastructure as the key to preserving parks for visitor enjoyment, and he was able to gain approval and funding for Mission 66, a program named in anticipation of the fifty-year anniversary of the National Park Service in 1966. The service-wide ten-year program sought to renovate and reinvigorate the national parks, focusing on the needs of auto tourists. Mission 66 funded improvements to roads and wayside viewing areas; upgrades to campgrounds and visitor centers; and enhancements to interpretive programs. It also upgraded employee housing for the growing numbers of permanent and seasonal rangers needed at national parks. Each individual park unit followed the guidance of the national program in developing its own Mission 66 plan.[28]

At Rocky Mountain National Park, Mission 66 projects included the construction of the Beaver Meadows Visitor Center, Administration Building, and Alpine Visitor Center, and the building of new entrance stations at Beaver Meadows, Fall River, and Grand Lake. The park upgraded and enlarged existing campgrounds, built new comfort stations, and enhanced roadside overlooks for scenic viewing on Trail Ridge Road. These major physical improvements included new informational and interpretive signage and exhibits for visitors. The park also upgraded and expanded the available employee housing, and it bought out remaining private inholdings in the park, subsequently demolishing the resorts and lodges that had long stood in these areas. Taken together, the Mission 66 improvements were intended to ensure that front-country visitors to Rocky Mountain National Park would be offered "a scenic and inspirational trip equaled nowhere else in the country" while most park land would be kept free from development.[29] Some critics decried the destruction of historical hotels and other structures, but park managers were eager to buy up and dismantle privately run resorts to protect and restore critical habitat and thereby facilitate visitors' observation of elk and other wildlife. The elimination of lodges was also meant to hasten Rocky's transition to a "day-use" park in which rapid visitor turnover would reduce crowds and traffic congestion.[30]

Though Longs had been an emblem of the park for decades, Rocky's Mission 66 program deflected attention from the grand peak to focus on the interests of automobile tourists. The park's Mission 66 prospectus highlighted the beauty of Rocky's terrain yet claimed, "While desirable, it is not essential for the visitor to leave the road to experience the inspiration of these surroundings. The Continental Divide on Trail Ridge Road opens many breath-taking vistas of great scenic beauty which portray the forces of nature." The prospectus recognized Bear Lake as "the natural destination of at least 60 percent of visitors on the eastern side of the Park," precisely because automobile tourists could drive very close to the lake, park their cars, and stroll along an easy perimeter trail while enjoying lovely views. By contrast, very few visitors had the stamina for a day-long excursion to Longs. Architectural designs for the park's new Beaver Meadows Visitor Center oriented the building to showcase a view of Longs Peak from a second-floor balcony, but most visitors remained in the main lobby on the first floor, where a wall of windows faced an undifferentiated view of the mountains. In a 1957 interview about Mission 66 at Rocky with Radio KCOL, Assistant Superintendent George B. Hartzog and Park Naturalist Norman Herkinham spoke enthusiastically about the "alpine vistas of glacier-carved mountains and tundra plateaus" that awaited visitors to Trail Ridge Road but said nothing about the climb to Longs Peak or the park's long history as a place of mountaineering adventure.[31]

With its emphasis on front-country improvements during Mission 66, Rocky took a piecemeal approach to infrastructure deficiencies on Longs. The park refurbished the Longs Peak campground near the East Longs trailhead and rebuilt the hitching rack for those who rode horses to the Boulderfield. Park rangers also replaced the *Cable* route's frayed cables with new ones and extended the emergency phone line on the peak, placing phones at Granite Pass, Jim's Grove, the Boulderfield, and the Longs Peak Ranger Station. The park did not, however, gain funding to repair the East Longs Peak Trail, despite obvious signs of erosion. Nor was it able to build new shelter cabins on Longs, though one at the Boulderfield might have been especially useful for rescue operations. Staff were forced to acknowledge that the "strong winds and adverse weather conditions at that location" made a durable building, however desirable, unfeasible.[32]

Physical improvements to Longs may not have been comprehensive, but Mission 66 was nonetheless critical to the celebrated peak. Over time, rangers applied the program's core value—dedication to visitor enjoyment—to the question of elite climbers' access to the Diamond. As early as 1956 the park abandoned its year-old outright ban on climbing the Diamond for a new rule that allowed climbing on the wall "only with the permission of the Superintendent." Though no such permission was granted until 1960, the superintendent had begun to admit the fundamental legitimacy of climbers' interest in tackling the sheer rock face, and rangers noted that they had been tasked with "formulating final plans for controlling the hazardous climb of the Diamond." Rangers discussed at length what they would need to see—comprehensive route and bivouac plans, evidence of experience, appropriate climbing equipment and clothing, adequate camp gear and first aid equipment, sufficient food supplies, and skilled support teams—before the superintendent granted climbers permission to ascend the Diamond. Simultaneously, they evaluated the types of climbing and rescue equipment the park would need to acquire if it were to aid injured climbers on the Diamond.[33] So, too, rangers participated in intensive training programs to upgrade their climbing skills and gain expertise in search, rescue, and recovery operations at high altitude. They also improved on existing climbing equipment—for example, designing and making three sets of a "new type [of] carabiner brake arm" for use in the park. Rangers placed emergency supplies for climbers and rangers on Longs in caches at Chasm View, Broadway, the Keyhole, and Jim's Grove, and the park assigned a second ranger to the station at the East Longs Peak trailhead, hoping thereby to improve oversight on the mountain and expedite communication between climbers and rangers, especially in case of injury.[34]

Rangers at Rocky also communicated actively with rangers at other mountainous national parks where climbing activity was increasing. In fact, throughout the 1950s the mountain parks regularly shared detailed information about technical and nontechnical ascents, accidents, and rescues and discussed emerging trends in climbers' interests and skills. Just as important, Rocky's rangers sought advice from other parks about the merits and disadvantages of climbing regulations. Correspondence suggests that rangers in the mountain parks generally viewed climbing regulations with skepticism, thinking it better to win the "voluntary cooperation" of climbers than to impose hard rules. Yosemite relied on the voluntary registration of climbers at most sites in the park, with stricter oversight of climbers only at Lost Arrow and Sentinel Rock. Mount Rainier required climbers to submit to equipment inspections and evaluations of their planned routes and competence, but these regulations had been developed with the close involvement and consent of local climbing organizations and thus were well accepted as a way to reduce accident risk.[35]

As rangers at Rocky developed cooperative relations with other mountain parks, they also worked to sustain their informal partnership with the Colorado Mountain Club and to strengthen ties to Boulder's Rocky Mountain Rescue Group, a recently formed organization of local climbers trained and ready to participate in mountaineering search, rescue, and recovery operations. Park rangers communicated as well with leaders at the American Alpine Club, wanting the organization to understand the park's reluctance to open the Diamond. Indeed, as the park considered how best to regulate the Diamond after rebuffing Johnson and Sutton, it requested meetings and advice from the CMC and the Rocky Mountain Section of the AAC. Though park files do not indicate how the climbing organizations responded to these queries, we can surmise that CMC members may have had mixed sentiments about Rocky's management of the Diamond. The club counted numerous expert rock climbers as members, Dale Johnson among them, and some in this cohort may have shared Johnson's frustration with the park.[36]

Publicly, however, relations between the park and the CMC remained positive and collaborative. *Trail and Timberline* published nothing about Rocky's refusal to give climbers access to the Diamond, suggesting it did not want to take a public stance on the issue. CMC members who participated in a technical climb on Mount Rainier in 1954 had already reported favorably in *Trail and Timberline* on the regulations in place there.[37] And for their part, Rocky's rangers appreciated the CMC's continuing efforts to promote education among technical rock climbers. As we saw in chapter 4, the CMC began offering rock-climbing instruction at its annual Summer Outings in 1939, and by the early 1940s a Denver Technical Climbing Committee had formed within the CMC to offer "thorough and competent instruction on technical climbing." The committee followed the doctrine that "a little knowledge is a dangerous thing" and put its students through a graded series of lectures and field trips that resulted, in successful cases, with students gaining the club's certification to climb and instruct others in subsequent years. Reporting in August 1950, the Technical Climbing Committee listed five women and seventeen men among the graduates of that season's beginner climber course; four women completed the advanced climber course along with ten men. The CMC continued to hold a multiday Technical Climbing School annually throughout the 1950s, each year attracting about one hundred women and men to sessions that offered lectures and field instruction in beginner, intermediate, and advanced rock-climbing skills.[38]

The park also appreciated the CMC's continued role in modeling "safe and sane" practices for nontechnical climbers on Longs. Perhaps because most climbers still had little contact with park rangers, the CMC sought to give mountaineers sound advice about appropriate backcountry conduct, both in club outings to Longs and in its monthly magazine. The CMC's outings to Longs attracted women and men, members and nonmembers. Leaders carefully guided climbers along designated routes and modified plans as necessary to accommodate individuals with different levels of fitness and skill. *Trail and Timberline* urged CMC members and guests to act responsibly and consider the interests of all on group trips, pointedly urging individuals not to ignore instructions or expect group leaders to offer them "effortless" excursions through the mountains. The magazine disparaged those who showed up for group trips with sloppy climbing habits and faulty equipment, noting that people of this type were likely to become lost, injured, or ill yet still hold group leaders responsible for their rescue and for "all their difficulties." On Longs, climbers who did not bother to carry clothing for cold and wet conditions were asking for "misery."[39] Meanwhile, behind the scenes, the president of the CMC corresponded with Rocky's superintendent, James Lloyd, about matters of climbing safety, such as how to manage overexcited climbers (not associated with the CMC) who thoughtlessly threw rocks upon reaching the summit of Longs, endangering climbers below; in this instance, Lloyd agreed to order a new sign for the peak warning against such behavior.[40]

Even as Rocky sustained a collaborative partnership with the CMC and moved toward the eventual opening of the Diamond, Superintendent Lloyd could not let go of his worries about the "extra hazardous" nature of the rock face. Serious climbing accidents continued to occur on Longs and other park mountains each year, and Lloyd feared the Diamond becoming a site of catastrophe, for climbers and rangers alike. With support from his regional director, Lloyd turned down a second request by Dale Johnson (and Ray Northcutt) to climb the Diamond in 1958, though the climbers' plans (submitted in 1957) were exceptionally "complete" and did not call for any use of bolts. In Lloyd's view, Johnson and Northcutt minimized the dangers they were likely to encounter while playing down the hazards facing their rescue-support party and the rangers "who would be primarily responsible for the climbing party and their rescue team." Variable weather conditions at high altitude made the Diamond far more dangerous than big-wall climbs at Yosemite and Devils Tower, and the park was not yet properly equipped for the "magnitude" of a rescue on the Diamond. Indeed, the park's "most qualified men, well trained in mountain rescue techniques and very familiar with this situation, feel that such a rescue would be too great a risk for them to assume." The park was mindful of a recent rescue attempt on the face of the Eiger in Switzerland, at a lower elevation than Longs, that had ended "in tragedy" with the abandonment of three climbers. Moreover, a climb on the Diamond could be attempted only in the summer months, but that was at the "height of the visitor season" when rangers were "critically needed in other capacities by the thousands of visitors scattered throughout the park." In summer 1957 Rocky deployed rangers to rescue climbers in four major accidents; it simply could not accept the additional burden of rescues on the Diamond during the busy summer season. And finally, the park's superintendent considered Johnson and Northcutt's proposed climb to be "in the stunt climb category," likely to "result in undesirable publicity for the National Park Service and Rocky Mountain National Park."[41]

Hesitation notwithstanding, unrelenting pressure to open the Diamond eventually made it impossible for Rocky Mountain National Park to avoid a change in policy. In summer 1959 Ray Northcutt and Layton Kor completed a first ascent of the *Diagonal* route on the wall below the Diamond, in hopes that "their success would convince the park service to lift the ban" on the Diamond itself. The triumphant climbers submitted a report to the park that rated the *Diagonal* as a 6, "severe" to "extremely severe" in difficulty, with seventeen pitches requiring delicate edge work, friction and tension climbing, and "lieback and lateral pressure techniques." Even by the park's reckoning, the *Diagonal* represented a climb harder than routes likely to be tried on the Diamond. To add to this pressure, Dale Johnson took his case for opening the Diamond to the mass media, speaking with the *Denver Post* about his quest. The newspaper circulated in seven western states, and the park fully expected the article about Johnson to spur other climbers to demand access to the Diamond wall.[42]

In the face of mounting pressure, Superintendent Lloyd sought guidance in late 1959 from John M. Davis, chief of the Division of Ranger Activities in the NPS's Washington Office. Perhaps to Lloyd's surprise, Davis took the side of the elite climbers. At a roundtable meeting with Davis in Estes Park, Lloyd and four of the park's rangers explained in detail why Rocky had thus far refused elite climbers access to the Diamond, highlighting the dangers of the Diamond to climbers, the limits of the park's rescue capabilities, and the park's reluctance to support climbers who seemed intent on burnishing their reputations with a needlessly "spectacular" endeavor. Davis was unimpressed. As Lloyd recalled in a long letter to his regional director, Davis stated that "after a thorough investigation of the proposed climb, including equipment and support group, the Superintendent's permission should, in most cases, be granted." The park need not give "blanket permission" to all Diamond aspirants, and the park's Ranger Division must certainly have "competent mountain climbers with adequate equipment, including necessary rescue gear." Also, climbers should "be forewarned that the Service would not be obligated to attempt a rescue beyond the capabilities of Service personnel/or equipment." Ultimately, however, the park must be prepared to comply with a proposed NPS policy on mountain climbing, expected to be finalized in late 1959, that reflected Mission 66's prioritization of visitor enjoyment. The proposed policy considered climbing "a proper park use [that] must be recognized and not discouraged." Davis "quite emphatically pointed out that under the Service's new policy park superintendents would not have the authority to deny permission to those who wish to engage in . . . difficult climbs such as the Diamond, if they were in all apparent respects qualified." Realizing he had no justifiable grounds for keeping experienced and well-prepared climbers away from the Diamond, Lloyd quickly produced a draft application form for aspirants along with a list of climbing and rescue equipment still needed by park rangers, with the expectation that climbers would open the Diamond the following summer. In the meantime, the park's chief ranger recommended "that no publicity be given to the possibility of obtaining permission to make these climbs." It appears that the park intended to wait until summer 1960 to contact elite climbers known to be interested in a first ascent of the Diamond, only then inviting submission of detailed applications.[43]

Inaction on Ecological Risk

Rocky Mountain National Park's commitment to visitor enjoyment began in the earliest years of the park's development, and it was reaffirmed and amplified by Mission 66. The park's determination during Mission 66 to facilitate the gratification of visitors—whether front-country automobile tourists or elite climbers—helped solidify Rocky Mountain National Park's standing as one of the most popular national parks in the nation. Yet it also validated an ethic of care that tended to disregard recreational tourism's harm to the environment.

To be fair, Rocky's Mission 66 plan gestured toward aligning visitation with ecological well-being. It touted a "development plan" that would make the park's "great beauty and scientific interest" accessible to visitors "in such ways as will preserve the natural landscape and avoid undue disturbance." Improvements to the park were to be concentrated in front-country areas and the park was to be administered as a "day-use" area, with the great majority of visitors driving along Bear Lake Road and Trail Ridge Road, viewing the park's "remote, primeval conditions" without damaging prized wilderness terrain. The park planned to continue research on topics including deer and elk populations, timberline ecology, forest insect problems, fish culture, and evaporation rates in high-altitude lakes. And it would look for opportunities to pursue needed research on the ecology of beavers, other small mammals, plants, and "aboriginal trout."[44]

These gestures did not, however, produce a meaningful turn toward the ecological management of wildlife and other natural resources. George Wright and his colleagues had urged the NPS to pursue ecological management two decades earlier, but Rocky continued to resist the resolution of documented wildlife management problems, such as elk overpopulation. Rocky's Mission 66 plan identified the elk and deer population in Rocky as a "potentially explosive problem" yet simultaneously claimed it was of "no immediate concern." Rangers worked in partnership with the Forest Service and Colorado Department of Fish and Wildlife to cull the park's elk herd, but relatively few animals were killed in the 1950s as park officials heard from visitors steadfastly opposed to the practice. This was despite the completion of a comprehensive study of range conditions that confirmed the serious damage caused by elk to winter range in the park in previous decades and the need for a continuing program of elk control. So, too, rangers in the 1950s became ever more dependent on pesticides and fire suppression to keep park vegetation verdant for visitors, though evidence of pesticides' toxicity to the biota was fast emerging, as was data linking fire suppression to uncontrollable fire events. Nor did the NPS or Rocky consider the potential impact of air pollution from cars on visitors, wildlife, or vegetation in national parks, though the nation had become acutely aware of the deadly effects of smog in and around American and European cities. The U.S. Congress passed the Air Pollution Control Act in 1955 to fund research on air pollution and management, but Mission 66 did not take note of growing concern about automobility and declining air quality. The only consequential ecological research of the Mission 66 era was Dr. Beatrice Willard's analysis of visitor impact on the alpine tundra along Trail Ridge Road at Forest Canyon and Rock Cut. Willard found that visitors who parked at these wayside areas to view the scenic terrain were trampling and destroying vegetation, lichen, and soil. The park responded by paving new wayside trails to help keep visitors off the delicate alpine tundra but did not fence off any of the fragile terrain until the 1970s.[45]

And though Rocky deliberately removed numerous lodges and resorts during the Mission 66 era to restore natural habitat and afford visitors additional areas for scenic viewing, especially in Moraine Park, it allowed plans for a ski resort at Hidden Valley to move forward. A prospective ski resort had been questioned in the 1930s by park rangers worried about natural resource damage, and plans were then delayed by World War II. Popular pressure for a ski area resumed, however, after the war, and the Hidden Valley Ski Area opened as a private concession in 1955, having won the enthusiastic support of Rocky's landscape architect and superintendent, the Estes Park business community, skiers along the Front Range, and NPS director Conrad Wirth. The resort boasted two new Austrian disk-type lifts—one capable of carrying four hundred skiers an hour, the other eight hundred—as well as new ski runs, a parking lot for 450 cars, and a warming shelter. The NPS's chief naturalist warned that cutting trees for ski runs would increase water runoff and soil erosion and change the forest's composition, but he found no listeners. Rocky's Mission 66 plan endorsed the resort and provided funding for a skating rink.[46]

Mission 66 was not, however, without critics. NPS biologist Victor Cahalane and University of Michigan research biologist Stanley A. Cain were among those in the scientific community who raised grave concerns, largely within their own professional circles, about allowing Mission 66 priorities rather than ecological principles and evidence to dictate natural resource management in national parks. The nationwide program also provoked exceedingly public and hostile reactions from the Sierra Club and Wilderness Society, whose leaders feared that the ten-year program would permit unlimited numbers of visitors in parks already crowded beyond capacity. These organizations claimed, too, that Mission 66 was distorting the meaning of wilderness. David Brower, the Sierra Club's executive director, accused the national parks of promoting a wholly inauthentic "roadside wilderness." In his view, Mission 66 tried to connect humans to nature through artifice, fostering development in the parks and reliance on human-made products and settings such as automobiles, roads, campgrounds, visitor centers, cafeterias, laundromats, boat-docking facilities, and winter resorts. The results, Brower said, were altogether fraudulent.[47]

As a fierce defender of "pristine wilderness," Brower was deeply suspicious of recreational tourism. Yet he was also an avid mountaineer and recognized that the pleasures of tourism and outdoor recreation often led people to support preservation. During the Echo Park Dam controversy, which began in 1949, Brower and other preservationists encouraged recreation in Dinosaur National Monument (on the border between Utah and Colorado) to bring attention to what would be lost if the dam at Echo Park was built and the monument's canyons and rivers were inundated. Brower overlooked the fact that Mission 66 funds subsequently improved the road that brought recreationists to Echo Park and helped safeguard its future. Instead, Brower and others began to push hard for a federal wilderness bill in 1949 and continued to do so even after the Echo Park Dam was conclusively defeated with the passage of the Colorado River Storage Project Act of 1956. The new legislation stated that "no dam or reservoir constructed under the authorization of the Act shall be within any National Park or Monument," but in the era of Mission 66, preservationists wanted a law with far greater clout. They saw new federal wilderness legislation as critical to defending national parks from myriad modern improvements and alterations.[48]

At the local level, the Colorado Mountain Club took no position on Mission 66, though the CMC Board of Directors and CMC Conservation Committee supported a range of preservation efforts in Colorado, including the opening of a new state park and campaigns to curb littering and limit backcountry jeep use on public lands. The club also put enormous effort into annual tree-planting weekends, during which members planted thousands of young trees at Forest Service sites. The CMC lacked expertise in ecological science and management but continued its long-standing commitment to educating members about existing wilderness regulations and problems in wilderness protection. Thus, when only a third of CMC members replied to an opinion survey on the Echo Park Dam controversy, CMC leaders realized it would be impossible for the organization to take a public stand on the issue and instead pivoted to instruction. Subsequently, *Trail and Timberline* published a statement in favor of the dam by a Bureau of Reclamation engineer as well as a sharp and thoughtful rebuttal written by Denver's leading landscape architect, CMC member M. Walter Pesman.[49]

As CMC climbers supported conservation efforts, they simultaneously constructed social identities that signaled their opposition to the postwar embrace of automobile tourism. Certainly, technical climbers' daring forays up the vertical walls of the East Face mocked common notions of physical comfort, safety, and aesthetic fulfillment. According to the two writers of one article for *Trail and Timberline*, nontechnical climbers also thought themselves quite different from the masses of auto tourists. A female climber who coauthored "Fourteeners or Foothills—Why Do We Climb Them?" said she wanted something different than did "the person whose idea of enjoying the mountains is to ride through them, dressed up in fashionable clothes, in an expensive automobile . . . stopping at a conventional tourist spot—the more popular and expensive the better—to order the most luxurious meal on the menu, and admire the mountains while sipping a dry martini." This woman would not have been satisfied to see Longs Peak from a restaurant in Estes Park or the second-floor window at the Beaver Meadows Visitor Center. She wanted the challenge and immediacy of immersion in wild nature, loved the "beauty and bigness" of mountains, the "chance to be . . . one's own self . . . not merely somebody's employee, spouse, parent or child." Climbing provided the companionship of people with shared ideals and gave those who were "not completely civilized" real opportunities for adventure and self-reliance. The woman's male coauthor admitted to "height fever" and interest in hard challenges. He and his companions liked to "knock ourselves out so we can revel in it in retrospect. It's the particularly tough trips that we remember; they're impressed on our mind." While *Trail and Timberline*'s editors produced a "her vs. him" story that playfully drew attention to gender differences in the two writers' motives for climbing, the authors themselves stressed how little they had in common with the tourists who were content to experience mountains through the glass of a windshield or visitor center window.[50]

For all their concern about preservation and mainstream consumerism, the CMC and its members nonetheless reflected the tensions embedded in recreational tourism. The organization promoted extensive international and domestic travel by car, rail, and airplane as well as the purchase and use of specialized equipment and gear, not acknowledging climbers' dependence on fuel, technologies, and manufacturing processes that contributed to environmental degradation. Backcountry climbers needed motorized vehicles and fossil fuel to reach trailheads, and they bought equipment, guidebooks, and specialized clothing from manufacturers who used fossil fuels and toxic chemicals in production, thereby contributing to air and water pollution. Their sport was enmeshed in America's consumer culture. Still, climbers were motivated by, and felt pride in, their physicality and love of direct experience in the mountains. Not yet inclined to consider how their own recreational technologies and practices affected the environment, they were nonetheless reliable advocates of public land and wilderness preservation.

Race and Free Access to Visitor Enjoyment

Just as Rocky resisted acknowledging the value of ecological management, it also resisted admitting the relevance of the burgeoning civil rights movement to national parks in the Mission 66 era. Clarion calls for freedom and equality by African Americans and other marginalized communities in the late 1940s and 1950s coincided with Mission 66's declaration that national parks were a symbol of American freedom and equality: "As much as any institution to be found in America, the National Park System is a symbol of a free people. Every American shares equally in the ownership of the System; and all Americans, regardless of race or creed, are free to use it on equal terms."[51] With statements such as this, the NPS appeared to endorse values at the core of civil rights reform. Yet, throughout the 1950s, the Park Service and its gateway towns proved unresponsive to the movement's urgent calls for sweeping change in culture and law. Racial equality and inclusivity in national park visitation remained an abstract principle, not an urgent agency objective for the NPS and managers at Rocky. For residents and business owners in Estes Park, changes in the racial status quo seemed more likely to yield harm than progress.

African American demands for civil rights in the postwar era built on the momentum of the Double Victory campaign during World War II, the United States' ideological defense of liberal freedoms in the Cold War, and the United Nations' adoption of the Universal Declaration of Human Rights. Working at the grassroots level as well as through state and federal legislatures and courts, Black women, men, and children in the 1940s and 1950s defied and challenged deeply embedded patterns of discrimination and segregation in education, employment, transportation, housing, public accommodation, and recreation. Efforts to dismantle racism were especially pronounced in southern cities and states where Jim Crow laws required and enabled cruel anti-Black oppression and violence, but civil rights activism also occurred in the North, Midwest, and West, including in Colorado. Activists knew that racism was embedded in economic, political, and social institutions across the nation, even when segregation was not required by state or municipal law. Over time, African Americans began to obtain favorable Supreme Court rulings and make modest legislative gains, to which a varied White response emerged. Some Whites offered social and institutional support, while others offered grudging acquiescence. Many Whites remained detached and uninformed, unwilling to consider the historical forces that produced a Black experience vastly different from their own. Especially in the South after the Supreme Court found racial segregation in education unconstitutional, large numbers of Whites mobilized in an overt show of "massive resistance" to racial equality.[52]

Throughout the postwar era, travel signified Blacks' interest in achieving equality and freedom. Most African Americans with disposable income pursued travel (usually by private automobile) to see beloved family and friends in distant locales, but some were interested in destinations with scenic and recreational value. For these African Americans, pursuit of the American Dream included accessing the experiential pleasures to be had in national parks. *Ebony* magazine, a leading "lifestyle" publication for Black audiences, commended this interest and encouraged readers to visit parks such as Yosemite, Yellowstone, and Rocky. Indeed, its 1957 "Vacation Guide" devoted eight pages to national parks, announcing, "One may vacation simply or luxuriously in America's greatest scenic wonderlands." The guide listed national parks around the country and identified what visitors might "do and see" at each one. It highlighted parks' easy accessibility by car and told readers where they might stay in (or near) each park and to whom they might write for further information. Trying to help readers imagine themselves enjoying national parks, the *Ebony* "Vacation Guide" also offered an eye-catching photo essay about two young Black women from Oakland, California—a pianist and a housewife—who had recently visited Yosemite. Readers followed the pretty young women as they explored Yosemite National Park's scenic beauty and experienced its recreational pleasures, interacted with the park's informative rangers, and enjoyed its fine lodging and dining.[53]

Ebony reminded Black travelers that the NPS prohibited racial segregation in its parks and privately run concessions. "Negroes should feel free, therefore, to use public accommodations of all types found within park boundaries. They are welcome in all hotels, lodges, restaurants and recreational areas which come under the supervision of the Federal Government." Yet, even as it recommended national parks, *Ebony* told prospective Black visitors not to take good service for granted. Reservations were needed precisely because the specter of ill treatment had not disappeared. "Park officials attempt to accommodate even those tourists who arrive without reservations, but wise travelers make it a rule to book space *well in advance.*"[54]

Indeed, *Ebony*'s optimism about national parks did not match the reality on the ground, even in Colorado, a state more responsive to appeals for civil rights legislation than many. Long before the 1950s, the state had passed and revised laws prohibiting racial discrimination in public accommodations at the urging of organized and enfranchised Blacks. Disappointed by the meager enforcement of these laws, Blacks and others pressed for political accountability. A task force commissioned by Mayor Quigg Newton to study Denver's minorities in 1947 found that Blacks, Latinx, Japanese Americans, and Jews faced persistent discrimination in housing, employment, restaurant service, and hospital admissions. While Newton responded cautiously to these findings, the Denver Urban League, labor unions, and myriad Black, Latinx, interracial, and human rights organizations collaborated with state legislators to strengthen Colorado's laws and promote measurable improvements in the lives of religious, ethnic, and racial minorities. The results included a 1951 Anti-Discrimination Act focusing on employment (subsequently amended in 1955 and 1957), the elimination of the state's antimiscegenation statute, new enforcement mechanisms for state prohibitions on discrimination in public accommodations, and the passage of an Anti-Discrimination Housing Bill in 1960.[55]

These reforms produced only small and incremental gains for people of color in Colorado's largest cities, including Denver. In mountain resort towns and gateway cities, the legal reforms had even less impact. During the 1950s African Americans from Denver and many other cities continued to enjoy the outdoors during visits to Lincoln Hills. Latinx children and parents in Boulder enjoyed fishing, hiking, and camping near the foothills and in the city's Chautauqua Park. We have no record of these communities traveling to Rocky Mountain National Park or its gateway cities for recreation. Restrictive covenants kept people of color and Jews from buying vacation properties in Estes Park or Grand Lake. Nor could they count on friendly service at restaurants, lodges, dude ranches, and resorts. *Ebony* urged Black travelers to national parks to book their accommodations well in advance of any visit, but this was not necessarily an easy task. At Rocky all lodging was beyond park boundaries and federal oversight, and while *Ebony* suggested that prospective Black travelers write to the Estes Park Chamber of Commerce for information about accommodations, the magazine identified no hotels or resorts known to serve Black visitors. Similarly, the *Green Book* and *Travelguide* (the latter a new offering for African Americans with an overt civil rights message) listed not a single hotel or restaurant in Estes Park or Grand Lake known to serve African Americans in the 1950s. *Go, Guide to Pleasant Motoring*, a short-lived travel guide for African Americans (1952–1959), began listing four hotels and resorts in Grand Lake and Estes Park in 1956, but we lack evidence that African Americans or other people of color actually tried to patronize these establishments. The park received occasional complaints about discrimination at local resorts from Jewish visitors (and perhaps from Blacks or other people of color), but it could do little more than remind resort owners of state law.[56]

Even if a few hotels near Rocky were willing to serve African Americans, the local media in Estes Park signaled the town's general disinclination to welcome them as visitors. Articles on the civil rights movement in the *Estes Park Trail* evinced considerable ambivalence, if not outright hostility, to Blacks' quest for integration and equality. One article reported that a judge from Mississippi, invited to present his views on *Brown v. Board of Education* to Estes Park Rotarians, "declared that the decision abrogates the sovereign rights of states." In his view the South should be "left alone" to "work with the Negro, 'since the South alone understands him.'" In another article, the *Estes Park Trail* reprinted portions of a booklet by the Mississippi State Sovereignty Commission that opposed school integration on the grounds that innocent six-year-old White children would be forced to share classroom space with much older, low-achieving Black children from illiterate homes. A third article deplored the mistaken Supreme Court "edicts" that preceded the Little Rock crisis, stating, "The whole affair is a shame on the nation and an occurrence which the Communists will review with great glee." And still other articles presented the contrarian views of African Americans who "deplored" integration on the grounds that it promoted racial tension and undermined Blacks' respect for the achievements of their community.[57]

Estes Park, Grand Lake, and Rocky Mountain National Park may also have discouraged visitation by African Americans and other people of color by collaborating in the production of summer events that reprised myths about stalwart White cowboys and savage Indians in the frontier West. In 1953 the Estes Park Chamber of Commerce, noting the results of a statewide survey of the tourist industry, opined, "Our visitors still expect to see cowboys and Indians when they visit us, so let's give them what they want." Estes Park offered a constant schedule of rodeo events and Native American performances during the summer season. A play performed at the YMCA of the Rockies near Estes told the story of "a little white girl who is taken captive by the Indians and then adopted into the tribe. When her mother tries to rescue her, the little girl is told that she cannot speak to her mother on pain of death." While the play reproduced the "color, excitement, and magic" of "legendary" Native American dances and ceremonies, it simultaneously stressed the essential violence of Native peoples. Grand Lake also offered visitors the spectacle of an "Indian Massacre Celebration" in which Arapahos and Cheyennes joined forces against the Utes, brutally killing a chief and hundreds of his warriors. Superintendent James Lloyd of Rocky Mountain National Park was one of the dignitaries at this event, which also included "Indian and pale face races," Native American ceremonial dances, and the re-creation of a "stone age" village with Natives "cooking in deer skin pots and working hides with stone tools actually discovered in Middle Park." Knowing that American tourists found satisfaction in watching displays of "exotic" and "primitive" cultures, Estes Park and Grand Lake sometimes hired Native dancers and singers to perform at these events. Town and park officials fully expected audiences to be White and invited them to imagine themselves as cowboys whose honor and fortitude gradually claimed the vast western frontier from Natives too coarse and untutored for modern life. It is difficult to imagine Native, Black, or Latinx peoples enjoying or identifying with storytelling that so thoroughly essentialized a socially constructed racial hierarchy. Summer performances in Rocky glaringly mispresented the histories and experience of Native peoples in the United States while signaling to other people of color that their experiences and identities were likely to be similarly distorted.[58]

And finally, Mission 66 appears to have readily accommodated tourism's racist tendencies. Tasked with managing vast numbers of visitors, the NPS saw visitors through a lens that emphasized numbers and uniformity, admitting no meaningful differentiation. Mission 66 declared a commitment to racial equality in its promotional materials, but the same publications also revealed expectations of racial homogeneity. One brochure distributed around the country that explained Mission 66 to the public described national park visitors simply as "Mr. and Mrs. America and their children." Visitors in the illustrations and photos were all White; every visitor was part of a White middle-class nuclear family unit composed of father, mother, and two young children. People of color had many reasons to feel unwelcome in national parks, and Mission 66 publicity would have done little to change that thinking.[59]

National parks had never functioned as places for the free and equal enjoyment of all Americans. As we saw in chapter 2, the early NPS systematically removed Native Americans from national park lands and treated Blacks as an impediment to the pleasure of White visitors. The NPS abandoned the formal separation of Black and White visitors at southern national parks in the early 1940s, but it was reluctant to consider how parks and gateway communities throughout the nation informally discouraged Black visitation. In the 1950s, especially as overcrowding and overuse became the NPS's paramount concern, idealistic messaging from the civil rights movement and Mission 66 documents did little to spur superintendents and rangers to pursue racially inclusive visitation. Rather, as Rocky and other parks implemented Mission 66 and tried to reverse a worrisome degradation of the visitor experience, they hung on to long-standing presumptions that White visitors' enjoyment required the exclusion of African Americans and other people of color.

AT THE END OF THE 1950S it seemed that Mission 66's efforts to serve automobile visitors in Rocky Mountain National Park had done little to advance the interests of elite climbers, preserve the environment, or welcome people of color. Elite climbers had not yet been told of plans to open the Diamond, and park managers apparently believed they were adequately preserving the park's natural resources by moving hordes of automobile tourists quickly through a front-county corridor. Despite heightened civil rights activism, national parks remained White spaces; historical records for Rocky Mountain National Park and Estes Park show no visual or textual evidence of visitation by African Americans or other people of color.

Starting in 1960, however, important changes would take place. The park opened the Diamond to technical climbers who quickly established routes on the sheer rock face. Their successes occasioned a revival of media and public interest in Longs and prompted sharp increases in the number of climbers on the peak. The park reported both a worrisome rise in climber accidents and new evidence of damage to Longs by recreational users. Park biologists called loudly for the ecological management of national parks at the same time as postwar Americans began to rethink their love affair with material consumption and embraced the Wilderness Act of 1964, a novel piece of legislation with significant implications for national parks' management of natural resources. So, too, the passage of major civil rights legislation placed additional pressures on the tourism industry and the NPS to welcome Americans of diverse racial and ethnic backgrounds into the great outdoors. As we will see in the following chapter, in combination, these changes finally pushed Rocky to reevaluate its ethic of care. Practical changes in management emerged slowly, but the park was thrust beyond the single-minded values and policies of the Mission 66 era.

SIX | Opening the Diamond in an Era of Reckoning

ACROSS THE UNITED STATES in the 1960s, Americans struggled to discern how the nation might become "a more perfect union." Activists for racial, religious, economic, gender, and sexual justice demanded an end to long-standing patterns of oppression and immiseration that prevented millions of men, women, and children from exercising their rights and freely fulfilling their dreams. Simultaneously, environmental scientists and activists demanded alterations to industrial technologies and practices harmful to human and nonhuman nature—across city and suburb, countryside and wilderness. Responding to these demands, Congress and Presidents Kennedy, Johnson, and Nixon approved new federal programs and legislation—most importantly, the "War on Poverty," the Civil Rights and Voting Rights Acts of 1964 and 1965, the Wilderness Act of 1964, and the National Environmental Policy Act of 1969—that revised the nation's obligation to protect both democratic freedoms and the natural world. Transformation proved far from easy, however, as the United States faced not just new laws but also the hard work of remaking its societal norms and institutions. Many Americans favored universal human rights and environmental protections in principle yet disagreed sharply on policy and process. Others resisted change altogether, fearing loss of privilege and unfettered liberty. Bitter controversy over U.S. involvement in Vietnam exacerbated differences on domestic policy; rancor and contention filled the body politic. When violent reaction became the preferred response of some on the Right, it provoked radicalism and the use of force among some on the Left.[1]

America's national parks largely escaped the antagonism, violence, and disorienting commotion of the 1960s, but this does not mean they were exempt from strife or calls for change.[2] With park visitation far exceeding Mission 66 projections and national concern about environmental and wilderness protections mounting, National Park Service leaders faced considerable pressure to remedy both severe overcrowding and the degradation of precious park biota.

Criticism came from disgruntled visitors, public leaders, and investigative journalists as well as park scientists. Scientists, especially, urged national parks to frame research and management programs around the goal of ecosystem preservation; in their view, this was the only way to ensure the long-term sustainability of natural resources.[3]

As the NPS struggled to do a better job of protecting the visitor experience and natural ecosystems in existing parks, it was asked to do still more. In a world experiencing a "population boom" as well as fierce debate over the relative merits of communist and democratic systems of governance, U.S. park leaders worried that their nation—the preeminent leader of the "free world"—had too few national parks to satisfy its people's right to wholesome leisure. Americans in densely populated cities, especially people of color, were those most often deprived of access to a National Park System that was expected to exemplify "democracy in action."[4] The NPS assumed responsibility for creating and managing new parks, recreation areas, and historic sites close to the places where Americans lived, including racially and ethnically diverse cities. Emerging legislation on civil rights and the environment served to consolidate and formalize the NPS's growing list of obligations. In effect, against the backdrop of an entire nation reckoning with demands for transformation, national parks were asked to demonstrate more overtly than ever before their ability to make good on *all* their central promises: to facilitate human enjoyment in the outdoors, preserve the natural environment, and manifest American ideals of freedom and democracy. It was a tall order. By the end of the decade, the process of reinvention was still in its early stages and the NPS had not yet developed a system-wide management plan to guide change. Creating a robust ethic of care with multiple core components proved extraordinarily complex and continues to this day.[5]

The story of Longs Peak and Rocky Mountain National Park during the 1960s reveals in rich detail the challenges of moving toward a truly multidimensional ethic of care at the local level. The history is one of complex interactions, as those capable of supporting or resisting change in visitor use, resource management, and park democracy included federal officials and park superintendents, rangers and scientists, back- and front-country visitors, residents and business owners in the park's gateway communities. Climbers were among those shaping the park's present and future. They were excited, finally, to gain permission to test their skills, endurance, and courage on Longs' "extra hazardous" Diamond wall, and Rocky developed detailed plans for managing their activity. Alpinists and park managers could not have anticipated that this one change in climbers' access to park resources would become intertwined with questions resonating across the nation and the park system—about how best to facilitate visitors' enjoyment and safety in overcrowded parks while also protecting threatened natural resources and advancing genuine democracy. Ready or not, Rocky and its climbers faced issues and choices about reward and risk in park settings that bore the imprint of a nation peering into its soul.

Open at Last

In the summer of 1960 Bob Kamps and Dave Rearick, two accomplished young climbers from California, traveled to Rocky Mountain National Park amid feverish speculation that officials were finally ready to open the Diamond. Rearick, a mathematician with a newly minted PhD from Cal Tech, and Kamps, a Los Angeles schoolteacher, were just two of numerous Californians with big-wall experience in Yosemite eager to climb the Diamond. Various Colorado climbers, including Dale Johnson, Layton Kor, and Ray Northcutt, were also vying to be first on the virgin wall. On July 20, the park sent applications to all eleven individuals who had inquired about climbing the Diamond since 1953. A cover letter explained that applications would be evaluated on a "first-come-first-serve" basis, with climbs permitted in August. Applicants would have to rely on their own support and rescue parties in an emergency, since the park had yet to "fabricate a cable-winch rescue device" suitable for an operation on the Diamond. Each application packet included a list of all those invited to apply.[6]

The race was on. Rearick and Kamps, already in Estes Park, filled out their application while seated on the steps of the chief ranger's office. They were quickly turned down. Most Colorado climbers viewed the Californians as "outsiders," not worthy of cooperative assistance, and the men were finding it difficult to assemble the support and rescue teams the park required. Undeterred, Rearick and Kamps turned to Roy Holubar, a venerated Boulder climber and manufacturer-retailer of climbing gear; he recruited local climbers for support and rescue and helped them gather necessary gear over "seven frantic days."[7] A second application demonstrated to the park's satisfaction that the young men had the technical experience, equipment, route plans, and support and rescue parties needed to make the daunting climb. It helped the California climbers' case that they were "fresh from a month of climbing in Yosemite" and had also proven their skills in Rocky by climbing the *Diagonal* on Longs. Meanwhile, the plans of the other contenders fell through. The park gave Rearick and Kamps permission to climb the Diamond, and on July 31, 1960, the four members of their support party "were promptly rewarded with the task of lugging a litter and 1,200 feet of rope up the mountain" to a base camp at Chasm Lake.[8]

The climb itself took two and a half days, following a route Rearick and Kamps had pondered for years that went straight up the center of the Diamond. It was named *D1* (or the *Ace of Diamonds*). According to Bob's wife, Bonnie, both men knew there was a lot at stake. Their climb had to be completed successfully and safely. If they "screwed up," they might be seriously hurt, and the sport of rock climbing would pay a steep price. On the first day, Rearick and Kamps climbed well above Broadway, using direct aid and free climbing. For hours they were "drenched by water falling free from the chimney near the top of the Diamond," and by four in the afternoon they were ready to retreat from their highest bolt. They spent the night back down on Broadway: "Our waterproof gear protecting us from the constant spray, we spent a reasonably comfortable night perched on our two by seven-foot ledge and talked over the remaining aspects of the climb." In the morning, the men used stirrups attached to the fixed line with Prusik knots to climb quickly to the top of the line. They then moved onto a ramp, discovered another narrow ledge (which they used that night as a bivouac), and began aid climbing a section of loose and fractured wall that leaned outward. For nearly four hundred feet they climbed behind a cascade of falling water. The rest of the day involved more direct aid climbing "up a series of blocks and overhangs." Kamps and Rearick reached the top of their eighth pitch before dark, placed a bolt, and returned to their bivouac ledge for the night. The next morning there was little distance left to climb after they used the Prusik knots to ascend back to the high point of the previous afternoon, but the climbers were worried that the "water-flowing upper chimney was impassable." Happily, they were able to negotiate the chimney, even though it had "several huge blocks of ice" and "was wet and sloppy throughout." The final (eleventh) pitch was a free climb up the chimney to the summit. "We made our entry in the register and dragged our weary bones back to the shelter hut at Chasm Lake."[9]

According to the Yosemite Decimal System devised during the 1960s, Rearick and Kamps's climb was a very challenging Grade V, 5.7, A4.[10] Interviewed by Superintendent James Lloyd a few days after their climb, "both men agreed the climb was considerably more difficult than had been expected and was certainly one of the hardest climbs in the country, primarily because of the extended areas of sheer overhang." Their equipment included about thirty-five of the chrome-moly pitons recently developed by Yosemite climber Yvon Chouinard, most of which they removed. These were far more durable and came in a wider range of sizes than the soft steel pitons used by most Colorado climbers, and they became the pitons of choice for subsequent Diamond climbs. Rearick and Kamps also used four expansion bolts as belay anchors, leaving them in place, and six ropes; of the latter, two were put in place for rescue purposes during the climb and subsequently removed by the support party. They pulled a pack stuffed with extra clothing, food, and water up behind them after each pitch of the climb. Trying to keep the weight and volume of their supplies as low as possible, the men chose foods with low water content and concentrated calories, sustaining themselves on a diet of salami, pepperoni, canned chicken, raisins, and chocolate.[11]

There had been no advance publicity about the climb, but, by the second day, word got out and people in the local area headed for the mountain. The *Rocky Mountain News* reported that "the narrow little trail up to the foot of Longs Peak began to resemble a thoroughfare." Rearick and Kamps could see "spectators perched high on Chasm View, staggered out in various spots along the ridge between Longs Peak and Lady Washington, and clustered at the edges of Chasm Lake. Now and then a Park Service radio crackled and reverberated across the thin air." Motorists stopped their cars along both sides of Highway 7 and "peered upward with everything from opera glasses to telescopes."[12] Simultaneously, their feat was written up in newspapers and magazines across the country. Two days after their momentous climb, Rearick and Kamps rode in the annual Estes Park Rooftop Rodeo parade as celebrated guests. The young climbers also appeared on television news programs. Relying on a frontier vernacular that evoked deeply held national values, most news media characterized the climb as a triumph of free will and ability: two young men's determination, daring, and astonishing skill made possible a great reward, "a victory over what was said to be the last unclimbed approach to a major mountain in the United States."[13]

Importantly, the editorial board of the *Denver Post* adopted a somewhat contrarian point of view. Yes, Rearick and Kamps had "shown what human determination can achieve." Their climb was a "lesson" for "a society grown soft and stale," with "much of our potentiality unrealized."[14] But their climb also provided a vital tutorial about the nation's ongoing struggles over difference and equal rights: Colorado alpinists who remained resentful of the Californians "because this 'Colorado peak' was submitted to the indignity of ascent by non-Coloradans" needed to understand that the Diamond and Longs Peak were situated in public lands owned by all Americans. "In fact, 37.73 percent of Colorado is owned by the federal government on behalf of all the country," and Californians had as much right to climb in Rocky Mountain National Park as any Coloradan. Indeed,

> to this national domain the poorest Puerto Rican bootblack in a New York slum has as much title, if not as much interest or proximity, as the most ardent Colorado sportsman. . . . In the last decade recreational use of the national parks increased by 76 percent . . . the national forests, 150 pct. . . . More and more Coloradans are going to have it brought home to them that more than a third of this state has 180 million hidden owners, who we seldom see but whose influence is beginning to bear more and more on the use of "our" land.[15]

The *Post*'s editorial board undoubtedly hoped to provoke reaction and debate; instead, there was silence. According to Rearick, "The excitement [about *D1*] died down as quickly as it started." The public's attention span was limited, affording only transitory consideration to dazzling climbing achievements and no consideration at all to questions about the rightful use of national parks. Questions of democratic access in Rocky would not emerge again until 1965, as we will see below. And no one else attempted to climb the Diamond in 1960, nor did the wall attract climbers the following year as severe weather conditions sharply limited alpine adventure. There were 1,691 ascents to Longs' summit in 1960, of which 168 were on the East Face, including *D1* on the Diamond. In 1961 the total number of summit ascents dropped to 785, with only 62 on the East Face and none on the Diamond wall.[16]

Managing Risk, Achievement, and Motivation

Rangers may have been relieved by this reprieve; 1960 was a year of astonishing achievement on the Diamond, but it was also a year of tragic climbing fatalities and grueling rescue and recovery missions. For six years, amid a modest decline in climbing activity on Longs, there had been no deaths on the peak. In 1960, however, as rangers prepared to open the Diamond, technical and nontechnical climbers returned to Longs in large numbers, and the peak again became a site of miscalculation, suffering, and loss. On April 19, four "very poorly equipped" young climbers from Boulder attempted a technical climb on Longs, even though rangers had closed the peak to visitors because of bad weather. Ignoring the posted closure, the group made it to the East Face and up *Lamb's Slide* about five hundred feet to the base of *Alexander's Chimney*. There, one of the four, James Greig, decided to return to the Longs Peak campground because he felt ill. The others continued up *Alexander's Chimney* and (probably) the Notch Couloir but encountered a spring blizzard and frigid temperatures as they reached a point about five hundred feet from the summit. Traversing to the Notch and the south side of the summit, the trio was able to rappel down a steep slope. Joan Bendixon and Prince Willmon took shelter under a rock overhang; David Jones, the most fit of the three, rappelled again and found cover in a small niche below them. After a bitterly cold night, Joan Bendixon survived a difficult rappel (and bad fall) on the south edge of Longs and walked to safety, though she subsequently required weeks of hospitalization for debilitating frostbite. Jones and Willmon, severely hypothermic and frostbitten, fell to their deaths while rappelling or climbing down the same steep slope. Recovery of the bodies took two days and involved park staff, partner organizations, local volunteers, and use of an air force helicopter. At least one of the young climbers, Willmon, was a member of the Colorado Mountain Club; sadly, the organization's focus on technical climbing skills and mountaineering safety had not kept him or his friends from danger. The accident gained "nationwide publicity" in the press and on radio and television.[17]

Still another climbing fatality occurred in 1960 when the leader of a CMC trip slipped and fell during a descent on a different peak, Chiefs Head. And there were four other backcountry accidents that year requiring search and rescue missions, one of them on Longs. The climbing deaths and accidents in 1960 unsettled rangers, reminding them that Rocky's grand mountains, especially Longs, could be places of grave harm, not reward, for those who had honed neither their powers of judgment nor their alpine skills. Looking for a silver lining, John Clark, a former park ranger and expert climber, told Chief Ranger Lyle McDowell that the local climbing community seemed eager to learn from the Willmon and Jones tragedy. The fatalities "had been foremost in the thoughts of mountaineers . . . in Boulder," and "a constructive development has come out of the tragic deaths of the Boulder climbers—there has been a wide re-evaluation of individual safety standards and I hope to see more caution exercised in the future."[18]

Rocky's rangers were not inclined to wait passively for the desired caution to emerge. As generally dry and clear weather finally replaced winter conditions in August and September 1961, technical and nontechnical climbers sought Longs in "near record" numbers. Climbing was gaining in popularity among Americans, and in Rocky climbers flocked not only to Longs but also to nearby Mount Meeker and Mount Lady Washington, and to peaks near Bear Lake, especially Hallett, where a solo climber had fallen to his death in July 1961. Keen to prevent accidents, rangers asked all technical climbers on Longs and in the Bear Lake area to register voluntarily with park staff. They also delivered bimonthly "camp-fire talks" on "safe mountaineering and the park's search and rescue missions" at the Glacier Basin Amphitheater—offering similar talks to the Boy Scouts and other outdoor organizations—and placed articles on mountaineering safety in the local media and park newspaper. Helpfully, the CMC continued to stress climbing safety in *Trail and Timberline* and kept up its annual rock-climbing schools. By one important measure the park's protective efforts paid off: 1,842 climbers summited Longs without mishap on nontechnical routes in 1962, as did 143 climbers on the technical East Face. And there were two accident-free attempts on the Diamond, one of them successful.[19]

Understandably, the climbs on the Diamond generated great excitement. Dale Johnson had wanted to climb the Diamond since 1954, and he finally gained permission to attempt the *D1* route with John Wharton, a schoolteacher from Princeton, New Jersey, in early August 1962. Sadly, the men had to retreat during their second morning on the wall. Wharton claimed he developed severe altitude sickness; Johnson thought otherwise, later remarking, "My climbing partner freaked out; I think he just got scared to death." Whatever Wharton's difficulty, Dave Rearick told the *Estes Park Trail*, "Johnson was in good spirits, but he must have been bitterly disappointed. It was rough to have [the Diamond] snatched from his grasp, after he'd waited so long."[20]

Johnson was still recovering from this setback when, Rearick recalled, "Layton Kor showed up on the scene and . . . he's not gonna fail." Rearick, by this time a math professor at the University of Colorado Boulder, had taken a summer job as a Longs Peak seasonal ranger, and it was he who inspected Kor's climbing equipment for the Diamond ascent.[21] Kor was a climber with "tremendous drive" and big ambitions. A Boulder bricklayer, he had put up the extremely difficult *Diagonal* route in 1959 (Grade V, 5.9, A3) as well as two other East Face routes earlier in the decade. He had also proven himself in California, lured to the big walls in Yosemite Valley in 1957 by elite climber Royal Robbins, who thought Kor would be outdone by the climbers there. To Robbins's surprise, in that "hotbed of rock climbing . . . this Colorado climber demolished any Californian pretensions to superiority, climbing our hardest routes in record time, and, even more annoyingly, without comment. He never talked up his own climbs or belittled the efforts of others."[22]

Now back in Colorado and determined to put up a new route on the Diamond, Kor won permission to climb it and lined up two partners, but they "turned up sick." Unwilling to abandon the ascent, Kor recruited Charlie Roskosz, a member of his support party (who had also provided support for Rearick and Kamps), to climb with him. Neither Kor nor Roskosz thought to inform the park (or even Roskosz's wife) of the last-minute change in the team's makeup, and Roskosz was eventually assessed a small fine for climbing the Diamond without permission. But that happened after the men's success in putting up the *Yellow Wall*. The new route was 150 feet to the left of *D1* on a section of smooth, slightly yellowed rock. Compared to *D1*, it had fewer overhangs, was less steep, and had more solid rock, but "the crack system . . . [was] not as continuous and more delicate traverses were necessary." Kor and Roskosz used both ordinary chrome-moly pitons and short pitons designed for hairline cracks (the latter were known as RURPs—Realized Ultimate Reality Pitons, made and named by Yvon Chouinard). They completed the climb after spending twenty-eight and a half hours on the Diamond, nineteen in actual climbing. The *Yellow Wall* was widely covered in the news media and rated a very difficult Grade V, 5.8, A4.[23]

If the *Yellow Wall* proved elite climbers' extraordinary abilities and ongoing enthrallment with the Diamond, it signaled to Rocky a real need for improved alpine search and rescue capabilities. The aborted Johnson and Wharton climb and the successful Kor and Roskosz ascent relied on support and rescue teams that the climbers themselves assembled, but park authorities wanted their own rangers to assume a central role in emergency missions on the Diamond. Hiring Rearick as a ranger on Longs in summer 1962 was a critical step toward that goal. As Rearick noted, "The park authorities saw there were going to be some more climbs on the Diamond . . . and so they wanted to have firsthand knowledge in case there was a rescue or something." Rearick climbed "on company time" to increase his familiarity with various routes on the East Face, and he and other rangers practiced rescue techniques that might be needed on the Diamond face. The nine-hundred-foot rock wall presented unusual difficulties, even for a big wall, because it "overhangs a little bit; it's not easy to reach somebody up there."[24]

As rangers prepared for the possibility of accidents among elite climbers on the Diamond, they simultaneously confronted the hard reality of accidents among climbers of lesser skill. In 1962, 1,985 technical and nontechnical climbers summited Longs without incident, but this was far from a complete story of the year's climbs. Indeed, the park reported that "accidents occurred in proportion to mountaineering use . . . resulting in above normal search and rescue demands." Two climbers fell to their deaths, in separate incidents on Longs, as they tried to take shortcuts from the *Keyhole* route to the Boulderfield. Dave Rearick helped with the recovery of both victims and with rescues on the lower East Face. And two other climbing deaths occurred elsewhere in Rocky in

1962—one on the Chaos Canyon snowfield, the other on Andrews Glacier—bringing the park to a "record high" of four mountaineering fatalities in a single year. Rocky counted a total of twenty-four mountaineering accidents in 1962, all requiring search and rescue operations, and one requiring "the services of a private helicopter."[25]

The climbing fatalities and accidents of 1962 alarmed rangers and prompted Rocky to adjust protective measures yet again. Most importantly, the park implemented a mandatory registration system for technical climbs throughout the park and all climbs above eleven thousand feet anywhere on Mount Meeker or Longs Peak, whether technical or nontechnical. The new rules effectively brought technical climbers on the lower East Face, the Diamond, and the North Face as well as nontechnical climbers on the *Keyhole* and *Cable* routes under the supervision of rangers. Even those going only as far as the Boulderfield needed to register, as that site was at 12,760 feet. The new rules prohibited solo climbing altogether and required registration for all backcountry winter excursions in the park, whether they involved climbing or not. Clearly, under the new system, registration was required of far more climbers and backcountry users than ever before. Yet it was also more streamlined than the original registration system for the Diamond, which had required that letters of interest, application forms, and letters of approval go back and forth in the mail. Under the new system, rangers filled out a form for climbers during a face-to-face interview or phone conversation, taking down personal data for each climber in a party and gathering information about the climbers' experience, equipment, routes, and bivouac plans.[26]

Rangers claimed their intent was not to "hinder" climbers' plans or pursuit of reward, but rather to use "persuasion . . . to keep obviously unqualified parties off of difficult routes." They informed climbers about "pertinent regulations," including the park's prohibition on solo climbing and the requirement that climbers notify a park ranger promptly when they returned from a climb. Rangers also gave climbers suggestions about safety and "back-country manners." Rangers expected cooperation from climbers and hoped they would appreciate that registration "facilitates rescue operations greatly, at no real sacrifice of the climber's time or independence." To enable the new registration requirements, the park increased the number of permanent rangers assigned to the Longs Peak Ranger Station from two to three. As of 1963 the park no longer required climbers on the Diamond to provide their own rescue teams, having handed primary responsibility for search and rescue on the steep wall to park staff. [27]

According to the park's rangers, rock climbers grumbled a bit about the new registration system, "particularly concerning the solo climbing prohibition." Nevertheless, rangers reported, compliance was generally good, "considering the type of temperament often encountered among climbers, the newness of the regulations, and difficulty of enforcement." In fact, rangers were quick to praise the registration system for helping to reduce the park's climbing fatalities—there were none in 1963—and subsequently incorporated the system into the park's

1964 *Master Plan*. The latter noted the efficacy of "a reasonable and prudent registration and screening procedure for visitors desiring to engage in recognized hazardous outings such as mountain climbing, winter back-country trips, etc."[28]

The mandatory registration system seemed promising, but Rocky's rangers pursued still further steps to reduce accidents, especially among inexperienced mountaineers who lacked any connection to safety-minded organizations such as the Colorado Mountain Club, the YMCA of the Rockies, or the Boy Scouts. Concerned about public misperceptions of Longs, they modified the language in Rocky's visitor brochures to discourage novice climbers from venturing to its alluring flanks. In 1963 the park brochure termed the *Keyhole* and *Cable* routes "exhausting for the unhardened climber." And in reviewing registration require-ments for those venturing above eleven thousand feet, the brochure stressed the inherent dangers of alpine environments: "Accidents in the mountains, even minor ones, may have very serious or fatal consequences. Severe storms come quickly, even in summer, with attendant exposure to low temperatures, rain, snow, sleet, and lightning. All hikers and climbers should observe the following precautions: *Never climb alone. Register before and after the climb. Avoid steep snowfields. Don't overextend your physical ability. Start early. Turn back in adverse weather.*"[29]

With the streamlined system for mandatory registration in place, Longs became a true mecca for elite and skilled rock climbers. In the summer of 1963 Kor returned to Longs with Royal Robbins as his partner, and the two men repeated *D1* before putting up another new route, the *Jack of Diamonds*, in a single day. Kor also climbed with Floyd "Tex" Bossier, of Boulder's Colorado Guide Service, establishing five other new routes on the East Face and Diamond. Still other climbers put up new routes rated 5.7 and harder on the lower East Face and other flanks of Longs Peak in the summer of 1963.[30] The following year, 190 people climbed the East Face of Longs Peak, the greatest number in any year thus far. Seventeen-year-old Pat Ament climbed the Diamond with Bob Boucher, establishing the *Grand Traverse*. And in 1966, 590 people registered for technical climbs on Longs, many of them on the East Face. Among them, Larry Dalke, George Hurley, and Wayne Goss put up *D7*, a moderate aid route requiring no A4 pitches, making it possible for people who were "competent but not daring on aid" to climb the Diamond. In the words of climber Roger Briggs, "following uninterrupted crack systems for hundreds of feet," the moderate aid climb "began to ease the Diamond's forbidding image."[31]

The next year, 1967, was another year of climbing achievements, as there were twenty-one technical climbs on the Diamond, eleven of them successful, and the first successful winter ascent of the Diamond, by Layton Kor and Wayne Goss.[32] And in 1968 there were 379 technical ascents on Longs, mostly on the East Face, surpassing previous records. By this time climbers had established nine routes on the Diamond. *D1* was still the hardest and most dangerous route; *D7* was the easiest and most frequently climbed. Twenty-four different parties had climbed the Diamond successfully by 1968, while thirty-one climbing parties had failed in their attempts to ascend the formidable wall. Chrome-moly pitons still greatly facilitated the placement and trustworthiness of aid, but big-wall climbers also benefited from the introduction of ascender devices. These replaced the Prusik knot and made the climbing of fixed lines much faster than before. Longs Peak continued to draw elite climbers excited by the prospect of putting up new routes on the Diamond, but technical climbers of modest skill were beginning to repeat the already-established routes, especially *D7*; they were also climbing shorter and less difficult routes on the lower East Face. Some of these climbers hired professional guides who had concession contracts with the park.[33]

Meanwhile, the number of nontechnical climbers on Longs also increased each year during the 1960s, though the new registration system and park messaging attempted to discourage those with little experience from venturing to the peak. The park reported 1,155 people ascending Longs Peak in 1961, 1,985 in 1962, 2,050 in 1963, and 2,100 in 1964; technical climbers never accounted for more than 190 of each year's total.[34] Snow and icy conditions deterred climbers in 1965, but in 1966 a total of 3,310 nontechnical climbers reached the summit of Longs; 2,290 did so in 1967.[35] And in 1968 the number of nontechnical climbers reaching the summit of Longs shot up to 3,847, setting a new annual record. Some of the nontechnical climbers took advantage of the stables within the park that offered guided trips on horseback to the Boulderfield, at which point they dismounted and climbed to the summit. The *Cable* route remained the most popular ascent route, with most people descending via the *Keyhole* route. Importantly, the figures for those summiting Longs must have undercounted the number of people on the mountain; many who wanted to summit were likely deterred by impediments including bad weather, fatigue, and inadequate food and water. And there were probably many visitors who intentionally climbed only partway up the peak.[36]

Rangers necessarily focused their time and energy on educating, monitoring, and protecting Longs' climbers. Yet they must also have pondered why the peak was rapidly gaining in popularity. Answers would not have been hard to find. From their interactions with technical climbers, rangers knew this cohort was drawn to the Diamond and East Face by values generated and sustained within the climbing community. Elite rock climbers participated in a sport that encouraged high levels of athleticism, skill, and ambition while also demanding resilience and courage under exceptionally daunting high-altitude conditions. Competition was important to some climbers, less so for others. As Dave Rearick explained, "Well, I like mountains. . . . Climbing is a mysterious thing, you know, when they ask 'why do you climb?' you know there's no real answer to that, it's just kind of in your blood. It's a, well, it's adventure, it's fresh air and sunshine, it's companionship, and it's also kind of a problem-solving process. It kind of exercises the mind, the brain, as well as the body." All elite climbers sought to master extreme levels of risk. Indeed, Dale Johnson, the Boulder climber who, in Pat Ament's words, helped "bring Colorado climbing into the modern age," promoted the notion of "calculated risk," believing it acceptable for lead climbers to choose maneuvers that put them at risk of falling during difficult ascents. Tackling the Diamond was a logical step for climbers who had acquired big-wall capabilities and wanted the additional challenge and stimulation of testing themselves in an alpine environment.[37]

Many of the moderately skilled technical climbers and nontechnical climbers who summitted Longs had probably been inspired by photos and stories that appeared in newspapers and magazines across the country as Rearick and Kamps, and then Kor, Robbins, and others put up astonishingly demanding routes on the Diamond. Knowing they could not attempt the same feats, these climbers adjusted their aspirations accordingly, settling for easier climbs on the East Face and Diamond or for Longs' nontechnical routes. And Paul Nesbit's *Longs Peak: Its Story and a Climbing Guide* (first published in 1946, frequently updated, and in its seventh edition by 1969) was probably read by climbers of widely varying abilities. It kept the legendary stories of Longs alive and informed readers of new climbing accomplishments on Colorado's most famous fourteener. So, too, climbers of modest skill were likely influenced by the growing popularity of adventure literature celebrating Longs and all of "Colorado's 14,000 foot mountains . . . as ideal landmarks in the American national identity." Climbers had been counting their ascents on fourteeners since the 1920s, but this pursuit gained in popularity in the 1960s. In 1967 J. Powell wrote "14,000 Feet: Where in the World?" for *Summit* magazine, publicizing the "cult of the fourteener." According to Powell, fascination with and worship of fourteeners "reaches its apex in Colorado, where fifty-three altars await the worshipper." Climbers who signed into the Longs summit registers used the idiom of this cult, describing the climb as an extraordinarily challenging and awe-inspiring endeavor.[38]

The growing popularity of the wilderness movement and the passage of the Wilderness Act in 1964 (discussed below) undoubtedly also inspired climbers. The wilderness movement had been building momentum for decades, and many Americans were inspired by best-selling authors Sigurd Olson, Aldo Leopold, and Wallace Stegner, whose writings described the aesthetic and spiritual renewal that wilderness experiences offered. In the view of these writers and others, wilderness was of critical scientific value but also essential to humans' spiritual fulfillment and their continued faith in the "abstract dream of human liberty and human dignity."[39] CMC member Jack Reed wrote frequently about wilderness values and protection in *Trail and Timberline*, turning to poets such as Nancy Newell to convey the meaning of human ventures into the wild: "You shall need the tongues of angels to tell what you have seen. / Were all learning lost, all music stilled / Man if those resources still remained to him, / Could again hear singing in himself and rebuild anew the habitations of this thought." Likewise, the breathtakingly beautiful images of wilderness created by contemporary photographers such as Eliot Porter and widely distributed by the Sierra Club and other wilderness protection organizations motivated Americans to discover their full humanity through immersion in wilderness settings. With "wilderness values" taking hold in the general population, it stands to reason that Rocky Mountain National Park and Longs Peak would become increasingly popular places to experience revitalization amid untamed grandeur.[40]

Park rangers and managers must have appreciated many of the motivations of climbers; after all, they too reveled in national parks and the wilderness experience, and some were skilled climbers themselves. Still, the rapidly increasing number of climbers in Rocky and on Longs, and the difficulty of East Face and Diamond ascents, complicated rangers' obligation to facilitate climbers' reward while limiting their risk. Fortunately, the mandatory registration of climbers on high peaks—in combination with the park's enhanced educational efforts, rangers' ongoing search and rescue training, the CMC's mountaineering classes, and the services of the Rocky Mountain Guide Service and Mountaineering School—seemed to reduce climbing fatalities. There was only one more climbing death on Longs in the 1960s after mandatory registration went into effect. Even so, two young boys died in separate accidents while scrambling on Thatchtop and Deer Mountain in 1966 and 1969.[41] And nonfatal accidents also continued on Longs, causing trauma for climbers and placing a heavy burden on their rescuers. Accidents among technical climbers never prompted park authorities to question access to climbing on either the Diamond or the East Face; NPS policies clearly established technical climbing on rock faces as a legitimate visitor use of park resources. Rather, accidents and rescue operations impressed upon rangers the importance of education, training, and preparedness for rangers and climbers alike. Backcountry emergencies also highlighted the value of collaboration with the climbing community and volunteer rescue organizations.

An extraordinarily difficult rescue that might well have failed without dedicated collaboration occurred in January 1968 after Richard Kezlan tumbled more than four hundred feet down *Lamb's Slide* and across Mills Glacier. Kezlan was part of a four-member party of moderately skilled alpinists who decided to abort a climb to their bivouac site on Broadway because two members of the group had become exhausted. Carelessly, the party began their descent in the dark without using ropes. Kezlan slid down the steep, icy slope and was unconscious and bleeding from a "gaping head wound" by the time the other members of his party reached him, none of them with more than a basic knowledge of first aid. Fortunately, they carried shortwave radios and were able to broadcast the details of the accident over radio station KLOV in Loveland, Colorado. Two local independent rescue groups, Rocky Mountain Rescue Group and Alpine Rescue, plus a park search and rescue team, set out to help the injured climber, but they were at least six hours away from the accident site.[42]

Realizing Kezlan might die before any outside help reached him, another member of the climbing party, James Disney, hiked down to the Chasm Lake Shelter Cabin where some other climbers were staying overnight and found that one member of the group was a physician. Dr. Dee Crouch climbed to Kezlan and cared for him for the next six hours, though the medical supplies in his pack were wholly inadequate for treating a patient in shock from massive blood loss. To make matters worse, the temperature was ten degrees Fahrenheit and winds were blowing at about fifty miles per hour. When the advance rescue team arrived with another physician, they stabilized Kezlan over a span of several hours and then moved him down to the Chasm Lake shelter. There, Dr. Crouch helped perform one of the most primitive operations he had ever participated in: "Kezlan's massive head wounds were opened and cleaned. Bleeding vessels were tied off. A portion of his skull was elevated to give his bruised brain more room to expand." Kezlan's blood pressure slowly rose from 70/50—"barely enough to sustain life"—to a normal reading of 120/80. "Until this point I had given the man less than a 10% chance of living, now it was boosted to perhaps 80%." The rescue team still had to carry Kezlan all the way down the mountain because poor visibility prevented a helicopter from landing near Chasm Lake. He reached Colorado General Hospital and underwent surgery "exactly twenty-four hours after his fall. After a six-day stay and an uneventful recovery, Kezlan walked out of the hospital, very thankful to be alive." Thirty-seven people had been involved in his rescue.[43]

Even more arduous, costly, and collaborative was the August 1969 rescue of sixteen-year-old Kordel Kor, a nephew of Layton Kor, who suffered serious head injuries and a broken femur and kneecap when he fell on the first pitch of the Diamond's *Grand Traverse* route. Kor's rescue took over twenty-four hours and involved a series of potentially disastrous complications: a helicopter with medical support could not land because of mechanical difficulties; a huge boulder crashed down the rock face during the rescue, just missing Kor and his rescuers; and finally, while being lowered from the Diamond in a litter, Kor, in shock and agitated, began trying to fight off those who were trying to save him. It took enormous skill and determination for the rescuers to get Kor to the Chasm Lake Shelter Cabin, where he was finally evacuated by helicopter to a Boulder hospital. Thirty-four members of the park staff and fourteen volunteers took part in the rescue effort.[44] Kor's accident prompted further rescue training: just two weeks after the incident, rangers at Rocky and volunteers with the Rocky Mountain Rescue Group participated in a trial during which rescuers descended to their "victim" on the Diamond from the edge of the North Face. "The event used the latest rescue techniques and answered many unknowns involved in evacuating an accident off the Diamond."[45]

Life-threatening accidents on Longs' East Face and Diamond demanded that rangers continually evaluate and improve search and rescue measures for technical climbers, but nontechnical climbers on the *Keyhole* and *Cable* routes also caused real worry. Rangers dutifully emphasized the dangers to be found on these routes during registration and in educational media, but accidents occurred nonetheless. In 1967 Longs Peak ranger Don Bachman decided it was time to study accidents and fatalities on the two routes, going back to 1925 when the cables were installed to improve safety after the Vaille tragedy. Records showed that going up and down the *Keyhole* and *Cable* routes, nontechnical climbers were sometimes hurt when rocks dislodged by climbers higher on the route fell onto them. Injuries from falls on the rocky (and often wet or icy) terrain were also common. Many injuries were slight, but others were extremely serious. And Bachman discovered that the six fatalities on the nontechnical routes had all been on the North Face cables. Five major accidents had occurred on the *Cable* route, but only two on the *Keyhole* route.[46] Compelled by these numbers to look closely at the cables, Bachman identified a host of physical dangers along their expanse, all exacerbated by climber inexperience, misapprehension, and crowding:

> They have a reputation of being quite simple, but they negotiate steep and often icy rock. It takes a certain amount of strength to pull yourself up over them, but there are ample resting spots. However, if a person lets go, he falls. The cables create a bottle neck on the route as more climbers ascend to the base only to find a slow party blocking their passage. This concentration of waiting people in a hazardous rock-fall area and in a location virtually surrounded by technical terrain is a deadly combination. There is a steep snow field that is totally unsafe to negotiate without equipment that must be coped with early and late in the season. Descent on the cable route is very hazardous but is often undertaken by the casual climber due to fatigue, sudden storm, and the lateness of the hour. Once above the cables, the route passes through technical terrain that can easily be blundered on by an inexperienced party, particularly during lightning storms. The North Face and the cables themselves attract considerable lightning.[47]

From Bachman's perspective, mandatory registration, "intensive visitor contact," and educational messaging were unlikely to remedy the risks to climber safety on the *Cable* route. Certain that the *Keyhole* route was safer than the North Face cables, Bachman recommended that the latter be removed. And with the cables gone, he wanted the North Face reclassified as a technical ascent.[48]

Notably, even as he focused on climber safety, Bachman urged park authorities to consider the *Cable* route in relation to wilderness values. Just three years after the passage of the Wilderness Act, he was inclined to see the cables as an installation that posed a risk to both visitors and wilderness, remarking, "Esthetically speaking, the removal of the cables will restore some of the park values on the peak 42 years ago." For Bachman, preserving Longs' wilderness was becoming as important as protecting the safety of inexperienced climbers looking for a "high mountain experience."[49] And as we will see below, rangers such as Bachman were not thinking about wilderness preservation solely in terms of aesthetic values. Influenced by scientific findings and by their own observations of backcountry visitors' harm to park resources, rangers believed the time had come to mitigate visitor impact and promote ecological preservation in Rocky Mountain National Park.

National Parks and the "Ecological Turn"

Ranger Don Bachman articulated concerns about the *Cable* route's contravention of wilderness values during a decade of growing environmental awareness. Americans were encountering dismaying evidence of environmental damage and hazard, in both the landscapes of ordinary life—suburbs, cities, small towns, farms—and the natural settings where they sought refuge and renewal. People across the United States worried about harm to humans and nature caused by industrial toxins, mining, automobile emissions, and the production and testing of atomic weapons. Many gained firsthand experience of the damaging effects of pollution and deforestation in and around their cities and suburban developments. Americans became aware of scientific evidence that common synthetic chemicals endangered all living things, and they heard of the harm that dams and other infrastructure caused to waterways and freshwater species. Prompted by the publication of Rachel Carson's *Silent Spring* in 1961, and by the media campaigns of Howard Zahniser for the Wilderness Society and David Brower for the Sierra Club, Americans debated curtailing the production of chemical pesticides and fertilizers and pondered the merits of proposed new wilderness legislation. They considered how best to restore landscapes and rivers already damaged by development. So, too, they worried about the state of their national parks and questioned the extent to which Mission 66 could be reconciled with the new environmentalism. For these Americans, national parks ought to be places that preserved wilderness and offered visitors an authentic "wilderness experience."[50]

Critics of Mission 66 had not gained much traction in the 1950s, but as environmental awareness and support for wilderness protection mounted in the 1960s, opposition to Mission 66 became widespread. Visitation to national parks far surpassed the predictions of Mission 66, calling into question the program's prioritization of visitor enjoyment and front-country improvement. Roads, lodges, visitor centers, campgrounds, and other amenities were making the parks too accessible. Indeed, front-country corridors and facilities in Yellowstone, Yosemite, Zion, Rocky, and other national parks were so crowded that both the visitor experience and the environment suffered. Visitors in crowds and traffic jams became irritable and uncooperative, disturbed one another, and abused the resources around them. And with backcountry use also rising, precious flora and fauna were under stress across park landscapes; to some, wild land seemed on the verge of ruination.[51]

National Park Service officials were surprised and unprepared to handle the criticism they encountered, having underestimated the strength of the environmental and wilderness movements and the degree to which antidevelopment and anticonsumerist messages resonated with Americans and fueled skepticism about Mission 66. In September 1962, NPS assistant director Daniel Beard of the Office of Public Affairs acknowledged the impact of the environmental movement on public support for Mission 66 projects. Speaking to a gathering of park superintendents at Rocky Mountain National Park about the impact of the environmental movement's criticism, Beard lamented especially the loss of support from women's organizations that had long been loyal champions of the Park Service: "The emotional appeal that they put out—that Mission 66 was harming the parks—actually got some of the women's organizations going away from us."[52] Indeed, the National Jaycees and the General Federation of Women's Clubs, the latter an organization with thousands of member clubs, had become allies of Brower and Zahniser. Beard went on to argue for a stepped-up public relations campaign, hoping that such a campaign would answer urgent questions about park conditions, restore the public's confidence in Mission 66, and preserve the "integrity of the National Parks."[53]

As architects of Mission 66 at the top levels of the National Park Service tried to insist that their plan was true to both the Organic Act and authentic wilderness protection, leading park biologists and rangers refuted them. Park biologists supported the environmental movement's legislative efforts while also urging the prioritization of scientific data and ecological principles. These skeptics within the service were advocates of a refined concept of wilderness, different from the landscape aesthetic that underlay the first fifty years of the National Park Service's policies and Mission 66. Rather than viewing wilderness solely in terms of the pleasure or uplift it brought to humans, the new generation of wildlife biologists and ecologists argued that wilderness needed to be studied and protected for its scientific value. Howard R. Stagner, chief of the Park Service's Branch of Natural History, argued in 1961 that the parks were "complex organisms" that were "rapidly becoming islands" in a nation of mixed land use and management. He believed the Park Service needed to do a better job of studying the ecological relationships and processes in the parks, the unnatural pressures on them, and the impact of visitors on fragile park environments. So, too, rangers at Sequoia and Kings Canyon National Parks proposed a backcountry management plan that recognized the critical value of wilderness to scientific knowledge and the need to balance visitors' desire for "personal freedom" in the wilderness with protection for wilderness resources. Major reports authored by Stagner, A. Starker Leopold, and William J. Robbins in the early 1960s urged the National Park Service to pursue extensive scientific research and manage resources for "ecosystem preservation."[54] Historian Ethan Carr describes the shift in thinking this way: "The social functionality of wilderness did not entail tourism or enjoyment. Its value to society was its intrinsic biological integrity, and that integrity was understood in scientific, not scenic, terms."[55]

Park biologists' calls for ecological management in the NPS rose in volume just as wilderness advocates closed in on legislative victory. With the support of Congress and President Lyndon Johnson, the Wilderness Act became law in 1964. Defining wilderness as areas of public land where "earth and its community of life are untrammeled by man," the new law specified that except for emergencies, there shall be "no use of motor vehicles, motorized equipment or motorboats, no landing of aircraft, no other form of mechanical transport, and no structure or installation within any such area." The act created some areas of wilderness and provided a process by which acreage within national parks and other public lands could gain wilderness designation.[56]

The Wilderness Act was a critical piece of legislation, providing a legal framework for identifying and protecting unspoiled land. Still, it did not resolve the tensions that had emerged in earlier decades as rangers and park superintendents tried to balance the preservation of undeveloped nature against the need to provide for humans' enjoyment of scenic vistas and recreation. And though biologists and other natural scientists endorsed the preservation of wilderness for its ecological integrity rather than for its aesthetic, spiritual, or recreational value to humans, the Wilderness Act retained, and may even have intensified, the ambiguities of the 1916 Organic Act. The 1916 legislation obligated the NPS to preserve parks' scenic natural resources for visitors' enjoyment without offering guidance on how the preservation of nature and the enjoyment of visitors were to be achieved in concert. Similarly, the Wilderness Act obligated the nation to preserve natural areas "untrammeled by man" and afford humans "outstanding opportunities for solitude or a primitive and unconfined type of recreation" but neglected to define the standards or practices land managers might use to keep humans from harming the cherished lands affording them a "wilderness experience." It made very little reference to scientific knowledge or principle, declining to define wilderness or its management and preservation in ecological terms. The new legislation advanced wilderness preservation but it did not authorize parks to limit visitation or downplay their prioritization of visitors' experience.[57]

The Land and Water Conservation Fund Act (1965), Concession Policy Act (1965), Wild and Scenic Rivers Act (1968), and National Trails System Act (1968) further obligated the NPS to preserve land and waterways within national parks and cooperate with other agencies and government entities in preserving trails and rivers that ran through and extended beyond park boundaries. As with the Wilderness Act, these laws highlighted the importance of preserving natural resources for human enjoyment without defining preservation in ecological terms. Federal agencies' obligation to pursue scientific study and apply ecological principles to environmental protection and regulation was made clear only with the passage of the Air Quality Act (1967), Clean Air Act (1970), and National Environmental Policy Act (1969), and with approval of the NPS's Administrative Policies for Natural Areas (1968).[58]

The National Park Service initially expressed skepticism about the Wilderness Act, taking the position that the legislation was unnecessary because national parks already treated all but their front-country corridors as wilderness. Over the course of the 1960s, the NPS and park staff at Rocky recognized that the Wilderness Act might serve them well, allowing them to question management practices and visitor impact that disturbed previously "untrammeled" park settings. Staff at Rocky realized, too, that their obligation to protect park wilderness would necessitate reliance on ecological science and management. Somehow, they had to align protection of the wilderness's ecological integrity with the preservation of its experiential benefits for humans.

One sign of park managers' quest to align the ecological and experiential meanings of wilderness was a report on Rocky's backcountry that was prepared in 1965 by three rangers as well as a park naturalist, civil engineer, and landscape architect. The team found that the number of hikers, campers, fishermen, horseback riders, and climbers in Rocky's backcountry had nearly doubled since 1960, all hoping "to escape the confines of more formal civilization in order to relax or stimulate the exaltation that so inspired their forefathers." Unfortunately, backcountry visitors appeared to lack scientific knowledge of wilderness areas or much understanding of how to behave responsibly in them. In fact, the various groups of backcountry users were badly eroding trails, trampling delicate plants, and endangering forests with unregulated campfires. Their trash and waste fouled land and water and was especially notable in Jim's Grove, a favorite camping area close to timberline on Longs Peak. "In 1964 one crew of five men spent five days in the Jim's Grove area and that effort was the entire 1964 clean-up program in the backcountry." The report urged the park to categorize the backcountry into three classes—essentially, scenic areas near the front country, wild areas, and backcountry areas with important historic remains or structures. It recommended many more backcountry privies; clear rules on backcountry camping, trash disposal, and fire use; restrictions on horseback riding; better signage; and more rangers to monitor backcountry visitors and engage in regular clean-up activities. Well aware of Beatrice Willard's work on the deleterious impact of visitors on the fragile alpine tundra near Trail Ridge Road and of support for ecosystems research and management among NPS scientists and rangers at other parks, the report also advised greater scientific study of the park's wilderness. Finally, it strongly opposed the proposed construction of a new paved road through the park to accommodate the rising number of automobile visitors, arguing it would seriously impair backcountry wilderness areas in the park.[59]

As it turned out, Rocky lacked funding and staff in the 1960s to fully implement the 1965 recommendations on ecologically informed backcountry management. Rocky counted 1,500,000 visitors to the park's front country in 1964, nearly eleven times more than the 138,500 who visited the backcountry, and the park's modest budget and labor force could not be diverted away from users putting heavy pressure on Rocky's roads, wayside facilities, campgrounds, and close-in trails.[60] That said, Rocky successfully defeated proposals for a new roadway. So, too, rangers made incremental improvements in monitoring backcountry conditions and prepared to integrate ecological principles and robust backcountry management practices in a new *Master Plan* for the park (forthcoming in 1976). Park managers also asked researchers in the Department of Recreation and Watershed Resources at Colorado State University to produce a report on park carrying capacity in both front country and backcountry. Preliminary in approach, the report defined carrying capacity as "the capacity of an area" to withstand visitor use "without irreversible deterioration of the physical environment and without diminishing user satisfactions to the point that the park experience is no longer pleasurable." The authors believed that "determination of an optimum level of use is primarily a value question," obligating the park to engage in "coordinated" research on changes over time in park use, visitor satisfaction, and qualitative and quantitative impact to park ecosystems. Ultimately, the park should be able to "exclude visitors . . . whose interest in the highest values of the park is only marginal," as long as they could be accommodated elsewhere. To get to that point, the NPS could "not afford to delay" further research. Unfortunately, in underfunded Rocky more research on visitor carrying capacity was nearly a decade away.[61]

Given Rocky's limited capacity for tackling backcountry problems, rangers at the park leaned on the Colorado Mountain Club, as they had in the past, hoping it would help educate backcountry users about the ecology and care of wilderness resources. A collaborative relationship with climbers had long been key to rangers' efforts to protect them from harm. Now, in moving toward ecological management, Rocky Mountain National Park deliberately widened the scope of its partnership with climbers. The CMC had worked hard for the passage of the Wilderness Act, and its members were already leading "litter trips," picking up the trash that other hikers and climbers left behind while climbing Longs and other peaks in Rocky.[62] *Trail and Timberline* reported on the CMC's other wide-ranging conservation efforts and offered its pages to foresters and national park rangers who thought it imperative to educate hikers and climbers about ecological principles and low-impact backcountry conduct. David Butts, one such ranger, informed *Trail and Timberline* readers in 1969 that Rocky was developing a "coordinated plan for all of the park's undeveloped areas, keyed to the ecosystems of the park," in order to facilitate wilderness preservation. To this end, he urged backcountry visitors to refrain from cutting switchbacks in trails, pack out all nonburnable trash, and desist from cutting tree boughs for bedding. If Rocky's wilderness backcountry was to remain unsullied, visitors had to adopt these "vital modern rules of the trail."[63] Butts was recommending crucial elements of what would emerge in the 1970s and 1980s as "minimal impact" and "leave no trace" principles.

Park staff may also have realized they had potential allies in wilderness protection among technical climbers who endorsed "clean climbing." Advocacy for clean climbing emerged in the 1950s and early 1960s among elite climbers as they watched peers ascend vast and nearly blank rock faces and cliffs in Yosemite. The climbs were made possible by using large numbers of bolts and other direct aid, and to some it seemed "there might be no limits to what climbers could master." Skeptics wondered, however, whether these ascents represented "true" climbing. Technical climbers had long debated "fair means" in their sport, and advocates of clean climbing charged that some aid climbers were gaining unfair advantage from bolting and technical aid. Soon, the debate about bolting moved beyond questioning whether direct aid compromised the authenticity of difficult climbs. Yvon Chouinard led the way in broadening the debate when he championed the aesthetic and environmental virtues of clean climbing in a 1961 article in *Summit* magazine. Chouinard was certain that bolts encouraged climbers to attempt routes that were beyond their abilities; more important, he lamented the permanent damage bolts did to rock faces. Bolts ought to be climbers' last resort, Chouinard declared, and climbers might even consider removing bolts already in place. In 1963, climber Steve Roper heeded Chouinard's suggestion, extracting thirty bolts from a classic route on Shiprock in New Mexico and publishing a defense of his actions in an article in *Summit* magazine in 1964.[64]

Sometime thereafter, "clean" climbers began to "chop" bolts from established routes, demonstrating a self-righteous disdain for aid climbers. Chopping or cutting a bolt was probably faster than pulling one out, but it left unusable hardware on marred rock faces and ratcheted up the potential for serious conflict among climbers. Worried that bolt chopping was doing more harm than good, Bob Kamps published an article in *Summit* magazine endorsing a climbing ethic that obligated mountaineers to consider their responsibilities to the mountains and to other mountaineers. He urged climbers to use bolts sparingly *and* desist from bolt chopping. Kamps wanted his peers to realize that clean climbers who asserted their superiority through bolt chopping harmed the entire climbing community in the long run.[65]

Boulder locals Pat Ament and Cleveland M. McCarty added their voices to this dialogue in their 1967 book, *High over Boulder.* Though the authors focused on climbing in the Flatirons and Eldorado Canyon near Boulder, their readers undoubtedly sought vertical adventure in Rocky as well as in the college town's backyard. And while Ament and McCarty articulated advocacy for clean climbing in terms more aesthetic than ecological, they highlighted the permanence of damage to rock. Specifically, the men disparaged climbers who

> have unknowingly ruined the personal enjoyment of others by defacing the aesthetic nature of a route. Thus, a few lovely climbs in the Boulder region have been converted to trash climbs. Rock is not replaceable as are divots in a golf course. Once the surface is changed, it will remain so. The rules are simple: Do not drill a previously unbolted route. Do not place extra bolts in a route. There is far more honor in retreat. Remove fixed ropes and pitons, too. In essence, leave the route clean for those who follow.[66]

Of course, ecosystem preservation depended on more than mitigating the environmental impact of climbers and other backcountry users. Like other national parks, Rocky had a long history of managing fire, nonnative fish, elk, and other wildlife largely on the basis of visitor preferences rather than sound ecological principles. Dedication to these patterns of management flagged but did not disappear as the NPS began its "ecological turn." By the late 1960s managers and biologists at Rocky and other national parks were beginning to rethink total fire suppression, recognizing that it produced heavy fuel loads and unnaturally homogeneous tree stands that invited megafires and catastrophic insect infestations. Rocky was not ready, however, to move toward a shift in policy. After all, fires left to burn might get out of control and endanger not only the park but also the gateway towns and small villages on its borders. On the management of fish, the park proved more inclined to action. Rocky abandoned fish stocking with nonnative species in 1968 and tried to rebuild its native trout population through new "catch and release" rules.[67]

Unfortunately, Rocky's management of elk became, if anything, more susceptible to nonscientific popular sentiment than ever before. According to historian Jerry Frank, by the early 1960s the park had "irrefutable scientific evidence" that its overlarge winter elk herd was in dire health and doing severe damage to willow and aspen groves. The park also knew that its decade-long culling program, though modest, was "working to ameliorate the situation." Still, nearby residents and visitors strongly opposed rangers' killing of elk inside the park. Over the next several years the park collaborated with the U.S. Forest Service and Colorado Fish and Game to study the seasonal movement of the park's elk herd beyond park borders. Once that data was gathered and the timing of migration outside park boundaries was understood, the park and its partners decided that Rocky could dispense with "the unseemly killing of a park icon" by displacing responsibility for lethal elk control onto hunters beyond park borders. Time would prove the new policy to be seriously flawed, allowing a threefold increase in the size of the park's elk herd over the next two decades. Ecological thinking was gathering momentum in Rocky during the 1960s, but the weight of limited funding, past practices, and public opinion severely constrained the park's options.[68]

Race and Democracy in Rocky Mountain National Park

Intransigence in the gateway community of Estes Park proved a particularly decisive impediment to changes in Rocky that might have advanced racial equality and inclusivity. In earlier decades, the NPS had declared parks open to all yet failed to welcome African Americans and other racial minorities, assuming they would discomfit White visitors. Gateway towns such as Estes Park and Grand Lake played an important role in discouraging visitation by Americans of color, as they provided essential services to park visitors while perpetuating the normative idea that national parks were meant for White middle-class Americans seeking pleasure and redemption in nature. By the 1960s the NPS was under pressure to acknowledge that it had a role to play in addressing the nation's long history of racial inequity. Still, resistance to change took place at many levels, including in national parks' gateway cities.

The civil rights movement had become a matter of urgent national concern early in the 1960s as grassroots activists and antiracist organizations put unrelenting pressure on southern states and the federal government to move decisively away from segregation. President Kennedy assumed office with little interest in civil rights, but the insistence of activists and the hideous violence of southern racists proved impossible to ignore. Moreover, the Soviet Union was using evidence of racial injustice as a weapon against the United States in the escalating Cold War. On June 11, 1963, President Kennedy declared his support for new civil rights legislation. Stepping in for the assassinated president a few months later, Lyndon Johnson wrapped himself in the mantle of racial justice, hoping thereby to guarantee his historical legacy.[69]

The Civil Rights Act of 1964, which outlawed discrimination in public accommodations and employment on the basis of race, national origin, religion, and sex, did not appear to be immediately relevant to the NPS. After all, segregation had already been disallowed at southern national parks and their commercial concessions, and no policies authorizing the formal exclusion or segregation of people of color existed elsewhere in the National Park System. The NPS thus appeared to satisfy the new law's prohibitions against overt racial discrimination in public accommodations. The NAACP and other civil rights organizations worked hard in the 1960s to compel corporate chains such as Hilton Hotels and Howard Johnson's to comply with the new legislation and welcome Black travelers, but these chains were not present in small gateway towns near western national parks like Rocky.[70] As for employment, procedures for implementing the workplace provisions of the Civil Rights Act of 1964 were slow to evolve, and an executive order requiring affirmative action in federal agencies was not issued until 1969, by President Nixon.[71]

Importantly, NPS leaders were not yet inclined to examine why or to what extent people of color, absent official policies of discrimination, rarely visited national parks, including Rocky. Certainly, Black travelers well understood the ubiquity of casual discrimination in hotels, restaurants, gas stations, stores, and recreational facilities and were actively involved in testing these places' compliance with the 1964 legislation, but national parks do not appear to have been subject to their scrutiny. Rather, African Americans who traveled for pleasure simply stayed away from Rocky and other national parks, as they had done in previous decades. According to scholar Beth Erickson, African Americans living in Colorado felt unwelcome in Rocky throughout the second half of the twentieth century. They also lacked the funds and material resources for park vacations and were disinclined to place high value on wilderness recreation, with most viewing it as a White activity.[72] The NPS was apparently unaware of these perceptions and impediments. Writing on park use in 1968, Ronald F. Lee, a retired NPS regional director, noted approvingly that travel in the United States had come to be recognized as a "right" consonant with the rights to freedom of movement, migration, rest, and leisure articulated in the 1948 Universal Declaration of Human Rights. And he opined that travel and outdoor recreation in parks had the "potential" to widen people's experience and thereby reduce prejudice based on race, religion, or political beliefs. Yet, without evidence, Lee claimed that national parks were in fact widely used by all Americans, noting that "the 133,000,000 visitors who came to the National Park System in 1966 are believed . . . to have included all segments of the American people."[73]

To the extent that the NPS engaged with questions of democratic and multiracial access, it did so in ways that left the big nature parks such as Rocky, Yosemite, and Yellowstone mostly untouched and unchanged. By the early 1960s the U.S. National Park Service was leading an international association of national parks, encouraging park leaders around the globe to share and debate park values and management practices. Park leaders consistently drew attention to two threats to national parks worldwide: environmentally harmful modern technologies and "uncontrolled growth of population." Stewart Udall, the U.S. secretary of the interior and keynote speaker at the First World Conference on National Parks (FWCNP) in 1962, argued that these twin forces threatened to destroy places that served simultaneously as "irreplaceable" scientific laboratories and "nature islands of solitude and repose . . . indispensable" to the happiness of humans in modern societies. For Udall, it was not acceptable that "park and wilderness experiences . . . be rationed out among the fortunate few." As leader of both the international parks movement and the "free world," the United States needed to show by example how to preserve and expand national park systems. And at home, where a "population boom" and environmental pressures overlapped with entrenched racial injustice, park leaders needed to acknowledge, in the words of NPS director Conrad Wirth, that national parks "symbolize democracy in action. They are created by the people for the use of the people. . . . They are a national resource, a scientific resource, an educational resource, and a recreational resource."[74]

Attempting to put idealism into action, Udall penned a letter in 1964 that identified three broad "categories" of units already extant within the National Park System—natural areas, historic areas, and recreational areas. Recreational areas need not have the magnificent features or ecological value of natural areas such as Rocky or Yosemite; still, they should offer excellent opportunities for reflection and play in nature. In fact, Udall declared it essential for the NPS to greatly expand this third category, as the "staggering demand for outdoor recreation projected for this country" would otherwise "inundate" the existing system. Soon thereafter, newly appointed NPS director George B. Hartzog moved to create dozens of new recreation areas, some of them in or near diverse cities such as New York, San Francisco, and Washington, DC. And in Washington, DC, Hartzog helped launch "an innovative, community-based recreational program called Summer in the Parks SITP" as the city contended with high levels of racial tension and unrest. Embracing the motto "parks for the people," Hartzog acknowledged that people of color had a right to safe and enjoyable parks and recreation areas. He also opened volunteer opportunities for youth of color in urban parks and appointed racial minorities and women to a few high-profile leadership positions in the NPS. For all his visionary action, however, it could be argued that Hartzog accepted the reality and constraints of residential segregation, trying to bring parks to people where they lived, but relieving pressure on the great nature parks such as Rocky to widen their doors to visitors of color, even to those who lived in the Denver area, just an hour's drive from the national park. [75]

If Rocky Mountain National Park and its gateway cities were under little pressure to welcome and serve visitors of color, they were briefly pressed to accept the presence of minority young men seeking employment opportunity and socioeconomic mobility via President Johnson's "War on Poverty." One of the programs in the War on Poverty was a Job Corps modeled on the New Deal Civilian Conservation Corps, and in early 1965 NPS leaders in Washington, DC, consulted with Superintendent Granville Liles about establishing a Job Corps Conservation Center in Rocky Mountain National Park. The center would be located in Hallowell Park, the site of one the park's former CCC camps, and with funding from the federal government, it would provide jobs for two years to two hundred unemployed young males between the ages of sixteen and twenty-one, many of them men of color from the nation's inner cities. The young men would gain valuable real-life job skills as they completed assignments in natural resource conservation, park maintenance, and landscaping, and they would be available to provide related services in the local community. [76]

Initially, the public response to the proposed Job Corps center was positive. Following informational meetings with park leaders, the Estes Park Chamber of Commerce endorsed the concept, as did the editors of the *Estes Park Trail* and civic leaders in Estes Park, Longmont, and Loveland. Polled for their response, "the majority of some 75 persons" who attended a public meeting with park officials in early March supported the Job Corps proposal. At a meeting a month later, Mayor Clarence Graves asked for a show of hands on the proposed Job Corps program at Rocky: the vote was 169 in favor, 41 against. [77] One supportive couple with a summer residence in Estes Park wrote a letter to the editor of the *Estes Park Trail*, declaring, "Unless we intervene to correct what slum rearing and slum schools have done, the vicious wheel of poverty rolls on and on and grows like a snowball. Job Corps Centers are the beginning of constructive intervention. What can be more appropriate than using some of the space of our National Parks for some of them? It is right in the tradition that brought our ancestors to America, the land of opportunity!"[78] This couple viewed young men of color from inner cities as individuals contending with disadvantages and problems that could be overcome by work in nature.

Other residents of Estes Park, however, saw young men of color as individuals with permanent pathologies and criminal tendencies. George Sykes, a resident of Estes Park, wrote an explicitly racist screed to the editors of the *Estes Park Trail*, stating that the boys enrolled in the Job Corps had not "had enough discipline to stay in established schools [and] up to 30% . . . are to be from minority racial groups." They were used to resorting to crime and violence to get their way and were sure to bring untamed passions and violence to Estes Park:

> Is a program of sports and other supervised activities carried out at the camp going to satisfy them? I feel not. They are going to want to socialize, particularly with girls. The animal energy of 200 boys in this age group is tremendous. They are going to seek an outlet for this very human drive, and Estes Park is not the sort of community . . . set up to provide for this natural outlet. . . . Their background will lead some of them to seek a more uninhibited, less regulated type of social outlet. Thwarted in obtaining their social desires in their accustomed ways, they can hardly be expected to do other than resort to force and violence. A percentage of the boys are from backgrounds where force and violence in the form of knifing and gang fights are accepted patterns of existence, where drunkenness and use of drugs are common and where prostitution and opportunities of promiscuity are readily available. We are expecting boys, largely from this background, to suddenly assume the responsibility necessary to become happy participants in the community life of a town such as Estes Park. From the standpoint of the boys themselves, this seems a great deal to ask.[79]

Sykes had opened the floodgates. Though Superintendent Liles tried in subsequent public meetings to offer realistic information about the backgrounds and interests of young men enrolled in Job Corps programs, he was unable to assuage program skeptics. Critics in Estes Park signed petitions in opposition to the Job Corps and sent the petitions and dozens of letters to Superintendent Liles. Liles chose not to fight back. In August, the *Estes Park Trail* reported that Otis Singletary, the Job Corps director in Washington, had decided that a Job Corps camp in Estes Park would be a "mistake." A recent "riot" by Job Corps participants at a former army and National Guard training site in rural western Kentucky had convinced him that diverse urban youth did not belong in the White countryside: "We're learning the hard way we've got to expect difficulties, particularly with this kind of clientele. . . . The camps' quality varied, and . . .

bigger urban centers had some advantage over the conservation centers, which are small and in rural areas."[80]

It is hardly surprising that the proposed Job Corps program in Rocky failed to materialize. Otis Singletary was apparently ambivalent about the entire national program and the young men it was supposed to serve. So, too, the town of Estes Park and its news media had a history of ignoring or belittling African Americans in the first half of the twentieth century, accepting them as menial employees, not visitors or residents. The *Estes Park Trail* had been highly skeptical of civil rights activism in the 1950s and offered scant and generally derogatory coverage of civil rights legislation in the 1960s.[81] And even though the newspaper's editors took a favorable position on the proposed program in early 1965, as hostility grew and Singletary decided a camp in Rocky was a "mistake," the *Estes Park Trail* joined the opposition: "Our Community is not large enough to absorb such a camp, be it 200 or 400 young men of under sixth-grade mentality. By Job Corps law, they are subject to no military discipline; they are free to come and go as they wish; they are subject to outside pressures and radical elements. Reluctantly, we come to the conclusion that we cannot handle a Job Corps Camp, no matter our humanitarian impulses."[82]

Rocky was just sixty-five miles from Denver, a city where African Americans, Latinx, and Native Americans pursued freedom with righteous vigor in the 1960s, building on decades of experience as they demanded equal rights and opportunity in education, housing, employment, politics, and civic leadership. The park was even closer to Boulder and Fort Collins, university towns where students of color and their allies demanded that municipal and school authorities recognize long-standing patterns of racism and endorse racial justice. Transformation did not come easily in any of these places, however, and in Estes Park there was no evidence of mobilization for meaningful change in race relations, whether at the local, state, or national level.[83] Rather, opposition to a Job Corps camp in Rocky points to the town's reluctance to transition away from racial exclusivity.

Where the climbing community stood on the Job Corps, civil rights reform, and the meaning of democracy in a multiracial nation in the 1960s is not easy to discern. As we have seen, many climbers in the 1960s were young and inclined to hold favorable views on environmental preservation and wilderness protection. At the same time, the Colorado Mountain Club had a significant presence in university towns such as Fort Collins and Boulder, and climbers enrolled at Colorado State University and the University of Colorado Boulder were presumably exposed to the debates on civil rights that animated those campuses. So, too, they must have become at least passingly familiar with controversies over feminism that roiled campuses in Colorado and other states. Still, photos and articles in *Trail and Timberline* and other climbing journals of the 1960s suggest that climbers saw little connection between their sport and demands that barriers of race and gender be dismantled. Climbing remained a White sport, dominated by men, even as it gained in popularity. Young White men were the elites; White women climbed enthusiastically and some developed great skill, but they did not garner the attention or high status of male climbers. Scholarship on the sport suggests that White male climbers in the 1960s thought masculinity had been weakened by the habits and demands of modernity; in their view risk-taking in outdoor endeavors such as mountaineering was a way to fortify an enfeebled manhood.[84]

One hint that Colorado climbers were being asked to reconsider their sport's relationship to democracy and race can be found in the July 1967 edition of *Trail and Timberline*. Colorado Outward Bound (COB) had begun to offer experiential outdoor education courses to urban adolescent boys, some of them Black or Latino with histories of delinquency, and COB's director, Joseph N. Nold, published an article in *Trail and Timberline* inviting "conservationists" to consider the role wilderness experience might play in resolving the nation's "social problems." Nold declared it a mistake for conservationists to "turn our backs on the city," where poverty, unemployment, and the collapse of family and community were commonplace. He urged CMC members to "break through our middle-class and romantic notions" in defining "what life is today." In his view, all those who supported conservation should consider "turning to Nature as a means of coping with Man's social problems." The *Trail and Timberline* staff must have held Nold and Outward Bound in some esteem or they would not have published his article. Ruth Wright, a CMC member from Boulder (subsequently a state legislator), agreed that Nold's piece had value given "the current tragic riots in our big cities" and suggested that the CMC's cabin at Brainard Lake be used for an experimental "one-or-two-week outdoor education camp" for urban youth.[85] Otherwise, however, Nold's piece was ignored by readers; it was the only article in *Trail and Timberline* on race, social ills, and reform in the 1960s, suggesting that the CMC did not want to engage with these issues. Nold assumed that youth of color shared an essential equality with Whites but also identified inner city youth and adolescent boys of color with persistent social pathologies. He offered juvenile delinquents, some of them of color, an Outward Bound experience as a chance at redemption. Wherever CMC members stood on the principle of civil rights and racial justice, they were apparently disinclined to enlist their club in the rehabilitation of youthful offenders.

THE OPENING OF THE DIAMOND in 1960 piqued interest in a mountain already celebrated for its sublime rewards—physical, aesthetic, mental, and spiritual. Elite climbers who succeeded in establishing new routes on the Diamond inspired climbers of all levels to test themselves on Longs' rugged granite, even if only on its nontechnical routes. Interest in Longs grew, too, as wilderness advocates conveyed the message that wild nature was essential not only to the environmental well-being of the planet but also to humans' quest for meaning and liberty. In the decade following the Diamond's opening, both technical and nontechnical climbers sought the summit of Longs in unprecedented numbers, eager to discover themselves in its stunning yet unforgiving landscape. Rangers were committed to climbers' enjoyment, but they faced the challenge of protecting both elite climbers on the Diamond and the growing numbers of lesser-skilled climbers on the East Face and the peak's nontechnical routes. Simultaneously, with pressures for ecological management mounting, rangers confronted the daunting task of monitoring and reducing backcountry visitors' adverse impact across the park wilderness, including on Longs Peak.

Rangers at Rocky generally responded deliberately and constructively to Longs' broadening appeal and to the challenges of protecting both climbers and natural resources on the peak. They did not pursue the impossible goal of eliminating fatalities and accidents on the peak but instead modified practices of protection, oversight, and education to fit the growing numbers and changing profile of technical and nontechnical climbers on Rocky's famous fourteener. So, too, rangers responded to emerging concerns about visitor harm to natural resources by monitoring trail erosion and human waste in the backcountry and partnering with the CMC to promote low-impact wilderness adventure. In doing so, rangers built on wilderness and environmental values already evident among some in the climbing community and expanded the terms of their decades-long partnership with mountaineers, encouraging them to identify as citizen visitors with substantial responsibility for their own safety and for the well-being of Rocky's natural resources.

Still, it remained to be seen how fully climbers and other backcountry visitors would match their ambitions and conduct to the environmental well-being of the peak. And in numerous ways the park itself wavered in the face of change. For one, park authorities did not heed rangers' recommendation to remove the *Cable* route to protect both visitor safety and wilderness values. The route had tremendous popular appeal, and removal seemed too radical a step; a decision on the route's fate waited for another day. And like other national parks, Rocky was able to invest in only limited ecological research and environmental monitoring. To the extent that it had ecological data at hand, it often hesitated to translate research findings into new management regimes. Park managers found it difficult to imagine and devise effective ecological approaches to the management of fire, insects, and elk, especially as they faced a tightening of budgets. So, too, park managers and rangers knew that Rocky's gateway communities and visitors preferred continuity with past practices that prioritized visitor enjoyment.

Rocky's gateway communities proved a particularly decisive impediment to change in the area of civil rights. Following the passage of the Civil Rights Act of 1964 and the creation of War on Poverty employment programs, the NPS and its parks pursued novel workforce initiatives as one pathway toward a multiracial democracy. Yet when Rocky proposed a new multiyear Job Corps conservation program that would have brought two hundred urban young men to Rocky and Estes Park, many of them of color, pushback from conservative residents in

Estes Park helped kill the program. Meanwhile, the local climbing community simply neglected to consider the extent of national parks' obligation to promote and exemplify multiracial democracy. By the end of the 1960s, climbing on Longs and management practices in Rocky were different than they had been a decade before, but much uncertainty remained about how, in the years ahead, to promote an ethic and practice of care that effectively balanced visitor enjoyment and safety with environmental protection and inclusive democracy.

SEVEN | Legends and Ethics in an Alpine Wonderland, 1970–2000

IN 1991 AND AGAIN IN 1993 hundreds of people gathered in Estes Park to celebrate climbing, past and present, on Longs Peak. Jim Detterline, a Longs Peak climbing ranger, organized the reunions after Clerin "Zumie" Zumwalt, Ev Long, and Hull Cook, men who had been climbing guides at the Boulderfield Shelter Cabin in the 1930s, showed up at the Longs Peak Ranger Station one day in September 1990. The men had not seen one another in over fifty years, but back at Longs, they reminisced excitedly about their summers on the starkly beautiful mountain. Detterline wanted to hear more and decided it was time to celebrate the people and legends of Longs Peak.[1]

The reunions of 1991 and 1993 brought together "Longs Peakers" of multiple generations, including the three Boulderfield guides. One after another, speakers shared accounts of Longs and mused about the grit and vision of the people who adventured there. Paul Stettner told the story of putting in *Stettner's Ledges* in 1927 with his brother Joe. The three former Boulderfield guides shared tales, alternately hilarious and harrowing, about entertaining, guiding, and rescuing the guests of Longs' short-lived alpine "hotel." Tom Hornbein, Dale Johnson, and Dave Rearick described the excitement of opening routes on the East Face and the Diamond in the 1950s and 1960s. Pat Ament and Bill Briggs recounted the challenges of "freeing" routes in the 1970s and 1980s that had previously been climbed only with direct aid; Briggs spoke, too, about an emerging era of "extreme free climbing." John Harlan described a thrilling descent on skis from the summit of Longs in the mid-1980s, and Derek Hersey shared a gripping story of "free soloing" the *Yellow Wall*, *Casual* route, and *Pervertical Sanctuary* in a single day in 1989 without ropes or protection of any kind.

And this was not all. Audience members listened to a retelling of John Wesley Powell's problematic yet successful summit of Longs in 1868, and they heard about daring women climbers on Longs, some of legendary status, such as Isabella Bird and Agnes Vaille, others long forgotten. Climbing rangers and physician climbers recalled extraordinarily difficult search and rescue missions. Every speaker used photographic slides to make the past come alive, and some went out of their way to recognize the people who summited Longs via the *Keyhole* route. Thus, Derek Hersey, in recounting his astonishing free solos on the Diamond, noted how impressed he had been by the pluck and enthusiasm of Longs' nontechnical climbers. "I was talking in the Boulderfield with all these hikers and they're great, I was amazed at the different kinds of people that were up there, old folks, young kids with garbage bags on, you know, everything from Kansas to New York City."[2]

The reunions were an opportunity to celebrate a shared understanding of Longs Peak, one built over time by climbers, the park, and publications such as Paul Nesbit's *Longs Peak: Its Story and a Climbing Guide* (in its ninth edition by 1990). In the discourse of the gatherings, Longs' meaning was familiar and gratifying: like Enos Mills and Roger Toll, speakers at the reunions characterized Longs as a place where generations of climbers tested themselves amid the glorious yet terrifying powers of nature. It was an alpine site for the most exalted recreational experiences and, occasionally, the scene of terrible fatalities. Longs brought out humans' capacity for athletic achievement, courage, problem solving, fellowship, and joyous wonderment, but it also made plain their susceptibility to accident and grave miscalculation. The mountain stirred women climbers to overstep societal conventions and inspired multiple generations of men to prove that society's faith in their ambition, audacity, and strength was well placed. Interestingly, in an era of growing awareness and debate about environmental harm and racial injustice, reunion participants did not acknowledge that climbers were being asked to reckon with their damage to rock surfaces, water, and plants on the beloved peak; nor did they notice that the history of recreational climbing on Longs was exclusively White or that Longs and other peaks in Rocky had been part of the sacred homeland of Utes and Arapahos who had been removed to reservations.[3]

Even as the reunions reaffirmed a familiar understanding of Longs and those who climbed it, Rocky was wrestling with demands for change, including on its famous fourteener. The park's founding legislation declared that "said tract is dedicated and set apart as a public park for the benefit and enjoyment of the people of the United States . . . with regulations being primarily aimed at the freest use of the said part for recreation purposes by the public and for the preservation of the natural conditions and scenic beauties thereof."[4] For decades, park superintendents assumed this legislation and the NPS Organic Act (1916) directed them to prioritize the public's enjoyment of Rocky, and they shaped natural resource management to visitors' interests and desires. The early laws remained in place, but by the 1960s and 1970s ecological scientists and environmental activists vocally opposed the laws' usual interpretation, insisting that the NPS place primary focus on ecological management and wilderness preservation. The Wilderness Act (1964), Administrative Policies for Natural Areas

(1968), National Environmental Policy Act (1969), and Clean Air Act (1970) reflected these concerns and, to varying degrees, established new environmental benchmarks and responsibilities for public lands.

In response to the new laws, Rocky outlined sweeping changes in environmental management in its 1976 *Master Plan*. The plan acknowledged that excessive hunting, resort development, mining, water diversion, and lumbering had compromised the ecological integrity of the park region even before Rocky was founded; ecological problems worsened over time as park managers allowed elk to overpopulate, suppressed fires, stocked nonnative fish, and otherwise tried to satisfy the interests and "contemporary comfort standards" of a rising tide of visitors. Recognizing the park's problematic history and obligation to chart a new course, the *Master Plan* committed Rocky to giving "major emphasis" to restoring "native ecosystems" and "the perpetuation of natural features in as near to pristine conditions as possible." Just a year later, UNESCO designated Rocky an International Biosphere Reserve possessing natural ecosystems of value for research, education, training, and sustainable resource use. The *Master Plan* and the park's recognition as a biosphere reserve marked a shift in managerial intentions. Yet, as we will see, neither of these developments spoke to the park's capacity to sustain the new intentions over time.[5]

So, too, the Civil Rights Act of 1964 and Executive Order 11478 (signed by President Nixon in 1969) obliged Rocky to make evident its commitment to diversity, equity, and inclusion. The 1964 law prohibited discrimination in public accommodations based on race, color, religion, or national origin. It similarly prohibited discrimination in employment, adding sex as a protected category. Nixon's executive order endorsed a proactive approach to workplace equality, requiring federal employers, including the National Park Service, to promote equal opportunity in the workplace "through a continuing affirmative action program."[6] Additionally, the National Historic Preservation Act (1966) and Archaeological Resources Protection Act (1979) deepened the NPS's obligation to recover, protect, and interpret historic and archaeological sites and objects, including those related to Native tribes and racial and ethnic minorities in the United States. The American Indian Religious Freedom Act (1978) recognized indigenous peoples' right of access to national parks and other public land for sacred and cultural ritual, and the Native American Graves Protection and Repatriation Act (1990) required the NPS to "inventory holdings of Native American human remains and funerary objects . . . and other cultural items" and consult and attempt to reach agreement with Native tribes "on the repatriation or other disposition of these remains and objects."[7]

Importantly, this evolving legal framework contradicted previously unquestioned values and practices at Rocky. The park derived inspiration and identity from White explorers, mountaineers, vacationers, and entrepreneurs of the late nineteenth and early twentieth centuries who set the stage for Rocky to become a "national playground" following the expulsion of the Arapaho and Ute tribes from the area. Since its founding, the park had attracted White middle-class visitors primed by privilege and culture to look for adventure in a natural setting presumably untamed and unoccupied. Rocky had not practiced formal segregation, but neither had it worked to attract or welcome people of color for visitation or sacred ritual, and its employees had always been White and mostly male. The new legal framework seemed to insist, however, that Rocky question its actions and beliefs, acknowledge the role of racial erasure and exclusion in its origin stories and development, and look for ways to revise its identity and pursue impartial inclusivity.

This chapter on Longs Peak and Rocky Mountain National Park between 1970 and 2000 shows that the park's founding mission and essential identity did not easily align with the new legal imperatives. Rocky made significant attempts to adapt to emerging ecological priorities, including on Longs, knowing that the park's future as a place of wilderness visitation and preservation was at stake. That said, entrenched patterns of management and inadequate resources limited change. Success in promoting multiracial democracy and inclusivity was even more modest, precisely because these goals were less intentionally and openly pursued. Still, as the park headed toward the twenty-first century, elements of a truly multidimensional ethic of care were emerging on Longs, at Rocky, and in leadership at the NPS.

Let's Climb!

As the 1970s began, technical climbers flocked to Longs Peak. Driven by ambition, remarkable innovations in technique and equipment, and their love of vertical nature, the most skilled among them sought to create new legends of daring and achievement on the mountain, surpassing those who had come before them. Within two decades they so brilliantly succeeded that Tom Hornbein felt compelled to tell his 1991 reunion audience, "People . . . are doing things now that those of us, as we went through our own generations, never dreamed could be done."[8]

Bill Forrest scored the first triumph of the 1970s when he completed a roped solo climb of the Diamond in July 1970, following the park's lifting of its ban on solo ascents.[9] Choosing a variation of the *Yellow Wall* that was named *Forrest Finish*, Forrest spent three days and two nights on the big wall, without the aid or camaraderie of companions. Though he enjoyed climbing with partners, Forrest thought "being alone in the mountain crucible can lend a vital, yet rational dimension to the sport. When soloing . . . using a hold, testing a piton, choosing the route—critical moves and decisions—become super-exciting and extremely meaningful." Moreover, solitude amplified Forrest's experience of the raw power and splendor of nature. During his first night on the Diamond, he slept in a small bivouac cave on Broadway. "Long before dawn, I was awakened by a terrible roar as an avalanche of rock cascaded down the North Chimney. Sparks shot through the darkness and the mountain seemed to groan and lurch, but my anchors held and the bottom didn't rip out of my hammock. I couldn't get back to sleep, and I hung in the chilly breeze waiting for the beautiful sunshine."

Of course, solo climbing heightened risk, and the following afternoon Forrest experienced severe anxiety as he encountered a badly cracked section of wall that seemed beyond his capabilities. It was only with great discipline that he summoned the calm and resolve needed to complete the ascent: "Thirty feet of easy nailing brought me to an evil crack—too wide to jam, too narrow to chimney. I cursed, prayed, chickened out and finally got on with it and struggled. I didn't dare lose my composure but it was awfully awkward. I fought and flailed. The crack took my best but once up it, I was glad it was there; it added zest to the route."[10]

Forrest's successful ascent inspired others to attempt solo climbs, this time on the right side of the Diamond, which was steeper than the left, with sections of overhung and chossy rock.[11] Because of its difficulty, the right side of the Diamond was still almost untouched, but Forrest's good friend Kris Walker, a nineteen-year-old, put up a right-side route in a roped solo climb in 1971, calling it *Waterhole #3* (Grade V, 5.8, A3). Two years later, Jim Beyer, only seventeen years old, put in *Sunshine* (Grade V, 5.7, A3) on a third solo climb. The flurry of solo activity on the right side of the Diamond prompted teams of climbers to venture onto the difficult rock surface, where they put up three more routes between 1971 and 1974. Renewing the quest for new routes on the left side of the Diamond, in 1974 Ron Olevsky and Bob Dodds put in *Pervertical Sanctuary*, which eventually became one of the wall's most popular climbs, with a rating of Grade IV, 5.8, A1.[12]

Dozens of other new routes went up on the Diamond in subsequent years. And many climbers eagerly tested themselves on routes established by others. Thus, Molly Higgins, Stephanie Atwood, and Laurie Manson completed the first all-female ascent of the Diamond's *D7* route in 1975. Men continued to dominate climbing, but talented White women made their mark on the sport across the United States as well as in Europe, reaching extraordinary levels of achievement and gaining well-deserved stature by the end of the century.[13]

The publication of Walter Fricke's *A Climber's Guide to the Rocky Mountain National Park Area* (1971) played a critical role in boosting technical climbers' interest in Longs and the other high peaks and low cliffs in Rocky. Fricke was a summer ranger in Rocky and an accomplished climber. He knew many of the climbing routes in the park and on Longs from firsthand experience, and he consulted extensively with other climbers to ensure the accuracy of his guidebook. Fricke made extensive use of park photographs, marking them to show the routes his text described. According to park staff, "With this text of previously unpublished climbs, RMNP climbing activity increased dramatically." Climber and author Jeff Achey confirmed this assessment, noting that Fricke's informative guide "transformed the scene," attracting climbers from across the country to Longs and Rocky's other mountains and cliffs. The park had reported 697 technical climbing attempts throughout Rocky in 1967, 270 of them on Longs. By 1977 there were 5,956 technical climbing attempts in the park, and in 1982 there were over 9,400. As park rangers wrote in 1983, "Where there was one climber back in 1967 there are now about 13."[14]

Admittedly, Longs and Rocky were not the only climbing attractions in Colorado. Eldorado Canyon near Boulder, the Black Canyon of the Gunnison, the Garden of the Gods in Colorado Springs, the San Juan Mountains near Telluride, and Colorado National Monument offered fantastically varied rock to ambitious climbers. Indeed, Longs Peak lost some allure relative to other sites after 1970, especially the North Chasm View Wall in the Black Canyon. Still, it was the nation's premier site for big-wall climbing in a true alpine setting.[15]

As technical climbers tested themselves on solo ascents and on the Diamond's overhung and chossy right side, they began to deliberately shift from direct aid climbing to free climbing. Until the 1970s most climbing on big walls in the United States, including the Diamond, had been accomplished with gear that served to both protect climbers and directly assist their movement upward. Climbers used rope threaded through bolts and pitons drilled or hammered into the rock, along with slings and stirrups attached to the ropes, for protection *and* as foot and handholds. Especially on featureless or badly fractured stretches of rock, they ascended the equipment rather than the rock itself. Direct aid worked well on big walls, but the gear was heavy and progress was slow. "Good style" on aid climbs in the 1960s "meant minimizing bolt placements and moving fast," but still, a climb on the Diamond typically took three days.[16]

In the "free" ascents of the 1970s, climbers challenged themselves to dispense with direct aid altogether. Instead, they looked for hand and footholds, however tiny, along the surface of the rock itself, using ropes and other gear only for protection. Free climbing required exceptional athletic ability and problem solving as well as newly designed sticky-soled climbing shoes and lightweight devices—chockstones and camming devices—that climbers placed in cracks, removed, and used again as they ascended a rock face. Climbers sought to carry as little equipment as possible and to move quickly, with the goal of completing a route on the Diamond in one day rather than three.[17]

After several teams made partial free ascents of the Diamond in the early 1970s, Wayne Goss and Jim Logan succeeded in free climbing most of *D7* in 1975, exiting at Table Ledge because of bad weather. Jim Dunn and Chris Wood followed just a week later, freeing a variation of the *Yellow Wall*. In 1977 John Bachar, a California climber known for his superbly confident free solos, freed the entire *D7*. Bachar returned to the Diamond with Billy Westbay in 1978, and the two men freed a version of *D1*. Roger Briggs and Jeff Achey freed the original *D1* route, put in by Rearick and Kamps, in 1980. Five years later Briggs and Dan Stone climbed the *King of Swords*, establishing the first free route on the Diamond with a difficulty grade of 5.12.[18]

As Bill Briggs (Roger's brother) explained at the 1991 reunion, *King of Swords* marked the start of a new era of "extreme free climbing," in which highly skilled climbers, often after multiple attempts, put in exceptionally difficult free routes. *Eroica*, another extreme free route, started on the *Casual* route but strayed from it quickly, going straight up a gray slab and into a corner that had never been climbed. Then, "the entire remainder of the route was entirely new. It just pieces its way up through a jungle of overhangs and flakes and inside corners . . . all the way to the top."[19]

"Sport climbing" also arrived on the Diamond, thanks to Alec Sharp, a British climber who moved to Boulder in 1977. Sport climbers roped from a summit *down* a rock face, inspected a potential route, and used power drills to install a permanent array of bolts that roped climbers might clip into as they ascended. The goal was to put up safe but fantastically challenging free routes, and sport climbing quickly gained popularity in Colorado. On Longs in the 1980s, sport climbers focused on the difficult right side of the Diamond, affixing routes with permanent protection.[20]

As technical climbers innovated new routes and methods on Longs, recreationists without technical skills were also showing keen interest in the peak. In 1975 nearly 11,198 climbers attempted to summit Longs, 9,393 of them on the *Keyhole* route.[21] Few of these climbers would have consulted Fricke's guide, since it focused on technical routes, but they may well have been inspired by other publications celebrating Longs Peak and Colorado's other fourteeners. Three years after J. Powell publicized "the cult of the fourteener" in *Summit* magazine in 1967, Perry Eberhart and Philip Schmuck published *The Fourteeners: Colorado's Great Mountains*, a coffee-table book filled with beautiful photographs, descriptions of Colorado's highest peaks, and text that encouraged readers to seek "closer communion" with these "miracles" of nature. Walter Borneman and Lyndon Lampert facilitated peak bagging with *A Climbing Guide to Colorado's Fourteeners*, published in 1978. Filled with essential information on nontechnical routes and conditions at each of Colorado's fourteeners, *A Climbing Guide* helped make summiting all the high mountains—a "Grand Slam"—an exciting and attainable goal.[22]

Whether they ascended the East Face, Diamond, or *Keyhole* route, the thousands of climbers chasing legends on Longs provoked a mix of admiration and concern among park rangers. Some of their concerns were very familiar, about climbers' risk of bodily harm. Accidents and injuries among climbers occurred frequently; even a relatively minor ankle sprain could become life threatening in an alpine setting where violent storms and lightning developed with little warning. Search and rescue missions were more necessary than ever as climbing gained in popularity, making heavy demands on park labor, volunteers, and equipment. Other concerns were newer, shaped by emerging environmental obligations. Rangers from the 1970s to the 1990s could readily see that the large numbers of climbers on Longs were eroding trails, harming fragile alpine plants, leaving trash and human waste on the mountain, and irreparably damaging granite surfaces. They were also crowding one another and diminishing access to wilderness solitude. For a park trying to preserve "pristine" conditions and facilitate climbers' safety and enjoyment in wild nature, conditions on Long were worrisome. The press of climbers on Longs threatened the peak and its celebrated status.[23]

Preserving Wilderness and the Wilderness Experience on Longs

Rangers responded to the problematic scene on Longs Peak in the 1970s, 1980s, and 1990s with varied strategies, some time honored, others new. Though they did not want to undercut Longs' reputation as a place for legendary encounters with a vertical wilderness, rangers were eager to reduce human injury and harm to the environment. The park had long displaced considerable responsibility for safety onto climbers themselves, and rangers deliberately built on this tradition, offering public lectures to educate climbers about preparedness and decision-making in hazardous alpine settings. More than ever, park brochures stressed Longs' dangers—especially for those with little mountaineering experience— rather than the awe and beauty awaiting alpine recreationists. When funding allowed, the park added rangers to its summer staff to monitor climbers and encourage those of limited skill to choose routes that matched their capabilities. Additionally, Rocky invested in advanced search and rescue training and new equipment, and rangers carefully evaluated the causes of climbing accidents on Longs as well as the efficacy of search and rescue missions. Some of their evaluations appeared in the American Alpine Club's annual report, *Accidents in North American Mountaineering*, for the edification of rangers and climbers across the United States. As in decades past, the Colorado Mountain Club supplemented park efforts by continuing to organize both climbing trips and technical climbing courses. The park also leaned on the expertise of the Colorado Mountain School, an Estes Park entity founded in 1981 that offered professional mountain guiding and courses in mountaineering, technical climbing, and avalanche safety.[24]

Adapting climbing management to increased visitor use was not without problems, however. Especially in the 1990s when budget cuts constrained hiring and innovation, Jim Detterline and other rangers wrangled with park managers over the climbing expertise required of rangers, the chain of command among park personnel, appointments to search and rescue teams, the presence of unpermitted commercial guides on Longs, and rangers' law enforcement duties. Moreover, despite the park's focus on safety, fatalities on Longs continued to occur—there were seventeen fatalities on the peak between 1961 and 1980 and eighteen between 1980 and 2000. Still, given the rising estimated number of climbers on Longs (over ten thousand annually by 1985, twenty thousand by 1994, and nearly thirty-five thousand by 2000), the rate of fatalities was diminishing over time.[25]

Rocky's response to environmental degradation on Longs reflected both its determination to gain wilderness status for nearly all its acreage under the 1964

Wilderness Act and its belief that doing so would require backcountry visitors' investment in good environmental stewardship.[26] Fortunately, the CMC vigorously promoted environmental conservation to its members and the larger public throughout the latter decades of the twentieth century, as did many other environmental organizations at the state and national level. So, too, in the 1970s nationally renowned climbers Yvon Chouinard and Tom Frost became vocal proponents of "free and clean" climbing, using publications such as the *1972 Chouinard Catalog* to dispense ethical values to a far-flung audience. In 1970 Warren Harding and Dean Caldwell had drilled three hundred holes for bolts and "bat hooks" while putting up a new aid route on El Capitan's Dawn Wall in Yosemite, bitterly dividing climbers, and Chouinard and Frost's *1972 Catalog* sought to clarify the stakes of the debate. Declaring that "mountains are finite, and despite their massive appearance, they are fragile," they urged climbers to stay off routes they did not intend to finish, abandon the use of direct aid on free routes, use chocks rather than pitons, and dispense with bolting. The men warned, too, against a "moral deterioration," whereby "advanced gadgetry" threatened to undermine genuine adventure and climbers' "appreciation of the mountain environment itself." They asked climbers to "re-examine your motives for climbing," to "employ restraint and good judgment," and to "remember the rock, the other climber." Chouinard and Frost urged ambitious climbers to consider how, in pursuing legendary achievements, they might do permanent environmental harm. They exhorted climbers to become citizens in nature, to balance their rightful pursuit of vertical adventure with their obligations to preserve rock walls for other climbers, present and future.[27]

Rangers in Rocky welcomed "free and clean" climbing, with Walter Fricke declaring in *A Climber's Guide*, "Ninety-five percent of all leads in Rocky Mountain National Park can be protected perfectly adequately with natural anchors, nuts, or pitons. Climbers ascending frequently climbed routes simply have no excuse for bringing a bolt kit along, much less for using it. Leave the damn bolts at home."[28] It should not be surprising, however, that the "free and clean" climbing ethic had a limited impact on Longs Peak. Direct aid climbing did not entirely disappear, and even committed free climbers may have had a relatively narrow understanding of their environmental impact. Chouinard and Frost recognized that "alpine tundra, meadows, trees, lakes and streams are all endangered," but the men admitted that their "primary concern" was "with deterioration of the rock itself." A few climbers were thinking in broader environmental terms, but they seemed to be a minority. Chris Landry, following a mixed ascent on Longs' *Yellow Wall* in 1972, decried technical climbers' egotism and obsession with the latest gear, as well as their habit of leaving all sorts of "junk" on the beautiful peak. To Landry, climbers were depressingly unaware of the varied ways in which they degraded mountain environments.[29]

To complicate matters, "sport climbing" competed unambiguously with "free and clean" methods and values. In the 1980s the "merely vertical" left side of the

Diamond remained in the hands of free climbers using removable protection, but sport climbers sought to claim the more difficult right side as their own, affixing "piton ladders" and bolt-intensive routes. According to Jeff Achey, "The overhanging Right Side was like a different wall, off limits to free climbers." Roger Briggs and Dan Stone challenged this binary by free climbing the *King of Swords* to the right of *D1* in 1985. But they could not stop climbers on Longs Peak and elsewhere in Colorado from "warring over the use of bolts to protect new free climbs. . . . The furor that arose over rappel bolting—in Colorado and elsewhere—would be hard to overstate."[30] To "free and clean" climbers, sport climbers seemed oblivious to environmental concerns, and their reliance on top-down inspection and bolt placement produced a fraudulent form of climbing. To sport climbing enthusiasts, free climbers (by this time often referred to as "trad" or "traditional" climbers) seemed sanctimonious and without ambition.

Recognizing climbers' limited investment in clean climbing, the park's backcountry and climbing rangers stepped up efforts to evaluate environmental conditions in climbing areas and develop new management practices and regulations as necessary. On Longs Peak rangers initially focused their attention on bivouac sites on Broadway (the ledge traversing the Diamond) and backcountry campsites in the Boulderfield and Jim's Grove, where climbers spent many hours resting and preparing for climbs. Finding evidence that both natural resources and climbers' wilderness experience were being degraded by overuse and heavy accumulations of trash and human waste, the park began as early as 1971 to require climbers planning to bivouac or camp in the backcountry to register with rangers. This was a small first step toward gathering information about the level and impact of overnight use at bivouac and camping sites on Longs and other popular climbing sites.[31]

Rangers also reevaluated the presence of the cables on Longs' North Face. In 1967 rangers had expressed concerns about the *Cable* route primarily in terms of safety, but by 1973 their focus had shifted to the cables' violation of wilderness values. Park managers ordered the removal of the *Cable* route in July 1973, hoping to bring the peak into closer compliance with new wilderness standards and give nontechnical climbers an authentic wilderness experience. In a memo to the park's East District ranger written on July 4, 1973, Walter Fricke noted that there was widespread agreement among rangers that the cables should come out, "the major reason for removal" being the "wilderness requirement." "Safety and discouragement of overcrowding" were "accompanying side effects."[32] Rangers took the cables down from the North Face on a snowy July 20, 1973, four days after the park issued a press release notifying the public of its intended action. The press release explained that the cables were being removed "on an experimental basis," apparently so the park could evaluate the public's response. The removal of the *Cable* route was "in keeping with the purpose and intent of the national parks—to manage them in as near their natural condition as possible." The cables had offered artificial aid, allowing people without experience or skill to attempt a climb far beyond their abilities. With the cables removed and the North Face reverting to a technical climb, people would be "meeting Longs Peak on its own terms." The Wilderness Act of 1964 supplied "added emphasis for the removal of the cables" because Longs Peak could not be considered for wilderness status as long as the cables remained. They were a human-made contrivance, not permissible in wilderness areas.[33] In supplementary actions, rangers removed "telephone lines and poles, great amounts of old trash, and other evidence of earlier man-made facilities to partially restore the naturalness of Longs Peak."[34]

To the park's relief, public response to the removal of the *Cable* route was overwhelmingly favorable. In a report written for the park's superintendent, Roger Contor, Walter Fricke declared: "It is my conclusion from a summer of close contact with Longs Peak users in the Ranger Station and on the trail that removal of the cables has met with overwhelming public acceptance (if not applause)." Formal petitions and letters favoring removal arrived in the park from the American Alpine Club, the Colorado Mountain Club, and the Colorado State University Mountaineering Club. As of March 1974, eight months after the cables had been removed, 384 individuals had contacted the park to applaud the decision; just 32 favored replacing the cables on the peak.[35]

Still, those who believed the park had erred in the cables' removal made it clear that rangers could not count on climbers being of one mind about access, safety, or wilderness values on Longs. Climber Norman Nesbit wrote a five-page letter in opposition to the removal of the cables, arguing that "abolishing the Cable Route seriously diminishes the value of the layman's climbing experience on Longs Peak." Similarly, other critics noted that the cables offered individuals of limited strength and endurance a way to reach Longs' summit and enjoy its sublime views. By removing the cables, the park was reducing access to the peak and, in the words of one writer, "penalizing those who are older or for other reasons do not have top physical ability." Some argued that the *Keyhole* route was also dangerous when crowded; the park was merely moving its safety problem from one route on the peak to another. Still others thought the park's real motive in removing the cables was to lessen visitation on Longs altogether. Bill Gingles, director of the Rocky Ridge Music Center at the foot of the peak, said about a meeting he had with Superintendent Roger Contor and Ranger Walter Fricke, "One thing I learned from this meeting was that the Park Service is definitely trying to discourage people from doing the Longs Peak climb." Finally, some letter writers disagreed with the park's interpretation of wilderness standards. As one writer declared: "Any argument that Long's Peak is a potential 'wilderness area' is ridiculous and founded on ignorance; historically and traditionally it has been a high-use playground area, and this will continue due to its location and fame. Only if one succeeds in cutting its use to about 1/100th of the present traffic can one imagine any 'wilderness.'"[36]

Critics who thought removal of the cables would do nothing to resolve overcrowding on Longs quickly proved themselves right. With the cables gone, nontechnical climbers shifted entirely to the *Keyhole* route, and their numbers continued to build. In 1974 a total of 5,845 climbers used the *Keyhole* route to summit Longs, considerably more than the 2,540 who had summitted via the *Cable* and *Keyhole* routes combined in 1971. In 1975, 9,393 climbers signed trail-head registers indicating their intention to summit Longs via the *Keyhole* route; an estimated 7,044 succeeded.[37] Growing traffic on the peak quickly became an urgent issue, as park managers admitted that Longs' status as a "high-use playground" did not align with obligations to preserve the peak as a wilderness area "untrammeled by man" with "outstanding opportunities for solitude."[38]

As we saw in chapter 6, park managers had requested an initial investigation of Rocky's "carrying capacity" in 1969, and they returned to this unresolved issue in the mid-1970s, asking whether there might be a maximum number of people that wilderness areas could accommodate before the environment and visitors' experiences were harmed. Other national parks were similarly inquiring into carrying capacity, as were some devoted wilderness climbers. Chris Landry, for example, coupled an account of climbing Longs' *Yellow Wall* with a plea to mountaineering equipment manufacturers, urging them to correlate the growth of their industry to emerging studies on the carrying capacity of America's wild lands. In his view, the mountaineering industry ought to aim for a "ceiling of consumption" based on "per person impact ratios."[39]

Responding to Rocky's renewed interest in carrying capacity, Richard Trahan, a faculty member at the University of Northern Colorado, led a survey team during the summer of 1976 that tried to assess the impact of rising visitation numbers on the quality of visitors' experience. Trahan found that "since 1968, the visitation rate has tripled in Rocky and the park has lost ten park-wide positions. The staff must deal with over one-half million day hikers per summer and they have faced a 700 percent increase in backcountry use since 1965." Team members queried visitors at six locations in the park, with one site on the East Longs Peak Trail, just above the junction with the Eugenia Mine Trail. There, climbers descending the peak were invited to answer questions about their experience and views on backcountry use. Of the 156 people interviewed by Trahan's study team on the East Longs Peak Trail, more than 60 percent were repeat visitors with considerable backcountry experience. Nearly 36 percent of the climbers had gone to the summit of Longs, and 30 percent had been to Chasm Lake, the remainder having been to intermediate destinations such as the Boulderfield or the Keyhole.[40]

Overall, nearly 80 percent of survey respondents reported that park trails were too crowded. On Longs, 48 percent of respondents expressed concern about high trail usage. Trahan learned that there were often crowds at the East Longs trailhead parking lot, crowding and safety hazards in the Trough, and congestion on the summit. Both backcountry and front-country visitors queried in the Trahan study accepted the concept of day-use limitations, especially to protect environmentally sensitive areas, yet most far preferred signage steering them away from heavily used trails or "first come, first served" measures over lottery, reservation, or ticketing systems. Park employees surveyed in the study also expressed concern about heavy visitor use in Rocky, but they were quite skeptical about day-use limitations, fearing complaints from visitors. Given visitors' dislike of overt restrictions, and park employees' uneasiness, Trahan recommended that Rocky rely on discreet methods, such as trail signs or small parking lots, to control visitor numbers at specific sites. The East Longs trailhead parking lot accommodated seventy-five vehicles in 1976; it already served, albeit imperfectly, to limit visitors on Longs. Trahan did not speak to the possibility of reducing its size.[41]

While Trahan focused on harm to the visitor experience on Longs, a second study in the mid-1970s explored technical climbers' harm to the flora on Longs' East Face. Milton "Chip" Salaun, a local climber and independent ecologist, did not use the term "carrying capacity" in his communication with park officials, yet he was clearly concerned that aid and free climbers on the East Face were surpassing plants' capacity to withstand disruption. Salaun began his study of Longs Peak flora in the early 1970s and extended it into the summers of 1976 and 1977, gathering scientific evidence about ecological harm that could be used to instruct climbers and improve management on Longs. Explaining his objectives to park authorities, Salaun stated: "With the recent upsurge in climbing activity on all the high alpine walls in the park it is of utmost importance to educate climbers concerning their impact on these ecosystems and of equal importance to the R.M.N.P. administration to be informed on what has happened or is liable to happen to this unique concatenation of ecosystems within their protectorate."[42]

Salaun discovered on the East Face plants "of some 15+ families living in compacted micro-ecosystems" including buttercups, mustards, stonecrops, saxifrage, roses, pea clovers, parsnips, primroses, and phlox. None had previously been known to live above twelve thousand feet. And climbing was having an adverse impact on the plants, with "severe damage to 100% . . . evident in some areas of climbing activity."[43] Quickly, he produced two magazine articles for climbers, informing them of his findings and exhorting them to evaluate and alter their practices. The first article appeared in the June 1976 issue of *Off Belay*, titled "A Hole in the Clean Climbing Philosophy," and the second, "The Diamond—a Different Perspective" appeared in the May–June 1978 issue of *Climbing*. Salaun admonished climbers to cease their practice of "gardening" the cracks on Longs Peak—that is, removing plants, soil, and organic matter to create a cleaner surface for hand and footholds or protection. For those who knew little about alpine flora, Salaun informed them, "Cleaning a crack is more than just temporarily easing the conditions for your own ephemeral passage. For all practical purposes, once it is done it will be forever."[44] Salaun also urged climbers to consider the impacts of littering, of leaving something as organic and innocent as a bit of orange peel on a rocky ledge. "Opaque and fairly dense in a land where no animals will eat it, where microorganisms, moisture and oxygen are scarce, it will remain intact for many years. If it lodges above an alpine plant it can kill that plant or portion of it in a season or two by depriving it of sunlight for photosynthesis and warmth."[45]

"Gardening" and littering might result from carelessness or ignorance, but Salaun also blamed the "human games" that climbers played on the Diamond. Climbers with large egos often took far more risk on the Diamond than they should; to save themselves from accident and injury they ended up using excessive protection and aggressively stripping plants from cracks in the rock. And climbers who tried to prove their superiority through a "free and clean" ascent sometimes did more harm than those using direct aid. "It might . . . be preferable," Salaun argued, "to drive an occasional piton or even a bolt than to kill off the area just to hang an environmentally 'clean' nut."[46] For Salaun the bottom line was that climbers had an obligation to be aware of "all the dimensions of our surroundings," and they had to assiduously protect both the Diamond's rare plants and its prized rock surfaces.[47] He revealed the environmental contradictions in free climbers' advocacy of clean climbing and tried to offer all technical climbers a primer on how to be authentically clean.

The Trahan and Salaun studies took place against the backdrop of an intense debate among wilderness advocates all around the country about recreationists' presence in the backcountry. In an era of tremendous growth in mountain recreation, some advocates in the Wilderness Society and Sierra Club endorsed the premises of carrying capacity studies and urged public land managers to limit visitor access to backcountry sites and climbing areas showing evidence of environmental damage. According to historian James Morton Turner, this position rather quickly lost out to a "new wilderness recreation ethic—minimal-impact camping—that promised to prop the doors to wilderness wide open for a better-educated wilderness visitor."[48] The new minimal-impact wilderness ethic, eventually popularized by the term "leave no trace," was formally endorsed by the U.S. Forest Service, National Park Service, and Bureau of Land Management in the 1980s, as well as by the National Outdoor Leadership School, the Wilderness Society, the Sierra Club, and the Access Fund, a climbing organization established in 1991 to defend access to climbing areas and promote constructive communication between public land managers and the climbing community on issues of regulation and access. So, too, the CMC favored continued emphasis on education in conservation and minimal-impact ethics.[49]

Campers and climbers who adopted minimal-impact ethics used lightweight gas stoves, tents, and sleeping bags. They abandoned older practices of "woodcraft," whereby overnight backcountry visitors gathered firewood to cook food and stay warm and collected tree boughs and other natural resources to build primitive shelters and beds. Skill in buying and using technical equipment produced in modern factories replaced skill in using and exploiting the resources of the wild. Minimal-impact practitioners packed out trash and human waste, anticipated and adapted to adverse conditions, and left all artifacts and natural resources as they found them. Certainly, climbers and others who adopted the new environmental ethics helped protect the immediate areas in which they recreated. At the same time, however, their dependence on equipment produced in factories that used petroleum for fuel and as a product ingredient was deeply problematic. Indeed, according to Gregory Simon and Peter Alagona, "Beginning in the 1970s, high technology consumer goods, composed mainly of synthetic materials derived from petroleum, came to mediate almost every aspect of the American wilderness experience. GORE-TEX jackets, Vibram rubber soles, foam sleeping pads, nylon tents, portable cooking stoves, and hand-held water purification devices proliferated as the market for camping products exploded, and as firms cultivated new consumer needs through technological advancements and marketing."[50]

Despite the contradictions embedded in the minimal-impact campaign, it encouraged rangers to view visitors as malleable, capable of altering their thinking and conduct to protect wilderness ecosystems and their own experience of the wild. Even so, Rocky never intended to "prop the doors to wilderness wide open" to educated visitors.[51] While the park rejected numerical limits on its millions of day-use visitors, it placed numerical restrictions on overnight backcountry users and front-country campground users and otherwise broadly incorporated concepts of carrying capacity into its 1976 *Master Plan*. The NPS defined visitor carrying capacity as "the type and level of visitor use that can be accommodated while sustaining acceptable resource and social conditions that complement the purpose of a park." In Rocky this definition underlay the park's reliance on channeling and zoning to manage visitors in the environmental era. Rocky's 1976 *Master Plan* stated that "the key to controlling man's impact is to channel use through facilities designed and grouped to insulate the resources." The 1978 National Parks and Recreation Act endorsed such planning and required all national parks to address carrying capacity in general management plans.[52]

Channeling visitors through roads and trails had always been a tool of park management, though perceptions of its value changed over time. In the 1930s, the park channeled visitors onto Trail Ridge Road to give them a superior aesthetic experience. During Mission 66, Rocky and the NPS used channeling to move people and cars efficiently through crowded front-country corridors and thereby protect the visitor experience. Protecting the wilderness from visitor impact was a secondary consideration. Now, as Rocky prioritized ecological preservation and pursued wilderness status, it identified channeling throughout the park—in the wilderness backcountry zone as well as the more developed front country—as the best way to acknowledge the park's carrying capacity and keep its "natural features in as near to pristine conditions as possible."[53] The successful channeling of front-country visitors would require public transportation, keeping walkers and horseback riders on formal roadside trails, building new picnic areas, and establishing wildlife viewing areas for visitors' use. Car campers would continue to be allowed only limited periods of stay at roadside campgrounds. In backcountry wilderness areas, channeling would mean keeping climbers and hikers on designated trails, such as Longs' East and North trails, and off fragile alpine tundra. Those who intended to camp or bivouac overnight would face both channeling and numerical restrictions, in the form of limited backcountry campsite availability and limitations on size of party and length of stay. As Trahan pointed out, signage pointing users to lightly used trails and parking lots of limited size could also become effective channeling techniques. Environmental education and monitoring by rangers would supplement all efforts to manage visitors, whether in front-country or backcountry settings.[54]

All of these tools—channeling and zoning, overnight restrictions, environmental education, and park monitoring—were built into a succession of plans, regulations, and decisions regarding climbing and backcountry use. The first was the 1975 *Backcountry Management Plan*, approved as the *Master Plan* underwent final review. Guided by emerging scientific knowledge about the park's distinct ecosystems and their relative fragility, the 1975 plan established goals and methods for improving trail maintenance and reconstruction, reducing conflict between horseback riders and hikers, and limiting the "short-cutting" that seriously eroded fragile soil and plant life. All of these were worrisome issues on Longs Peak. The plan identified "loop trail construction" as a promising way "to minimize wilderness encounters" among backcountry users and required advance registration for backcountry camping and bivouacking at climbing sites. It established limits on the size of camping and bivouac parties and the number of nights to be spent in the park, restricted most camping to designated sites, prohibited wood fires on bivouac, regulated the use of firewood at other campsites, and regulated where and how to dispose of human waste and use soaps and detergents. The plan also called for the installation of vault toilets, to be evacuated by helicopter, "at high density use areas such as Longs Peak."[55]

The 1975 *Backcountry Management Plan* expanded backcountry rangers' responsibilities, tasking them with evaluating the condition of the backcountry and preventing it from being "changed ecologically by human use." They were to remove litter, repair water bars, fix signs, eradicate illegal campfires, keep trails clear, and clean campsite pit toilets. And they were to spend time speaking with visitors to encourage their investment in environmental stewardship. Rangers on patrol were expected to be "friendly and helpful in nature, with the primary objective being education and *prevention* of possible violations. . . . A useful tactic is to offer some form of helpful information; this almost always establishes the friendly rapport that we seek." Helpful information might cover how to wash dishes, clean fish, and dispose of trash, garbage, and human waste at a designated campsite. "Let the novice know that the days of 'burn, bash, and bury' were outdated over a decade ago." When necessary, rangers were expected to issue written citations to visitors who violated park regulations.[56] Given rangers' sizable responsibilities, park officials increased the budget allotment going to backcountry management and recommended that Rocky Mountain National Park try to obtain funding to increase the number of backcountry rangers. Managers established a new training program for backcountry rangers and prepared a series of new handouts for backcountry visitors about minimal-impact backcountry ethics and the park's new regulations.[57]

Rangers also spoke with climbers in settings outside the park, hoping to gain their support for new backcountry policies. In March 1976, for example, rangers met with local conservation groups and climbers to discuss climber congestion and trash on Longs Peak, especially on Broadway, along with "technical climbing regulations and bivouac policies." According to rangers who attended the meeting, there had been considerable concern among park staff about "a general state of apathy for regulation compliance among the climbing community," yet the meeting went well. Climbers accepted the park's proposals "to designate specific routes for bivouacs," to implement an "up at dusk, down at dawn policy," and to prohibit nonclimbing members of climbing parties from staying overnight at bivouac sites, including Broadway.[58] Rangers met with climbers again in January 1978 to discuss bivouac regulations and climbers' ongoing competition for bivouac sites on the East Face of Longs Peak. And in 1979 climbers met with rangers in Boulder to continue discussion of bivouac policies and hear Chip Salaun give a presentation on fragile plant communities on the Diamond. The rangers in attendance reported climbers' support for both bivouac limits and more education on the Diamond's plant ecology.[59]

As the park continued to evaluate backcountry conditions, it refined and fortified its regulations and restrictions. A 1979 case study of the cirque drainage below Longs' East Face bivouac sites found that human waste was contaminating water at Chasm Lake's inlet and outlet and in the stream of a nearby alpine meadow.[60] This and other evidence prompted rangers to recommend tighter restrictions on bivouac use (subsequently included in the 1984 *Backcountry Management Plan*):

> Agree that all bivouacs will be off vegetation, sites need only be large enough for one person, relatively flat, adequate drainage, 100 feet from water, clear of rock fall, that little consideration is given protection from weather, no tents, stoves only, pack out trash, human waste buried 4–6 inches 100' from water or more, evidence of bivouac up no earlier than dusk—down no later than dawn, actual climbers only, no pets. Also recommended is limiting climbing party size to 4 people.[61]

So, too, rangers found that efforts to keep visitors on formal trails had not ended climbers' or horseback riders' use of a shortcut through Jim's Grove on their way to the Boulderfield. "A plethora of use trails have been imprinted on the tundra, and trail braiding on the two steep sections of the trail has become a critical problem." And people who camped at the grove badly damaged soil and fragile alpine plants whose regeneration was "painfully slow." Rocky announced a prohibition on travel by horses through the grove in its 1982 *Trails Plan*. Two years later the park closed Jim's Grove to camping because of overcrowding and erosion, though it still allowed hikers to use the "single trail transecting its center." Rangers eventually removed signs leading to the grove to discourage human traffic altogether.[62]

Vault privies on Longs were yet another issue of growing concern. The vault privies in use since 1975 were subjected to heavy use, and the helicopters that removed the full vaults were expensive to use and very noisy. Also, as the vaults were carried away by helicopter, they dangled on 100-foot-long cables and occasionally spilled human waste. In 1978 a helicopter crashed at Granite Pass, depositing waste over the mountain landscape. Fortunately, a sustainable solution was at hand. In 1984 rangers replaced the vault privies at Chasm Junction and the Boulderfield with solar toilets. The new toilets were dehydrating, and burros or llamas could be brought in occasionally to haul out dried waste.[63]

Even as Rocky's backcountry rangers responded diligently to problems of bivouacking, shortcutting, and waste management on Longs, they grew concerned about other unregulated climbing impacts on the environment. In 1989 Rocky established a Climbing Task Force to evaluate climbing's continuing impact on the "limited areas suitable for the sport," hoping to "provide a long-term perspective and . . . the necessary planning . . . for park policies" that would prevent "serious degradation of natural resources and a reduced quality of visitor experience."[64] By this time at least ten thousand climbers were attempting to summit Longs each year, with thousands of others going to intermediate destinations on the peak. The park's other peaks and cliffs also drew thousands of climbers annually.[65]

Issuing its findings in a 1990 report, the Climbing Task Force offered an overview of climbing history in the park, evidence and analysis of climbers' impact on the park's resources and one another, and recommendations for a climbing management plan. The report focused entirely on technical climbers, highlighting this group's increased interest in Rocky during the 1970s and the development of "nondestructive" protective devices and clean climbing ethics. It noted as well the advent of sport climbing in the 1980s, which brought climbers with portable power drills and bolts into the park. Many of these climbers had trained extensively on artificial climbing walls and had reached "extreme levels" of skill. They were ready to "surpass the earlier standards of difficulty" and were interested in "previously unclimbed blank rock faces." Using power drills, the new generation of climbers put up bolted routes on "remote high peaks" and in "accessible day-use climbing areas" in the park. Members of the task force acknowledged with understated tact the conflict between clean climbers and sport climbers that ensued: "In the 1980's 'ethics' or the manner in which a route is constructed and ascended, became topical. . . . Climbers often find themselves at philosophical odds with each other. This had occasionally led to confrontation or sabotage of routes."[66]

Rather than take sides in the dispute between trad and sport climbers, members of the task force let science be their guide. Researchers sent out into the field documented climbers' varied environmental harms. They found that climbers disrupted wildlife—especially the raptors nesting at Lumpy Ridge—while moving over rock walls and ledges and "stressed or displaced" other wildlife. At every climbing site, especially heavily used Longs and Lumpy Ridge, climbers' trash accumulated at the base of climbs and on bivouac sites. Exposed human waste presented health hazards to humans and wildlife while degrading nearby water sources. Climbers who bushwhacked to the base of cliffs produced serious "soil loss, trenching, and loss of vegetation," and those who "gardened" vegetation by hand or used brushes to "scrub away loose debris" on rock faces destroyed fragile plant life. Climbers' chalk "accumulate[d] over time," with the potential to adversely affect lichen, moss, and rock. And climbers who "chisel[ed] the rock when natural holds [were] not available" or drilled holes and filled them with epoxy and bolts permanently damaged precious granite surfaces.[67]

Finally, climbers produced noise and visual impacts. Their power drills, audible to other climbers, hikers, and wildlife, "can be considered intrusive in a wilderness setting." They shouted to one another across wide distances, sometimes played loud music on portable audio devices, and created a visual disturbance on the rock. "Bright colored slings, shiny bolts or pitons, white chalk, and the very sight of climbers and ropes on an otherwise undisturbed rock formation can all be viewed as intrusive. The sight of people, shiny metal, or cloth material swaying in the wind could cause some wildlife, such as raptors, to shy away from perches or affect nesting behavior."[68]

Task force members knew that technical climbers in many parts of the country faced loss of access to climbing areas because land managers had decided they could tolerate neither the degrading impact of climbers on the natural resources in public parks and forests nor their problematic interactions with one another. They hoped to steer Rocky Mountain National Park away from this solution. The task force did not recommend new strategies; rather, it doubled down on the varied methods already in use, calling for further research on climber impact, the construction of new approach trails to popular climbing sites, limited regulation, and a "rigorous information and education campaign" designed to produce "cooperation through ethics." The task force outlined a proposed system of ethics comprising "clean climbing" and "leave no trace" principles, including "[accepting] responsibility for yourself and others." It recommended only one new restriction, a prohibition on the use of motorized drills. That recommendation immediately became a park-wide regulation. By 1992 the park was also temporarily closing climbing areas "to protect nesting raptors and raptor habitat."[69]

Clearly, the task force hoped that climbers exposed to instruction and ethics would respect the concepts of carrying capacity and channeling and stay on trails, refrain from shouting, pack out trash, and desist from "gardening" rock. Unfortunately, the park was unable to follow all its recommendations. Rocky was chronically understaffed in the 1990s, suffering the loss of seventy-five seasonal positions between 1986 and 1992, and it could ill afford to implement new and potentially costly science- and education-based management initiatives. Park managers tried hard to place rangers on Longs, but there were fewer of them on the peak in the 1990s than there had been in the 1970s. Fortunately, most climbers had become day users, tackling Longs in a single long day whether on the *Keyhole* route or the Diamond, and problems associated with bivouacking and camping appeared to be declining over time.[70]

Meanwhile, the number of climbers on the peak continued upward. A 1994 park study estimated that "an average of 20,000 people venture up Longs Peak" between June and September. And a 2002 study using infrared trail monitors on Longs concluded that approximately 35,000 visitors hiked the East Longs Peak Trail between May 30 and October 14, with an estimated 9,600 reaching the summit via the *Keyhole* route. The 2002 figures were probably a reasonable estimate for the late 1990s.[71]

Former ranger Jane Gordon recalled that when she worked on Longs Peak in the mid-1990s, during the summer months "there was *no* time when there was no one on the trail, the main trail, any hour of the day." And on technical routes on the Diamond, "on a nice day, you're in line for routes up there. . . . On the Casual Route, you'll see parties stopped having to set up intermediate belays because they're all piling up on top of one another."[72] The limited number of rangers on Longs could not possibly provide close monitoring of climber safety; nor could they thoughtfully educate more than a few climbers on environmental issues. If climbers were gaining exposure to leave-no-trace ethics or had a good understanding of climbing regulations and safe climbing protocols, it was not through interaction with backcountry staff. Rocky made significant advances between 1970 and 2000 in devising ecologically sensitive backcountry management plans, but the park lacked the resources to implement these plans fully.

Ecological Imperatives in Context

Challenges to ecological management on Longs occurred against the backdrop of environmental difficulties throughout Rocky and the NPS. Reducing ecological disturbance and restoring ecosystem health became an avowed NPS priority in the 1960s and 1970s, but the NPS's 1980 *State of the Parks Report* found inadequate research and monitoring of at least 75 percent of "threats" to the environment across the park system, whether from external sources such as industrial emissions, or from internal sources such as overabundant elk, invasive species, and high visitor use. Seven years later, the U.S. General Accounting Office found documentation, monitoring, and protection of resources still insufficient across the NPS, despite increases in resource management funding from 1980 to 1984.[73] Again, in the early 1990s, both the National Academy of Sciences and the National Parks Conservation Association criticized the national parks for their persistent failure to use sound scientific research and ecological principles as the basis for management plans and decisions. Most park managers seemed reluctant to put preservation values ahead of the public's immediate interest in accessing sites of scenic beauty, and most visitors still behaved like "recreational tourists at a theme park."[74]

NPS historian Richard Sellars contends that park superintendents deserved particular criticism for their misreading of A. Starker Leopold's influential 1963 report, *Wildlife Management in the National Parks*, interpreting it in aesthetic rather than ecological terms. Leopold stated, "As a primary goal, we would recommend that the biotic associations within each park be maintained, or where necessary recreated, as nearly as possible in the condition that prevailed when the area was first visited by the white man. A national park should represent a vignette of primitive America." He also said that "a reasonable illusion of primitive America" would require "using the utmost in skill, judgment, and ecologic sensitivity." Leopold was speaking of a primitive "vignette" in both visual and scientific terms, but park superintendents versed in scenic management and visitor satisfaction read Leopold as though he were speaking only about aesthetic values. And so, over numerous decades, superintendents distorted Leopold's intentions and pushed aside ecological recommendations to cull elk and other animals, allow the controlled use of fire, reduce pesticide use, and control invasive and exotic species.[75]

It did not help, of course, that the NPS suffered from inadequate funding for scientific research and long-term monitoring throughout the latter part of the twentieth century. The NPS expanded dramatically in the 1960s and 1970s with the addition of dozens of new parks, historic sites, and recreation areas, but congressional appropriations were inadequate and sporadic. The resource management increases of 1980–1984, for example, came without complementary research funding. Problems in funding deepened as the Republican Party and Reagan administration promoted antigovernment sentiment, questioned the legitimacy of public lands and environmental regulation, and pushed for cuts in federal spending. Rocky superintendent James Thompson reported in his 1986 *Annual Report* that the Gramm-Rudman-Hollings Balanced Budget and Emergency Deficit Control Act of 1985 had resulted in "reduced budgets" for the park, a reduction in productivity, and "a noticeable decline in employee morale and confidence." The Democratic Clinton administration responded to public skepticism about the federal government by vowing to make it more efficient; for the NPS this manifested in a 1993 Department of Interior decision to move nearly all NPS biologists to a new agency, the National Biological Survey. The new agency was tasked with ecological and biological research on land management issues but not with oversight or responsibility for resource management in the field. Meanwhile, threats to parks continued to mount, ranging from invasive species and human overcrowding to air and water pollution, industrial and residential development on park borders, and climate change.[76]

Given what we know of Rocky's 1976 *Master Plan* and efforts to manage climbers' and other backcountry users' environmental impact, it might seem that the park tried harder than most to pursue ecological management. Other actions similarly reflect a genuine interest in reducing environmental threats. For example, the park's shuttle bus system, implemented in 1978, reduced automobile traffic and pollution along a corridor from Estes Park to Bear Lake, and its capacity, hours of operation, and designated stops expanded over time.[77] So, too, the park shut down the (economically unviable) Hidden Valley Ski Area as park staff found that its tree removal practices, septic system, and snowmaking machines harmed the park's forests and waterways and thwarted the recovery of greenback cutthroat trout. In 1992 the park declared the ski area "fundamentally inconsistent with the purposes for which Rocky Mountain National Park was established" and thereafter dismantled the operation.[78]

Rocky's commitment to ecological preservation also seems evident in its support for scientific research between 1970 and 2000. The park's annual reports show that it approved (and was somehow able to fund or cost share) hundreds of studies on subjects ranging from nitrogen deposition to fire suppression, beetle infestations, hydrology, pika, elk, and global warming. Some of the studies were conducted by park scientists, others by scientists at research universities and other federal agencies. The park also invested in projects aimed at restoring critical species to Rocky, including greenback cutthroat trout, otters, and peregrine falcons. And in print media, campfire talks, environmental education presentations, and interpretive walks, the park attempted to educate backcountry and front-country visitors about natural history and environmental ethics and practices.[79]

Other evidence, however, suggests that ecological preservation at Rocky suffered from administrative unwillingness to steer the park away from conventional priorities and practices. Backcountry users and the shuttle to Bear Lake notwithstanding, Rocky remained a park for scenic viewing by automobile. Annual visitation reached two million in 1968, three million in 1978, and three million again in 1998, 1999, and 2000.[80] Nearly all these visitors drove in private automobiles from Front Range cities to Estes Park, as public transportation was nonexistent. Once in the park, many visitors drove on Trail Ridge Road, stopping at viewing areas, wayside trails, and visitor centers. The cars emitted pollutants and visitors often strayed from designated trails, trampling fragile plants and soil, but the park never seriously considered numerical limits or a reservation system for day users. Admittedly, none of the nation's other "crown jewel" parks thought numerical limits on day-use visitation were an option in the twentieth century, though all reported overcrowding, and it would have been impossible for Rocky to impose limits on its own.

Equally important, on two critical issues, fire and elk management, park superintendents were reluctant to pursue needed changes in policy, regardless of the emerging scientific data. By the 1970s decades of fire suppression had resulted in unhealthy forests and dangerous accumulations of fuel for fire. Park scientists documented unnatural expanses of lodgepole pine, the encroachment of ponderosa pine, spruce, and fir into grasslands and meadows, loss of aspen groves, and massive die-offs of Douglas fir. Rocky initiated a poorly conceptualized let-burn policy for natural fires in 1972 but canceled it after the lightning-caused Ouzel Fire of 1978 provoked anxiety about potential damage to private property among nearby residents. The park returned to fire suppression, waiting until 1992 to begin using prescribed burns and closely managed lightning-ignited fires as tools for restoring forests to health.[81]

Rocky's elk policy was similarly problematic. In 1968 the park turned to hunters beyond its borders to cull its elk population during winter migration, but new land development limited elk migration beyond park borders and the hunting season was not timed to match elk migration. By 1982, the winter elk population in the park was estimated at three thousand, and the animals were severely impacting willow, aspen, wet meadows, dry grassland, and beaver. A succession of superintendents evaded the warnings of park scientists, however, not wanting to consider in-park culling operations that would surely provoke public backlash. Rocky's refusal to listen to scientists reached a high point in 1991 when Superintendent James Thompson got rid of the park's science staff, eliminating two ecologist positions and reassigning another to administrative duties. Responding to criticism by scientists beyond the park, Rocky subsequently contracted for extensive study of elk and their impact on Rocky, but it did not implement a revised elk and vegetation management plan until 2008.[82]

Retrospectively, we can see that Rocky's 1976 *Master Plan* established a formal commitment to ecological preservation. At sites such as Longs Peak, scientific research, detailed management plans, and efforts to gain climber support for "leave no trace" ethics and practices helped advance and align ecological and visitor values. Still, inconsistent implementation, loyalty to the park's traditional focus on scenic viewing by car, and a welter of external political and environmental factors limited the park's overall success in protecting its natural resources.

Democracy in a Mountain Park

Rocky pursued inclusivity in access and interpretation even more tentatively than it did ecological management. The park's 1976 *Master Plan* acknowledged emerging laws and scientific standards that prioritized ecological and wilderness preservation, but it was silent on recent civil rights and historic preservation legislation and seemed not to notice that visitation, employment, and interpretation had been compromised by racial and gender hierarchies. A 1982 *Annual Statement for Interpretation and Visitor Services* estimated that African Americans, Hispanics, and Native Americans accounted for just 3 percent of Rocky's visitors, but the statement declined to notice the discrepancy between these figures and the 1980 census data, which showed that racial and ethnic minorities (Hispanic, Black, Indian/Eskimo, Asian, Other) accounted for 17.7 percent of the population in Colorado and 20.44 percent in the nation. The statement further observed that there were no "special arrangements" at Rocky for interpretation or outreach to "minorities/ethnic/cultural groups," and it did not recommend that any be put in place. A decade later, the park reported again that it did not engage in interpretation or outreach with "minorities/ethnic/cultural groups."[83] Discussion of race and ethnicity in outdoor and wilderness recreation was similarly absent from the CMC's *Trail and Timberline* and other popular climbing magazines, though as we will see below, small numbers of African Americans were becoming members of the CMC.

Rocky was not unusual among national parks in doing little to encourage communities of color to visit the park. NPS recreation areas near Washington, DC, New York City, Atlanta, and Boston were intended for use by diverse urban populations, while the big nature parks continued to serve an overwhelmingly White visitor base throughout the latter part of the century and accepted this pattern as normative, not requiring outreach to communities of color.[84] Visitation numbers that continued to increase by the year and media reports on Rocky, Yosemite, Yellowstone, and Grand Canyon being "loved to death" may have dissuaded superintendents from reaching out to underserved populations, including communities of color. Importantly, national parks also remained beyond the radar of civil rights organizations, which were preoccupied with evidence of egregious discrimination against racial and ethnic minorities in housing, employment, education, criminal justice, and governance, especially in urban settings. Though the legislative gains of the civil rights era had been significant, a fierce backlash quickly developed in the 1960s and 1970s against governmental measures promoting racial and gender equality. Nativism also increased, targeting Latinx and Asian immigrants, and as Reagan's antigovernment and neoliberal ideology gained ascendancy in the GOP after 1980, the American public grew increasingly divided over the extent to which racism existed or needed to be addressed through formal action at the federal, state, or local level. Mirroring national trends, Denver became mired in controversy over mandatory court-ordered busing to achieve desegregated schooling. Talented Black and Latinx men and women became forceful advocates for reform, and some, such as Betty Benevídez, Wilma and Wellington Webb, and Federico Peña, obtained state and local political office in Colorado. Still, change was very slow. With so much at stake in cities and towns across Colorado and the nation, racial justice activists had no incentive to focus attention on national parks.[85]

Moreover, the few academics concerned about the overwhelming Whiteness of national parks chose not to identify park inclusivity as a priority. In a 1971 article, "Is the National Parks Movement Anti-Urban?," Peter Marcuse, a professor of urban planning at Columbia University, accused conservation organizations and the NPS of being antiurban as well as "antiblack, anti-minority, and anti-poor." In his view, national parks and their boosters were "trying to preserve a corner of the world for the exclusive preserve of a white upper-middle class for their play and recreation, insulated from the pressures and needs of the majority of the people of the real world." Marcuse had "seen no racial statistics on national park use" (as none were collected), but during a camping trip in the summer of 1970 that took him from Connecticut to California, he observed only two Black families at more than thirty campgrounds run by the NPS or other public land agencies. Certainly, Marcuse wanted conservation organizations to engage in outreach and collaboration that would create opportunities for urban minority children to experience national parks and nature beyond the city. Yet he thought it far more important for conservationists to dedicate themselves to making the home environment "of those at the bottom end of the ladder as healthful, beautiful, and enjoyable as that of those at the upper end."[86]

In 1973 Joseph W. Meeker, a former NPS ranger and professor of literature and environmental studies at the University of California, Santa Cruz, went even further than Marcuse in rejecting the goal of multiracial inclusivity in parks. Like Marcuse, Meeker found national parks in the United States "expressive of a myth" created by and for White Euro-Americans. Parks were Edenic places where White visitors found refuge from urban turmoil, enjoyed nature's scenic splendor, and basked in their own privilege. But in his view, since African Americans and Native Americans did not believe in Whites' Edenic mythology, parks were unlikely to attract them, even if they tried. Referencing Eldridge Cleaver, Meeker noted that Black Americans had learned from slavery "to hate the land." When they needed refuge from hardship, Blacks sought it not in "any wilderness setting, but among other Black people where they [could] expect to find understanding and human compassion." And for Native Americans, national parks were places of humiliation that celebrated White conquest and the appropriation of their lands. Native Americans were present in parks only to be "displayed and exploited." Meeker seemed not to know of African Americans who viewed recreation in natural settings in positive terms or of Black vacation communities such as Lincoln Hills in Colorado and Oak Bluffs on Martha's Vineyard. Nor was he aware of Native Americans who still viewed national parks as homeland. Finding the Edenic mythology of national parks to be bankrupt yet being an ardent advocate of both racial justice and environmental preservation, Meeker suggested that national parks revise their mission, abandoning their Edenic mythologies and any notion of becoming "settings for [inclusive] mass recreation." They should instead prioritize environmental protection and the discovery of "knowledge of equilibrium among biological species, including our own species." Denied places for privileged play, White Americans might learn from Blacks and Native Americans about "tolerance and brotherhood among humans and how to adapt human activities to the conditions of natural environments."[87]

Organizers for environmental justice in the 1980s and 1990s articulated views similar to those of Marcuse and Meeker as they responded to evidence that people of color were suffering catastrophic harm from toxic waste and air pollution in towns and cities across the nation. Community organizers developed sophisticated analyses of the ways in which systemic racism forced people of color to live, work, and play in degraded environments. They became convinced, as well, that the nation's most important environmental organizations cared little about racism or environmental justice in minority urban and rural neighborhoods, precisely because these organizations prioritized the protection of wilderness areas and parks where people of privilege went to play. Environmental justice advocates put groups such as the Sierra Club on notice about the racist values embedded in their organizations and their all-White staff, and they successfully pressured the Clinton administration to issue an executive order requiring the federal government to pursue environmental justice for minority and low-income populations. They did not attempt to change visitation trends in national parks.[88]

Yet, even as the attention of most racial justice advocates focused on reform in urban and rural habitats, some organizations and individuals sought to inspire people of color to pursue adventure in wilderness areas and national parks. Throughout the latter decades of the twentieth century, Colorado Outward Bound (COB) worked actively to draw urban youth—male and female, Black and White, Latinx and Native—along with high school and college teachers, into its orbit. COB programs included wilderness and national park expeditions, urban service activities, extended trips to the Navajo reservation in northern Arizona and rural communities in Mexico, and seminars on ecological science and habitats. East High School in Denver, with a diverse population and racial tensions to match, became a hub of COB activities. COB found that students who were admitted to its programs regardless of demographic background or academic achievement gained self-confidence, learned to navigate class and racial differences, and worked constructively in unified teams. At the same time, they developed a deep appreciation for wild nature and acquired outdoor skills. Similar Outward Bound programs emerged in other states, with deliberate outreach across racial, ethnic, gender, and class differences. Numerous public and private high schools also embraced outdoor wilderness experience as one element of successful programming for diverse and inner-city students, including the Eagle Rock School, which opened outside Estes Park and Rocky in 1993 under the auspices of the nonprofit American Honda Education Corporation. Rocky was not yet inclined to pursue diversity in visitation as a formal park goal, yet the superintendent noted, "From the standpoint of environmental education, and other societal goals, the park was very supportive of the school."[89]

Building on the COB model, in 1993 Denverite Jerry L. Stevens, a Black attorney who had been an Outward Bound instructor, collaborated with twenty other volunteers, mostly people of color, to make the outdoors more accessible to inner city adults and youth. Stevens was also a CMC member, though it is not clear when he joined or what his experience was like in the predominantly White organization. The James P. Beckwourth Mountain Club (BMC) organized annual outings to Rocky Mountain National Park and visited many other NPS sites in Colorado and neighboring states. Stevens offered presentations on the BMC to potentially supportive organizations and government agencies, including the NPS, to make them aware of the club's goals: "to bring together a diverse group of people to explore the outdoors, to uncover and share the historical contributions of African Americans and minority adventurers, and to affect the destiny of urban youth by using the outdoors as a vehicle for defining self-worth." The NPS published a supportive article about the BMC in an agency bulletin in 1996, by which time the Colorado Mountain Club was making its library of guidebooks and other printed materials available to BMC members. Michael Richardson, another BMC member with concurrent membership in the CMC, became the first African American to successfully climb all of Colorado's fourteeners in 1995, inspiring others to seek fulfillment through mountain adventure.[90]

Two years later Cheryl Armstrong led the BMC in opening the James P. Beckwourth Outdoor Education Center to train urban youth in hiking, kayaking, map and compass reading, and other backcountry skills. The BMC's presence in Rocky did not have a noticeable impact on park visitation estimates, yet it marked the start of a trend among communities of color. Similar organizations were emerging elsewhere across the United States in the 1990s to facilitate wilderness experience and the cultivation of preservation ethics among adults and youth of color.[91] As we will see in the epilogue, this trend has become powerful in the twenty-first century. Outdoor organizations established by and for people of color are inspiring diverse communities to participate in wilderness recreation while simultaneously embracing preservation, honoring indigenous connections to public lands, and pressuring traditionally White environmental and outdoor organizations to pursue justice, diversity, and inclusivity in wilderness areas and public lands.

While federal law did not require Rocky to promote diversity among its visitors in the latter part of the twentieth century, the Civil Rights Act of 1964 and Nixon's executive order on affirmative action demanded that the park pursue equity and diversity in employment. From the 1970s through the 1990s the NPS employee newsletter, *Courier*, devoted considerable attention to equal opportunity programs and policies while also highlighting the achievements of minority and women employees in the agency.[92] Similarly, Rocky's superintendents dutifully reported on efforts to recruit and hire minorities and women to permanent and seasonal positions in their annual reports. In 1985, for example, the superintendent reported that park EEO staff made three trips to Colorado colleges and universities to recruit minorities and women, allowing the park to place thirteen minorities in 5 percent of Rocky's seasonal jobs, and four minorities and three women in 7 percent of the park's permanent jobs. By 1987 women had been hired into 33 percent of seasonal positions and minorities into 6 percent of seasonal jobs. Rocky also quietly hired racially and ethnically diverse teams of young people through the Youth Conservation Corps and related programs, relying on them for essential conservation and maintenance work in the summer months. When the YCC was terminated by the federal government in 1981, Rocky's superintendent reported great disappointment, as the young corps members had performed important work at low cost.[93]

Still, affirmative action policies seem to have had a limited impact on employment in the park. In 1987 the Equal Employment Opportunity Commission (EEOC) eliminated the requirement that federal agencies "set annual goals for underrepresented groups in categories where vacancies were expected" and instructed them instead "to devise flexible approaches to improving the representation of women and minorities in their workforces."[94] It is hard to know exactly what impact the changed approach had on employment numbers in Rocky, for 1987 also marks the year when discussion of affirmative action dropped out of the superintendent's annual reports. Documentation recently collected and analyzed by the NPS about employment across the agency in the latter decades of the twentieth century shows very slow change away from a permanent workforce in which White males dominated positions of high pay, stature, and leadership.[95]

Meanwhile, Rocky was also supposed to promote comprehensive historical and archaeological research and interpretation in accordance with the National Historic Preservation Act (1966) and Archaeological Resources Protection Act (1979). And it needed to comply with the American Indian Religious Freedom Act (1978) to accommodate indigenous cultural and sacred use of parks, and with Native American Graves Protection and Repatriation Act (1990) requirements to inventory, protect, and consult with lineal descendants and Native tribes about the repatriation or transfer of human remains, funerary objects, sacred objects, and objects of cultural patrimony.

From the 1970s through the 1990s the park used the framework provided by the National Historic Preservation Act (NHPA) to nominate buildings, sites, trails, and roads of historic significance to the National Register of Historic Places. Rocky's nominations highlighted the mining and ranching era before the park was founded, or dude ranching and park visitation during Rocky's first several decades. The East Longs Peak Trail and the Agnes Vaille Shelter were among the places named to the National Register. The park's overworked Division of Interpretation and Education (responsible for educating visitors about natural resources and for historical and cultural interpretation) lacked the staff and resources to promote historical and archaeological research on indigenous peoples or to consult with the Ute, Arapaho, and other tribes about park sites, resources, or objects and artifacts of significance to them. Not surprisingly, the park's interpretive exhibits continued to neglect Native tribes whose homeland encompassed the park region.[96]

In truth, historical preservation and interpretation remained focused on the Euro-American experience across the NPS system, despite evidence of interest in innovation. From the 1970s through the 1990s, the *CRM Bulletin*, the

NPS's professional bulletin on cultural resource management (CRM), regularly published articles about CRM projects related to the history and culture of Native Americans, African Americans, immigrants, and women. And Muriel Crespi, the NPS chief ethnographer, worked diligently throughout the 1980s and 1990s to "democratize NPS management decisions" about cultural resource management and preservation "by directing its attention to people who were 'traditionally associated' with park lands and resources" and trying to provide them "a voice through planning and consultations." "Traditionally associated" people might be of diverse backgrounds, including Native American, Latinx, or African American. Crespi's ideas were well received, yet the work she envisioned went largely unfunded.[97]

So, too, as legal scholar Amanda M. Marincic has argued, the NHPA and its 1992 amendments (meant to facilitate the preservation of historical properties of religious and cultural significance to Native tribes) did not do enough to protect tribal preservation efforts and rights. Reno Keoni Franklin, chair of the National Association of Tribal Historic Preservation Officers (THPOs), has pointed to funding deficiencies for tribal preservation in the 1990s (and beyond), despite local THPOs' persistent efforts to champion preservation projects. Cultural heritage consultant Ned Kaufman argues that preservation results for other minority populations were also disappointing. The NPS "mounted important diversity initiatives," with more than 77,000 properties listed in the National Register as of April 20, 2004, yet "only about 1,300 are explicitly associated with African-American heritage, 90 with Hispanic, and 67 with Asian. Taken together, these properties amount to 3 percent of what is intended to be a comprehensive inventory of the nation's heritage." New sites associated with the nation's diverse heritage drew visitors of color, even as long-standing interpretive habits and inadequate funding for staff and research kept nature parks such as Rocky from exploring their own histories of difference or from attracting more diverse visitors.[98]

Rocky finally began to pursue meaningful reform and innovation after it hired Bill Gwaltney as chief of interpretation in 1997. An African American with a long career in the NPS, Gwaltney took seriously the imperatives of the Archaeological Resources Protection Act and oversaw the launch of a systematic archaeological survey and the development of new interpretive materials for the park inclusive of indigenous culture and history. He also started a program to bring Ute and Arapaho adults and children to the park from tribal reservations to experience for themselves the place where their ancestors had once lived.[99]

It would take time, of course, for this work to bear fruit. Thus, even as Gwaltney identified new possibilities for research, interpretation, and consultation, most park visitors experienced a park unchanged in meaning and identity: Rocky was a grand nature park that recalled conditions extant in the late nineteenth century when White Americans took an apparently "unoccupied" region and made it into a glorious vacation ground. Without indulging in overt racism, Rocky's outdated exhibits normalized indigenous peoples' disappearance and rendered unproblematic Whites' many decades of privileged access to the stunning mountain region.

AS THE UNITED STATES approached the end of the twentieth century, the NPS established an Advisory Board of twelve citizens representing science, education, public lands, and recreation and chaired by the distinguished African American historian John Hope Franklin. The board's charge was to examine the park system and prepare a vision statement for the NPS's next twenty-five years. Members of the board carefully examined the NPS's legal obligations as well as recent studies evaluating recreation, scientific research, resource management, and interpretation at NPS sites across the nation. Its report, *Rethinking the National Parks for the 21st Century* (2001), was eloquent and optimistic. The board deemed the NPS a critically important agency. Its mission to conserve parks "unimpaired for the enjoyment of future generations" echoed "the promise of the Constitution 'to secure the blessings of liberty to ourselves and our posterity.'" Still, there was much room for improvement: the NPS was "beloved and respected, yes; but perhaps too cautious, too resistant to change, too reluctant to engage the challenges that must be addressed in the 21st century." The 1916 Organic Act had established the foundational mandates of the NPS, but the agency's understanding of its mission needed "to evolve as society and conditions change."[100]

Most important, the Advisory Board urged NPS leaders and the public to understand that the national park mission went far beyond providing cultural or natural sites for Americans' pleasure. Rather, the NPS fostered enjoyment and preservation with a larger goal in mind: to honor and protect the nation's ideals and its historical and environmental heritage. The board wrote, "As a nation, we protect our heritage to ensure a more complete understanding of the forces that shape our lives and future. National parks are key institutions created for that purpose, chapters in the ever-expanding story of America. It is the founding mission of the Park Service to insure that these special places will never be impaired, and will be available forever to inspire and inform future generations."[101]

The Advisory Board thus conceived the NPS mission as "multi-dimensional," with distinct yet overlapping obligations to visitors, the nation's founding ideals, and the environment. And because "the larger purpose of this mission is to build a citizenry that is committed to conserving its heritage and its home on earth," the Advisory Board began with two recommendations on field-based education about culture, history, and nature. First, "parks should be not just recreational destinations but springboards for personal journeys of intellectual and cultural enrichment." They needed to promote deep appreciation for "Congress's description of the National Park System as 'cumulative expressions of a single national heritage.'" They needed to tell histories of the nation's long and difficult "journey" toward liberty and justice "faithfully, completely, and accurately" and thereby produce a "civic glue" that strengthened the "national character." And second, parks needed to immerse visitors in learning about the environment and promote understanding of "humanity's relationship to the natural world."[102]

In the board's view, education about culture, history, and nature would facilitate action on its other recommendations. Education that "seamlessly presented" human and environmental history as "inseparable chapters of our life on this planet" would "encourage public support of resource protection at a higher level of understanding" and facilitate NPS efforts to put "greatly increased focus on the conservation of natural systems and the biodiversity they encompass." So, too, environmental education would help the NPS as it worked to "model sustainability . . . practicing what is preached." Crucially, cultural and historical learning would facilitate the board's recommendation that parks do more to foster "the irreplaceable connections that ancestral and indigenous people have with the parks," allowing them to become "sanctuaries for expressing and reclaiming ancient feelings of place." In honoring indigenous connections to place, both Native and non-Native Americans would benefit, the latter learning that "parks become richer when we see them through the cultures of people whose ancestors once lived there." Finally, visitors who fully understood NPS values—"appreciation of the out-of-doors, caring for our shared natural and cultural heritage, and providing opportunities for personal challenge and adventure"—would support NPS collaborations to "build a national network of parks and open spaces across America." And they would aid efforts to "improve the Service's institutional capacity by developing new organizational talents and abilities and a workforce that reflects America's diversity."[103]

In 2001 conditions and efforts in Rocky Mountain National Park did not match the Advisory Board's multidimensional vision. Yes, it was a place of great and exhilarating experiences in montane and alpine settings. Yes, its natural resources were increasingly appreciated and well understood. That said, natural resources were far from fully protected. And in cultural and environmental history and education, in preserving and interpreting the Native American past and promoting tribal connections to the park in the present, much work remained to be done. Visitors and staff still did not reflect the diversity of the nation. Fortunately, despite its shortcomings, the park was far from static. As we will see in the epilogue, critical trends and developments of the twenty-first century have pushed the park to embrace change. As always, Longs Peak and its climbers are part of that story.

Epilogue

Climbers, National Parks, and a Twenty-First-Century Ethic of Care

LONGS PEAK IN THE NEW MILLENNIUM remains a place where climbers pursue vertical adventure amid natural splendor, the elite among them making remarkable first ascents. Since 2001, climbers have established four new routes on the Diamond with difficulty ratings of 5.13 and one with a rating of 5.14. Chris Weidner, who put up *Gambler's Fallacy* (V 5.13b) in 2020 after more than fifty days (spread over two years) of arduous practice and route finding, calls Longs' East Face "the highest and hardest free climbing arena in the world. Nothing comes easily."[1] Yet, even as Longs retains its legendary stature, those who strive to gain its summit also illuminate notable changes in the climbing community. Climber demographics and identity are in flux. Perceptions of reward and risk, ethics and practices of care—all are undergoing scrutiny, debate, and revision.

Take Steph Davis, born in 1973. As she began rock climbing in the 1990s, women were "dramatically narrow[ing] the gap" between women and men in both sport and free climbing, gaining recognition for "cutting edge first ascents" around the globe.[2] Davis's 1996 all-female first free ascent with Elaine Lee on the Diamond's *Obelisk* (IV 5.11) went largely unnoticed, but between 2003 and 2005 she won acclaim for spectacular firsts on Yosemite's El Capitan, including the first free ascent by a woman of Salathé Wall (VI 5.13b/c, 35 pitches). Davis also won approbation for free climbing firsts in Patagonia, on Baffin Island, and in Kyrgyzstan.[3] And when she free soloed four climbs on the Diamond in the summer of 2007, becoming the first female climber to ascend routes of 5.10+ on the celebrated wall without a partner, rope, or protection, Davis pushed gender boundaries again. Writing about her experience on Longs, Davis explained that she loved the "seductive danger" of climbing without protection and "relished the absolute focus" it required, "knowing that every move I made counted more than anything else in the world at that moment." Free soloing demanded audacity and—for this classically trained former pianist—a familiar dedication to hard practice. Before ascending *Pervertical Sanctuary* in 2007, Davis got to know every inch of the route on roped climbs. She cultivated physical and mental discipline to "extinguish" the fear that might compromise her abilities and put her in danger. When she finally ascended the route without protection, Davis felt free, confident, and safe:

> I had no rope, no gear, no partner to wait for. All I had to do was climb. It was the simplest thing in the world. . . . Fifteen hundred feet above the glacier, I reached a tiny ledge before the steep finger crack, the crux of the route. . . . There was nothing to fear. . . . I envisioned the moves I would make. . . . I watched myself climbing perfectly, easily. . . . I raised my hands and twisted my fingers into the rough granite and stepped high with my feet against the wall. Every lock felt solid, every foot perfectly fractioned. . . . I was safe. I looked down at the exposure. Empty space dropped down for over a thousand feet, snow, boulders, and granite walls spreading all around the floor beneath me. I observed it dispassionately. I looked up at the deep gash above, the final difficulty of the route, and wriggled into it gladly. Granite pressed around me, holding me safe.[4]

Or consider Tommy Caldwell. Caldwell, a Colorado native born in 1978, displayed talent on rock at an early age and climbed the Diamond's *Casual* route with his father when he was just twelve. By his late teens he was a world-class climber, initially focused on sport climbing, then turning to big-wall trad climbing, especially in Yosemite. In 2013, Caldwell returned to Longs to free the Diamond's *Dunn-Westbay* with partner Joe Mills, deliberately making the climb much harder than the original 5.10+ ascent: "I had the vision of trying to do it ledge to ledge (with no hanging belays), and that meant doing an 80-meter pitch, which made it fully 5.14," Caldwell said. "It was extraordinary. I never expected to find anything like that on the Diamond."[5] Caldwell went on to achieve the seemingly impossible in Yosemite in 2015, freeing the Dawn Wall (5.14d, 32 pitches) on El Capitan with Kevin Jorgeson in an epic climb of nineteen days. They had been preparing and practicing for seven years.

Yet Caldwell represents more than relentless ambition and problem-solving on rock. He has endured trauma and hardship—capture by Islamic militants in Kyrgyzstan during a climbing trip in 2000, the loss of his index finger in a table saw accident in 2001—and reflected openly on the human relationships, ethics, and adversities that make resilience possible. More willing to disclose his feelings and interior life than male climbers of previous generations, Caldwell speaks freely about how becoming a husband and father have shaped his perception of acceptable risk. And he has become an activist with the Access Fund, Protect Our Winters, and other organizations, defending climbers' access to public lands, promoting solutions to the climate crisis, and working to protect indigenous sacred sites and ritual on public land. Leave-no-trace and clean-climbing practices have been supported by many climbers for decades, but Caldwell is among those urging climbers to up their game and tackle climate change. And by working with indigenous tribes at Bears Ears National Monument and other sites, he is trying to turn the page on the late twentieth century when rock climbers flocked to Bear Lodge (Devils Tower National Monument) in Wyoming, defaced the rock, left litter and waste, and disrupted indigenous rituals important to dozens of tribes. Even after the NPS helped negotiate an annual ban on climbing at Bear Lodge each June when most spiritual ceremonies occur, some climbers fought the ban in court. They eventually lost, but indigenous people's distrust of climbers has not easily been put aside, and with good reason, as the desecration of sacred sites by climbers has not ended.[6]

Beyond Davis and Caldwell, other signs of change in the climbing community are striking. For one, Black, Brown, Asian, and Native women and men are participating enthusiastically in climbing, as are LGBTQ individuals; some are moving to the top ranks of climbing, as are some extraordinarily talented White women.[7] It is not yet evident that climbers of color are heading to Longs or other peaks in Rocky in significant numbers, but climbing organizations that inspire and train climbers from diverse backgrounds have emerged all over the country, including Brothers of Climbing, Brown Girls Climb, Brown Ascenders, Climbing for Change, Flash Foxy, Never Stop Moving, and Sending in Color. Natives Outdoors, Latinos Outdoors, and Afro Outdoors promote climbing and a range of other outdoor sports. Cruxing in Color works to support and empower climbers of color in Denver. Vibe Tribe Adventures, based in Colorado, promotes hiking and has a program, Black 14ers, directly relevant to nontechnical climbing on Longs Peak. It offers "educational clinics, equipment sponsorship, and backcountry adventures for Black people and Allies to summit 14,000-foot peaks safely."[8]

In addition, the new organizations manifest goals that go well beyond encouraging a diversity of people to claim their rightful places in climbing and the great outdoors. Simply put, they unequivocally oppose humans' abuse of power, whether the target of abuse is the environment or other humans. Many of the organizations' founders and members have deliberately embraced environmental stewardship and broad conceptions of social justice, and they insist that an increasingly diverse climbing community respect indigenous cultures and honor the sites sacred to them. Len Necefer, a Navajo climber and the founder of Natives Outdoors, is geotagging mountains in the West and giving them back their indigenous names. He has renamed Longs Peak Neníisótoyóú'u, the mountain's long-forgotten Arapaho name, and seeks to repudiate the "myth" that national parks were created in "untouched wilderness areas" devoid of human presence.[9] So, too, Brown Girls Climb deliberately embeds environmental stewardship, respect for the values of indigenous communities and people of color, and awareness of historical injustice in their approach to climbing:

We value our own interpretation and representation of what climbing is for each of us. We continue to educate ourselves about the rich and dynamic histories of climbing, the multitude of methods by which humans have interacted and appreciated the mountains over time, and the ways by which our cultures have practiced environmentalism in their own communities and language. . . . We aim to continue this education so that we and others can appreciate this knowledge so that our identities as climbers can be uniquely rooted in our identities as people striving to learn, adapt, and treat others with the respect and dignity that we would like in the outdoors. . . . We strive to honor the current and previous ethnic communities which have contributed to the land that we appreciate today. We acknowledge the complexity of our own positions in this history, recognizing that our ancestral histories are rooted in the earth we enjoy *and* that we occupy stolen land from Indigenous communities and areas in which Communities of Color may have been displaced. We recognize that outdoor recreation and every extension of the outdoor industry is a colonial concept that can be both limiting and harmful to the communities we are connected to. We move forward with this appreciation and acknowledgement in all the work we do with the goal of reducing harm and restoring land and resources to impacted communities.[10]

The growing prominence in climbing of people who identify with the BIPOC (Black, Indigenous, People of Color) movement to fight "Native invisibility, anti-Blackness and white supremacy"[11] has gained strong support from influential climbing media outlets and prominent climbing organizations, including *Climbing* magazine, the CMC, the American Alpine Club, and the Access Fund. So, too, environmental organizations such as the Sierra Club and the Wilderness Society have made new commitments to centering justice, equity, diversity, and inclusion in their work. Like Caldwell, these organizations have affirmed their dedication to finding solutions to environmental crises, including climate change, yet they also insist that environmentalism be aligned with social justice and protecting indigenous connections to public lands.[12] It is impossible to tell how successful any of the organizations will be in overcoming tenacious patterns of privilege in climbing or in fusing work for human justice with environmental activism. The American Alpine Club's 2019 *State of Climbing* report showed that climbing in the United States was still disproportionately male and over 80 percent White. Still, possibilities for transformation clearly exist.[13]

If change is evident in the demographics, ethics, and practices of the climbing community in the new millennium, what can be said about Rocky and the NPS? *Rethinking the National Parks for the 21st Century* offered ideas and recommendations that generally align with emerging values among climbers, but have those recommendations been translated into policy and action? What are Rocky and the NPS doing to deepen visitors' experience of NPS sites and to effectively protect the nation's complex historical and cultural inheritance as well as its environmental heritage? Are they promoting diversity and inclusivity in visitation, employment, and interpretation? And if change is happening in national parks, how is it affecting climbers and places such as Longs?

My discussion in this epilogue is brief and provisional, as the implications of events and developments in the recent past are still emerging, and circumstances remain dynamic. So, too, much documentation about work in Rocky and the NPS in recent decades is not yet archived or accessible to historians. With complete certainty beyond reach, it is nonetheless evident that the NPS has attempted to implement many of the recommendations in *Rethinking the National Parks for the 21st Century.* The report prompted innovative efforts, including at Rocky, to enrich the visitor experience, redefine the management of cultural and natural resources, and make the NPS fully representative of the nation's diverse citizenry, complex history, and founding ideals. Indeed, in *A Call to Action*, the document marking the NPS's 2016 centennial, the agency announced a vision for its second century that drew quite obviously on *Rethinking the National Parks* (emphasis in original):

> In our second century, the *National Park Service must recommit to the exemplary stewardship and public enjoyment of these places. . . .* We must use the collective power of the parks, our historic preservation programs, and community assistance programs to expand our contributions to society. . . . IN OUR SECOND CENTURY, *we will* fully represent our nation's ethnically and culturally diverse communities. To achieve the promise of democracy, *we will* create and deliver activities, programs, and services that honor, examine, and interpret America's complex heritage. By investing in the preservation, interpretation, and restoration of the parks and by extending the benefits of conservation to communities, the *National Park Service will* inspire a "more perfect union," offering renewed hope to each generation of Americans.[14]

Not surprisingly, the NPS has also encountered a range of obstacles to change and reform. Below, I examine innovations on Longs, in Rocky, and broadly across the NPS that reflect the agency's enlarged vision and evolving ethics and practices of care while also identifying critical obstacles that stand in the way of "exemplary stewardship" of the nation's natural and cultural inheritance.

Climbing in the New Millennium

Though climbing received no mention in *Rethinking National Parks for the 21st Century,* the report made clear national parks' enduring obligation to provide visitors with recreational opportunities for "personal challenge and adventure."[15] Certainly, in the twenty-first century Longs Peak remains exceedingly popular.

Recent monitoring with automated counters and photos (2011–2015) has shown that the East Longs Peak Trail attracts up to thirty-five thousand visitors during the summer and early fall each year, with about six hundred people on the trail each Saturday in August, when visitation is at its highest. As in the past, hikers and nontechnical climbers vastly outnumber rock climbers in warm weather months. Recent data does not account for winter visitors, though rangers have noted that snow and ice climbing and backcountry skiing are increasingly popular in Rocky, including on Longs.[16]

Not surprisingly, with visitor use very high on Longs, especially during the summer and early fall, Rocky has found that crowding and the improper disposal of human waste and trash are persistent and worrying problems. Injury and other health emergencies, often related to inadequate equipment, clothing, food, and preparation, are also continuing challenges. The park continues a busy search and rescue operation, relying on park staff and skilled volunteers from the Rocky Mountain Rescue Group and Larimer County Search and Rescue. The most recent available figures, for 2010–2016, show between ten and twenty-two SAR incidents on Longs annually. SAR teams are called out for everything from hypothermia and altitude sickness to sprains, rope lacerations, and falls. Thirteen people have died on Longs since 2000.[17]

Climber education has always been important to Rocky, but, following a trend evident across the NPS since the publication of *Rethinking the National Parks*, the park has redoubled its efforts to educate climbers about safety and environmental ethics. In decades past, the park used printed flyers, articles in local media, ranger presentations, and on-trail encounters between rangers and visitors to educate climbers, relying on the CMC and other organizations to supplement its guidance and provide practical training. The park's goal was to build consensus and understanding with climbers about safety and conservation standards.

In the new millennium, Rocky continues to rely on others to provide formal rock-climbing instruction, but it has expanded its public outreach on the fundamentals of safe and low-impact climbing, offering presentations at popular outdoor retailers such as REI and Neptune Mountaineering. Some presentations have targeted nontechnical climbers with interest in the *Keyhole* route; others have targeted technical climbers, especially those who learned to climb in gyms and need help thinking about the realities of climbing outdoors. Presentations have also covered technical snow and ice climbing, backcountry skiing, and avalanche safety at sites such as Longs. The Covid-19 pandemic has put the presentations on hold for now, but the park keeps two permanent climbing rangers on staff all year, hiring another six to eight for the summer season. The climbing rangers maintain a presence at all of Rocky's popular climbing sites; during the summer on Longs, there is usually one ranger each day walking the East Longs Peak Trail and *Keyhole* route. The climbing rangers interact with visitors, answer their questions, and "spread the good word" on safety, climbing ethics, and leave-no-trace practices. Volunteers greet hikers and climbers at the East Longs Peak trailhead to answer questions about weather and trail conditions.[18]

With climbers' numbers high and climbing rangers' numbers rather modest, it is not surprising that online learning has become an important educational tool for the park. Rocky's "Climbing and Mountaineering" web page provides critical information for nontechnical climbers about the different sections of the *Keyhole* route and their distinct challenges. It describes the glorious alpine environment on Longs but also advises climbers about variable weather, adequate preparation, essential equipment, and the dangers posed by lightning, rapidly moving storms, and falling rock. It instructs technical climbers about overnight bivouac rules and permits and identifies climbing concessions licensed to provide formal rock-climbing instruction and guided ascents in Rocky. So, too, the climbing web page clearly defines leave-no-trace ethics and practices; discusses the plants, animals, soils, and rock that climbers will encounter and how easily they can be harmed; and explains why the park prohibits climbing at specific sites during the falcon nesting season. And though Rocky does not categorically prohibit the placement of new climbing bolts and other fixed anchors, the climbing web page stresses local climbers' historical investment in clean climbing and the need to continue this ethic in the present day:

> RMNP and the surrounding area has long been known for a strong traditional climbing ethic and concern for the resource by its users. The local climbing community does not accept practices such as placing bolts on existing routes or establishing new bolt-intensive routes and chipping or gluing new holds. Clean-climbing techniques are generally the norm. It is incumbent on the local climbing community, along with the park, to inform and educate climbers new to the area of this fact for the ultimate protection and maintained access to climbing areas.[19]

The Boulder Climbing Community, established in 2010 by climber Roger Briggs and affiliated with the Access Fund, augments Rocky's communications, educating the public about low-impact climbing, conservation, and the importance of working closely with public land managers. Other websites established by and for climbers, such as SummitPost and Mountain Project, offer helpful information on climbing routes. They describe nontechnical routes such as *Clark's Arrow* that are not as well known as the *Keyhole* route, as well as the most popular technical routes on Longs' East and North Faces. They also provide a space for climbers to post climbing accounts that others may read, learn from, and respond to. Technical climbers have also continued to publish comprehensive climbing guides on Rocky Mountain National Park; the most recent, by Richard Rossiter, includes brief but pointed remarks about visitor overuse in Rocky and the need to adhere to leave-no-trace and clean-climbing methods.[20] Older organizations such as the CMC also continue to educate and instruct climbers, enhancing their work with an online presence. And many other organizations and publications, from the American Alpine Club to *Climbing*, play important roles in educating climbers about safe and environmentally sound ethics and practices.

Occasionally, climbers in Colorado and other states have pushed back against emerging NPS policy, as happened after the NPS issued Director's Order 41 on Wilderness Stewardship in 2013. The order attempted to cover many elements of wilderness stewardship, including climbing management. It did not categorically prohibit fixed anchors (bolts and pitons) in wilderness climbing areas but stated that they should be "rare." Moreover, the order noted that authorization would be required for the placement of new fixed anchors and might be required for the replacement or removal of existing fixed anchors. Climbers across the country were incensed, arguing that they could not possibly predict when they might need to place a new fixed anchor or remove and replace an old one and would thus be unreasonably limited by a requirement for prior authorization.[21]

The Access Fund and the American Alpine Club stepped in, consulting with the NPS, providing feedback on the new order, and developing a shared policy for the climbing organizations. The AF-AAC policy (2015) explained how fixed anchors were actually used by climbers, described their value for climber safety and wilderness resource protection when used properly, and highlighted language in the new Director's Order that required the NPS to work with stakeholders to tailor the order to each park. The AF-AAC policy also stated emphatically that wilderness fixed anchor management policy must recognize the legitimacy of climbers' decisions to use fixed anchors for safety, or because they sometimes facilitated "the purest forms of wilderness exploration." The Access Fund had already signed a General Agreement with the NPS in 2014, acknowledging the mutual interests of the two organizations and the Access Fund's willingness to collaborate with the NPS on climbing management plans and the promotion of responsible and environmentally sound climbing practices.[22]

With the General Agreement and the AF-AAC policy in place, many parks, including Rocky, chose not to impose new restrictions or outright prohibitions on fixed anchors. They appeared to view the climbing provisions of Director's Order 41 (along with a detailed reference manual on the order) as a requirement for consultation and collaboration around fixed anchors, not a call for new prohibitions. Authorities at other parks, most importantly Joshua Tree National Park (one of the most popular areas for climbing in the United States), were considerably more restrictive, announcing the necessity of permits for any rebolting and confirming the park's right to remove bolts in fixed anchor "free zones" without notice. Finding the varied and conflicting rules on bolts deeply troubling, the Access Fund and collaborating organizations attempted, without success, to promote federal legislation on the management of fixed anchors in wilderness areas that reasonably aligns natural resource protections with protection of the wilderness climbing experience. Recently, concerns over bolting rules have intensified as a 2021 proposed Climbing Management Plan for Joshua Tree National Park would treat all bolts as "installations" prohibited under the Wilderness Act of 1964. As of 2022, the Access Fund and climbing community remain very concerned that the proposed regulations on fixed anchors in Joshua Tree could be adopted for use in wilderness areas across the NPS and Forest Service, thereby undermining climbing and misconstruing the intentions of the Wilderness Act without substantively protecting rock surfaces from damage.[23]

Civic Engagement in National Parks

The new term for consultation and collaboration between visitors and park staff in the twenty-first century is "civic engagement." *Rethinking the National Parks for the 21st Century* was a product of civic engagement, written by an Advisory Board of citizens with expertise and professional responsibilities germane to the Park Service. The board's report did not use the term, yet in recommending that the NPS do more to immerse visitors in learning about the nation's natural environment, founding values, diverse cultures, and complex history, it held out hope that better-educated Americans would actively engage with national parks to help them fulfill their multidimensional mission. And soon after *Rethinking the National Parks* was released, the NPS sponsored meetings and developed programming to build the agency's capacity for civic engagement. With a "Director's Order on Civic Engagement and Public Involvement" in 2003 and the NPS's revision of its *Management Policies 2006*, the NPS identified civic engagement as an essential component of formal park policy:

> The Service will embrace civic engagement as a fundamental discipline and practice. The Service's commitment to civic engagement is founded on the central principle that preservation of the nation's heritage resources relies on continued collaborative relationships between the Service and American society. Civic engagement will be viewed as a commitment to building and sustaining relationships with neighbors and other communities of interest—both near and far. This will require that the Service communicate by both talking and listening. Through its practice of civic engagement, the Service will actively encourage a two-way, continuous, and dynamic conversation with the public.[24]

Rethinking the National Parks had imagined engagement between educated citizens and parks as positive and straightforward, with visitors learning to support NPS goals. The 2003 Director's Order and *Management Policies 2006* were less rosy-eyed but also more ambitious. Without being explicit, the language in the documents acknowledged that civic engagement could involve contention among multiple stakeholders and require compromise on all sides. It was an essential tool of democracy but not a tool that was easy to use. Still, civic engagement would allow the NPS to fulfill its obligations more successfully than it could with one-way communication and top-down decision-making. These insights had emerged from the NPS's experience in soliciting public input and consulting with tribes on proposed projects as required under the NHPA, NEPA, AIRFA, and NAGPRA. Involving the public in decision-making on historical preservation and environmental planning, and consulting with tribes on historical preservation, environmental planning, access to parks for sacred ritual, and the transfer and repatriation of cultural materials were of great value, though they involved difficult conversation and conflict. The new policy announced the NPS's interest in using civic engagement broadly across the agency and in building competency with this tool. The Access Fund's efforts to work with the NPS and other land managers on the use of fixed anchors is one example of civic engagement in action.[25]

Science, Resource Stewardship, and an Engaged Public

Rocky's concerted efforts to advance environmental education and leave-no-trace practices at Longs and other climbing sites are consistent with recent efforts across the NPS to advance the scientific management of parks, in part by fostering civic engagement in environmental stewardship. *Rethinking the National Parks* warned the NPS it could wait no longer to prioritize scientific research and ecological management and urged it to implement efforts to curb pollution, save fuels, and reduce waste. And because parks are not isolated islands but parts of large, complex ecosystems, the report also advised the NPS to "cooperate extensively with its neighbors—federal agencies, states, counties, cities, tribes, the private sector, even other countries." So, too, it exhorted the NPS to educate the American public about humans' complex relationship to the environment and thereby win broad support for enhanced environmental protection.[26]

A significant body of evidence documents NPS efforts since 2001 to adopt the Advisory Board's recommendations. Even in the face of interference by the George Bush Jr. (2000–2008) and Donald Trump (2016–2020) administrations, the NPS moved decisively toward increased scientific rigor and efficacy in resource stewardship. Thus, in 2006, after years of meddling from President Bush's secretary of the interior, Gale Norton, the NPS was able to publish a revised edition of *Management Policies*, its service-wide policy document, that put new emphasis on protecting the integrity of park resources by managing them "in the context of their larger ecosystems."[27] The Advisory Board report and *Management Policies 2006* presumed the presence of multiple environmental threats to park resources but did not name climate change as one of them. Four years later, in announcing the NPS's *Climate Change Response Strategy*, Director Jonathan Jarvis acknowledged climate change as a game changer, "the greatest threat to the integrity of our national parks that we have ever experienced." Long-recognized problems such as periodic drought, invasive species, and loss of predators had always presented complex problems in parks, but climate change posed a monumental challenge to resource protection and restoration because its "long-range and *cascading effects* . . . are just beginning to be understood." Jarvis committed the NPS to a response strategy with four key components: scientific research; mitigation (reducing parks' carbon footprint); adaptive management; and communication about climate change with NPS staff and the public. All these components were crucial, none more so than communication, which would provide staff with essential knowledge and promote citizens' support for the entire range of climate change strategies.[28]

Director Jarvis also asked the Science Committee of the National Park Service Advisory Board to "revisit" the highly influential 1963 *Leopold Report.* The Science Committee's report, *Revisiting Leopold: Resource Stewardship in the National Parks* (2012), found much of continuing value in the original report, especially its emphasis on the "enormous complexity" of ecological systems, continual scientific research, and the legitimacy of resource management that involved the "active manipulation" of plants and animals. In other ways, the committee parted ways with Leopold. Where he had recommended that "biotic associations within each park be maintained or where necessary recreated as nearly as possible in the condition that prevailed" before the arrival of Euro-Americans in an area, the committee urged the NPS to acknowledge and manage for "unrelenting and dynamic" change caused by "development pressures, pollution impacts, climate change, terrestrial and marine biodiversity loss [and] habitat fragmentation." If the parks were to fulfill their obligations to promote "ecological integrity" and "cultural and historical authenticity" and to provide "transformative experiences" for visitors, the NPS would need to invest in continual scientific research and expand its "capacity to manage natural and cultural resources efficiently across large-scale landscapes." Collaboration with academic institutions and other federal agencies and partnerships with states, tribes, and the private sector would be crucial. The American public (particularly youth) could assist in these efforts by performing resource monitoring and "citizen science" activities under the direction of scientists and park resource managers.[29]

After 2012 the NPS issued directives and released agency-wide planning guidelines to improve the efficacy of its responses to climate change, directing NPS units to protect the "wilderness character" of parklands even in the face of rapid change; improve sustainability through the reduction of carbon emissions, water use, and waste; and advance research, preservation, and the restoration of park resources—ecological, historical, and cultural—within the context of national and international networks for resource protection. The directives and planning documents stressed the agency's obligations to engage with the public and consult with indigenous tribes as required by NEPA, AIRFA, NAGPRA, *Management Policies 2006,* and the NPS "Planning, Environment and Public Comment (PEPC) System."[30] The Trump administration attempted to undo much of this work, politicizing the NPS and working to undermine the agency's reliance on science, commitment to preservation in perpetuity, adherence to NEPA, engagement with the public, and government-to-government consultations with indigenous tribes. Not wanting to appear altogether hostile to national parks, the Trump administration signed the Great American Outdoors Act (2020), which passed Congress with rare bipartisan support and addressed the need for billions of dollars in deferred maintenance in the NPS. Unfortunately, the new law ignored the agency's underfunded capacities for ecological, historical, and cultural preservation. The Biden administration has worked to roll back Trump initiatives and restore the integrity of the agency, though it faces sharp opposition in Congress and the distrust of millions of Americans. In the face of these external forces of resistance, in 2021 the NPS issued new management guidelines on climate change, clarifying processes for defining adaptive response strategies and making management decisions.[31]

Rocky is a good place to see how the NPS's twenty-first-century efforts to advance scientific stewardship and civic engagement with science have developed on a local scale. It is likely that in addition to *Rethinking the National Parks*, a 2002 *State of the Parks Report* produced by the National Parks Conservation Association helped push Rocky to improve scientific research and the management of both natural and cultural resources. The report evaluated the park on a scale of 1 to 100, giving it a set of mediocre scores: 75 in natural resource conditions, 67 in cultural resource conditions, and 77 in stewardship capacity. Much work was needed in scientific and cultural research, monitoring, planning, and the protection of the park's archaeological and historic sites.[32]

Then, as now, Rocky had a small staff of park scientists, but it was gradually developing capacity to conduct research through collaborations and partnerships with scientists in regional and agency-wide NPS offices, other federal agencies, and research universities. Scientists from the U.S. Geological Survey and Colorado State University have worked in partnership with Rocky since the 1980s to monitor "ecological response[s] to nitrogen deposition, climate variability and change, microbial activity in sub-alpine and alpine soils, hydrologic flow paths, and the response of aquatic organisms to disturbance" in the Loch Vale watershed. This ongoing work has provided critical data to park managers, and in the twenty-first century the scientists working at Loch Vale have become affiliated with Rocky's Continental Divide Research Learning Center (established in 2000). Reflective of a deepening commitment to rigorous research and ecological management, the CDRLC is one of seventeen NPS units with research learning centers. At Rocky the CDRLC coordinates and supports research by university natural and social scientists and graduate students on a range of environmental changes that are affecting air, water, climate, fire, vegetation, and wildlife in the park and northern Rockies. Researchers share their results with park staff in papers, meetings, and conferences and offer recommendations on resource management. The CDRLC is also committed to improving science literacy and thus supports opportunities for middle and high school teachers and students to assist CDRLC staff with scientific monitoring of species at various park sites. In collaboration with Eagle Rock School in Estes Park, which has a diverse body of students from the United States and abroad, the CDRLC runs an internship program that brings students into the park to gain an understanding of the scientific challenges facing public lands and explore careers in the NPS. And numerous projects at the CDRLC have a citizen science component, drawing volunteers to the park to assist scientists in monitoring species and recording scientific data.[33]

Rocky has also established a record of drawing the public into environmental planning as required by NEPA and the NPS's new policies on civic engagement. Most importantly, after decades of missteps and seven years of intensive research (1996–2003), park scientists and collaborators began the long process of developing an effective elk and vegetation plan to reduce the size of the park's elk population and restore willow and beaver habitat. Outreach was extensive, and citizens showed up at meetings and submitted thousands of comments, many expressing great concern about efforts to reduce the number of majestic elk in Rocky. The process was slow; eventually the park was able to win EPA approval of a plan that has successfully reduced the elk population through culling and contraception and led to improvements in vegetation in affected areas. So, too, the public supported the park's efforts to gain wilderness status for 95 percent of the acreage within Rocky's border, which was finally approved in 2009.[34]

Rocky's twenty-first-century commitment to scientific management is also evident in a 2015 comprehensive synthesis of research and stewardship related to the park's physical environment. *Natural Resource Vital Signs* summarized data on various threats to the park, including warming temperatures, increased fire risk, pollution, invasive species, and increased visitor use. The synthesis was prepared to help decision-makers engaged in adaptive management identify "preferred alternative actions" and learn of "early warning signs of declines in ecosystem health" that called for intervention. The report identified climate change and visitor congestion at both front-country sites such as Bear Lake and backcountry sites such as Longs Peak as the park's greatest challenges to natural resource stewardship. And it noted that "alpine vegetation, the spread of nonnative plants and aquatic organisms, wildlife distribution and habituation, soundscapes, and water quality are particularly susceptible to visitor impacts."[35]

And this brings us back to the climbers on Longs Peak. By 2015, when *Natural Resource Vital Signs* identified Longs as a backcountry site with levels of congestion harmful to the visitor experience and the environment, the peak had been a site of crowding for decades. Visitor use increased from over 10,000 annually in 1985, to 20,000 by 1994, and approximately 35,000 in 2000. Overall visitation in Rocky has also gone up. Since 1987 Rocky has never had fewer than 2.5 million visitors annually; after 1998 it began to see annual figures that frequently topped 3 million and never went below 2.7 million. From 2015 to 2019 visitation figures topped 4 million each year. In 2020, though Covid-19 closed the park entirely in April, visitation reached 3.3 million. Between 2012 and 2019, Rocky's overall visitor use rose 44 percent.[36]

As we saw in previous chapters, at no point in the twentieth century was Rocky in a position to restrict day-use visitation. In contrast, the twenty-first century has provided an unexpected opportunity to tackle the issue of visitor congestion. Covid-19 closed the park entirely in April 2020; by the time it reopened in May, park leadership had a timed-entry reservation system in place to reduce contact and contagion among visitors. Quickly, Superintendent Darla Sidles realized that some version of a timed-entry reservation system could be a long-term tool for reducing both visitor congestion and visitor impact on the environment. Whether the park will try to reduce the number of visitors overall or just spread out their presence in the park over time is not clear; in 2021 park visitation figures again topped 4 million, though timed entry was in place from late May through October. The park is developing plans for a permanent Day Use Visitor Access Strategy, which must go through the NEPA process. Public commentary has been solicited in a preliminary phase and will be solicited again as the park's Environmental Impact Statement undergoes evaluation. This initial public input shows that "commentors are fairly evenly divided on whether a reservation (timed-entry), crowds, traffic, or lack of parking interfere the most with their desired park experience. Poor human behavior, such as irresponsible interactions with wildlife, lack of a 'leave no trace' ethic, or general inconsideration or rudeness, was also raised repeatedly as an issue that interferes with a desired park experience, along with other visitor use issues, such as noise."[37]

The 2020–2021 timed-entry system had no real impact at Longs Peak, since it limited entry only from 9:00 a.m. to 3:00 p.m., a time frame irrelevant to many climbers who start their day well before dawn. But the park is considering day-use hiking permits for Longs Peak as part of the permanent Day Use Visitor Access Strategy. Certainly, park staff will face a challenge in gaining technical and nontechnical climbers' support for a timed-entry system that might reduce access to the peak. The park's growing experience in navigating the NEPA process and using civic engagement to work with stakeholders should, however, serve the park and climbers well. For the first time, the park, its climbers, and other stakeholders have an opportunity to devise a visitor day-use plan that could sustain visitors' enjoyment in, and engagement with, the park yet also protect its vulnerable environment.[38]

Diversity and Inclusion in Interpretation, Employment, and Visitation

As the Advisory Board was working on *Rethinking the National Parks for the 21st Century*, diverse community groups, Native tribes, and professional historians were already pressuring the NPS to heed their knowledge and expertise in developing interpretive exhibits and programming at various NPS historic sites, both old and new. The sites were reflective of human oppression and pain, resilience and hope, related to slavery and sharecropping, the incarceration of Japanese Americans during World War II, criminal punishment and reform in the federal prison system, and violence between southern plains tribes and the U.S. military in the late nineteenth century. In the early 2000s, with new policies on civic engagement emerging, the NPS completed educational and interpretive projects at some sites and made measurable progress at others. Available documentation on the sites, including the African Burial Ground National Monument in lower Manhattan, the Eastern State Penitentiary Historic Site in Philadelphia, the Washita Battlefield National Historic Site in Oklahoma, and the Sotterley Plantation in Maryland, points to the complexities of civic engagement and the very hard work of building trust among stakeholders. Simultaneously, it points to the vital contributions diverse stakeholders are making to the public's historical knowledge and understanding.[39]

The NPS also moved civic engagement in history education online. *Rethinking the National Parks for the 21st Century* imagined that most educational and interpretive work would take place *inside* national parks and NPS historic sites; the internet has made it possible to deliver complex stories of the nation's past into Americans' homes and schools. The NPS's web page "Telling All Americans' Stories" offers rich thematic and place-based histories of the United States, its diverse peoples, and its troubled journey toward liberty and justice. The histories are accessible, yet they acknowledge the complexity of the past and are based on meticulous research. The people who have produced the histories are NPS professionals, activists, community members, NPS student interns, and professional historians with deep ties to the places, people, and subjects they explore. The NPS has openly admitted that some of its efforts to utilize civic engagement in historical research and education have stumbled as NPS staff encountered skepticism and distrust in communities of color. Nonetheless, historical education in the NPS is reaching new levels of achievement in providing an inclusive, multilayered, and accurate portrait of the nation's past.[40]

Not surprisingly, individual parks and historic sites vary greatly in their capacity to promote civic engagement and meet the NPS's increasingly high standards of history education and interpretation. Funding and staffing at NPS sites are chronically insufficient, leaving a few highly dedicated interpretive professionals stretched very thin. History education on Rocky's website still neglects indigenous tribes' centuries-long presence in the Northern Rockies before the park was founded. The park's visitor centers feature outdated exhibits on indigenous cultures that provide little narrative history or interpretation. The park has put up a couple of wayside signs about indigenous culture at specific sites such as the Ute Trail, but much remains to be done. Neither on-site exhibits nor online materials have yet made much use of the results of the extensive archaeological research conducted at Rocky by Dr. Robert Brunswig and coinvestigators between

1998 and 2003, which seeks to explain "how past Native Americans integrated spiritual beliefs and spiritually-inspired behavior with socio-economic systems to both define and cope with their often challenging physical worlds through time."[41] Nor does the park offer coverage of Euro-American encroachment in the Northern Rockies, warfare between the U.S. government and indigenous peoples, the coerced removal of tribes to reservations, or the experiences and resilience of the Utes, Arapahos, Cheyennes, and other indigenous groups on and off reservations since removal. Not surprisingly, the park's educational and interpretive programming also neglects to discuss values and practices that kept Rocky Mountain National Park a place for Whites' exclusive enjoyment throughout the twentieth century. There is no coverage of discrimination at local resorts and businesses or of the KKK's presence in Colorado or Estes Park; no mention of African Americans' creation of an alternative space for outdoor enjoyment and inspiration at Lincoln Hills; no discussion of persistent bias and discrimination against Blacks, Latinx, Jews, and Asians in communities all along the Front Range, or of opposition in Estes Park to a Job Corps program for diverse urban youth inside Rocky during the 1960s.

Fortunately, Rocky is building relationships with the Ute, Arapaho, and Cheyenne Tribes that have the potential to both improve history education at Rocky and strengthen the tribes' connections to their homelands. Under Bill Gwaltney's leadership (1997–2005), Rocky's Division of Interpretation and Education worked to develop collaborative relations with Arapaho and Ute tribal members and hosted annual or biannual visits by Ute and Arapaho adults and children to Rocky for about a decade. In 2011 loss of funding for indigenous travel to Estes Park ended those visits. Nonetheless, the park helped Arapaho tribal members organize a successful centennial celebration of the Arapaho Pack Trip in 1914 in downtown Estes Park. And in recent years, the Division of Interpretation and Education at Rocky has partnered with leaders at the University of Colorado Boulder (the Center of the American West and the Center for Native American and Indigenous Studies), the NPS Intermountain Region (Cultural Anthropology Program), and representatives from the Cheyenne and Arapaho Tribes in Oklahoma, the Northern Arapaho Tribe in Wyoming, the Northern Cheyenne Tribe in Montana, the Southern Ute Tribe in Colorado, the Ute Tribe of Uintah and Ouray in Utah, and the Ute Mountain Ute Tribe in Colorado to promote better representation of indigenous Americans at Rocky and other national parks. The workshops held thus far have focused on developing processes and goals for improving interpretive exhibits and online materials about indigenous tribes at Rocky. Current collaborative work between the park and tribal entities, with funding from the Rocky Mountain Conservancy, should result in the mounting of new interpretive exhibits in 2024 on indigenous cultures, their histories in Rocky, and their abiding connections to it.[42]

Participants in this collaborative effort are also contributors to a forthcoming anthology of case studies, tentatively titled *Native Peoples and National Parks:*

Pathways to Collaboration. Some case studies will illuminate the process of building collaborative relationships between researchers, Native partners, and public lands representatives. Others will highlight difficulties that have arisen at sites with very difficult and contested histories. A final group of case studies will examine the experiences of tribal nations that have developed successful shared governance arrangements related to land access and management. The efforts underway by the Division of Interpretation and Education at Rocky have the potential to greatly enhance the educational experience of visitors at Rocky and create the basis for a collaborative relationship between Rocky and Native tribes that sustains tribal connections to park lands. No plans are yet underway to develop interpretive materials on other people of color and their histories of outdoor recreation and exclusion from Rocky, but recent collaborations between indigenous tribes and Rocky may inspire interpretive work on these issues.[43]

RETHINKING NATIONAL PARKS FOR THE 21ST CENTURY highlighted the need for a diverse workforce in national parks. It said little about the lack of diversity among visitors in the big nature parks, focusing instead on the NPS's obligation to partner with other federal, state, and local agencies to create park and recreational opportunities in and near urban areas where most Americans live, including people of color. The imperative to establish more parks in urban settings remains. Nonetheless, after 2001 the Whiteness of visitors at the big nature parks such as Yosemite, Yellowstone, and Rocky became an increasingly urgent topic among scholars and journalists. NPS studies showed visitor populations across all regions of the NPS and at all types of NPS units (parks, historic sites, battlefields, recreation sites, etc.) to be on average 95 percent White, though the 2010 census showed the U.S. population to be 72 percent White. Rocky conducted separate studies of visitors in summer 2010 and winter 2011 and found visitors to the park to be 94 to 95 percent White. A smaller 2006 study of visitors to sites along the Highway 7 corridor in Rocky Mountain National Park, which included Longs Peak, found that 7 percent of visitors identified as non-White or Hispanic.[44]

Scholars generated a range of explanations for the relative absence of people of color in national parks, including socioeconomic marginality, differing cultural norms, legacies of discrimination, and geographic distance. Journalists and scholars also pointed to census data showing that ethnic and racial minorities will account for more than 50 percent of the U.S. population before 2050. The United States is on the way to becoming a "majority-minority" nation. And numerous authors have noted that the NPS might become increasingly irrelevant to Americans if the agency does not work to gain the support and interest of ethnic and racial minorities.[45]

As evidence of the system's lack of diversity grew, the NPS acknowledged the need to modify both its visitor base and workforce and established an Office of Relevancy, Diversity, and Inclusion (RDI), articulating support for inclusivity regardless of race, ethnicity, gender and sexual identity, or disability. The NPS issued a series of Director's Orders that reaffirmed its commitment to hiring and retaining a workforce that represented the diversity of the nation with regard to race and ethnicity, gender identity and sexual orientation, and disability, and its refusal to tolerate discrimination or harassment of any kind, including sexual harassment. In addition, it established an Urban Agenda program to encourage communities of color to connect to parks, whether as visitors or potential employees. With 80 percent of Americans living in urban settings, the NPS committed to building more parks for cities and making big nature parks like Rocky more accessible to urban populations through alliances with governmental agencies and community organizations, outreach, transportation initiatives, and other strategies.[46]

Innovations related to the NPS's RDI initiatives and Urban Agenda have slowly taken shape at Rocky, though no data on their impact is yet available. The Latinx population in Estes Park has grown recently, reaching 11.6 percent by 2019, with nearly 25 percent of school-age children from Latinx homes. When staffing and funding has allowed, Spanish-speaking and African American interns and rangers in the Division of Interpretation and Education at Rocky have engaged in direct outreach with the growing Latinx community in Estes Park and with the African American community in Denver. The park has staffed tables at the Estes Park Cinco de Mayo celebration, organized dozens of other outreach events, and provided transportation and picnic meals for Latinx families wishing to visit Rocky. Meanwhile, Ben Baldwin, the Youth and Volunteer Programs manager for the Intermountain Region of the NPS, has worked to attract diverse youth to the NPS's Youth Conservation Corps (YCC) at numerous parks in the Intermountain Region, including Rocky. YCC crews at Rocky are funded by the park's friends' group, the Rocky Mountain Conservancy (RMC), and the RMC now has a Diversity Internship Cohort coordinator leading efforts to build diverse youths' interest in becoming the next generation of park stewards. Superintendent Darla Sidles led a successful Urban Agenda initiative with the city of Tucson as superintendent of Saguaro National Park before moving to Rocky in 2016, and her experience could prove highly beneficial for Rocky. Denver is only sixty miles away and the entire Front Range is increasingly urban and diverse. As we have seen, interest in outdoor recreation is building in communities of color in the United States, and Rocky could be an important site of adventure and education for people of color living in Colorado's cities and in urban settings across the nation. The Estes Valley Land Trust (EVLT), an organization devoted to preserving land in the area near Rocky through conservation easements with willing landowners, is also promoting diversity, equity, and inclusion in the park. The EVLT is creating opportunities for its local membership (predominantly White and of retirement age) to hear from young people of color who are organizing their peers and encouraging them to recreate in national parks, become outspoken advocates of democratic access, and gain knowledge about environmental imperatives.[47]

CERTAINLY, IT IS ESSENTIAL to acknowledge and applaud the changes that Rocky has embraced since the turn of the twenty-first century, following the lead of the NPS. Building on historical examples of partnership between climbers and rangers in the park, Rocky has scaled up its efforts to engage visitors in the NPS's multifaceted mission. Facilitating their enjoyment is no longer enough. Rocky has thus worked to enhance visitors' education, devoting resources to educating climbers and other visitors about safety, leave-no-trace practices, and the threats posed by climate change and loss of biodiversity. It has gained expertise in meaningful engagement with stakeholders, prioritized scientific approaches to park management, recognized the necessity of devising a plan to manage visitor day use, and worked to improve its outreach to diverse populations in Estes Park, Denver, and the Front Range. The park is slowly developing collaborative processes with indigenous tribes that will make it possible for tribes to rebuild connections to their homeland and improve the park's interpretive offerings for visitors.

These are good signs. It is imperative that the park continue this work and embark on other initiatives. For example, with the proliferation of climbing and outdoor organizations for communities of color in recent years, including in Colorado, the park has a real opportunity to make climbing in Rocky and on Longs a sport of adventure that is truly inclusive. In addition, the park could engage Native climbers such as Len Necefer and members of consulting tribes to help educate climbers and park staff about the history and culture of indigenous peoples in Rocky and the meaning they have attached to places such as Longs Peak.

We must also be mindful of the enormous obstacles that stand in the way of constructive change in Rocky and other parks. Engaged citizens, academic partners, and park staff play critical roles in promoting reform both in and beyond the NPS, but the agency is a slow-moving bureaucracy. In 2020, the NPS was still 78.5 percent White and disproportionately male, especially in higher-ranking professional positions. And the agency buried the results of a 2018 survey of agency staff that revealed high levels of "disrespectful and abusive behavior" in employment settings. An independent watchdog group, Public Employees for Environmental Responsibility, obtained and released the report in November 2021. The U.S. Supreme Court, now with a conservative supermajority, will hear a case on affirmative action in its next term (2022–2023), and it is widely anticipated that it will overturn affirmative action law, thus upsetting NPS policy and the agency's Relevancy, Diversity, and Inclusion programs.[48]

Moreover, we need the federal government, other nations, and global alliances to demonstrate a willingness to act against climate change and loss of biodiversity. Scientific management by staff at Rocky and other parks has very limited capacity to mitigate in park settings the effects of environmental challenges that are global in scope. The East Troublesome and Cameron Peak Fires burned thirty thousand acres in Rocky in just a couple of days in 2020, moving over the Continental Divide, forcing the evacuation of Estes Park, and demonstrating how climate change has increased fire danger. The wildfire season in Colorado is now twelve months long, as the December 31, 2021, Marshall Fire (about fifty miles from Rocky) made clear, and Colorado's famously bright blue skies are increasingly obscured by smoke, ash, and pollution for months of the year.[49] Yet as of mid-2022, bitter political division and gridlock in Congress and a radically conservative Supreme Court majority stand in the way of the policy changes and action needed to preserve parks and the world around them from environmental devastation.

If national parks are to remedy past wrongs and fulfill the promises offered at their founding, visitors and citizens, NPS leaders and government officials must all be on board. Progress has been made, but further progress is not inevitable. In the present day, though much has been learned from mistakes and omissions of the past, stewardship of the nation's national and cultural heritage at Rocky Mountain National Park is not yet ensured.

NOTES

INTRODUCTION

1. Philpott, *Vacationland*.
2. Automated infrared counts of estimated visitor use, East Longs Peak Trail, 2011–2013, 2015, unpublished park documentation from Mike Lukens, Wilderness and Climbing Program supervisor, in email to author, January 25, 2022. The recent counts are similar to those obtained between 2002 and 2004. See Paul McLaughlin, "Climbing the Longs Peak Keyhole Route," October 20, 2008, accessed December 18, 2021, https://www.nps.gov/articles/climbing -the-longs-peak-keyhole-route.htm; Mike Caldwell, interview by Ruth Alexander, August 12, 2009, transcript, ROMO-01851.
3. Nesbit, *Longs Peak*, 79–81 (note: all citations of this source are of the 12th ed. [2015] unless otherwise indicated); Jeffrey J. Doran, "A Statistical Analysis on Fatalities while Climbing Longs Peak," *Rocky Mountain Journal* (blog), March 25, 2021, accessed December 18, 2021, http://rockymountainhikingtrails .blogspot.com/2021/03/a-statistical-analysis-on-fatalities.html.
4. A 2010 study of visitors to Rocky Mountain National Park showed that Whites were 95 percent of park visitors, Asians were 2 percent, and other races and ethnicities constituted 1 percent or less each. See Blotkamp et al., *Rocky Mountain National Park*. See also Shoemaker, "Mountains Are Calling"; Taylor and Grandjean, "Visitor Satisfaction"; Roberts, "Ethnic Minority Visitors."
5. An Act to Establish a National Park Service, and for Other Purposes, approved August 25, 1916, 39 Stat. 535, 16 U.S.C. 1, 2, 3, and 4.
6. Frederick Law Olmsted, "The Yosemite Valley and the Mariposa Big Tree Grove," (1865), in Dilsaver, *America's National Park System*, 10–15.
7. Olmsted, "Yosemite Valley," 9, 15–17; Carr, *Wilderness by Design*, 20–22, 27–31; Shaffer, *See America First*; Ross-Bryant, *Pilgrimage to the National Parks*; Button, "American Liberalism."
8. Charles E. Beveridge, introduction to Olmsted, *Papers of Frederick Law Olmsted*, 1–37; Olmsted, "Yosemite Valley," 16; Grinde and Johansen, *Exemplar of Liberty*.

9. Diamant, "Olmsteds and the Development."
10. Theodore Roosevelt, "Remarks at the Laying of the Cornerstone of the Gateway to Yellowstone National Park in Gardiner, Montana," American Presidency Project, April 24, 1903, accessed December 18, 2021, https://www.presidency.ucsb.edu/node/343416.
11. An Act to Establish a National Park Service, and for Other Purposes, approved August 25, 1916, 39 Stat. 535.
12. See, for example, Smith, *Civic Ideals*; Blight, *Race and Reunion*; Bederman, *Manliness and Civilization*; Hoxie, *Final Promise*.
13. Leopold, *Sand County Almanac*, 201–7, 224–25.
14. Sauvajot, "National Parks."
15. Lanisha Renee Blount, "Anti-Racism Resources for Climbers," *Climbing*, June 15, 2020, accessed January 8, 2022, https://www.climbing.com/news/anti-racism-resources-for-climbers; Stanfield McCown, "Evaluation of National Park Service."
16. Nesbit, *Longs Peak*; Donahue, *Longs Peak Experience*; Randall, *Longs Peak Tales*; MacDonald, *Longs Peak*; Robertson et al., *100 Years Up High*; Robertson, *Magnificent Mountain Women*.
17. Sellars, *Preserving Nature*; Runte, *National Parks*; Frank, *Making Rocky Mountain National Park*; Keiter, *To Conserve Unimpaired*.
18. Andrews, *Coyote Valley*; Warren, *Hunter's Game*; Keller and Turek, *American Indians and National Parks*; Spence, *Dispossessing the Wilderness*; Burnham, *Indian Country*; Jacoby, *Crimes against Nature*. Scholars have also examined the expulsion of Native peoples from national parks and other protected landscapes on a global scale. See, for example, Dowie, *Conservation Refugees*.
19. Stevens, *Indigenous Peoples*.
20. In addition to Sellars, Runte, and Frank, see especially Rothman, *Devil's Bargains*.
21. Johnson, *This Grand and Magnificent Place*; Mittlefehldt, *Tangled Roots*.
22. Turner, "From Woodcraft to 'Leave No Trace'"; Taylor, *Pilgrims of the Vertical*; Chamberlin, *On the Trail*. See also Sutter, *Driven Wild*; and Young, *Heading Out*.
23. See, for example, Tuler and Golding, *Comprehensive Study of Visitor Safety*.
24. See, for example, Finney, *Black Faces, White Spaces*; Stodolska et al., *Race, Ethnicity, and Leisure*; O'Brien, "State Parks and Jim Crow."
25. See, for example, Foster, "In the Face of 'Jim Crow'"; Sorin, *Driving while Black*; Bay, *Traveling Black*; Taylor, *Overground Railroad*; Young, "'Contradiction in Democratic Government'"; McCammack, *Landscapes of Hope*; Wolcott, *Race, Riots, and Rollercoasters*.
26. NPS Advisory Board and Franklin, *Rethinking the National Parks*, 7; NPS, *Management Policies 2006*; Reynolds, "Whose America?"
27. NPS Advisory Board and Franklin, *Rethinking the National Parks*, 8, 14, 15, 21, 24–25, 27.
28. NPS Advisory Board and Franklin, 30.
29. NPS, *Management Policies 2006*; NPS, "Director's Order #16B: Diversity in the National Park Service"; NPS, "Director's Order #75A: Civic Engagement

and Public Involvement." See also Taylor et al., "National Park Service Comprehensive Survey"; Schultz et al., "Whose National Park Service?"

30. Gonzalez et al., "Disproportionate Magnitude of Climate Change"; Mott, "Mind the Gap"; Thakar et al., "Building a More Inclusive National Park System." Rocky has become the third most popular national park in the nation, with high levels of traffic and crowding. See John Meyer, "Rocky Mountain National Park Sets Another Attendance Record with 4.6 Million Visitors in 2019," *Denver Post*, February 14, 2020, https://theknow.denverpost.com/2020/02/14/rocky-mountain-national-park-attendance-2019/233799/. On environmental conditions at Rocky as of 2015, see Franke et al., *Natural Resource Vital Signs*.

CHAPTER 1

1. Estes, *Memoirs of Estes Park*, 6.

2. U.S. Congress, *Hearing Before the Committee on the Public Lands on S. 6309, a Bill to Establish the Rocky Mountain National Park in the State of Colorado*, 63rd Cong., 3rd Sess. (1914), 8, 19, 40, 56, 60, 62.

3. Rocky Mountain National Park was established by congressional act on January 26, 1915 (Pub. L. No. 63–238, 38 Stat. 796).

4. Buchholtz, *Rocky Mountain National Park*, 34–37; Goetzman, *Exploration and Empire*, 58–62.

5. Fuller and Hafen, *Journal of Captain John R. Bell*, 142.

6. Brunswig, *Prehistoric, Protohistoric*, 63–77, 87–94, 590, 622, 624, 634.

7. Brunswig, *Prehistoric, Protohistoric*, 88–92, 590, 622, 624; Andrews, *Coyote Valley*, 19–62.

8. Brunswig, *Prehistoric, Protohistoric*, 92–93; Brunswig, "Apachean Archaeology," 20–36; Brett, *Ethnographic Assessment*, 35–53.

9. Brunswig, *Prehistoric, Protohistoric*, 93–94; Oliver W. Toll, "Report of Arapaho Indian Trip, 1913 [*sic*]," typescript, 1931, 17, ROMO Library #2133. Toll rearranged and slightly revised the original typescript for publication in 1962. See Toll, *Arapaho Names and Trails*.

10. Toll, "Report of Arapaho Indian Trip," 34; Cowell and Moss, "Arapaho Place Names."

11. Toll, "Report of Arapaho Indian Trip," 30–31. See also Kroeber, *Arapaho*, 22; Metcalf and Black, *Archaeological Excavations*, 7, 10; McBeth, *Native American Oral History*, 139–42.

12. Bowles, *Parks and Mountains of Colorado*, 145–46; Anderson, *One Hundred Years*, 33–40, 55–59; West, *Contested Plains*; Berwanger, *Rise of the Centennial State*, 23–40; Andrews, *Coyote Valley*, 63–94; Decker, *"The Utes Must Go."* See also the website for the Sand Creek Massacre National Historic Site, accessed December 20, 2021, https://www.nps.gov/sand/learn/historyculture/index.htm.

13. Buchholtz, *Rocky Mountain National Park*, 49. On the growth of tourism in the United States, see Sears, *Sacred Places*; Gassan, *Birth of American Tourism*; Shaffer, *See America First*; Stewart, *"What Nature Suffers to Groe"*; Stradling, *Making Mountains*; Aron, *Working at Play*; Sterngrass, *First Resorts*; Olmanson, *Future City and the Inland Sea*; Mackintosh, *Selling the Sights*.

14. Buchholtz, *Rocky Mountain National Park*, 44, 52.

15. Buchholtz, 57–60; Keplinger, *First Ascent of Longs Peak*; Mazel, *Pioneering Ascents*, 227–31. Dougald MacDonald notes that *Rocky Mountain News* published an account of a Longs Peak summit by J. W. Goss and R. L. Woodward in 1865, three years prior to Powell and Byers's successful ascent. He finds the account credible, though other historians do not. MacDonald, *Longs Peak*, 46–47.

16. Bartlett and Goetzman, *Exploring the American West*, 92–95, 116–19, 515–29; Bueler, *Roof of the Rockies*, 31–33; Holland, *Rocky Mountain National Park*, 28–29; Robertson, *Magnificent Mountain Women*, 9–11. For a useful discussion of visual theory and the process of learning to see through cultural and political cues, see Harris and Ruggles, *Sites Unseen*, 5–29.

17. Isserman, *Continental Divide*, 115–20; Robertson, *Magnificent Mountain Women*, 7–8; Willard, "Evans and the Saint Louis Western Colony," 5–11.

18. Pickering, *"This Blue Hollow,"* 53–81.

19. Bird, *Lady's Life in the Rocky Mountains*, 83–101; Robertson, *Magnificent Mountain Women*, 11–17.

20. Sears, *Sacred Places*, 122–23, 156–81; Ross-Bryant, *Pilgrimage to the National Parks*.

21. Bird, *Lady's Life in the Rocky Mountains*, 82, 109–15. Bird stayed with the Evans family in Estes Park for several weeks after her climb on Longs Peak.

22. Pickering, *"This Blue Hollow,"* 81–106, 192–94; Buchholtz, *Rocky Mountain National Park*, 77–86; Musselman, *Rocky Mountain National Park*, 7–9; Kropp, "Wilderness Wives," 5–30; Aron, *Working at Play*, 156–77.

23. Lamb, *Past Memories*, 86–87; Pickering, *"This Blue Hollow,"* 99–101.

24. Pickering, *"This Blue Hollow,"* 154–65; Standish, "East Longs Peak Trail," 6; Perry, *It Happened*, 11–15.

25. Quin, *Rocky Mountain National Park Roads*, 6–7.

26. Pickering, *"This Blue Hollow,"* 111–19, 130–36, 154–56.

27. See, for example, Bowles, *Parks and Mountains of Colorado*; Tice, *Over the Plains*; Crofutt, *Crofutt's Grip-Sack Guide*.

28. Pickering, *Frederick Chapin's Colorado*, 30–31, 34–63.

29. Buchholtz, *Rocky Mountain National Park*, 124–26; Drummond, *Enos Mills*; Nesbit, *Longs Peak*, 3–5.

30. Mills, *Adventures of a Nature Guide*, 155–81. Most of the chapters in Mills's book had been published previously in popular magazines. See also Armitage, *Nature Study Movement*; Herron, *Science and the Social Good*, 147–54; Worster, *Passion for Nature*; Musil, *Rachel Carson and Her Sisters*, 12–52, 57, 92–93.

31. Buchholtz, *Rocky Mountain National Park*, 116–32.

32. Pickering, *"This Blue Hollow,"* 220–35; Musselman, *Rocky Mountain National Park*, 19–27; Drummond, *Enos Mills*, 222–47.

33. The literature on race relations after the Civil War and into the twentieth century is vast. See, for example, Smith, *Civic Ideals*; Blight, *Race and Reunion*; Bederman, *Manliness and Civilization*; Hoxie, *Final Promise*; Lears, *Rebirth of a Nation*; Newman, *White Women's Rights*; Hahn, *Nation under Our Feet*; Slotkin, *Gunfighter Nation*; Richardson, *How the South Won the Civil War*.

34. "City News," *Statesman*, September 25, 1909; "40 Miles of the Grandest Mountain Scenery on Earth," *Statesman*, January 13, 1905; "City News,"

Statesman, May 20, 1911; "To the Public," *Statesman*, September 16, 1911; Hansen, "Entitled to Full and Equal Enjoyment."

35. Shaffer, *See America First*, 55–59, 68–71.

36. Robertson, *Magnificent Mountain Women*, 44–47; Toll, "Report of Arapaho Indian Trip"; Arps and Kingery, *High Country Names*, 1–3.

37. Toll, "Report of Arapaho Indian Trip," 1, 3, 8–10, 14.

38. Toll, "Report of Arapaho Indian Trip."

39. U.S. Congress, *Hearing Before the Committee on the Public Lands on S. 6309, a Bill to Establish the Rocky Mountain National Park*, 16–22.

40. On touristic development and its environmental impact in Estes Park, see Pickering, *"This Blue Hollow,"* chap. 9; Frank, *Making Rocky Mountain National Park*, 120–21, 147–55; Zietkiewicz, "Nature's Playground," 21–27; Packard, "Ecological Study of the Bighorn Sheep," 3–28.

41. The Estes Park area began stocking rivers with nonnative fish in the 1880s and began to import elk from Yellowstone National Park in 1913. See Frank, *Making Rocky Mountain National Park*, 120–24, 147–55. See also the correspondence between Peter Hondius and the U.S. Forest Service, February 4, 1913, through May 10, 1913, on the shipment of elk to Estes Park from Wyoming, in ROMO-01572, series 3, folder 22.

42. Mills, *Rocky Mountain National Park*, 73–74.

43. U.S. Congress, *Hearing Before the Committee on the Public Lands on S. 6309, a Bill to Establish the Rocky Mountain National Park*, 3–12.

44. An Act to Establish the Rocky Mountain National Park in the State of Colorado, Publ. L. No. 238, 63rd Cong., 3rd Sess. (January 26, 1915), 800.

45. National Park Service Organic Act, 39 Stat. 535, 16 U.S.C. 1, 2, 3, and 4; "Auto Use in the National Park," Proceedings of the National Park Conference Held at the Yosemite National Park, October 14, 15, and 16, 2012, in Dilsaver, *America's National Park System*, 30–33; Runte, *National Parks*, 56–60; Buchholtz, *Rocky Mountain National Park*, 116–23, 144–45; Drummond, *Enos Mills*, 376–86.

CHAPTER 2

1. U.S. Department of the Interior, *Rocky Mountain National Park*, 8.

2. The Colorado State Highway Commission held formal responsibility for road construction and maintenance until 1922, but actual supervision fell to the skeleton park staff. Descriptions of park roadwork can be found in the *Superintendent's Monthly Reports (SMR)* and the *Superintendent's Annual Reports (SAR)*, ROMO-01571. See also Musselman, *Rocky Mountain National Park*, 77–83.

3. Wells, *Car Country*; Dauvergne, *Shadows of Consumption*, 37–40; Jackie Powell, "Fill 'Er Up! A History of the Gas Pump," *Colorado Central Magazine*, September 1, 2011, accessed December 20, 2021, https://coloradocentralmagazine.com/fill-er-up-a-history-of-the-gas-pump/; Shaffer, *See America First*; Louter, *Windshield Wilderness*; NPS, *General Information regarding Rocky Mountain National Park, Season of 1918*; U.S. Railroad Administration, *Rocky Mountain National Park, Colorado*; Union Pacific System, *Colorado Mountain Playgrounds*; Mather, *Progress in the Development*, 5.

4. On visitation, see *SAR*, 1915, 34d; *SAR*, 1919, 133–38d; letter from Superintendent Roger Toll to the Director of the National Park Service, August 30, 1926, in *SAR*, 1926, 368–69d; *SAR*, 1929, 436d. All page numbers for *SAR* and *SMR* are for the digitized reports (d). See also "Park Reports," NPS Stats: National Park Service Visitor Use Statistics, https://irma.nps.gov/STATS /Reports/Park/ROMO.

5. *SAR*, 1928, 1929, 1930; Buchholtz, *Rocky Mountain National Park*, 167; Musselman, *Rocky Mountain National Park*, 77–87; Quin, *Rocky Mountain National Park Roads*.

6. NPS, *General Information regarding Rocky Mountain National Park, Season of 1918*, 5–9; NPS, *Rules and Regulations, Rocky Mountain National Park, 1920*, 7, 24–27.

7. NPS, *Rocky Mountain National Park, Season of 1918*, 21–23; NPS, *Rules and Regulations, Rocky Mountain National Park, 1920*, 24–27.

8. Toll and Yard, *Mountaineering*, 49.

9. Roger Toll, "Analysis of Register on Longs Peak 1915–1916," and Park Registers Committee, "Report, February 10, 1933," in CMC Peak Registers, Reports of Conditions, 1912–1936, CMCC, AAL; *SAR*, 1922, 249d; "The Resistless Urge," *Trail and Timberline*, December 1921, 3. By 1918 the CMC had placed registers on twenty-nine peaks in Colorado. See *Trail and Timberline*, August 1918, 3. Over the next decade, the geographic reach of the CMC extended to all mountain ranges of the Colorado Rockies and to Wyoming. See Ellingwood, "Technical Climbing." Paul Nesbit estimates that three-quarters of all Longs Peak climbers went in "guided parties" in 1915–1916, but only one-quarter "went with guides" by 1931. See Nesbit, *Longs Peak*, 5.

10. See, for example, comments on the need for new and improved trails throughout the park in *SAR*, 1916, 44d; *SAR*, 1923, 285d.

11. *SMR*, July 1918, 144d; Drummond, *Enos Mills*, 215; *Estes Park Trail*, August 19, 1921, 1; *SAR*, 1921, 218d.

12. *SAR*, 1922, 249–50d. The local newspaper reported favorably on the new trail markers. See *Estes Park Trail*, August 25, 1922, 1.

13. Toll and Yard, *Mountaineering*. By 1919 the CMC had a large central group in Denver and chapters developing in Boulder, Estes Park, Fort Collins, and Colorado Springs. The organization's magazine for members, *Trail and Timberline*, began monthly publication in 1918.

14. F.M.F., "Roger Toll, 1883–1936, in Memoriam," *American Alpine Journal* 3, no. 1 (1937): 92–94; Buchholtz, *Rocky Mountain National Park*, 158–60.

15. Quote by Robert Sterling Yard, "By Way of Introduction," in Toll and Yard, *Mountaineering*, 7.

16. Toll and Yard, *Mountaineering*, 20–38, 46–56.

17. Toll and Yard, 41–43.

18. Toll and Yard, 9–10, 12–13, 43.

19. Schrepfer, *Nature's Altars*; Hansen, *Summits of Modern Man*.

20. Kingery and Kingery, *Colorado Mountain Club*, i.

21. Toll and Yard, *Mountaineering*, 10; Ross-Bryant, *Pilgrimage to the National Parks*; Hyde, *American Vision*; Runte, *National Parks*.

22. See photos of CMC members in *Trail and Timberline*; scrapbooks in the CMC archival collection at the AAL; and Ina Teresa Aulls, "Colorado Mountain Club Album," 1919–1929, Western History and Genealogy, Denver Public Library. See also Colorado Mountain Club, "Constitution and By-Laws and Directory of Members," supplement to *Trail and Timberline*, March 1922, 2.

23. For example, James Grafton Rogers, the CMC's first president, was an attorney and professor of law at the University of Colorado. Among other founding and early members, Roger Toll was an engineer, William Smedley was a dentist, Charles Partridge Adams was a well-regarded landscape artist, Lucretia Vaile was a reference librarian, Florence Sabin and Elsie Pratt were physicians, and Mary Sabin was a schoolteacher. For further information on the backgrounds and civic associations of CMC members, see the Western History Subject Index of the Denver Public Library, accessed December 25, 2021, https://history .denverlibrary.org/research-tool/western-history-subject-index. For the names of early members, consult the first years of *Trail and Timberline*, and Kingery and Kingery, *Colorado Mountain Club*.

24. On race relations in Colorado and the American West, see Atkins, *Human Relations in Colorado*, 53–59, 109–16; Leonard and Noel, *Denver*; Taylor, *In Search of the Racial Frontier*; Whitaker, *Race Work*; Brenner, "Women of the Ku Klux Klan."

25. Atkins, *Human Relations in Colorado*; Leonard and Noel, *Denver*, 122, 169–74; Labode, "'Defend Your Manhood,'" 173; Wasinger, "From Five Points to Struggle Hill," 28–39; Goldstein, "Breaking Down Barriers"; Reid, *Negro Population in Denver*; Dickson, "Early Club Movement"; Newsum et al., *Lincoln Hills and Civil Rights*.

26. Williams, *Torchbearers of Democracy*.

27. Quoted in Shaffer, *See America First*, 126. Shaffer's endnote 101, p. 358, cites the primary source as "Accommodations for Colored People," Entry 6, General, Minutes, Sixth National Parks Conference, 1922, RG 79, National Archives, Maryland.

28. "Klan Presents Minister with Handsome Purse, Farewell Reception Tendered Rev. and Mrs. Harris," *Estes Park Trail*, May 1, 1925; "Fiery Crosses Burned at Half-Way Place," *Estes Park Trail*, April 17, 1925; "On His Way," *Estes Park Trail*, June 22, 1923.

29. Labode, "'Defend Your Manhood,'" 166–73; Newsum et al., *Lincoln Hills and Civil Rights*.

30. Toll and Yard, *Mountaineering*, 50, 60, 68.

31. Lears, *Rebirth of a Nation*; Putney, *Muscular Christianity*; Bederman, *Manliness and Civilization*.

32. Longs Peak summit registers, ROMO-01132; CMC trip reports and scrapbooks, CMCC, AAL; Roger Toll, "Analysis of Register on Longs Peak 1915–1916," in CMC Peak Registers, Reports of Conditions, 1912–1936, CMCC, AAL.

33. Kingery and Kingery, *Colorado Mountain Club*; Taylor, *Pilgrims of the Vertical*; Chamberlin, *On the Trail*; Sayre, "Urban Climbers in the Wilderness," 92–110.

34. Matthews, *Rise of the New Woman*; Baker, *Votes for Women*; Grimshaw and Ellinghaus, "Higher Step for the Race"; Marilley, *Woman Suffrage.*

35. *SAR*, 1917, 65–66d; Robertson, *Magnificent Mountain Women*, 25–30. Esther Burnell became the wife of Enos Mills in 1918. "The Storyteller at Work: Selected Stories of Anne [Pfifer] Austill as Told the Summer of 1987, YMCA of the Rockies, Estes Park, Colorado," transcribed by Elizabeth Winans, typescript, file 7, box AR012, YMCA of the Rockies Archives; Kaufman, *National Parks*, 65–87.

36. Kingery and Kingery, *Colorado Mountain Club*, i.

37. Kingery and Kingery, 21–25; Brady, "Colorado Mountain Club," 36–42.

38. Turner, "From Woodcraft to 'Leave No Trace.'"

39. Kingery and Kingery, *Colorado Mountain Club*, 71–75; Brady, "Colorado Mountain Club," chap. 2; "And You Helped Do It," *Trail and Timberline*, April 1921, 5; Colorado Mountain Club, *Colorado Mountain Club*, 6.

40. "Superintendents' Resolution on Overdevelopment," prepared at the National Park Service Conference, November 13–17, 1922, Yosemite Park, California, with explanatory letter by Roger W. Toll, in Dilsaver, *America's National Park System*, 44–47; Buchholtz, *Rocky Mountain National Park*, 161.

41. On roadways, campgrounds, predator control, fire suppression, and the stocking of lakes with nonnative trout, see *SAR*, 1915–1925.

42. Buchholtz, *Rocky Mountain National Park*, 149–57; Musselman, *Rocky Mountain National Park*, 59–76; Frank, *Making Rocky Mountain National Park*, 28–34, 91–96, 120–24; Sellars, *Preserving Nature*, 47–90.

43. Adams, "Ecological Conditions."

44. Musselman, *Rocky Mountain National Park*, 150–53.

CHAPTER 3

1. Ferrel Atkins, "Longs Peak Deaths," typescript, ROMO-01572, series 3, folder 27; *SAR*, 1921, 227–28d; *SAR*, 1922, 262d; *SAR*, 1925, 356d. See also Evans, *Death, Despair*, 165–69, 269; Woody Smith, "Deadly Monarch: Death on Longs Peak," *Trail and Timberline*, Summer 2011, 36–39.

2. Evans, *Death, Despair*, 268.

3. Ellingwood, "Technical Climbing"; Blaurock and Euser, *Climber's Climber*, 2–3; Chamberlin, *On the Trail*, chaps. 2–3; Taylor, *Pilgrims of the Vertical*, chaps. 3–4.

4. Roger Toll, report to Colorado Mountain Club, "Long's Peak from the North Side," September 28, 1917, CMCC, AAL.

5. Nesbit, *Longs Peak*, 66. From *Alexander's Chimney*, Zimmerman climbed what became the *Eighth Route* and *Gorrell's Traverse*.

6. Moomaw, *Recollections*, 46–48; *SMR*, September 1922, 456d; Roger Toll, "Routes up Longs Peak," August 18, 1924, typescript based on letter from James Alexander to Toll on August 15, 1924, and Carl Blaurock, "A Trip up the Northeast Side of Longs Peak," September 10, 1922, ROMO-01192, subseries 1.7:800, folder 7, Travel—Mountain Climbing, 1922–1928.

7. Gillett, *Rocky Mountain National Park: The Climber's Guide, High Peaks*, 43.

8. Mills, *Adventures of a Nature Guide*, 87, 89; "Mr. Enos A. Mills Latest Book," *Trail and Timberline*, March 1920, 7; Moomaw, *Recollections*, 20–27.

9. *SMR*, September 1921, 373–74d; Ferrel Atkins, "Longs Peak Deaths," typescript, ROMO-01572, series 3, folder 27; Evans, *Death, Despair*, 37, 60, 165–69, 269.

10. Robertson, *Magnificent Mountain Women*, 47–56; Blaurock and Euser, *Climber's Climber*, 5–6; Howard T. Vaille, "Early Years of the Telephone in Colorado," *Colorado Magazine* 5, no. 4 (August 1928): 121–33; Roger Toll, "Report to Colorado Mountain Club on Trip to Longs Peak, 14,255 Feet," August 20, 1920; "Leader's Report to Outing Committee, Colorado Mountain Club," trip no. 245, July 30–August 1, 1921, CMCC, AAL.

11. Blaurock and Euser, *Climber's Climber*, 57–59; Robertson, *Magnificent Mountain Women*, 48–56; Pickering, "Tragedy on Longs Peak," 18–31. Janet Robertson's account of the Vaille tragedy relies on two important sources, an unpublished manuscript written by Charles Edwin Hewes that records Kiener's narration of the event, and an unpublished manuscript written by Elinor Eppich Kingery. The two accounts are not in complete accord, especially regarding Kiener's responsibility for Vaille's death. Kiener's story, based on the Hewes manuscript, is also included in its entirety in Pickering's article, though Robertson was the first to learn of this important source.

12. Robertson, *Magnificent Mountain Women*, 53; Pickering, "Tragedy on Longs Peak," 18–31.

13. Roger Toll, report to Colorado Mountain Club, "Long's Peak from the North Side," September 28, 1917, CMCC, AAL.

14. Robertson, *Magnificent Mountain Women*, 54–55; Roger Toll, "Official Report," *Trail and Timberline*, February 1925, 4; "Conquering Heroine Surrenders to Storm King on Longs Peak: Miss Agnes Vaille, Conqueror of Most of Peaks of County, Loses Life on Longs Peak, and Her Rescuer, Herbert Sortland, Lays Down Life in Attempted Rescue," *Estes Park Trail*, January 16, 1925; Carl Blaurock, "Tragedy on Longs Peak," *Denver Westerners Roundup*, September–October 1981. Blaurock was a friend of Vaille's and participated in the recovery of her body. The Vaille tragedy continues to fascinate mountaineers and researchers. See Woody Smith, "Agnes Vaille vs. Longs Peak," *Trail and Timberline*, Winter 2005, 36–39.

15. Robertson, *Magnificent Mountain Women*, 54–55; "Conquering Heroine Surrenders to Storm King," *Estes Park Trail*, January 16, 1925; Moomaw, *Recollections*, 34–39; Carl Blaurock, "Tragedy on Longs Peak," *Denver Westerners Roundup*, September–October 1981. After the Vaille tragedy, Kiener's injuries prevented him from returning to his job as foreman of a small sausage-making factory. He took a position as a ranger for Rocky Mountain National Park, serving as a fire lookout on Twin Sisters, directly east of Longs Peak. While serving as a ranger, Kiener met some students and faculty from the University of Nebraska and soon thereafter entered the University of Nebraska–Lincoln to pursue a formal education, earning an AB degree in 1930, a master's degree in botany in 1931, and the PhD in botany in 1939. His master's thesis and

doctoral dissertation were well-regarded works on the alpine vegetation of Longs Peak, and Kiener was subsequently hired by the University of Nebraska. He never married and died of cancer in 1955. See Walter Kiener, "On the Vegetation of an Isolated Peak in the Rocky Mountains" (master's thesis, University of Nebraska–Lincoln, 1931); Walter Kiener, "Sociological Studies of the Alpine Vegetation on Longs Peak" (PhD diss., University of Nebraska–Lincoln, 1939). Kiener's papers are housed at the University of Nebraska–Lincoln. A short biography may be accessed on the website of the university's Archives and Special Collections. See https://archives.nebraska.edu/repositories/8/resources/1795.

16. *SMR*, January 1925, 634–36d.
17. "The Tragedies of Longs Peak," *Estes Park Trail*, January 16, 1925.
18. "Agnes Wolcott Vaille," *Trail and Timberline*, April 1925, 2–3; Toll and Yard, *Mountaineering*, 46.
19. Moomaw, *Recollections*, 66–68.
20. "Trails," *SMR*, August 1925, 695d.
21. Moomaw, *Recollections*, 45. Jack Moomaw also described work on the upper portion of the East Longs Peak Trail in a 1955 interview with William Ramaley: "Then the trail used to end way down at the lower end [of the Boulderfield]. Used to be flat rocks and iron rings and cement and rock—people tied their horses there and then—but I built that trail clear across the Boulder Field up to that Boulder Field cabin when it was there and right across . . . the expenses there—you just wouldn't realize how much money that would run into." Jack Moomaw, interview by William Ramaley, 4.
22. *SMR*, June 1925, 673d.
23. *SMR*, June 1925, 673d. Though Toll was optimistic about the usefulness of the Boulderfield telephone, Jack Moomaw claimed it was nearly impossible to keep the phone line working during the winter and said he was forced to frequently repair it during its first winter of operation. Repairs to the line by Moomaw and other members of the "telephone patrol" lessened over the next several winters and were virtually suspended by the winter of 1930. Presumably, the phone worked more smoothly and was better maintained during the warmer months of the year. Moomaw, *Recollections*, 40.
24. *SAR*, 1926, 381d; D. Ferrel Atkins, "Longs Peak Timberline Cabin—Historic Structures and Buildings Survey," 1964, ROMO-01822.
25. *SMR*, May 1926, 775d.
26. "Aged Veteran Scales a Peak," *New York Times*, October 3, 1926.
27. Merrill J. Mattes, "The Boulderfield Hotel: A Distant Summer in the Shadow of Longs Peak," *Colorado Heritage*, no. 1 (March 1986): 30–41. Mattes worked at the "Boulderfield Hotel" in 1929. He was then an eighteen-year-old Longs Peak guide in the employ of Robert Collier, the park concessionaire for the cabin, but later entered the NPS, serving over his long career as park ranger, superintendent, planner, historian, and chief of historical preservation.
28. Robert Collier Jr., interview by Merrill Mattes and Chet Harris, November 21, 1961.
29. "Agnes Vaille Storm Shelter," *Trail and Timberline*, January 1928, 1, 3; Nesbit, *Longs Peak*, 66.

30. Nesbit, *Longs Peak*, 66; D. Ferrel Atkins, "Longs Peak Ranger Station and Campground—Historic Sites and Buildings Survey," ROMO-01822; *SAR*, 1929, 440d; *SAR*, 1930, 479d.

31. When the Boulderfield cabin opened in 1927 it charged climbers $2.00 for a night's lodging and $1.25 to $1.75 for meals. See *Estes Park Trail*, June 3, 1927; D. Ferrel Atkins, "Boulderfield Cabin—Historic Structures and Buildings Survey," 1964, ROMO-01822.

32. Longs' Peak [Annual] Summit Reports, folder: Peak Registers, Reports of Conditions, 1912–1926, CMC Administrative Files, part 1, box 1, CMCC, AAL.

33. *SMR*, June 1927, 882d.

34. Paris, *Children's Nature*; Wall, *Nurture of Nature*; Ward and Hardy, *Goodnight Campers!*; Blankers, "'Tonic of Wildness.'"

35. Pickering, *America's Switzerland*, 242–50; *Random Ramblings: A Brief History of the Colorado Cheley Camps, 1921–1970* (Estes Park, CO: Cheley Colorado Camps, n.d.), 9, YMCA of the Rockies Archives, box AR002, folder 1.

36. "The Storyteller at Work: Selected Stories of Anne Austill, as Told the Summer of 1987," YMCA of the Rockies Archives, box AR012, folder 7.

37. Longs Peak Reunion, 1991, transcript, 17–31, Estes Park Museum and Archives.

38. Gorby, *Stettner Way*, 63–64.

39. Gorby, 64–68.

40. *Random Ramblings*, 10; "Accidents," *SAR*, 1929, 444d; Robert Collier Jr., interview.

41. Blake, "Colorado Fourteeners," 161.

42. "Carl A. Blaurock, 1894–1993," American Alpine Club, 1994, https://publications.americanalpineclub.org/articles/12199432300/Carl-A-Blaurock-1894-1993.

43. Toll and Yard, *Mountain Peaks of Colorado.*

44. Hart, *Fourteen Thousand Feet* (1925), 32–37; Hart, *Fourteen Thousand Feet* (1931), 32–35.

45. Woody Smith, "Climbing the 'High Tops' with Mary Cronin and the Colorado Mountain Club," *Colorado Heritage* 28, no. 3 (2008); Gore Galore, "Mary Cronin Completes Her List—The First Woman to Climb All the 14,000 Foot Peaks in Colorado, 1934," 14ers.com, April 15, 2015, https://www.14ers.com/forum/viewtopic.php?f=7&t=46162.

46. Pickering, *America's Switzerland*, 246–48; "Highlander Boys," accessed December 22, 2021, https://www.highlanderboys.org/history; Laura Ruttum Senturia, "Neighborhood Ties: Highlands; a Brief History of the Highland Neighborhood," Go Play Denver, January 11, 2017, accessed December 22, 2021. https://www.goplaydenver.com/neighborhood-ties-highlands/.

47. Dervin, *Father Bosetti in America*, 86–97, 105–6; Kearnes, *Chapel on the Rock*, 14–15.

48. Taylor, *Overground Railroad*, 133; Craig Leavitt, "A Shelter from Harsh Times: The African American Mountain Resort of Lincoln Hills," *History Colorado*, April 14, 2021, accessed December 29, 2021, https://www.historycolorado.org/2021/04/14/shelter-harsh-times; advertisement for Lincoln Hills in

Newsum et al., *Lincoln Hills and Civil Rights*; letter from Dr. J. H. P. Westbrook to the Lincoln Hills Company, ARL39-Lincoln Hills Records, Denver Public Library; Shellenbarger, *High Country Summers*, 126–50; Goldstein, "Breaking Down Barriers," 73–78; Simmons and Simmons, "Wink's Panorama"; Andrea Juarez, "Lincoln Hills: An African-American Monument in Colorado's Mountains," *Denver Urban Spectrum*, May 2007, http://www.urbanspectrum.net /may07/writers/home_hills.htm.

49. Ellingwood, "Technical Climbing"; Nesbit, *Longs Peak*, 5.
50. Robert Collier Jr., interview.
51. Evans, *Death, Despair*, 70–72, 101; Woody Smith, "Deadly Monarch: Death on Longs Peak," *Trail and Timberline*, Summer 2011, 38; *SMR*, August 1929, 1070d; "Ranger Tells a Thrilling Story of Peak Rescue," *Estes Park Trail*, April 6, 1934; Nesbit, *Longs Peak*, 79.
52. Robert Collier Jr., interview. The Boulderfield cabin had a latrine, but sources do not mention how this facility was maintained.
53. Nesbit, *Longs Peak*, 66; Moomaw, *Recollections*, 46. Moomaw served as a ranger at Longs from the early 1920s to the early 1940s, during which time there were nine deaths on Longs Peak. See Nesbit, *Longs Peak*, 79–81, for a list of fatalities on Longs Peak.
54. Ellingwood, "Technical Climbing," 146.
55. Mattes, "Boulderfield Hotel," 37–38; Robertson, *Magnificent Mountain Women*, 56–59.
56. Mattes, "Boulderfield Hotel," 38. Mattes, one of the guides in the summer of 1929, estimated that of the 1,700 people who summited the peak that year and entered their names in the summit register, half stayed at the Boulderfield cabin overnight, whether they had hired a commercial guide or not.
57. *SAR*, 1929, 443d.

CHAPTER 4

1. FDR radio address at Two Medicine, Glacier National Park, August 5, 1934, accessed January 29, 2022, https://www.nps.gov/glac/learn/historyculture/fdr -radio-address.htm.
2. Maher, *Nature's New Deal*.
3. NPS, *Motorists Guide*, 1938; Unrau and Williss, *Expansion of the National Park Service*; Lily Rothman, "The Story behind Those Gorgeous National Parks Posters from the 1930s," *Time*, April 18, 2016, https://time.com/4282408 /national-parks-posters-wpa/.
4. Wright et al., *Fauna of the National Parks*; Shafer, "Conservation Biology Trailblazers," 332–44; Sellars, *Preserving Nature*, chap. 4; Buchholtz, *Rocky Mountain National Park*, 182–83, 187–97; Maher, *Nature's New Deal*, chap. 5; Frank, *Making Rocky Mountain National Park*, 124–27; Woody Smith, "Deadly Monarch: Death on Longs Peak," *Trail and Timberline*, Summer 2011, 38; Young, "'Contradiction in Democratic Government.'"
5. Young, "'Contradiction in Democratic Government'"; Wagar, "Visitor Concepts."

6. Cohen, *Making a New Deal*; Unrau and Williss, *Expansion of the National Park Service*; Gross, "'See, Experience, and Enjoy'"; Swain, "National Park Service"; Pillen, "See America"; Maher, *Nature's New Deal*.

7. NPS, *Motorists Guide*. Visitors to Rocky paid no entrance fees until 1939, when the NPS succumbed to administrative pressure to charge fees at all national parks and monuments. See Mackintosh, *Visitor Fees*, chap. 1.

8. Vandersall, "Building the View"; Musselman, *Rocky Mountain National Park*, chap. 6, Buchholtz, *Rocky Mountain National Park*, 177; Sellars, *Preserving Nature*, 4–5; Runte, *National Parks*; Frank, *Making Rocky Mountain National Park*, 34–36; Sutter, *Driven Wild*; Louter, *Windshield Wilderness*.

9. NPS, *Rocky Mountain National Park, Colorado* (1937), 1.

10. "*Travel Magazine* Tells of Park in Pictures," *Estes Park Trail*, July 6, 1934, 11.

11. NPS, *Circular of General Information*, 21.

12. "Foreign Countries Contribute Climbers," *Estes Park Trail*, August 10, 1934; Nesbit, *Longs Peak*, 67. When the Boulderfield cabin opened in 1927 it charged climbers $2.00 for a night's lodging and $1.25 to $1.75 for meals. See *Estes Park Trail*, June 3, 1927. Subsequently, it adopted a single-fee system, charging $2.50 to cover food, lodging, and a guided climb. See *Estes Park Trail*, August 30, 1935, 7.

13. *SAR*, 1937, 146d.

14. "Two Climb Peak," *Estes Park Trail*, June 8, 1934; Mattes, "Boulderfield Hotel"; Robert Collier Jr., interview; Nesbit, *Longs Peak*, 67.

15. "*American Weekly* Has Story on Local Hotel," *Estes Park Trail*, June 1, 1934.

16. "The Hull Cook Journals," *Climbing Narc* (blog), May 7, 2010, accessed February 17, 2022, http://climbingnarc.com/2010/05/the-hull-cook-journals/.

17. Nesbit, *Longs Peak*, 66; Longs Peak summit registers, 1915–1945, ROMO-01132.

18. Paris, *Children's Nature*; Miller, *Growing Girls*; Wall, *Nurture of Nature*.

19. "Allsebrook Camp for Girls Located in Estes Park Region," *Estes Park Trail*, July 18, 1930; Elaine Allsebrook Hostmark, "Allsebrooks in Estes Park," typescript, 1994, 30, YMCA of the Rockies Archives, box 3, folder 10.

20. Jessie Burrell Eubank, Lois Elliott, and Elaine Moore, "Sunrise Meditations," Allsebrook Camp for Girls, mimeograph, YMCA of the Rockies Archives, box 3, folder 10; Betty Lou Bolce, "From the Top," *Allsee News*, August 1934, 2, 6, YMCA of the Rockies Archives, box 3, folder 10.

21. Gore Galore, "1930's Colorado Climbers," 14ers.com, October 4, 2014, https://14ers.com/forum/viewtopic.php?t=45140; Gorby, *Stettner Way*, 75–78; Nesbit, *Longs Peak*, 67; "Notes on the 1932 Climbing Season," *Trail and Timberline*, January 1933, 9; Clerin Zumwalt, "The North Face of Longs Peak," *Trail and Timberline*, February 1933, 20; Robert Collier Jr., interview; "Tops Long's Peak, 14,255 Feet, Alone," *New York Times*, January 3, 1939; "Long's Peak Conquered," *New York Times*, January 8, 1939; Taylor, *Pilgrims of the Vertical*, chap. 4; Isserman, *Continental Divide*, chap. 4.

22. Musselman, *Rocky Mountain National Park*, chap. 7; William B. Butler, "The Archaeology of the Civilian Conservation Corp in Rocky Mountain National Park," internal study by the park archaeologist for ROMO, 2006, ROMO-01822.

23. D. Ferrel Atkins, "Longs Peak Ranger Station and Campground—Historic Sites and Buildings Survey," ROMO-01822.

24. Musselman, *Rocky Mountain National Park*, chap. 7; Buchholtz, *Rocky Mountain National Park*, 177–78.

25. Maher, *Nature's New Deal*, 60–69; Phillips, *This Land, This Nation*.

26. Wright et al., *Fauna of the National Parks*, Fauna Series No. 1, 2, 4–5, 37; Wright et al., *Fauna of the National Parks*, Fauna Series No. 2, vi.

27. Maher, *Nature's New Deal*, 165–76.

28. Wright et al., *Fauna of the National Parks*, Fauna Series No. 1, 40–41.

29. Fauna Series No. 1 cited John L. McLaughlin, "Report on Conditions of Portions of Elk and Deer Winter Range in Rocky Mountain National Park," Rocky Mountain National Park, Colorado, January 15, 1932. It undoubtedly also used Joseph S. Dixon's "Report on Needed Winter Range for Big Game in Rocky Mountain National Park," June 30, 1931. Additional studies completed by the park in the 1930s included John A. Rutter, "Report on Carrying Capacity of the Winter Range of Rocky Mountain National Park," January 5, 1937; and Joseph S. Dixon, "Special Report on the Elk Problems at Rocky Mountain National Park," December 16, 1939. All these reports are cited in Packard, "Study of the Deer and Elk Herds.

30. *SAR*, 1936, 121d; Buchholtz, *Rocky Mountain National Park*, 187–97; Frank, *Making Rocky Mountain National Park*, 174–77.

31. *SAR*, 1935, 84d; Evans, *Death, Despair*.

32. Field quoted in Evans, *Death, Despair*, 169–70. See also "Rockies Climber Dies on Rescue in Snow," *New York Times*, August 8, 1939.

33. Evans, *Death, Despair*, 38, 41, 225; *SMR*, September 1931, 1339–40d.

34. "New Yorker Hurt on Long's Peak," *New York Times*, September 1, 1939.

35. "Accidents," *SMR*, August 1934.

36. Robert Collier Jr., interview.

37. "Jim's Grove—Natural Area," Jim's Grove File, Office of Jeff Connor, ROMO-01761; Robert Collier Jr., interview.

38. Frank, *Making Rocky Mountain National Park*, 126–27; Maher, *Nature's New Deal*, 214–26.

39. Frank, *Making Rocky Mountain National Park*, 174–80; *SMR*, January 1938, 1408d; *SMR*, October 1938, 1652d.

40. T. Melvin Griffiths, "Rock Climbing," *Trail and Timberline*, August 1932, September 1932; "Modern Rock Technique," *Trail and Timberline*, May 1933.

41. Clerin Zumwalt, "Is Rock Climbing Dangerous?," *Trail and Timberline*, May 1933, 65–66; John S. McLaughlin, "A Ranger's Side of the Story," *Trail and Timberline*, March 1934, 36.

42. Robert Collier Jr., interview, transcript, tape 2, 1, 14; D. Ferrel Atkins, "Longs Peak Shelters—Historic Sites and Buildings Survey," 3, ROMO-01822.

The barn in the Boulderfield was left standing, and its remains were not removed until 1959.

43. "Colorado Mountain Club School of Mountaineering," supplement to *Trail and Timberline*, May 1939; Ernest K. Field, "Rock Work on Long's Peak," *Trail and Timberline*, June 1939, 71–72; "Attention Mountain Climbers," *Trail and Timberline*, May 1940, 78–79; Nesbit, *Longs Peak* (2005), 67. See also correspondence between Ernest K. Field, the Colorado Mountain Club, and the U.S. Forest Service, Rocky Mountain Region, November 8, 1939, February 21, 1940, March 5, 1940, on the "code of ethics" to be communicated in the posters encouraging "safe and sane" climbing, CMC Administrative Files, 1912–36, part 1, box 1, folder: CMC Correspondence, 1938–42, CMCC, AAL.

44. Joseph Bosetti, "Philosophy of Mountaineering," *Trail and Timberline*, February 1937, 22–24.

45. M. Walter Pesman, "Man, the Troublemaker," *Trail and Timberline*, June 1935, 67–68, 73; M. Walter Pesman, "Should Mountain Lions be Killed?," *Trail and Timberline*, July 1933; Francis Ramaley, "The Preservation of Natural Areas," *Trail and Timberline*, June 1935, 69; Earl Davis, "Nature Protection," *Trail and Timberline*, June 1935, 68, 74.

46. Young, "'Contradiction in Democratic Government'"; Ariel Schnee and Ruth Alexander, "The African American Visitor Experience at Shenandoah National Park," unpublished report, Rocky Mountain Collaborative Ecosystem Studies Unit, Public Lands History Center, Colorado State University, and Shenandoah National Park, 2019; Devlin, "Under the Sky."

47. Newsum et al., *Lincoln Hills and Civil Rights*. One of the last pages in the Camp Nizhoni scrapbook refers to "God's Wonderland." See Camp Nizhoni Album, 1928–1937, Phyllis Wheatley YWCA, Lincoln Hills Records, Blair-Caldwell African American Research Library, Denver Public Library.

48. Leonard and Noel, *Denver*, 190–202; Wasinger, "From Five Points to Struggle Hill," 28–39; Foster, "In the Face of 'Jim Crow,'" 130–49; Neverdon-Morton, *Finding History's Forgotten People*, 89–94; Taylor, *Overground Railroad*, chap. 1; Goldstein, "Breaking Down Barriers," 77–79; Juarez, "Lincoln Hills"; Shellenbarger, *High Country Summers*, 140–50; Cherland, "No Prejudice Here"; McIntosh, *Latinos of Boulder County*; Carpio, *Collisions at the Crossroads*; Brock, "Creating Consumers," 58–62. Readers may access a complete digital collection of *The Negro Motorist Green Book* (1936–1967) at the New York Public Library, https://digitalcollections.nypl.org/collections/the-green-book#/?tab=about&scroll=3.

49. Young, "'Contradiction in Democratic Government,'" 651–82.

50. Hirsch, "For the Benefit and Enjoyment," 29–31; "Recommendations of the National Park Superintendents' Conference," January 1939, quoted in Rick Caceres-Rodriguez, "From Jim Crow to Diversity," 2018, 53, National Archives and Records Administration, RG 79, NPS Central Classified File 1933–1949, box 9; O'Brien, "State Parks and Jim Crow," 169; Katznelson, *Fear Itself.*

51. CMC Membership Committee (Denver) to Board of Directors, May 18, 1938, in folder: Denver Group, Membership Correspondence, 1938;

Membership Application, Isadore Karl Silverman, April 23, 1938; and membership data card with dates of membership, in folder: Application and Waivers, CMC Administrative Files, 1912–1936, part 1, box 2, CMCC, AAL.

52. Shaffer, *See America First*, 126; Brock, "Creating Consumers," 59–62; H. R. Gregg, "Museums in Rocky Mountain National Park," *Estes Park Trail*, April 23, 1937, 11, 30; Beals, *Ethnology of Rocky Mountain National Park*.

53. "Church Notes," *Estes Park Trail*, July 31, 1936; "St. Walter's Catholic Church," *Estes Park Trail*, July 13, 1934.

54. J. V. K. Wagar, "Visitor Concepts of National Park Policies and Conservation Needs," Colorado State College, Fort Collins, January 1941, Wagar Collection, Colorado State University Archives.

55. Wagar, 1.

56. Wagar, 3.

57. Wagar, 5, 8, 10.

58. Wagar, 6, 10.

59. McDonnell, "Far-Reaching Effects," 89–110; Sellars, *Preserving Nature*, 151–55.

60. *SMR*, January 1943; *SAR*, 1942, 1943. For ROMO visitation statistics, see "Park Reports," NPS Stats: National Park Service Visitor Use Statistics, https://irma.nps.gov/STATS/Reports/Park/ROMO; Nesbit, *Longs Peak*, 67.

61. *SAR*, 1943 (rough draft), 344d; Frank, *Making Rocky Mountain National Park*, 127–29.

62. "Nazis Hurled back in Italian Thrust; Suffer Heavy Casualties as U.S. 10th Mountain Division Holds Recent Gains," *New York Times*, February 28, 1945, 11.

63. Henry Buchtel, "And So Endeth the Last Lesson," *Trail and Timberline*, January 1942, 179; Dorothy Sethman, "Longs Peak or Bust," *Trail and Timberline*, October 1943, 129; Molly Sethman, "Junior Journeys," *Trail and Timberline*, October 1943, 127–28; Kingery and Kingery, *Colorado Mountain Club*, 25.

64. Gorby, *Stettner Way*, 109; *SMR*, January 1943; "Estes Park Publicity for Post-War Travel," *Estes Park Trail*, January 29, 1943.

65. *SMR*, June 1942, 2021d.

66. Ernest K. Field, "Technique of Mountain Climbing Told," *Estes Park Trail*, April 25, 1941, 29, 36–37. "Ranger Ernest K. Field perfected plans and completed two emergency rescue equipment caches. The caches so concentrate equipment in a minimum of space that efficiency of rescue parties is expected to be substantially improved in reaching stranded or injured climbers. Loss of time in gathering ropes, pitons and other equipment from a number of different points is to be eliminated by the caches. The comparatively small weatherproof chests include such articles as climbing ropes, pitons, carabiners, piton hammers, ice axes, crampons, headlamps, signal flares, emergency rations, wool blankets, complete sets of woolen clothing, chemical heating pads, pack sacks, thermos bottles, mess kits, first aid kits, canteens, miner helmets and rappelling hooks. Two central caches were established at the park utility area and at the Hewes-Kirkwood Inn near the base of Longs Peak. Three more chests, slightly smaller, are to be placed later at the Boulder Field and

Chasm Lake shelter cabins and at the Bear Lake ranger station." *SMR*, October 1940, 1867d; *SMR*, July 1942.

67. "Twenty-Ninth Annual Summer Outing and Fourth Annual School of Mountaineering, August 13–23, 1942," *Trail and Timberline*, May 1942, 67; Myrle Cammack, "Club Policy and Practice," *Trail and Timberline*, November 1943, 135; Harold M. Dunning, "Climbing Longs Peak—Hints for Beginners," *Trail and Timberline*, August 1945, 100–101. See also Roy R. Murchison, "Some Observations on Climbing," *Trail and Timberline*, August 1945, 98–99.

68. *SAR*, 1945, 344–46d.

69. *SMR*, July 1945, 2232d.

70. Pickering, *America's Switzerland*, 372–75; Schnee and Alexander, "The African American Visitor Experience at Shenandoah National Park"; Devlin, "Under the Sky." The NPS's 1941 *Study of the Park and Recreation Problem of the United States* called humans' need for recreation "fundamental" to their well-being and simultaneously recognized that "the human wealth of the United States is composed of many racial backgrounds." It did not, however, acknowledge racial discrimination as an obstacle to recreation (see 1–4, 5). On resistance to racial oppression on the domestic front, see, for example, Wynn, *African American Experience*; Murray, *Historical Memories*; Bernstein, *American Indians and World War II*; U.S. Latino and Latina World War II Oral History Project Collection, [ca. 1999]–2008, Dolph Briscoe Center for American History, University of Texas at Austin, https://txarchives.org/utcah/finding_aids/01369.xml.

71. M. Walter Pesman to CMC Board member Joy Swift, December 10, 1945; Post War Planning Committee to M. Walter Pesman, January 1, 1946; Anna Timm to CMC Board of Directors, December 2, 1945, CMC Administrative Files, 1912–1972, box 4, folder: CMC Denver Group Membership, 1937–1946, CMCC, AAL.

CHAPTER 5

1. Cohen, *Making a New Deal*; Katznelson, *When Affirmative Action Was White*; Rothstein, *Color of Law*; May, *Homeward Bound*; Weiss, *To Have and to Hold*; Rugh, *Are We There Yet?*; Philpott, *Vacationland*; Runte, *National Parks*.

2. NPS, "Mission 66 for the National Park System," 10; Appleman, "History of the National Park Service."

3. Taylor, *Pilgrims of the Vertical*, chaps. 6–7; Isserman, *Continental Divide*, chap. 6; Achey et al., *Climb!*, chaps. 2–3.

4. Conrad L. Wirth, foreword to NPS, "Mission 66 for the National Park System," iii–iv; NPS, *Mission 66: Our Heritage*.

5. Bzdek and Ore, *Mission 66 Program*.

6. See, for example, Lawson, *Civil Rights Crossroads*; Vargas, *Crucible of Struggle*; Valandra, *Not without Our Consent*; Svonkin, *Jews against Prejudice*; Kanfer, *Summer World*.

7. Rugh, *Are We There Yet?*, 147–51; NPS, *Mission 66: Our Heritage*, 1.

8. *"Cool, Colorful Colorado Invites You!"* (Denver: Department of Public Relations, [1954?]); Philpott, *Vacationland*.

NOTES TO CHAPTER 5

9. NPS, *Rocky Mountain National Park*, brochure (1951), see http://www
.npshistory.com/publications/romo/index.htm#brochures. For ROMO visitation statistics, see "Park Reports," NPS Stats: National Park Service Visitor Use
Statistics, https://irma.nps.gov/STATS/Reports/Park/ROMO.

10. Carr, *Mission 66*; ROMO, "Mission 66 for Rocky Mountain National
Park," ROMO-01192, series 2.3, folder 073: Prospectuses; Bzdek and Ore,
Mission 66 Program; Philpott, *Vacationland*; Rugh, *Are We There Yet?*; Wells,
Car Country, 269–77.

11. *SMR*, August 1952, 523d; ROMO, "Mission 66 for Rocky Mountain
National Park," 8d; ROMO, "1952 Master Plan for Rocky Mountain National
Park," 7, 11–12, ROMO-01192, series 2.3, folder 073: Prospectuses; Buch-
holtz, *Rocky Mountain National Park*, 201–3, 206.

12. Estes Park Vacation Guides, box 1, folder 1 (1950–59), Estes Park Museum;
Knudten, "Diminishing Shadow," 34–35; NPS, *Rocky Mountain National
Park*, brochure (1951); Dwight Hamilton, "Long's Peak, an Old Friend," *Trail
and Timberline*, July 1950, 99. Paul Nesbit published the first edition of *Longs
Peak: Its Story and a Climbing Guide* in 1949, drawing on an extensive range
of printed sources, from newspaper articles to memoirs and guidebooks. *SAR*,
1950, 1951, 1952, 1953; Nesbit, *Longs Peak*, 68.

13. *SMR*, August 1952, 523d.

14. *SAR*, 1953, 554d; Nesbit, *Longs Peak*, 68.

15. Isserman, *Continental Divide*, 276, chaps. 5–6; Taylor, *Pilgrims of the Vertical*,
124–32; Ullman, *Age of Mountaineering*; Megan Walsh, "Can't Keep Her Down:
A Consolidated History of Women's Climbing Achievements," *Climbing*, February 13, 2018.

16. Isserman, *Continental Divide*; Achey et al., *Climb!*, 22; Bright, "History
of Rock Climbing Gear," 8; Dave Robertson, interview by Ruth Alexander,
October 18, 2016; Bruce B. Johnson, "Holubar Mountaineering, Boulder,
Colorado," http://www.oregonphotos.com/Holubar1.html.

17. Isserman, *Continental Divide*, 264–68, 277–78, 396n18; Wexler, "Theory
of Belaying," 380–404; Ullman, *Age of Mountaineering*, 306; Nesbit, *Longs
Peak*, 43–49.

18. Achey et al., *Climb!*, 24–26; Harold P. Walton, "Through the Window—
Pioneer Climb of a Delicate New Route up Longs Peak," *Trail and Timberline*,
February 1951, 15–17; Tom Hornbein, interview by Ruth Alexander, Octo-
ber 28, 2016; Gillett, *Rocky Mountain National Park*, 284–86.

19. Paul Nesbit reported that in 1952 only 11 percent of all ascents on Longs
were led by commercial guides, but of the total number of guided ascents,
more than half were technical climbs on the mountain's East Face. Nesbit,
Longs Peak, 5; *SAR*, 1950, 1951, 1952, 1953.

20. Achey et al., *Climb!*, 25; Roger Briggs, "The Diamond," *Alpinist*, Spring
2007, 26; Acting Superintendent Peterson to National Park Service Director,
July 27, 1954, temporary box: Climbing, folder 1954, ROMO Archives;
"Minutes of Staff Meeting, August 30, 1955, Protection Division," temporary
box 44, ROMO Archives.

21. Evans, *Death, Despair*, 49–50, 52, 61, 73, 213–14; "Boy Dies Climbing
Longs Peak," *New York Times*, September 2, 1946.

22. NPS, "Summary of Annual Mountain Climbing Reports from Areas Administered by the National Park Service, 1954," 3, temporary box: Climbing, folder 1955, ROMO Archives; *SMR*, June 1954, 749d; "500 Foot Fall Kills Student," *New York Times*, June 7, 1954.

23. Edward J. Kurts, "Annual Mountain Climbing Report, 1954, Rocky Mountain National Park," 2, temporary box: Climbing, folder 1954, ROMO Archives; Colorado Mountain Club trip report, "Longs Peak," August 21, 1954, folder: Trip Reports, Longs Peak, CMCC, AAL.

24. Teletype from Peterson, Acting Superintendent, to NPS Director, July 27, 1954, temporary box: Climbing, folder 1954, ROMO Archives; David H. Canfield, Superintendent, to Vaughn Ham, President of the CMC, August 5, 1954, temporary box: Climbing, folder 1954, ROMO Archives.

25. Rocky Mountain National Park, "Notice of Closed Area," September 5, 1955; Acting Regional Director George Baggley to Superintendent, Rocky Mountain National Park, "Subject: Climbing East Face of Longs' Peak," August 26, 1955, temporary box: Climbing, folder 1955, ROMO Archives.

26. Isserman, *Continental Divide*, 306; Taylor, *Pilgrims of the Vertical*, 118–32, NPS, "Summary of Annual Mountaineering Reports from Areas Administered by the National Park Service, 1957," temporary box: Climbing, folder 1955, ROMO Archives.

27. Carr, *Mission 66*; Dilsaver, *America's National Park System*; Sellars, *Preserving Nature*; Appleman, "History of the National Park Service," 2–6.

28. Carr, *Mission 66*.

29. Bzdek and Ore, *Mission 66 Program*; ROMO, "Mission 66 Prospectus, Rocky Mountain National Park and Shadow Mountain Recreation Area," July 15, 1957, 6, ROMO-01192, series 2.3, folder 073: Prospectuses; Frank, *Making Rocky Mountain National Park*, 43–49.

30. Buchholtz, *Rocky Mountain National Park*, 205–6; ROMO, "Mission 66 for Rocky Mountain National Park"; Bzdek and Ore, *Mission 66 Program*.

31. ROMO, "Mission 66 for Rocky Mountain National Park," 5; Allaback and Carr, "Rocky Mountain National Park," 35–36; "Radio KCOL, Fort Collins, Colorado, Interview by Dorothy Collier of George Hartzog, January 26, 1957," transcript, ROMO library; Knudten, "Diminishing Shadow," 52.

32. Fricke, *Climber's Guide*, 29; *SMR*, July 1953; Nesbit, *Longs Peak*, 68; "Minutes of Staff Meeting, October 6, 1955," 5, ROMO-01192, series 1.7. See also "Minutes of Staff Meeting, Protection Division," August 30, 1955, 5, temporary box 44, ROMO Archives. This document reports a difficult two-day rescue on the *Cable* route, which prompted Assistant Chief Ranger Ruben Hart to remark, "The accident on Sunday pointed out the need for a shelter at the Boulder Field . . . a rescue party returning from the cable route would nearly always involve an overnight operation, as was the case this time, and if the weather is bad it could prove very rough on everyone involved."

33. Memorandum from NPS Director Conrad Wirth to Assistant Solicitor, Branch of National Parks, "Addition to Section 1.14 of General Rules and Regulations," November 14, 1956; Memorandum to Assistant Chief Ranger, RMNP from Robert Weldon, District Ranger, Central District, "Suggestions for a form to use in regard to revised climbing regulations on the Diamond,

East Face of Longs," December 6, 1956, temporary box: Climbing, folder 1956, ROMO Archives.

34. *SMR*, August 1953, on Mountaineering Training and Rescue Conference, 646; NPS, "Summary of Annual Mountain Climbing Reports from Areas Administered by the National Park Service, 1954," temporary box: Climbing, folder 1955; Rocky Mountain National Park, "Annual Mountain Climbing Report, 1957," temporary box: Climbing, folder 1957; Rocky Mountain National Park "Annual Mountain Climbing Report, 1959," temporary box: Climbing, folder 1959, ROMO Archives.

35. NPS, "Summary of Annual Mountain Climbing Reports from Areas Administered by the National Park Service, 1954," temporary box: Climbing, folder 1955, ROMO Archives; Harthon L. Bill, Acting Superintendent, Yosemite, to Superintendent, Rocky Mountain National Park, August 13, 1954; Superintendent, Rocky Mountain National Park, to Superintendent, Mt. Rainier, August 10, 1954; Superintendent, Mt. Rainier, to Superintendent, Rocky Mountain National Park, August 13, 1954; David H. Canfield, Superintendent, to Vaughn Ham, President of the Colorado Mountain Club, August 5, 1954; David H. Canfield to G. A. Cunningham, American Alpine Association, August 11, 1954, temporary box: Climbing, folder 1954, ROMO Archives.

36. David H. Canfield, Superintendent, to Vaughn Ham, President of the Colorado Mountain Club, August 5, 1954; David H. Canfield to G. A. Cunningham, American Alpine Association, August 11, 1954, temporary box: Climbing, folder 1954, ROMO Archives; Don Laing and Baker Armstrong, "Boulder's Rocky Mountain Rescue Group," *Trail and Timberline*, May 1966, 71.

37. Robert Ellingwood, "Chairman's Report," *Trail and Timberline*, December 1954, 167–68; Allen Auten, "The Climb of Mount Rainier," *Trail and Timberline*, December 1954, 169–73.

38. Lewis V. Giesecke, "Report of the Denver Technical Climbing Committee," *Trail and Timberline*, September 1946, 186–87; John Devitt, "Education for Thrills," *Trail and Timberline*, August 1950, 115–17; Allen Auten, "Technical Climbing School," *Trail and Timberline*, July 1955, 132; Allen W. Greene, "The Climbing Schools," *Trail and Timberline*, August 1959, 109–10.

39. Henry Buchtel, "Don't Be an 'X' Climber," *Trail and Timberline*, July 1949, 101; Bill Burky, "A Midnight Climb of Longs Peak," *Trail and Timberline*, September 1956, 131–32; Colorado Mountain Club trip report, "Longs Peak via Chasm Lake," August 30–31, 1947; "Longs Peak," August 21–22, 1954, folder: Trip Reports Longs Peak, CMCC, AAL.

40. Superintendent James V. Lloyd to James C. Gamble, July 21, 1959, temporary box: Climbing, folder 1960, ROMO Archives.

41. Memorandum, Superintendent James Lloyd to Regional Director, Region Two, "Subject: Climbing the East Face of Longs Peak," October 30, 1957; Rocky Mountain National Park, "Major Climbing Accidents, 1957," temporary box: Climbing, folder 1957. See also an editorial in *Estes Park Trail*, June 27, 1958, critical of Rocky's policy and in support of Johnson and Northcutt's application, temporary box: Climbing, folder 1959, ROMO Archives.

42. Achey et al., *Climb!*, 25; Roger Briggs, "The Diamond," *Alpinist*, Spring 2007, 26; Roy Northcutt, "Technical Report on the *Diagonal*," August 11, 1959; memorandum, Park Ranger Cantor to Park Superintendent, "Subject: Comparison of Advanced Technical Climbing on Longs Peak," August 5, 1959; memorandum, Superintendent James Lloyd to Regional Director, "Subject: Extra Hazardous Mountain Climbing in Rocky Mountain National Park," October 5, 1959, temporary box: Climbing, folder 1959, ROMO Archives; Mark Bearwald, "Boulder Man Hopes to Scale Long's Diamond Face," *Denver Post*, September 1, 1959, 19.

43. Memorandum, Superintendent James Lloyd to Regional Director, October 5, 1959; ROMO, "Application to Make Extra Hazardous Rock Climbing Attempt" and "Mountain Rescue Equipment Needed for Rocky Mountain National Park"; U.S. Department of the Interior, National Park Service, "National Park Service Mountain Climbing Policy and Guidelines," November 4, 1959; Memorandum, Chief Park Ranger, Lyle H. McDowell, to Superintendent, "Extra Hazardous Mountain Climbing," November 23, 1959, temporary box: Climbing, folder 1959, ROMO Archives; Superintendent Lloyd James to Robert Kamps, July 20, 1960, letter in possession of Dave Rearick, shared with author.

44. "Mission 66 Prospectus: Rocky Mountain National Park and Shadow Mountain National Recreation Area," final draft, July 15, 1957, 4–6, ROMO-01192, series 2.3, folder 073: Prospectuses.

45. Frank, *Making Rocky Mountain National Park*, 49–51, 101–3, 129–32; Bill Kovarik, "Air Pollution Timeline," Environmental History, https://environmentalhistory.org/about/airpollution/; Stern, "History of Air Pollution Legislation," 44–61; ROMO, "Mission 66 for Rocky Mountain National Park," 29, ROMO-01192, series 2.3, folder 073: Prospectuses; Hess, *Rocky Times*, 15–27, 54–60; Rocky Mountain National Park, National Register of Historic Places Registration Form, "Beatrice Willard, Alpine Tundra Research Plots," September 10, 2007, 42–43, ROMO-01822; Willard et al., " Natural Regeneration," 177–83.

46. Buchholtz, *Rocky Mountain National Park*, 176–77, 188–91, 194–98; Musselman, *Rocky Mountain National Park*, chap. 11; "Two New Lifts Will Be at Hidden Valley," *Estes Park Trail*, July 8, 1955; Frank, *Making Rocky Mountain National Park*, 180–94; Sellars, *Preserving Nature*, 155–73; Stanley A. Cain, "Ecological Islands as Natural Laboratories," in Dilsaver, *America's National Park System*, 177–86.

47. Sellars, *Preserving Nature*, 155–73; Stanley A. Cain, "Ecological Islands as Natural Laboratories," in Dilsaver, *America's National Park System*, 177–86; Louter, *Windshield Wilderness*, 255–63; Sutter, *Driven Wild*, 117–21.

48. Barringer, "Mission Impossible," 22–26; Carr, *Mission 66*; Sellars, *Preserving Nature*, 177–94; Harvey, *Symbol of Wilderness*.

49. See, for example, Raymond R. Lanier, "Some Wilderness Area Problems in Colorado," *Trail and Timberline*, September 1958, 120–21; E. H. Brunquist, "Wilderness Areas—Pros and Cons," *Trail and Timberline*, December 1958, 169, 175; C. B. Jacobson, "Why Echo Park," and M. Walter Pesman, "Let's

Not Jump in the Dinosaur Lake," *Trail and Timberline*, March 1954, 31–34, 35–37. For a summary of conservation actions taken by the Colorado Mountain Club between 1954 and 1961, see "CMC Conservation Action," *Trail and Timberline*, September 1961, 159.

50. C. A. and R. R., "Fourteeners or Foothills—Why Do We Climb Them? The Feminine Viewpoint—Enjoy the Trip; The Masculine Idea—Get to the Top," *Trail and Timberline*, April 1956, 60–61, 66.

51. NPS, "Mission 66 for the National Park System," 1.

52. The scholarly literature on the civil rights movement is extensive. Useful historiographic essays include Hall, "Long Civil Rights Movement," 1233–63; Lawson, "Freedom Then, Freedom Now," 3–28.

53. Seiler, "'So That We as a Race,'" 1091–117; "Annual Vacation Guide," *Ebony*, June 1957, 99–108.

54. "Annual Vacation Guide," *Ebony*, June 1957, 102–4.

55. Atkins, *Human Relations in Colorado*, 143–56; Leonard and Noel, *Denver*, 366–73; Neverdon-Morton, *Finding History's Forgotten People*, 94–97; McIntosh, *Latinos of Boulder County*, 63–66.

56. Leonard and Noel, *Denver*, 373–76; Zach Clemens, "Estes Park Neighborhood Covenants Reflect a Divided Past," *Estes Park Trail-Gazette*, October 4, 2017. For digital copies of the *Green Book*, *Travelguide*, and *Go, Guide to Pleasant Motoring*, see the website of the New York Public Library: https://libguides.nypl.org/greenbook/more. Craig Leavitt, "A Shelter from Harsh Times," *History Colorado*, April 14, 2021; McIntosh, *Latinos of Boulder County*, 64–66; *SMR*, August 1952, 523d; *SMR*, September 1953, 535d; *SAR*, 1953, 554d; Rodnitzky, "Recapturing the West," 111–26; Ariel Schnee, "Race and Ranching at Rocky Mountain National Park," *History Colorado*, August 21, 2020.

57. "Case of the South in Segregation Ruling Presented to Rotary," *Estes Park Trail*, July 18, 1955; "In the Interest of Better Understanding," *Estes Park Trail*, July 12, 1957; Booker T. Washington Centennial Commission, "An Appeal to Americans of All Races and Creeds," *Estes Park Trail*, November 23, 1956; "A Negro Deplores Integration Idea," *Estes Park Trail*, November 29, 1957; "After Integration Repeal, What?," *Estes Park Trail*, October 17, 1958.

58. Fred P. Clatworthy, "Seeing Ourselves as Others See Us," *Estes Park Trail*, November 20, 1953; "Exciting Indian Play at Children's Playhouse," *Estes Park Trail*, July 14, 1950; Carolyn Rhone, "Grand Lake Schedules Mid-Week Massacre to Cooperate with the Rooftop Rodeo in Estes Park," *Estes Park Trail*, July 24, 1959; Deloria, *Playing Indian*.

59. NPS, *Mission 66: Our Heritage*.

CHAPTER 6

1. On the politics of the 1960s, see, for example, Isserman and Kazin, *America Divided*; Bloom and Breines, *"Takin' It to the Streets."*

2. A violent confrontation between young countercultural partiers and rangers occurred in Yosemite National Park in 1970. See Childers, "Stoneman Meadow Riots."

3. Cahn, *Will Success Spoil*; Dilsaver, *America's National Park System*, 175–98, 211–34.
4. Wirth, "National Parks," 20.
5. Lee, *Public Use*, 12–20; Mackintosh et al., "National Parks," 43–54; Dilsaver, *America's National Park System*, 198–210, 234–38, chap. 6.
6. Briggs, "Diamond," 22–24; Lyle H. McDowell, Chief Park Ranger, to Superintendent, re: "First Ascent of the Diamond, East Face of Longs Peak, August 1–3, 1960," August 23, 1960; letter and enclosures from James V. Lloyd, Superintendent, to Robert Sutton, July 20, 1960, temporary box: Climbing, folder: Climbing Diamond Face, Longs Peak 1960, ROMO Archives.
7. Though considered an "outsider," Dave Rearick was not a newcomer to Colorado climbing or Longs Peak. He had vacationed in Estes Park with his family as a boy, worked at the YMCA camp in Estes as a teenager, and climbed Longs Peak (both the nontechnical routes and the East Face) a total of nine times before he and Kamps ascended the Diamond in 1960. Bob Kamps, on the other hand, had never been to Rocky Mountain National Park before 1960. Dave Rearick, interview by Ruth Alexander, June 9, 2009, ROMO-01851, Longs Peak Oral Histories.
8. Briggs, "Diamond," 22–24; Robert Kamps, "The Diamond Climbed," *Trail and Timberline*, September 1960, 123–24; Chief Park Ranger to Superintendent, re: "First Ascent of the Diamond, East Face of Longs Peak, August 1–3, 1960," August 23, 1960; Superintendent to Regional Director, Region Two, re: "Permission for Granting or Denying Permission to Climb the Diamond (East Face, Longs Peak)," July 22, 1960; letter from James V. Lloyd, Superintendent, Rocky Mountain National Park, to Robert F. Kamps, July 20, 1960; letter from James V. Lloyd to Robert Kamps and David F. Rearick, July 27, 1960, temporary box: Climbing, folder: Climbing Diamond Face, Longs Peak 1960, ROMO Archives. The original letters from the park to Kamps and Rearick are in the possession of David F. Rearick and were shared with the author.
9. Bonnie Kamps, phone interview by Ruth Alexander, August 26, 2009, ROMO-01851, Longs Peak Oral Histories; Robert Kamps, "The Diamond Climbed," *Trail and Timberline*, September 1960, 122–23.
10. Climbers created the Yosemite Decimal System during the 1960s as they recognized the necessity of evaluating the distinct elements of a climb. For a full discussion of the rating system as understood in that era, see Fricke, *Climber's Guide*, 2–6. The V, 5.7, A4 rating for the *D1* climb in 1960 translates as follows:

"Grade" describes the general magnitude of the undertaking and considers the length of time required, the number of leads/pitches, and the number of feet of hard climbing. A Grade V designation on a scale of I to V means a climb requires more than one day and involves more than five leads/pitches and more than four hundred feet of hard climbing.

"Class" describes the severity of the pitches. Class 5.7 on a scale of 1 to 5.10 means a climb requires protection for pitches of "very severe" difficulty. All Class 5 climbs require protection. "Aid Difficulty" describes the difficulty of placing protection and the trustworthiness of the protection. An aid difficulty of A4 on a scale of A1 to A5 means a climb involves the very difficult placement of aid; pitons might (or might not) hold body weight.

The present-day Yosemite Decimal System has expanded the Grade scale up to VII and the Class scale up to 5.15d. The Aid Difficulty category is sometimes supplemented with a Protection Category. On contemporary rating systems in the United States and the world, see "Climbing Rating Systems," *Mountain Madness*, accessed December 27, 2021, https://mountainmadness .com/resources/climbing-rating-systems.

11. Chief Park Ranger to Superintendent, re: "First Ascent" August 23, 1960, 3, temporary box: Climbing, folder: Climbing Diamond Face, Longs Peak 1960, ROMO Archives; Briggs, "Diamond"; David F. Rearick and Robert F. Kamps, "Report of the First Ascent of the Diamond East Face of Longs Peak," *Trail and Timberline*, September 1960, 125–26 (this report was initially sent to Rocky Mountain National Park and subsequently published, unedited, in *Trail and Timberline*); Achey et al., *Climb!*, 39.

12. Rudy Chelminski, "Two Start Climb on East Face of Longs Peak," *Rocky Mountain News*, August 2, 1960.

13. Dave Rearick, "First Ascent," sidebar in Briggs, "Diamond"; "Two Climbers Triumph over an Unscaled Cliff," *New York Times*, August 4, 1960.

14. "The Triumph over Longs' Diamond Is a Lesson for a Soft Society," *Denver Post*, August 4, 1960, 30.

15. "The Hidden Owners of Colorado," *Denver Post*, August 8, 1960, 14.

16. Rearick, interview; Rocky Mountain National Park, "Annual Mountaineering Report, 1962," temporary box: Climbing, folder 1962, ROMO Archives.

17. Rocky Mountain National Park, "Annual Mountaineering Report, 1960," temporary box: Climbing, folder 1961; Superintendent James Lloyd to Richard Collier, May 6, 1960; John Clark to Chief Ranger Lyle McDowell, May 6, 1960, temporary box: Climbing, folder: Climbing Longs Peak, Diamond Face, 1960, ROMO Archives; Evans, *Death, Despair*, 73–75.

18. John Clark to Chief Ranger Lyle McDowell, May 6, 1960, temporary box: Climbing, folder: Climbing Longs Peak, Diamond Face, 1960; Rocky Mountain National Park, "Annual Mountaineering Report, 1960," temporary box: Climbing, folder 1961, ROMO Archives.

19. Rocky Mountain National Park, "Annual Mountaineering Report, 1962," 2, temporary box: Climbing, folder 1963, ROMO Archives; Evans, *Death, Despair*, 101.

20. Gerry Caplan, oral history interview by Dale L. Johnson, November 23, 2002, transcript, 28, Maria Rogers Oral History Program, Boulder Public Library, Boulder, CO; Tom Chapman, "Diamond Climb Story: Altitude Ends Attempt at 550-Feet," *Estes Park Trail*, August 10, 1962, 1.

21. Rearick, interview.

22. Briggs, "Diamond," 27–28.

23. Rearick, interview; Nesbit, *Longs Peak*, 55–57; Briggs, "Diamond," 27–28; "East Face of Longs Peak Conquered for Second Time," *New York Times*, August 13, 1962.

24. Rearick, interview.

25. Rearick, interview; Rocky Mountain National Park, "Annual Mountain-eering Report, 1962," 4–5, temporary box: Climbing, folder 1963, ROMO Archives; Nesbit, *Longs Peak*, 79.

26. Rocky Mountain National Park, "Annual Mountaineering Report, 1963," 2–3, temporary box: Climbing, folder 1964, ROMO Archives.

27. Rocky Mountain National Park, "Annual Mountaineering Report, 1963," 2; "Summary of Annual Mountaineering Reports from Areas Administered by the National Park Service, 1963," 2–5, temporary box: Climbing, folder 1964, ROMO Archives; Nesbit, *Longs Peak*, 69.

28. Rocky Mountain National Park, "Annual Mountaineering Report, 1963," 2–3; "Summary of Annual Mountaineering Reports from Areas Administered by the National Park Service, 1963," 5, temporary box: Climbing, folder 1964, ROMO Archives; "Master Plan for the Preservation and Use of Rocky Mountain National Park," vol. 1, chap. 1, "Objectives and Policies," revised 1964, 50d, ROMO-01192.

29. NPS, *Rocky Mountain National Park, Colorado* (1963).

30. Nesbit, *Longs Peak*, 69; Rocky Mountain National Park, "Annual Mountaineering Report, 1964," 1, temporary box: Climbing, folder 1964, ROMO Archives; Royal Robbins, "North America, United States, Colorado, Longs Peak, the Diamond," *American Alpine Journal*, 1964, accessed February 28, 2022, http://publications.americanalpineclub.org/articles/12196419500/North-America-United-States-Colorado-Longs-Peak-The-Diamond. According to Roger Briggs, the *Jack of Diamonds* has been climbed only rarely since 1963, and "it is uncertain whether anyone has again made a one-day ascent." Briggs, "Diamond," 30.

31. Fricke, *Climber's Guide*, 66; Briggs, "Diamond," 30; Nesbit, *Longs Peak*, 69.

32. *SMR*, March 1967, ROMO-01571; Nesbit, *Longs Peak*, 69–70.

33. Nesbit, *Longs Peak*, 69–70; Achey et al., *Climb!*, 103.

34. Rocky Mountain National Park, "Annual Mountaineering Report, 1964," 1, temporary box: Climbing, folder 1965, ROMO Archives.

35. Rocky Mountain National Park, "Annual Mountaineering Report, 1965," ROMO-01192, series 2.6.1, file 73; Rocky Mountain National Park, "Annual Mountaineering Report, 1966," temporary box: Climbing, folder 1967; "Mountaineering Statistics, Longs Peak, 1968," temporary box: Climbing, folder 1969, ROMO Archives; Fred J. Novak, Superintendent, ROMO, "High Point in the Park," *Trail and Timberline*, January 1968, 3.

36. Nesbit, *Longs Peak*, 70.

37. Rearick, interview; Brad Johnson and Eric Ming, "Dale Johnson, 1931–2012," *American Alpine Journal*, 2013, accessed February 28, 2022, http://publications.americanalpineclub.org/articles/13201212376/Dale-Johnson-1931–2012.

38. Powell's article is discussed and quoted in Blake, "Colorado Fourteeners," 160; Colorado Mountain Club, Longs Peak summit registers, CMCC, AAL; Nesbit offers selected quotes from the Longs Peak register in *Longs Peak*, 58.

39. Olson, "Spiritual Aspects of Wilderness"; Leopold, *Sand County Almanac*; Wallace Stegner, "Wilderness Letter" to the Outdoor Recreation Resources

Review Commission, 1960, https://www.wilderness.org/articles/article/wallace -stegner.

40. James Reed, "Book Review," *Trail and Timberline*, June 1960, 90–91. Eliot Porter's most famous book of photography, *In Wildness Is the Preservation of the World* (1962), explored the scenery of New England through the words and perspective of transcendentalist and naturalist Henry David Thoreau. Porter subsequently published books of photography that offered stunning images of Glen Canyon, Maine, the Adirondacks, and Baja California, as well as numerous other sites around the world. Porter's imagery emphasized aesthetics rather than science, and his iconic photographs of the wild always showed it as a place without any human presence. The Eliot Porter Archives are housed at the Amon Carter Museum of American Art; some of his papers have been digitized. See https://www.cartermuseum.org/artists/eliot-porter (accessed February 28, 2022).

41. Blake Hiester Jr. fell 1,200 feet to his death from the Notch Couloir Chimneys to Mills Glacier in 1966. The recovery was exceedingly difficult and traumatic, as Hiester's body was broken into pieces during his precipitous fall. Bryan Harts, the chief guide at the Rocky Mountain Guide Service, assumed responsibility for locating Hiester's body parts. See Rocky Mountain National Park, "Annual Mountaineering Report, 1966," temporary box: Climbing, folder 1967, ROMO Archives; Evans, *Death, Despair*, 50–51, 62, 76–77.

42. Dee B. Crouch, MD, "Midwinter Rescue on Longs Peak," *Trail and Timberline*, March 1969, 41–44.

43. Crouch, "Midwinter Rescue"; MacDonald, *Longs Peak*, 153–54.

44. Nesbit, *Longs Peak*, 70; MacDonald, *Longs Peak*, 150–52.

45. Nesbit, *Longs Peak*, 70–71. Rescuers involved in the trial included personnel from the park and volunteers with the Rocky Mountain Rescue Group, an all-volunteer association serving Boulder County since 1947. See http://www.rockymountainrescue.org/history.php. American Alpine Rescue, another volunteer group, also participated in search and rescue operations in Rocky Mountain National Park, though it is not known whether it was involved in the 1969 trial rescue.

46. Memorandum from Longs Peak Ranger Don Bachman to Wild Basin Sub-District Ranger, July 27, 1967, 2–3, ROMO-01192, series 2.1, folder 53.

47. Memorandum from Bachman to Sub-District Ranger, 3–4.

48. Memorandum from Bachman to Sub-District Ranger, 3–4.

49. Memorandum from Bachman to Sub-District Ranger, 4–5. The available evidence from park files does not explain why Rocky did not remove the *Cable* route in 1967 at rangers' recommendation. There is a gap in documentation between 1967 and 1973, at which point park managers again considered the *Cable* route's removal. The story of the *Cable* route is continued in chapter 7.

50. Carson, *Silent Spring*; Sale, *Green Revolution*, 12–24; Sellars, *Preserving Nature*, 173–91; Rome, *Bulldozer in the Countryside*.

51. Mission 66 was supposed to guide continued growth in park visitation, and it anticipated that visitor numbers would rise from fifty million in 1955 to eighty million in 1966. In fact, there were 129,282,100 national park visitors

in 1966. NPS, "Mission 66 for the National Park System," 14. See also annual park statistics in "Annual Summary Report," https://irma.nps.gov/STATS /SSRSReports/National%20Reports/Annual%20Summary%20Report%20 (1904%20-%20Last%20Calendar%20Year); Cahn, *Will Success Spoil*; Everhart, *National Park Service*, 65–69.

52. Don Beard, "Public Affairs," presentation to superintendents meeting, September 16, 1962, 8, ROMO, museum catalog no. 21369.

53. Beard, "Public Affairs," 13.

54. Sellars, *Preserving Nature*, 168–73, 193, 200–201; Dilsaver, *America's National Park System*, chap. 5.

55. Carr, *Mission 66*, 307.

56. Publ. L. No. 88–577 (16 U.S.C. 1131–1136), 88th Cong., 2nd Sess. (September 3, 1964). Full text available at https://www.govtrack.us/congress /bills/88/s4.

57. Publ. L. No. 88–577.

58. See text of the new laws and brief discussion in Dilsaver, *America's National Park System*, 239–30.

59. U.S. Department of the Interior, ROMO, "A Report to the Superintendent for a Backcountry Management Plan in Rocky Mountain National Park," 1965, 12, ROMO-01192, series 2.6, folder 225.

60. U.S. Department of the Interior, ROMO, "A Report to the Superintendent," 8.

61. Held et al., *Study to Develop Practical Techniques*, pp. b–f; Richard G. Trahan, "Day-Use Limitation in National Parks: Visitor and Park Personnel Attitudes toward Day-Use Limitation Systems for RMNP," 1977, ROMO Library Vertical Files.

62. Baker, "Conservation Congress," 104–19; Schulte, *Wayne Aspinall*, 130–62; E. H. Brunquist, "Wilderness Areas—Pros and Cons," *Trail and Timberline*, December 1958, 169, 175.

63. Kingery and Kingery, *Colorado Mountain Club*, 79; David B. Butts, "Perpetual Back Country, a Turn in the Trail," *Trail and Timberline*, May 1969, 90–92.

64. Perkins, "Rock Climbing Ethics," part 1, 1–2, 4–5, part 2, 3.

65. Bob Kamps, "Bolt Ethics," *Summit*, 1966.

66. Ament and McCarty, *High over Boulder*, 4.

67. Frank, *Making Rocky Mountain National Park*, 105, 165–66; Hess, *Rocky Times*, 54–57.

68. Frank, *Making Rocky Mountain National Park*, 133–37.

69. Sitkoff, *Struggle for Black Equality*; Dudziak, *Cold War Civil Rights*.

70. Sorin, *Driving while Black*, 256–57; Bay, *Traveling Black*, 285–305.

71. Anderson, *Pursuit of Fairness*, 115–25; Jackie Mansky, "The Origins of the Term 'Affirmative Action,'" *Smithsonian*, June 22, 2016, https://www.smithsonianmag .com/history/learn-origins-term-affirmative-action-180959531/.

72. Beth Erickson and her colleagues discovered during interviews with African Americans in Denver in 2001 that the Black community in Colorado tended to view Rocky Mountain National Park as unwelcoming and economically

inaccessible, and to see wilderness recreation as a White activity. These views were widely held by African Americans in Colorado in the mid-twentieth century, including the tumultuous 1960s, and they still held sway in 2001. See Erickson et al., "Rocky Mountain National Park," 529–54.

73. Lee, *Public Use*, 15, 17, 51.

74. Stewart L. Udall, "Nature Islands for the World," and Conrad L. Wirth, "National Parks," in Adams, *First World Conference*, 2–6, 20.

75. Secretary Stuart Udall to NPS Director, July 10, 1964, in Dilsaver, *America's National Park System*, 241–45; Morath, "Park for Everyone," 1–21; Garland-Jackson, "Missing Voices," 1.

76. "500,000 Jobs Corps Center Being Considered for Rocky Mountain National Park," *Estes Park Trail*, February 26, 1965. Rocky hired eight African Americans, all students or faculty at historically Black colleges and universities, as temporary summer employees in 1962. The historical record does not indicate how they were received. "Eight Negroes Will Be on Summer Staff of National Park," *Estes Park Trail*, May 4, 1962.

77. "Jobs Corps Approved by Chamber during Busy Monday Nite Session," *Estes Park Trail*, March 5, 1965; "A Second Trail Ridge," *Estes Park Trail*, March 5, 1965; "Local Leaders Favor Job Corps Establishment," *Estes Park Trail*, March 5, 1965; "Majority Favor Youth Corps Camp Establishment," *Estes Park Trail*, March 5, 1965; Luis A. Gastellum, "Citizens Vote Four-to-One That Job Corps Camp Should Be Here; Proposal Now Goes to Washington," *Estes Park Trail*, April 2, 1965.

78. J. McV. and Esther D. Hunt, "Speak Up," *Estes Park Trail*, March 19, 1965.

79. Letter to the editor, *Estes Park Trail*, March 19, 1965.

80. "National Park Recommends Job Corps Here," *Estes Park Trail*, March 26, 1965. See petitions opposing the Job Corps in Rocky Mountain National Park, Land Holdings and General Subject Files 1932–1966—NRG-079-97-534, box 23, K34—Newspaper Clippings 1–65–12–65, National Archives, Denver; Erickson et al., "Rocky Mountain National Park," 34; "A Reluctant Decision," *Estes Park Trail*, August 27, 1965.

81. "Campaign Promises Versus Realities," *Estes Park Trail*, October 4, 1963; "What Is This Civil Rights Bill?," *Estes Park Trail*, March 20, 1964.

82. "A Reluctant Decision," *Estes Park Trail*," August 27, 1965.

83. Leonard and Noel, *Denver*, 369–74, 390–402; Lee, "Forgotten Alliance," 1–25; "Report of the 1965 Workshop on American Indian Affairs," *Anuario indigenista* 26 (January 1966): 237–49; Abbott et al., *Colorado*, 347–61; "Black/African American History in Fort Collins," City of Fort Collins, accessed December 27, 2021, https://www.fcgov.com/historicpreservation/blackfortcollins.

84. For analysis of masculinity and mountaineering in Canada, see Dummitt, "Risk on the Rocks," 3–29; Robertson, *Magnificent Mountain Women*, 152–55.

85. Joseph N. Nold, "Conservation and Social Problems," *Trail and Timberline*, July 1967, 137–41; Ruth Wright, letter to the editor, *Trail and Timberline*, November 1967, 203. Subsequent to writing this letter, Wright obtained a law degree, became an environmental activist, and served as a member of the Colorado House of Representatives.

CHAPTER 7

1. Jim Detterline, oral history interview by Bryon Hoerner, November 12, 2013.

2. Longs Peak Reunion, 1991, 1993, transcript of reunion program, Estes Park Museum.

3. In one important and widely covered manifestation of the nation's reckoning with race in the early 1990s, activists and scholars reinterpreted the legacy of Christopher Columbus from the perspective of indigenous peoples in anticipation of the 1992 quincentennial of his first voyage to the Americas. Axtell, "Columbian Encounters."

4. An Act to Establish the Rocky Mountain National Park in the State of Colorado, Publ. L. No. 238, 63rd Cong., 3rd Sess. (January 26, 1915), 800.

5. Dilsaver, *America's National Park System*, 245–54, 315–21, 325–30; NPS, *Foundation Document*, 6; NPS, *Rocky Mountain National Park: Final Master Plan*, 1, 10, 13–16, 18.

6. Exec. Order No. 11478, "Equal Employment Opportunity in the Federal Government," 34 Fed. Reg. 12985, 3 C.F.R., 1966–1970 Comp. (August 8, 1969), 803.

7. Dohnalek, "Native American Religious Accommodations"; Native American Graves Protection and Repatriation Act, Publ. Law No. 101–601, 25 U.S.C. 3001–13.

8. Tom Hornbein at Longs Peak Reunion, 1991, transcript, 4. As many readers will know, Hornbein was a highly accomplished rock climber and mountaineer; in addition to putting up East Face routes in the 1950s, he attempted a West Ridge ascent of Mount Everest in 1963 as part of the American Everest Expedition.

9. Nesbit, *Longs Peak*, 70–71. Rocky lifted the ban on solo climbing after a successful trial rescue from the top of the Diamond increased the park's confidence that search and rescue teams could aid climbers stranded or injured on the wall. Jonathan Hough described the trial rescue in "The Diamond," *Trail and Timberline*, March 1970, 52–59.

10. William Forrest, "Solo on the Diamond," *American Alpine Journal* 17, no. 2 (1971): 285–87.

11. Chossy rock is friable, unstable, crumbly, or loose. The term has apparently been used by climbers since the 1960s. See "Chossy," Slang Define, accessed December 29, 2021, https://slangdefine.org/c/chossy-6cc4.html.

12. Achey et al., *Climb!*, 104–5.

13. Briggs, "Diamond," 24–25; Nesbit, *Longs Peak*, 71; Robertson, *Magnificent Mountain Women*, 154–55; Megan Walsh, "Can't Keep Her Down: A Consolidated History of Women's Climbing Achievements," *Climbing*, November 14, 2017.

14. Climbing Task Force, "Task Force Findings: Climbing in Rocky Mountain National Park," May 1990, 3, ROMO-01761, series 17.5, folder 2; Jeff Achey, "Longs Strange Trip," *Climbing*, June 15–August 1, 1994, 124; "Climbing Activity, Rocky Mountain National Park, 1975," ROMO-01192, central files,

series 2.6, folder 55; "Bivouac Use Management: Overview and Recommendations," December 1983, 1, ROMO-01761, series 17.1, folder 4.

15. Achey et al., *Climb!*, part 3, 80–168.
16. When Dave Rearick and Bob Kamps climbed the Diamond in 1960, they removed nearly all their pitons and placed just four bolts. Over time, Rearick created a set of wooden nuts for his own use "and was one of the first climbers in Colorado to pursue free climbing as a worthwhile end in itself." Achey et al., *Climb!*, 56.
17. Bill Briggs, Longs Peak Reunion, 1991, transcript, 33–35.
18. Achey et al., *Climb!*, 142–43; Briggs, "Diamond," 31–34.
19. Longs Peak Reunion, 1991, transcript, 39.
20. Achey et al., *Climb!*, 172–73; Climbing Task Force, "Task Force Findings: Climbing in Rocky Mountain National Park," May 1990, ROMO-01761, series 17.5, folder 2.
21. ROMO, "Annual Mountaineering and Search and Rescue Report," 1975, 2, ROMO-01192, series 2.6, folder 55.
22. Eberhart and Schmuck, *Fourteeners*, 1; Borneman and Lampert, *Climbing Guide*; Blake, "Colorado Fourteeners," 162–65.
23. Climbing Task Force, "Task Force Findings: Climbing in Rocky Mountain National Park," May 1990, ROMO-01761, series 17.5, folder 2. For a good description of crowding on the Diamond and technical climbing parties' irritation and competition with other parties, see Dean Tschappat, "Diamond," *Climbing*, March–April 1976, 2–8. Jim Detterline earned a PhD in biology before becoming a climbing ranger at Longs. See his 2013 interview with Bryon Hoerner for discussion of his commitments to visitors' wilderness experience and ecological preservation.
24. For park language on the dangers of climbing, see, for example, *Rocky Mountain National Park Brochure*, 1982, accessed November 10, 2021, http://npshistory.com/brochures/romo/1982.pdf. For accident reports, see, for example, American Alpine Club, *Accidents in North American Mountaineering*, 1972, 9–11; American Alpine Club, *Accidents in North American Mountaineering*, 1994, 39–41. On improvements to search and rescue capability, see *SARs*, ROMO-01571.
25. On disputes between rangers and park managers, see the notes, correspondence, and newspaper coverage in box 3, folders 15 and 25, James L. Detterline Collection, AAL. On fatality numbers, see Kela Fetters, "The Legend of Longs Peak, One of Colorado's Most Popular 14ers," *Outdoor Journal*, February 18, 2019. For estimates on the number of climbers on Longs, see ROMO, *1985 Interpretive Prospectus*, 37–38, ROMO-01192; NPS, Rocky Mountain Region, "Draft Environmental Assessment Management/Development Concept Plan: Longs Peak/Wild Basin/Lily Lake," July 1994, 25; Paul McLaughlin, "Climbing the Longs Peak Keyhole Route," research summary (ROMO, CDRLC, 2008), accessed November 10, 2021, https://www.nps.gov/articles/climbing-the-longs-peak-keyhole-route.htm.
26. Rocky Mountain National Park did not obtain wilderness designation for most of the area within its borders until 2009, but the park began adopting

Wilderness Act standards in the 1960s and first applied for wilderness status in 1974. See "Wilderness," Rocky Mountain National Park, https://www.nps.gov/romo/planyourvisit/wilderness.htm.

27. On the CMC's persistent commitment to conservation, see, for example, "Report of the Long Range Planning Committee," April 12, 1982, in *CMC Minutes, 1980–82*, CMC Collection, AAL; *1972 Chouinard Catalog*, 2–3, https://thesenecaproject.org/wp-content/uploads/2017/10/ChouinardCatalog.pdf; Jones, *Climbing in North America*, 367–69.

28. Fricke, *Climber's Guide*, 12.

29. *1972 Chouinard Catalog*, 2–3; Chris Landry, "*The Yellow Wall:* A Climb of the Times," *Climbing*, March–April 1972, 6; "Task Force Findings: Climbing in Rocky Mountain National Park," May 1990, ROMO-01761, series 17.5, folder 2.

30. Achey et al., *Climb!*, 172–73, 187, 198, 206.

31. Memorandum from Superintendent to Director, Midwest Region, April 6, 1971, "Wilderness-Backcountry Management," ROMO–01192, series 2.6, folder 206; Fricke, *Climber's Guide*, 10; *Backcountry Management Plan, Rocky Mountain National Park*, 1975, ROMO Library, 1. The 1975 plan notes that park rangers had studied the steadily increasing impact of climbers and hikers on backcountry bivouac and camping sites since 1967 and had determined a 390 percent increase in overnight backcountry use in the park between 1967 and 1974. See also "Bivouac Use Management: Overview and Recommendations," December 1983, ROMO-01761, series 17.1, folder 4.

32. Memorandum from Fricke to East District Ranger, July 4, 1973, "Rationale for Removal of Cables from Longs Peak," ROMO-01192, series 2.1, folder 53.

33. ROMO, press release, July 16, 1973, ROMO-01192, series 001, folder 53-A3415 / A3615—Comments and Complaints—Longs Peak Cables 1967–1976.

34. ROMO, press release, March 18, 1974, ROMO-01192, series 2.1, folder 53.

35. Memorandum from Walter Fricke to Superintendent, October 8, 1973; memorandum from Backcountry Subdistrict Ranger Steven Hickman to East District Ranger, March 7, 1974, ROMO-01192, series 2.1, folder 53.

36. Norman Nesbit to Rocky Mountain National Park, August 15, 1973; W. R. Downs to Park Superintendent, August 15, 1973; Dale McNeal to Roger Contor, Superintendent, November 19, 1973; Bill Gingles to Swiss Village Inn, August 18, 1973; Karl Gustafson to ROMO, August 21, 1973, ROMO-01192, series 2.1, folder 53.

37. ROMO, "Annual Mountaineering and Search and Rescue Report," 1971, 2; ROMO, "Annual Mountaineering and Search and Rescue Report," 1974, 2; ROMO, "Annual Mountaineering and Search and Rescue Report," 1975, 8, ROMO, Temporary Climbing Collection.

38. The Wilderness Act, Publ. L. No. 88–577, 16 U.S.C. 1131–1136, 88th Cong., 2nd Sess. (September 3, 1964) (as amended), https://www.law.cornell.edu/uscode/text/16/1131.

39. On the necessity of using carrying capacity standards in the NPS, see the 1972 report "Preservation of National Park Values," produced by the Conservation Foundation as part of its National Parks for the Future Project, in

Dilsaver, *America's National Park System*, 343–45; Chris Landry, "*The Yellow Wall:* A Climb of the Times," *Climbing*, March–April 1972, 6.

40. Trahan, "Day-Use Limitation," chap. 1, p. 4, chap. 5.
41. Trahan, "Day-Use Limitation."
42. Milton Salaun, "Synopsis and Prospectus," ROMO-01761, series 21.02, folder 514.
43. Milton M. Salaun, "Investigator's Annual Report," January 19, 1977, and "Taxonomic Table," ROMO-01761, series 21.02, folder 514.
44. Chip Salaun, "A Hole in the Clean Climbing Philosophy," *Off Belay*, June 1976, 37.
45. Salaun, "Hole in the Clean Climbing Philosophy."
46. Salaun, "Hole in the Clean Climbing Philosophy," 35.
47. Chip Salaun, "The Diamond," *Climbing*, May–June 1978, 19.
48. Turner, "From Woodcraft to 'Leave no Trace,'" 473.
49. Marion and Reid, "Development of the U.S. Leave No Trace Program," 81–92. During the 1980s the AAC was involved in difficult discussions with public land managers over climbers' impact on the environment. By 1991 climbers had established a new organization, the Access Fund, to defend access to climbing areas and reduce climbers' impact on the environment across the nation. See "History," Access Fund, accessed December 27, 2021, https://www.accessfund.org/meet-the-access-fund/our-history. On the CMC and minimal impact ethics, see "Report of the Activities Subcommittee, Long Range Planning Committee, Colorado Mountain Club, to the Board of Directors and Membership of the Colorado Mountain Club," April 17, 1982, in *CMC Minutes 1980–1982*, CMC Archives.
50. Turner, "From Woodcraft to 'Leave no Trace,'" 473–79; Simon and Alagona, "Beyond Leave No Trace Ethics," 17–34.
51. Turner, "From Woodcraft to 'Leave no Trace,'" 473.
52. NPS, *VERP: The Visitor Experience and Resource Protection (VERP) Framework*, 8; NPS, *Rocky Mountain National Park: Final Master Plan*, 15.
53. NPS, *Rocky Mountain National Park: Final Master Plan*, 1, 15.
54. NPS, *Rocky Mountain National Park: Final Master Plan*, 1, 7, 13, 15, 18, 33.
55. ROMO, *Backcountry Management Plan*, 1975, 6–14, ROMO-01761, series 17.2, folder 3.
56. ROMO, *Backcountry Management Plan*, 1975, 1–8, appendix H, ROMO-01761, series 17.2, folder 3.
57. ROMO, *Backcountry Management Plan*, 1975, 15, appendix H-8, appendix I.
58. "Bivouac Use Management: Overview and Recommendations," December 1983, 1–2, ROMO-01761, series 17.1, folder 4.
59. "Bivouac Use Management," 2–3; typescript, no title, 1979, on meeting in Boulder, Backcountry Office File, "Climbing," ROMO-01850.
60. William H. Tipton, "A Case Evaluation of Excessive Bivouac Use, Rocky Mountain National Park," [1979?], ROMO-01850.
61. "Bivouac Use Management," 3–4; Stuart W. Schneider, "Rocky Mountain National Park Bivouac and Climbing Proposal, 1982," ROMO-01761, series

17.5, folder 1; NPS, *Rocky Mountain National Park Backcountry Management Plan* (1984).

62. Peter D. Armitage, "Unimproved Trail, Jim's Grove to Granite Pass," 1–5; "Jim's Grove—Natural Area," 1, n.d., Office of Jeff Connors, Resources Stewardship Division, ROMO-01761; Nesbit, *Longs Peak*, 71; NPS, *Trails Plan: Rocky Mountain National Park*, 66, 68.

63. Superintendent Chester L. Brooks to Director, Denver Service Center, February 20, 1979, ROMO-01192, central files, series 2.7, folder 137; Mark Magnuson, interview by Ruth Alexander, June 11, 2009, ROMO-01851; Joe Arnold, "Solar Toilets on Longs Peak," *Rocky Mountain Highlights*, July 1984, 6–7. Rocky has found solar toilets in the Boulderfield to be satisfactory, though their design has required modification over time, especially to withstand high wind. See Joe Arnold, "Solar Dehydrating Toilets in Rocky Mountain National Park," YouTube, December 19, 2016, https://www.youtube.com/watch?v= F_rMIed2dDo.

64. *SAR*, 1987, 1d; Climbing Task Force, "Task Force Findings: Climbing in Rocky Mountain National Park," May 1990, 2, ROMO-01761, series 17.5, folder 2.

65. ROMO, *1985 Interpretive Prospectus*, 37–38, ROMO Library.

66. Climbing Task Force, "Task Force Findings: Climbing in Rocky Mountain National Park," May 1990, 1–2, 6, ROMO-01761.

67. Climbing Task Force, "Task Force Findings, 3–6.

68. Climbing Task Force, 5.

69. Climbing Task Force, 9–11; NPS, *Statement for Management*, June 1992, 13.

70. Climbing Task Force, "Task Force Findings," and Project Statement Sheets, "Rock Climbing Management," ROMO-N-380.000, ROMO-N-380.001, ROMO-N-380.200, 1992, in ROMO-01761, series 17.5, folder 2; NPS, *Statement for Management*, June 1992, 15, 67–71; Mark Magnuson, interview.

71. U.S. National Park Service, Rocky Mountain Region, "Draft Environmental Assessment Management/Development Concept Plan: Longs Peak/Wild Basin/Lily Lake," July 1994, 25; Paul McLaughlin, "Climbing the Longs Peak Keyhole Route," research summary (ROMO, CDRLC, 2008).

72. Mark Magnuson, interview; Jane Gordon, interview by Ruth Alexander, July 30, 2009, ROMO-01851.

73. Dilsaver, *America's National Park System*, 365–70, 375–78.

74. Sellars, *Preserving Nature*, 283–88.

75. Leopold, *Wildlife Management*, 5; Sellars, *Preserving Nature*, 243–49, 269–76, 281–84.

76. *SAR*, 1986, 1d; Ansson, "Our National Parks," 1–144; Shafer, "Rise, Fall, and Legacy," 29–46; Turner, "'Specter of Environmentalism,'" 123–48; Sellars, *Preserving Nature*, 262, 272–73, 288–90, 294; Oreskes and Conway, *Merchants of Doubt*.

77. Parsons, Brinkerhoff, Quade, and Douglas, Inc., *Rocky Mountain National Park Transportation Study*.

78. NPS, *Economic Feasibility Study*; Frank, *Making Rocky Mountain National Park*, 196–205; NPS, *Statement for Management*, June 1992, 19.

79. Each *Superintendent's Annual Report* from the 1970s through the 1990s identifies scientific studies and restoration projects being pursued in Rocky as well as environmental education initiatives. ROMO-01571.

80. For park visitor statistics, see "Park Reports," NPS Stats: National Park Service Visitor Use Statistics, https://irma.nps.gov/STATS/Reports/Park/ROMO.

81. Hess, *Rocky Times*, 60–71, 77–78, 92–93; Gootz, *Transformation*, 114–21; NPS, *Board of Review Report for the Ouzel Fire.*

82. Hess, *Rocky Times*, 14, 23–49, 77–90; Gootz, *Transformation*, 134–39; U.S. Geological Survey (U.S. Department of the Interior) and Natural Resources Ecology Lab, Colorado State University, *Ecological Evaluation.*

83. ROMO, *Annual Statement for Interpretation and Visitor Services, 1982*, 15, 20, 32; ROMO, *Annual Statement for Interpretation, 1993*, 32, ROMO-01192, series 2.5, folder 23. See census data on race at CensusScope, accessed November 10, 2021, https://www.censusscope.org/us/s8/chart_race.html (for Colorado) and https://www.censusscope.org/us/chart_race.html (for the United States).

84. Mackintosh et al., "National Parks," 68–69; Floyd, "Managing National Parks," 41–51.

85. See, for example, Natasha Gardner, "The Legacy of Denver's Forced School Busing Era," *5280*, June 2018, accessed December 29, 2021, https://www.5280.com/2018/05/the-legacy-of-denvers-forced-school-busing-era/; Leonard and Noel, *Denver*, 366–406; Cherland, "No Prejudice Here"; Sanchez, "Face the Nation," 1009–30. Omi and Winant, *Racial Formation.*

86. Marcuse, "Is the National Parks Movement," 16–21, 48.

87. Meeker, "Red, White, and Black," 3–7; McCammack, *Landscapes of Hope*, chap. 4; Ruth Terry and Michelle Jackson, "Preserving Black Historical Resorts Is a Radical Act," *Yes! Magazine*, June 24, 2021, accessed December 31, 2021, https://www.yesmagazine.org/social-justice/2021/06/24/preserving-black-historical-resorts-is-a-radical-act.

88. DeLuca and Demo, "Imagining Nature," 541–60; Carder, "American Environmental Justice Movement"; Renee Skelton and Vernice Miller, "The Environmental Justice Movement," NRDC, March 17, 2016, https://www.nrdc.org/stories/environmental-justice-movement; William J. Clinton, Exec. Order No. 12898, "Federal Actions to Address Environmental Justice in Minority Populations and Low-Income Populations," Fed. Reg. Presidential Documents 59, no. 32 (February 16, 1994), https://www.archives.gov/files/federal-register/executive-orders/pdf/12898.pdf.

89. Miner and Boldt, *Outward Bound U.S.A.*, 283–305; Weinbaum et al., *Expeditionary Learning Outward Bound*; "Eagle Rock School—History," https://eaglerockschool.org/about-us/history/; Alex Kotlowitz, "The High School at the End of the Road," *New York Times Magazine*, July 5, 1998, accessed November 3, 2021, https://www.nytimes.com/1998/07/05/magazine/the-high-school-at-the-end-of-the-road.html; *SAR*, 1991–1992, 5d.

90. Kathy McKoy, "The James P. Beckwourth Mountain Club," *CRM Bulletin: A National Park Service Technical Bulletin* 19, no. 4 (1996): 42; Maggie Magoffin, "A 'Tailing Tale' of Winston Walker and Lincoln Hills," *Weekly Register-Call*,

December 2017, accessed November 21, 2021, https://weeklyregistercall.com
/a-tailing-tale-of-winston-walker-and-lincoln-hills/history/postmaster/4864/;
Bryan Wendland and Erin Powell, "First Black Man to Hike All Colorado
14ers Celebrates Other Man Trying to Achieve Same Feat," *9News*, September 20, 2020, https://www.9news.com/article/news/local/next/army-veteran
-trying-to-become-first-african-american-to-summit-all-colorados-14ers/73
-017de4a8-2040-4b94-99b1-b183e46abc0c.

91. Edmondson, *Black and Brown Faces*, 23–27.
92. See the complete digital collection of the *Courier* at the National Park Service History eLibrary, http://npshistory.com/newsletters/courier/index.htm.
93. On equal opportunity at Rocky, see *SAR*, 1985, 9d. On the YCC and
related conservation programs, see each *SAR* from 1972 to 1981.
94. The White House, "Affirmative Action Review: Federal Civilian Employment Affirmative Action: History and Results," https://clintonwhitehouse4
.archives.gov/WH/EOP/OP/html/aa/aa08.html.
95. "By the Numbers," National Park Service, May 4, 2021, accessed January 3,
2022, https://www.nps.gov/articles/000/by-the-numbers.htm. See also the
oral history interview by historian Lu Ann Jones with African American park
ranger Kevin Cheri and his experience working at the newly formed Buffalo
National River in Arkansas in 1978, "The National Park Service Reckons with
Representation," https://www.nps.gov/subjects/oralhistory/podcasts-episode-8
.htm; U.S. Government Accountability Office, "EEO at the National Park Service," GGD-94–54R, published March 3, 1994, publicly released March 15,
1994, 2–3, https://www.gao.gov/products/ggd-94-54r.
96. "National Register of Historic Places Listings in Rocky Mountain National
Park," Wikimedia Foundation, accessed November 30, 2021, https://en
.wikipedia.org/wiki/National_Register_of_Historic_Places_listings_in_Rocky
_Mountain_National_Park; Rocky Mountain National Park, *Statement for Interpretation, 1993*, ROMO-01192, central files, series 2:5 Interpretation, folder 86.
97. "CRM Bulletin / CRM / CRM Journal: Master Table of Contents,"
National Park Service History eLibrary, http://npshistory.com/newsletters/crm
/contents.htm; Wray et al., "Creating Policy," 43–50.
98. Marincic, "National Historic Preservation Act"; testimony of Reno Keoni
Franklin (Kashia Pomo), chair, National Association of Tribal Historic Preservation Officers, to U.S. Senate Subcommittee on National Parks, November 5, 2011, accessed January 2, 2022, https://www.nathpo.org/assets/pdf
/NATHPOtestimonyJune2011/; Kaufman, "Historic Places," 70.
99. Ranger Sue Langdon, Division of Interpretation and Education, ROMO,
phone conversation with Ruth Alexander, October 3, 2021; Daniel P. Baker II,
"Interpreting Rocky Mountain National Park's Past People," unpublished
paper, [1999?], ROMO-01192, series 2.5, folder 108.
100. NPS Advisory Board and Franklin, *Rethinking the National Parks*, 7, 8, 28.
101. NPS Advisory Board and Franklin, 30.
102. NPS Advisory Board and Franklin, 9, 10, 14, 30.
103. NPS Advisory Board and Franklin, 8–9, 11–15, 23, 26, 28.

1. Chris Weidner, "Epic Proportions: New Routing on the Diamond," *Climbing*, July 13, 2021, accessed January 3, 2022, https://www.climbing.com/places /east-face-diamond-longs-peak-rock-climbing-history/; Derek Franz, "Two New 5.13 Routes Freed on the Diamond of Longs Peak (Neniisotoyou'u) on August 9," *Alpinist*, August 17, 2020, accessed January 15, 2022, http://www .alpinist.com/doc/web20c/newswire-gamblersfallacy-beethovenshoneymoon -diamond-longs-peak.

2. Megan Walsh, "Can't Keep Her Down: A Consolidated History of Women's Climbing Achievements," *Climbing*, November 14, 2017, accessed April 21, 2022, https://www.climbing.com/people/cant-keep-her-down-a-consolidated -history-of-womens-climbing-achievements/.

3. Katie Arnold, "Steph Davis Rocks," *Outside*, June 2, 2006, accessed January 9, 2022, https://www.outsideonline.com/outdoor-adventure/climbing/she -rocks/; Victoria Robinson, *Rock Climbing: The Ultimate Guide* (Westport, CT: Greenwood, 2013), 56; "Salathe Wall," *Alpinist*, March 1, 2006, accessed January 7, 2022, http://www.alpinist.com/doc/ALP15/climbing-notes-editors.

4. Davis, *Learning to Fly*, 56–57, 121, 125–27; Ryan Minton, "Steph Davis Free Solos the Diamond Four Times," *Alpinist*, October 15, 2007, accessed January 10, 2022, http://www.alpinist.com/doc/web07f/newswire-solo -diamond-steph-davis; Conroy and Gonzalez, "Off Belay!"

5. Dougald MacDonald, "Tommy Caldwell, Joe Mills Climb First 5.14 on the Diamond," *Climbing*, August 23, 2013, accessed January 6, 2022, https:// www.climbing.com/news/caldwell-mills-climb-first-5-14-on-the-diamond/; Chris Van Leuven, "Free at Last: Caldwell, Jorgeson Top Out the Dawn Wall," *Alpinist*, January 14, 2015, accessed January 13, 2022, http://www.alpinist .com/doc/web15w/newswire-caldwell-jorgeson-free-dawn-wall; Dougald MacDonald, "2015 Golden Pitons: Climb of the Year," *Climbing*, February 1, 2016, accessed January 13, 2022, https://www.climbing.com/people/2015 -golden-piton-awards-the-dawn-wall-is-climb-of-the-year/.

6. William Finnegan, "Finding a Way Up," *New Yorker*, November 29, 2021, 46–57; Tommy Caldwell, interview by Ruth Alexander, August 9, 2009; Caldwell, *Push*, 86–116; "Climate Change Makes Mountaineering Riskier," Adventure Alternative, n.d., accessed January 20, 2022, https://www.adventurealternative .com/adventure-blog/climate-change-makes-mountaineering-riskier/; J. D. Simkins, "Tommy Caldwell Climbs toward a Future of Climate Change Activism," *Sunset*, November 19, 2021, accessed January 10, 2022, https://www.sunset .com/travel/wild-lands/tommy-caldwell-climate-change; Angelo Baca and Tommy Caldwell, "Op-Ed: There's More Work to Do at Bears Ears," *Outside*, October 12, 2021, accessed January 7, 2022, https://www.outsideonline.com /culture/opinion/bears-ears-national-monument-native-utah-restoration/; Kevin Johnson, "Coloradan Called Out for Bolting over Petroglyphs," *Outside*, April 16, 2021, accessed January 20, 2022, https://www.outsideonline.com /outdoor-adventure/climbing/moab-area-petroglyphs-climbing-controversy/; Cody Nelson, "Defaced Petroglyphs Force Rock Climbers to Reckon with Sport's

Destructive Past," *Guardian*, May 4, 2021, accessed January 20, 2022, https://www.theguardian.com/sport/2021/may/04/rock-climbing-native-american-indigenous-people. See also Dustin et al., "Cross-Cultural Claims."

7. Amanda Machado, "Is Rock-Climbing a 'White' Sport? These Epic Climbers of Color Are Proving Otherwise," Matador Network, April 13, 2016, accessed January 20, 2022, https://matadornetwork.com/sports/rock-climbing-white-sport-epic-climbers-color-proving-otherwise/; Noel Phillips, "No Man's Land: The Rise of Women in Climbing," *Climbing*, October 25, 2017, accessed January 20, 2022, https://www.climbing.com/people/no-mans-land-the-rise-of-women-in-climbing/.

8. Vibe Tribe Adventures, accessed January 8, 2022, https://vibetribeadventures.org/; Lanisha Renee Blount, "Anti-Racism Resources for Climbers," *Climbing*, June 15, 2020, accessed January 8, 2022, https://www.climbing.com/news/anti-racism-resources-for-climbers. See the database that Climbing for Change has developed "to enable people to connect with outdoor DEI initiatives," accessed January 9, 2022, https://climbing4change.org/connections.

9. Cameron Fenton, "Giving Mountains Back Their Indigenous Names," *Outside*, February 13, 2018, accessed January 16, 2022, https://www.outsideonline.com/outdoor-adventure/environment/giving-mountains-back-their-indigenous-names/; Ryan Dunfee-Sierra, "Meet the Native American Climber Restoring Indigenous Place Names," *Adventure Journal*, June 25, 2018, accessed January 10, 2022, https://www.adventure-journal.com/2018/06/meet-native-american-climber-restoring-indigenous-place-names/; Art Hughes, "Responsible Rock Climbing," *Native America Calling*, November 5, 2019, accessed January 10, 2022, https://nativeamericacalling.com/tuesday-november-5-2019-responsible-rock-climbing/; Len Necefer, "Water Is Life," *Alpinist* 71 (October 5, 2020), accessed January 13, 2022, http://www.alpinist.com/doc/web20f/wfeature-a71-wired-water-is-life. See also Aaron Mike, "A Navajo's Creation Story," *Natives Outdoors*, September 1, 2021, accessed January 28, 2022, https://natives-outdoors.com/temoajournal/2021/9/1/a-navajos-creation-story.

10. "About Brown Girls Climb," accessed January 10, 2022, https://www.browngirlsclimb.com/about/.

11. For an excellent overview of the BIPOC movement, see the BIPOC Project website, accessed January 10, 2022, https://www.thebipocproject.org/. See also Sandra E. Garcia, "Where Did BIPOC Come From?," *New York Times*, June 17, 2020, accessed January 10, 2022, https://www.thebipocproject.org/.

12. For coverage of antiracism in *Climbing*, see "Anti-Racism Resources for Climbers," accessed January 10, 2022, https://www.climbing.com/news/anti-racism-resources-for-climbers/, and "Climbing Magazine Supports Racial Justice," accessed January 10, 2022, https://www.climbing.com/news/climbing-magazine-supports-racial-justice/. For CMC bylaws (2020), and CMC anti-harassment (2000) and antidiscrimination policies (2007), see "Governing Documents," Colorado Mountain Club, accessed January 20, 2022, https://www.cmc.org/about/governing-documents. For Access Fund commitments to social justice and inclusivity and its collaborative work with indigenous tribes,

see "Our JEDI Journey," accessed January 13, 2022, https://www.accessfund
.org/meet-the-access-fund/our-jedi-journey. For AAC commitments to justice and inclusivity, see "About Climb United," accessed January 10, 2022,
https://americanalpineclub.org/climb-united. For the Sierra Club, see "Equity,
Inclusion, and Justice," accessed January 10, 2020, https://www.sierraclub
.org/equity, and "Climate Change," https://www.sierraclub.org/topics/climate
-change. For the Wilderness Society, see "Our Commitment to Diversity,
Equity and Inclusion," December 1, 2021, accessed November 7, 2022, https://
www.wilderness.org/articles/article/our-commitment-diversity-equity-and
-inclusion, and "Public Lands Should Be Part of the Climate Change Solution,"
accessed November 10, 2022, https://www.wilderness.org/key-issues/climate
-change-solutions.

13. American Alpine Club, *State of Climbing* (2019), 6–7, https://aac
    -publications.s3.amazonaws.com/articles/State_of_Climbing_Report_2019
    _Web.pdf.

14. NPS, *Call to Action*, 5. See also NPS, *America's Great Outdoors*; NPS,
    National Parks Second Century Commission, *Advancing the National Park
    Idea*; NPS, *Future of America's National Parks*.

15. NPS Advisory Board and Franklin, *Rethinking the National Parks*, 23.

16. Unpublished park documentation provided to author via email by Mike
    Lukens, Wilderness and Climbing Program supervisor, ROMO, January
    25, 2022; Kevin Sturmer, climbing ranger, interview by Ruth Alexander,
    October 18, 2016; Roger Leverton, park volunteer, conversation with Ruth
    Alexander, Longs Peak Ranger Station, September 13, 2021.

17. Unpublished park documentation from Mike Lukens, January 25, 2022;
    Kevin Sturmer, interview; Jeff Doran, "A Statistical Analysis on Fatalities while
    Climbing Longs Peak," *Rocky Mountain Journal* (blog), March 25, 2021,
    accessed January 25, 2022, https://rockymountainhikingtrails.blogspot.com
    /2021/03/a-statistical-analysis-on-fatalities.html.

18. Unpublished park documentation from Mike Lukens, January 25, 2022;
    Kevin Sturmer, interview.

19. See "Climbing," Rocky Mountain National Park, https://www.nps.gov
    /romo/planyourvisit/climbing.htm; Kevin Sturmer, interview.

20. See "Climbing," Rocky Mountain National Park, https://www.nps.gov/romo
    /planyourvisit/climbing.htm; "Boulder Climbing Community," https://www
    .boulderclimbers.org/about-bcc; "Long's Peak," Mountain Project, https://www
    .mountainproject.com/area/105857350/longs-peak; "Longs Peak," SummitPost
    .org, http://www.summitpost.org/longs-peak/150310 (all accessed January 13,
    2022); Rossiter, *Rocky Mountain National Park*.

21. NPS, "Director's Order #41: Wilderness Stewardship," May 13, 2013,
    accessed January 28, 2022, https://www.nps.gov/policy/DOrders/DO_41
    .pdf; Jeff Achey, "Fixed Anchors in the Wilderness," *Climbing*, April 8, 2013,
    accessed January 30, 2022, https://www.climbing.com/people/fixed-anchors
    -in-the-wilderness/.

22. "Access Fund and American Alpine Club Policy on Fixed Anchors,"
    April 27, 2015, accessed January 15, 2022, https://d1w9vyym276tvm

.cloudfront.net/assets/pdf/AF-AAC_FixedAnchorPolicy_20150428.pdf ?mtime=20200711221300&focal=none; "General Agreement between the U.S. Department of the Interior, National Park Service, and the Access Fund," August 18, 2014, https://d1w9vyym276tvm.cloudfront.net/assets/Access -Fund-NPS_MOU_-2014-2019.pdf; "Managing Climbing Activities in Wilderness," NPS Reference Manual #41, 2013, accessed January 29, 2022, https://www.nps.gov/orgs/1981/upload/Managing-Climbing-in-W_508.pdf.

23. "Bolting," Joshua Tree National Park, accessed January 30, 2022, https:// www.nps.gov/jotr/planyourvisit/fixed_anchors.htm; "Access Fund Makes Historic Move to Pass Law Legitimizing Climbing Bolts," December 5, 2018, accessed January 30, 2022, https://www.accessfund.org/news-and-events/news /access-fund-makes-historic-move-to-pass-law-legitimizing-climbing-bolts; Erik Murdock, Access Fund vice president of policy and government affairs, meeting with Ruth Alexander, Estes Park, CO, March 31, 2022; memoran- dum from Chris Winter, Executive Director, Access Fund, and John Lauretig, Executive Director, Friends of Joshua Tree, to Superintendent David Smith, Joshua Tree National Park, March, 11, 2022, "Comments on Joshua Tree National Park Climbing Management Plan Scoping" (copy of memorandum in possession of author).

24. NPS, *Management Policies 2006*, 14. See also NPS, "Director's Order #75A: Civic Engagement and Public Involvement," 2003 (renewed 2007).

25. See, for example, Christopher Zheng, "31 Years of NAGPRA: Evaluating the Restitution of Native American Ancestral Remains and Belongings," *Center for Art Law*, May 15, 2018, accessed January 23, 2022, https://itsartlaw.org /2021/05/18/31-years-of-nagpra/; Harms, "NAGPRA in Colorado"; Antolini, "National Park Law in the U.S."; Force and Forester, "Public Involvement."

26. NPS Advisory Board and Franklin, *Rethinking the National Parks*, 17.

27. On Bush, see Sellars, *Preserving Nature*, 297–306; on Trump, see Union of Concerned Scientists, "Surveying the National Park Service: Scientist Voices under President Trump," 2018, accessed January 22, 2022, https://ucsusa.org /sites/default/files/2019-09/science-under-trump-nps.pdf; Laura Bloomer, Peter Daniels, Eric Wriston, and Joseph Goffman, "Managing Public Lands under the Trump Administration and Beyond," Harvard Law School, Environ- mental and Energy Law Program, October 2020, accessed January 28, 2022, http://eelp.law.harvard.edu/wp-content/uploads/Managing-Public-Lands -Under-the-Trump-Administration-and-Beyond.pdf; NPS, *Management Pol- icies 2006*, 36.

28. NPS, *Climate Change Response Strategy*, 1, 3, 5, 21.

29. NPS Advisory Board Science Committee, *Revisiting Leopold*, 3–5, 7–8, 11–13, 20, 23.

30. NPS, Wilderness Character Integration Team, *Wilderness Stewardship Plan Handbook*; NPS, "Director's Order #100: Resource Stewardship for the 21st Century," 2016; Department of the Interior, "Notice of Creation of a New System of Records," Fed. Reg. 79, no. 102 (May 28, 2014), 30641, accessed January 26, 2022, https://www.govinfo.gov/content/pkg/FR-2014-05-28 /html/2014-12298.htm; NPS, *Green Parks Plan: Advancing Our Mission*

through Sustainable Operations, 2016, accessed January 27, 2022, https://www.nps.gov/subjects/sustainability/green-parks.htm.

31. Laura Bloomer, Peter Daniels, Eric Wriston, and Joseph Goffman, "Managing Public Lands under the Trump Administration and Beyond," Harvard Law School, Environmental and Energy Law Program, October 2020, accessed January 28, 2022, http://eelp.law.harvard.edu/wp-content/uploads/Managing-Public-Lands-Under-the-Trump-Administration-and-Beyond.pdf; Kizer, "Great American Outdoors Act," 143–45. For an overview of all the executive orders and memoranda issued by the Biden administration in 2021 to reverse the negative impact of the Trump administration on the NPS, see Coalition to Protect America's National Parks, "This Land Is Our Land, Restoring the National Park Service and Our National Parks: Recommendations from the Coalition to Protect America's National Parks, Executive Summary," accessed January 30, 2022, https://protectnps.org/this-land-is-our-land-restoring-our-national-parks/; NPS, *Planning for a Changing Climate.*

32. National Parks Conservation Association, *State of the Parks*, July 2002.

33. On long-term monitoring at Loch Vale in Rocky, see "Loch Vale Watershed: Long-Term Ecological Research and Monitoring Program," accessed January 27, 2022, https://www2.nrel.colostate.edu/projects/lvws/; on the Continental Divide Research Learning Center, research undertaken by academic scientists, Eagle Rock School internships, and "citizen science," see "Rocky Mountain National Park Research and Discovery," accessed January 27, 2022, https://www.nps.gov/rlc/continentaldivide/index.htm.

34. Rocky Mountain National Park, "Final Environmental Impact Statement, Elk and Vegetation Management Plan, Record of Decision," 2008, https://www.nps.gov/romo/learn/management/upload/rod_evmp_signed_2-15-08.pdf; NPS, *Foundation Document: Rocky Mountain National Park*, 2013, 56, https://www.nps.gov/romo/learn/management/upload/ROMO_Foundation_Document.pdf; Franke et al., *Natural Resource Vital Signs*, 17.

35. Franke et al., *Natural Resource Vital Signs*, 1, 29.

36. For statistics on visitor use, see "Park Reports," NPS Stats: National Park Service Visitor Use Statistics, accessed January 27, 2022, https://irma.nps.gov/STATS/Reports/Park/ROMO.

37. ERO Resources Corporation, "Rocky Mountain National Park Day Use Visitor Access Strategy (Pre-NEPA) Public Comment Summary Report," unpublished report, January 2022, 5, https://parkplanning.nps.gov/showFile.cfm?projectID=100042&MIMEType=application%252Fpdf&filename=RMNP%5FDUVAS%5FPreNEPA%5FPublic%5FComment%5FSummary%5F508compliant%2Epdf&sfid=560978.

38. "Day Use Access Visitor Strategy (pre NEPA)," Rocky Mountain National Park, documents and public slide presentation, accessed January 27, 2022, https://parkplanning.nps.gov/projectHome.cfm?projectID=100042#:~:text=The%20purpose%20of%20the%20Rocky,which%20the%20park%20was%20created; Tori Peglar, "How to Save Rocky Mountain National Park from Its Growing Popularity," *Outside*, Colorado National Park Trips, June 24,

2021, accessed January 27, 2022, https://www.mycoloradoparks.com/park/conservation/save-rocky-mountain-national-park/.

39. Martin Blatt, guest editor, "Civic Engagement at Sites of Conscience: Introduction and Essays," *George Wright Forum* 19, no. 4 (2002): 9–74, accessed January 11, 2022, http://www.georgewright.org/194.pdf; National Park Service, "Civic Engagement, Case Studies," accessed January 11, 2022, https://www.nps.gov/civic/casestudies/index.html.

40. "Telling All Americans' Stories," https://www.nps.gov/subjects/tellingallamericansstories/index.htm; Glassberg, "Reflections on the Past."

41. Brunswig, "Modeling Eleven Millennia," 45–104 (quote 96).

42. Sue Langdon, park ranger, Division of Interpretation and Education, ROMO, phone conversation with Ruth Alexander, October 7, 2021; Brooke Neely, Center of the American West, University of Colorado Boulder, phone conversation with Ruth Alexander, June 30, 2021; Estee Rivera (Rocky Mountain Conservancy), Jeffrey Boring (Estes Valley Land Trust), Erik Murdock (Access Fund), Walt Borneman (Rocky Mountain Conservancy), meeting with Ruth Alexander, Estes Park, March 31, 2022.

43. Project description, "American Indian Cultures and Rocky Mountain National Park," typescript, n.d.; project abstract, "Indigenous Connections at Rocky Mountain National Park," typescript, n.d.; book proposal, "Native Peoples and National Parks: Pathways to Collaboration," provided to Ruth Alexander by Brooke Neely. See also Center of the American West, "Indigenous Connections at Rocky Mountain National Park," accessed January 27, 2022, https://outreach.colorado.edu/program/indigenous-connections-at-rocky-mountain-national-park/.

44. Vaske and Lyon, *Linking the 2010 Census*; NPS, Resource Systems Group, and Wyoming Survey and Analysis Center, *National Park Service Comprehensive Survey*; Blotkamp et al., *Rocky Mountain National Park*; Papadogiannaki et al., *Rocky Mountain National Park*; Taylor and Grandjean, "Visitor Satisfaction," 16–17.

45. See, for example, Weber and Sultana, "Why Do So Few"; Floyd and Stodolska, "Theoretical Frameworks"; Scott and Lee, "People of Color"; U.S. Census Bureau, "U.S. Census Bureau Projections Show a Slower Growing, Older, More Diverse Nation a Half Century from Now," December 23, 2012, accessed January 28, 2022, https://www.census.gov/newsroom/releases/archives/population/cb12-243.html; Todd Wilkinson, "The Cultural Challenge," *National Parks*, January–February 2000, 20–23.

46. Director's Orders 16A through 16E specify policy on accommodation for disability, diversity, nondiscrimination, equal opportunity, and antiharassment in employment. See "Director's Orders and Related Documents," accessed January 30, 2022, https://www.nps.gov/policy/DOrders.cfm; NPS, *Urban Agenda: Call to Action Initiative*, March 2015.

47. Chelsea Hernandez, interpretive ranger, conversation with Ruth Alexander, July 12, 2019; "Rocky Mountain Conservancy Staff," https://rmconservancy.org/get-to-know-us/rocky-mountain-conservancy-staff/; Estes Valley Land

Trust, "Summer Breakfasts: Embracing Inclusivity in the Outdoors," newsletter, Summer 2022, 3, https://evlandtrust.org/wp-content/uploads/2022/06/Newsletter-Summer-2022-_digital.pdf; Rocky Mountain National Park, news release, "Darla Sidles Named Superintendent of Rocky Mountain National Park," June 6, 2016, https://www.nps.gov/romo/learn/news/pr_darla_sidles_named_superintendent_of_rocky_mountain_national_park.htm.

48. "By the Numbers," National Park Service, May 4, 2021, accessed January 3, 2022, https://www.nps.gov/articles/000/by-the-numbers.htm; Chandra Rosenthal and Kevin Bell, "Park Service Shelved Employee Harassment Review," November 15, 2021, accessed January 30, 2022, https://peer.org/park-service-shelved-employee-harassment-review/; Adam Liptak and Anemona Hartocollis, "Supreme Court Will Hear Challenge to Affirmative Action at Harvard and U.N.C.," *New York Times*, January 24, 2022, accessed January 30, 2022, https://www.nytimes.com/2022/01/24/us/politics/supreme-court-affirmative-action-harvard-unc.html.

49. "Current Fire Information and Regulations," accessed January 30, 2022, https://www.nps.gov/romo/learn/fire-information-and-regulations.htm.

SELECTED BIBLIOGRAPHY

MANUSCRIPT COLLECTIONS

Boulder, Colorado

Boulder Public Library, Carnegie Library for Local History
    Maria Rogers Oral History Program

Denver, Colorado

Denver Public Library
    Lincoln Hills Records, Blair-Caldwell African American Research Library
    Western History and Genealogy Repository
National Archives, Denver
    Rocky Mountain National Park Records

Estes Park, Colorado

    Estes Park Museum and Archives
    Rocky Mountain National Park Archives
        ROMO-01132 Colorado Mountain Club Summit Registers
        ROMO-01192 Rocky Mountain National Park Historic Records and
            Central Files
        ROMO-01348 Patrol Cabin and Ranger Station Logbooks
        ROMO-01434 Native American Oral History and Cultural Interpretation
        ROMO-01571 Superintendent's Monthly and Annual Reports, 1915–2008
        ROMO-01572 Ferrel Atkins Collection
        ROMO-01605 Visitor Use Patterns on Longs Peak and Survey of Highway 7
        ROMO-01689 Beatrice E. Willard Collection
        ROMO-01747 JVK Wagar Manuscript Collection
        ROMO-01761 Natural Resource Management Records
          ROMO-01822 Cultural Resource Management Records, unprocessed
          ROMO-01850 Backcountry Wilderness Program Records, unprocessed
          ROMO-01851 Longs Peak Oral Histories

ROMO Library Vertical Files
ROMO Museum Catalog
ROMO Photographic Collections
ROMO Temporary Climbing Collection
YMCA of the Rockies Archives, Lula Dorsey Museum

Fort Collins, Colorado

Colorado State University, Morgan Library, Archives and Manuscript Collections
    Colorado State University Photographic Collection
    Wagar Collection
Fort Collins Local History Archive, Fort Collins Museum of Discovery

Golden, Colorado

American Mountaineering Center, American Alpine Library
    Colorado Mountain Club Collection
    Jim Detterline Collection

National Park Service, Harpers Ferry Center

NPS Oral History Collection

NEWSPAPERS, MAGAZINES, WEBSITES

Adventure Alternative
Adventure Journal
Alpinist
American Alpine Journal
The BIPOC Project
Boulder County News
Climbing
Climbing for Change
Colorado Central Magazine
Colorado Heritage
The Colorado Magazine
Courier
Denver Post
Denver Urban Spectrum
Denver Westerners Roundup
Ebony
Estes Park Trail
Go Play Denver
Guardian
History Colorado
Matador Network
Native America Calling
Natives Outdoors
New Yorker

New York Times
Outdoor Journal
Outside
Pittsburgh Courier
Rock and Ice
Rocky Mountain Highlights
Rocky Mountain News
Smithsonian
The Statesman
Summit
Sunset
Time
Trail and Timberline

BOOKS, ARTICLES, UNPUBLISHED REPORTS, THESES, AND DISSERTATIONS

Abbott, Carl, Stephen J. Leonard, and Thomas J. Noel. *Colorado: A History of the Centennial State.* 4th ed. Boulder: University Press of Colorado, 2005.

Achey, Jeff, Dudley Chelton, and Bob Godfrey. *Climb! The History of Rock Climbing in Colorado.* Seattle: Mountaineers Books, 2002.

Adams, Alexander B., ed. *First World Conference on National Parks, Proceedings.* Washington, DC: National Park Service, U.S. Department of the Interior, 1962.

Adams, Charles C. "Ecological Conditions in National Forests and in National Parks." *Scientific Monthly* 20, no. 6 (June 1925): 561–93.

Agnell, Shirley. *Pinnacle Club: A History of Women Climbing.* Glasgow, UK: Pinnacle Club, 1988.

Alberts, Edwin C. *Rocky Mountain Park, Colorado.* Washington, DC: U.S. Superintendent of Documents, 1963.

Allaback, Sarah, and Ethan Carr. "Rocky Mountain National Park Administration Building." National Historic Landmark Nomination, September 2000. https://npgallery.nps.gov/NRHP/GetAsset/NHLS/01000069_text.

Ament, Pat, and Cleveland M. McCarty. *High over Boulder: A Climber's and Hiker's Guide to Boulder, Colorado.* Boulder: High Over Publications, 1967.

Anderson, Helen. *For Your Pleasure Directory of Longs Peak and Allens Park Regions, Rocky Mountain National Park, 1931.* Colorado, 1931.

Anderson, Jeffrey D. *One Hundred Years of Old Man Sage: An Arapaho Life.* Lincoln: University of Nebraska Press, 2003.

Anderson, Terry H. *The Pursuit of Fairness: A History of Affirmative Action.* New York: Oxford University Press, 2004.

Andrews, Thomas. *Coyote Valley: Deep History in the High Rockies.* Cambridge, MA: Harvard University Press, 2015.

Ansson, Richard J., Jr. "Our National Parks—Overcrowded, Underfunded, and Besieged with a Myriad of Vexing Problems: How Can We Best Fund Our Imperiled National Park System?" *Journal of Land Use and Environmental Law* 14, no. 1 (1998): 1–144.

Antolini, Denise E. "National Park Law in the U.S.: Conservation, Conflict, and Centennial Values." *William and Mary Environmental Law and Policy Review* 33, no. 3 (2008–2009): 851–921.

Appleman, Roy E. "A History of the National Park Service Mission 66 Program." Typescript report. National Park Service, U.S. Department of the Interior, January 1958. Accessed January 17, 2022. http://npshistory.com/publications/mission66 /history.pdf.

Armitage, Kevin C. *The Nature Study Movement: The Forgotten Popularizer of America's Conservation Ethic.* Lawrence: University Press of Kansas, 2009.

Arnold, Anne Morrison, Elyse Deffke Bliss, Jackie Elliott, Charmayne Gooch, and Karen Stopfer Stapleton. *Steads Ranch and Hotel: Echoes within the Moraines.* Bellvue, CO: Elyse Deffke Bliss, 2000.

Aron, Cindy. *Working at Play: A History of Vacations in the United States.* New York: Oxford University Press, 1999.

Arps, Louisa Ward, and Elinor Eppich Kingery. *High Country Names: Rocky Mountain National Park and Indian Peaks.* Estes Park, CO: Rocky Mountain Nature Association, 1994.

Atkins, James A. *Human Relations in Colorado: A Historical Record.* Denver: Colorado Department of Education, 1968.

Avila, Eric. *Popular Culture in the Age of White Flight: Fear and Fantasy in Suburban Los Angeles.* Berkeley: University of California Press, 2004.

Axtell, James. "Columbian Encounters: 1992–1995." *William and Mary Quarterly* 52, no. 4 (1995): 649–96.

Baker, Jean H. *Votes for Women: The Struggle for Suffrage Revisited.* New York: Oxford University Press, 2002.

Baker, Richard A. "The Conservation Congress of Anderson and Aspinall, 1963–1964." *Journal of Forest History* 29, no. 3 (July 1985): 104–19.

Bancroft, Caroline. *Estes Park and Trail Ridge: Their Dramatic History.* 2nd rev. ed. Boulder, CO: Johnson, 1981.

———. *Trail Ridge Country: The Romantic History of Estes Park and Grand Lake.* Boulder, CO: Johnson, 1968.

Barringer, Mark. "Mission Impossible: National Park Development in the 1950s." *Journal of the West* 38 (1999): 22–26.

Barron, T. A. *High as a Hawk: A Brave Girl's Historic Climb.* New York: Philomel Books, 2004.

Bartlett, Richard A., and William H. Goetzman. *Exploring the American West, 1803–1879.* Washington, DC: National Park Service, U.S. Department of the Interior, 1982.

Bay, Mia. *Traveling Black: A Story of Race and Resistance.* Cambridge, MA: Belknap Press of Harvard University Press, 2021.

Beals, Ralph L. *Ethnology of Rocky Mountain National Park: The Ute and Arapaho.* Berkeley, CA: National Park Service, Field Division of Education, U.S. Department of the Interior, 1935.

Bederman, Gail. *Manliness and Civilization: A Cultural History of Gender and Race in the United States, 1880–1917.* Chicago: University of Chicago Press, 1995.

Bernstein, Alison R. *American Indians and World War II: Toward a New Era in Indian Affairs.* Norman: University of Oklahoma Press, 1991.

Berwanger, Eugene H. *The Rise of the Centennial State: Colorado Territory, 1861–76.* Urbana and Chicago: University of Illinois Press, 2007.

Bickel, Marjorie Hannen, Helen Hannen Donahue, and Irene Hannen St. John. *Three Sisters Remember Longs Peak in 1927.* Loveland, CO: Indiana Camp Supply, 1993.

Bird, Isabella L. *A Lady's Life in the Rocky Mountains.* Norman: University of Oklahoma Press, 1960.

Birkett, Bill, and Bill Peascod. *Women Climbing: 200 Years of Achievement.* Seattle: Mountaineers Books, 1990.

Blake, Kevin S. "Colorado Fourteeners and the Nature of Place Identity." *Geographical Review* 92, no. 2 (April 2002): 155–79.

Blankers, Ellen. "'The Tonic of Wildness': Religion and the Environment at the YMCA of the Rockies." Master's thesis, Colorado State University, 2015.

Blatt, Martin, ed. "Introduction: The National Park Service and Civic Engagement." In "Civic Engagement at Sites of Conscience." Special issue, *George Wright Forum* 19, no. 4 (2002): 9–14.

Blaurock, Carl, and Barbara J. Euser. *A Climber's Climber: On the Trail with Carl Blaurock.* Louisville, CO: Cordillera Press, 1984.

Blight, David W. *Race and Reunion: The Civil War in American Memory.* Cambridge, MA: Harvard University Press, 2001.

Bloom, Alexander, and Wini Breines. *"Takin' It to the Streets": A Sixties Reader.* 4th ed. New York: Oxford University Press, 2015.

Blotkamp, Ariel, William F. Boyd, Douglas Eury, and Steven J. Hollenhorst. *Rocky Mountain National Park Visitor Study: Summer 2010.* Natural Resource Report NPS/NRSS/SSD/NRR—2011/121/10758. Fort Collins, CO: National Park Service. https://sesrc.wsu.edu/doc/235.1_ROMO_rept.pdf.

Borneman, Walter, and Lyndon Lampert. *A Climbing Guide to Colorado's Fourteeners.* Boulder, CO: Pruett, 1978.

Bowles, Samuel. *The Parks and Mountains of Colorado: A Summer Vacation in the Switzerland of America, 1868.* Edited by James H. Pickering. Norman: University of Oklahoma Press, 1991.

Brady, Tracy L. "The Colorado Mountain Club and the Growth of Environmentalism in Colorado." Master's thesis, Colorado State University, 1994.

Brenner, Betty Jo. "Women of the Ku Klux Klan." *Colorado Encyclopedia.* Accessed December 22, 2021. http://coloradoencyclopedia.org/article/women-ku-klux-klan.

Brett, John A. *Ethnographic Assessment and Documentation of Rocky Mountain National Park.* Denver: University of Colorado, Department of Anthropology, 2003.

Briggs, Roger. "The Diamond." *Alpinist* 19 (March 1, 2007). Accessed February 28, 2022. http://www.alpinist.com/doc/_print/ALP19/mountain-profile-longs-diamond.

Bright, Casandra Marie. "A History of Rock Climbing Gear Technology and Standards." Undergraduate honors thesis, University of Arkansas, Fayetteville, 2014.

Brock, Julia. "Creating Consumers: The Civilian Conservation Corps in Rocky Mountain National Park." Master's thesis, Florida State University, 2005.

Brown, Douglas A. "The Modern Romance of Mountaineering: Photography, Aesthetics, and Embodiment." *International Journal of the History of Sport* 24, no. 1 (2007): 1–34.

Brown, Rebecca A. *Women on High: Pioneers of Mountaineering.* Boston: Appalachian Mountain Club Books, 2002.

Brunswig, Robert H. "Apachean Archaeology of Rocky Mountain National Park, Colorado, and the Colorado Front Range." In *From the Land of Ever Winter to the American Southwest: Athapaskan Migrations, Mobility, and Ethnogenesis,* edited by Deni J. Seymour, 20–36. Salt Lake City: University of Utah Press, 2012.

————. "Modeling Eleven Millennia of Seasonal Transhumance and Subsistence in Colorado's Prehistoric Rockies, USA." In *Contributions in New World Archaeology,* 45–104. Krakow, Poland: Polish Academy of Arts and Sciences and Jagiellonian University Institute of Archaeology, 2015.

————. *Prehistoric, Protohistoric, and Early Historic Native American Archeology of Rocky Mountain National Park.* Vol. 1, *Final Report of Systemwide Archeological Inventory Program Investigations by the University of Northern Colorado (1998–2002).* Prepared for the National Park Service, Rocky Mountain National Park, 2005.

Buchholtz, C. W. *Rocky Mountain National Park: A History.* Boulder: Colorado Associated University Press, 1983.

Bueler, William M. *Roof of the Rockies: A History of Colorado Mountaineering.* 3rd ed. Golden: Colorado Mountain Club, 2000.

Burnham, Philip. *Indian Country, God's Country: Native Americans and the National Parks.* Bloomington, IN: iUniverse, 2014.

Button, Mark E. "American Liberalism from Colonialism to the Civil War and Beyond." In *The Cambridge Companion to Liberalism,* edited by Steven Wall, 21–41. Cambridge: Cambridge University Press, 2015.

Bzdek, Maren, and Janet Ore. *The Mission 66 Program at Rocky Mountain National Park: 1947–1973.* Fort Collins: Colorado State University, Public Lands History Center, and Rocky Mountain National Park, 2010.

Cahn, Robert. *Will Success Spoil the National Parks?* Boston: Christian Science Publishing Society, 1968.

Caldwell, Tommy. *The Push: A Climber's Search for the Path.* New York: Penguin Books, 2017.

Carder, Eddy F. "The American Environmental Justice Movement." *Internet Encyclopedia of Philosophy.* https://iep.utm.edu/enviro-j/.

Carpio, Genevieve. *Collisions at the Crossroads: How Place and Mobility Make Race.* Oakland: University of California Press, 2019.

Carr, Ethan. *Mission 66: Modernism and the National Park Dilemma.* Amherst: University of Massachusetts Press, 2007.

————. *Wilderness by Design: Landscape Architecture and the National Park Service.* Lincoln: University of Nebraska Press, 1998.

Carson, Rachel. *Silent Spring.* 40th anniv. ed. Boston: Mariner Books, 2002.

Cassell, Colleen Estes. *The Golden Pioneer: Biography of Joel Estes, the Man Who Discovered Estes Park.* Seattle: Peanut Butter Publishing, 1999.

Chamberlin, Silas. *On the Trail: A History of American Hiking.* New Haven, CT: Yale University Press, 2016.

Chapin, Frederick H. *Mountaineering in Colorado: The Peaks about Estes Park.* Lincoln: University of Nebraska Press, 1987.

Chapman, Arthur. *Enos A. Mills: Author, Speaker, Nature Guide.* Longs Peak, CO: Trail Book Store, 1921.

Cherland, Summer Marie. "No Prejudice Here: Racism, Resistance, and the Struggle for Equality in Denver, 1947–1994." PhD diss., University of Nevada, Las Vegas, 2014.

Childers, Michael. "The Stoneman Meadow Riots and Law Enforcement in Yosemite National Park." *Forest History Today,* Spring 2017, 28–34.

Cohen, Lizabeth. *Making a New Deal: Industrial Workers in Chicago, 1919–1939.* New York: Cambridge University Press, 1990.

Colorado Mountain Club. *The Colorado Mountain Club: Its History, Activities, and Purposes.* Denver: Hartmann-Bruderlin, 1922.

Conroy, Christina, and Gina Blunt Gonzalez. "Off Belay! The Morality of Free Soloing." *Sport, Ethics and Philosophy* 13, no. 1 (2019): 62–77.

Cowell, Andrew, and Alonzo Moss. "Arapaho Place Names in Colorado: Form and Function, Language and Culture." *Anthropological Linguistics* 45, no. 4 (2003): 349–89.

Crofutt, George A. *Crofutt's Grip-Sack Guide of Colorado.* Omaha, NE: Overland, 1881.

Dauvergne, Peter. *The Shadows of Consumption: Consequences for the Global Environment.* Cambridge, MA: MIT Press, 2008.

Davis, Steph. *Learning to Fly: A Memoir of Hanging On and Letting Go.* New York: Touchstone, 2013.

Decker, Peter R. *"The Utes Must Go": American Expansion and the Removal of a People.* Golden, CO: Fulcrum, 2004.

Deloria, Philip J. *Playing Indian.* New Haven, CT: Yale University Press, 1998.

DeLuca, Kevin, and Anne Demo. "Imagining Nature and Erasing Class and Race: Carleton Watkins, John Muir, and the Construction of Wilderness." *Environmental History* 6, no. 4 (October 2001): 541–60.

Dent, C. T. *Above the Snow Line: Mountaineering Sketches between 1870 and 1880.* London: Longmans, Green, 1885.

Dervin, Dan. *Father Bosetti in America: A Biographical Study.* Denver: Cache Glade Publications, 2004.

Devlin, Erin Krutko. "Under the Sky All of Us Are Free: African American Travel, Visitation and Segregation in Shenandoah National Park." Washington, DC: National Park Service, 2010.

Diamant, Rolf. "The Olmsteds and the Development of the National Park System." In *The Master List of Design Projects of the Olmsted Firm, 1857–1979,* edited by Lucy Lawliss, Caroline Loughlin, and Lauren Meier, 9–14. Washington, DC: National Association for Olmsted Parks and National Park Service, 2008.

Dickson, Lynda. "The Early Club Movement among Black Women in Denver: 1890–1925." PhD diss., University of Colorado, 1982.

Dilsaver, Larry M., ed. *America's National Park System: The Critical Documents.* Lanham, MD: Rowman and Littlefield, 2016.

Dohnalek, James. "Native American Religious Accommodations, National Parks, and the Cutter Test." *University of St. Thomas Law Journal* 15, no. 3 (2019): 715–44.

Donahue, Mike. *The Longs Peak Experience and Trail Guide.* Allenspark, CO: Wildbasin Summits, 1992.

Dotson, John, ed. *Radiant Days: Writings by Enos Mills*. Salt Lake City: University of Utah Press, 1994.

Dowie, Mark. *Conservation Refugees: The Hundred-Year Conflict between Global Conservation and Native Peoples*. Cambridge, MA: MIT Press, 2011.

Drummond, Alexander. *Enos Mills: Citizen of Nature*. Niwot: University Press of Colorado, 1995.

Dudziak, Mary. *Cold War Civil Rights: Race and the Image of American Democracy*. Princeton, NJ: Princeton University Press, 2000.

Dummitt, Christopher. "Risk on the Rocks: Modernity, Manhood, and Mountaineering in Postwar British Columbia." *BC Studies: The British Columbian Quarterly* 141 (2004): 3–29.

Dunning, Harold M. *Facts about Longs Peak*. Boulder, CO: Johnson, 1970.

———. *The History of the Trail Ridge Road: One of the Most Famous Roads in the World*. Boulder, CO: Johnson, 1967.

———. *Over the Hill and Vale: In the Evening Shadows of Colorado's Longs Peak*. Boulder, CO: Johnson, 1956.

Dustin, Daniel L., Ingrid E. Schneider, Leo H. McAvoy, and Arthur N. Frakt. "Cross-Cultural Claims on Devils Tower National Monument: A Case Study." *Leisure Sciences* 24, no. 1 (2002): 79–88.

Eberhart, Perry, and Philip Schmuck. *The Fourteeners: Colorado's Great Mountains*. Chicago: Sage Books, 1970.

Edmondson, Dudley. *Black and Brown Faces in America's Wild Places*. Cambridge, MN: Adventure Publications, 2006.

Ellingwood, Albert Russell. "Technical Climbing in the Mountains of Colorado and Wyoming." *American Alpine Journal* 1, no. 2 (1930): 140–47.

Emerick, John C. *Rocky Mountain National Park: Natural History Handbook*. Niwot, CO: Roberts Rhinehart and Rocky Mountain Nature Association, 1995.

Erickson, Beth, Corey W. Johnson, and B. Dana Kivel. "Rocky Mountain National Park: History and Culture as Factors in African-American Park Visitation." *Journal of Leisure Research* 41, no. 4 (2009): 529–54.

Estes, Milton. *The Memoirs of Estes Park*. Fort Collins: Friends of the Colorado State College Library, 1939.

Evans, Joseph R. *Death, Despair, and Second Chances in Rocky Mountain National Park*. Boulder, CO: Johnson Books, 2010.

Everhart, William C. *The National Park Service*. Boulder, CO: Westview Press, 1983.

Fazio, Patricia M. "Cragged Crusade: The Fight for Rocky Mountain National Park, 1909–15." Master's thesis, University of Wyoming, 1982.

Finney, Carolyn. *Black Faces, White Spaces: Reimagining the Relationship of African Americans to the Great Outdoors*. Chapel Hill: University of North Carolina Press, 2014.

Floyd, Myron F. "Managing National Parks in a Multicultural Society: Searching for Common Ground." *George Wright Forum* 18, no. 3 (2001): 41–51.

Floyd, Myron F., and Monika Stodolska. "Theoretical Frameworks in Leisure Research on Race and Ethnicity." In *Race, Ethnicity, and Leisure: Perspectives on Research, Theory, and Practice*, edited by Monika Stodolska, Kim J. Shinew, Myron F. Floyd, and Gordon J. Walker, 9–20. Champaign, IL: Human Kinetics, 2014.

Force, Jo Ellen, and Deborah Forester. "Public Involvement in National Park Service Land Management Issues." *Social Science Research Review* 3, no. 1 (Summer 2002): 1–28.

Foscue, Edwin J., and Louis O. Quam. *Estes Park: Resort in the Rockies*. Dallas: University Press, 1949.

Foster, Lisa. *Rocky Mountain National Park: The Complete Hiking Guide*. Englewood, CO: Westcliffe, 2005.

Foster, Mark S. "In the Face of 'Jim Crow': Prosperous Blacks and Vacations, Travel and Outdoor Leisure, 1890–1945." *Journal of Negro History* 84, no. 2 (Spring 1999): 130–49.

Foster, Shirley, and Sara Mills, eds. *An Anthology of Women's Travel Writing*. New York: Manchester University Press, 2002.

Frank, Jerry J. *Making Rocky Mountain National Park: The Environmental History of an American Treasure*. Lawrence: University Press of Kansas, 2013.

Franke, Mary Ann, Therese Johnson, Isabel Ashton, and Ben Bobowski. *Natural Resource Vital Signs at Rocky Mountain National Park*. Natural Resource Report NPS/ROMO/NRR—2015/946. Fort Collins, CO: National Park Service, 2015.

Freudenberg, Betty. *Facing the Frontier: The Story of the MacGregor Ranch*. Estes Park, CO: Rocky Mountain Nature Association, 1998.

Fricke, Walter, Jr. *A Climber's Guide to the Rocky Mountain National Park Area*. Boulder, CO: Johnson, 1971.

Fuller, Harlin M., and LeRoy R. Hafen, eds. *The Journal of Captain John R. Bell, Official Journalist of the Stephen H. Long Expedition to the Rocky Mountains, 1820*. Glendale, CO: Arthur H. Clark, 1957.

Garland-Jackson, Felicia. "Missing Voices: Participants' Narratives of the National Park Service's Summer in the Parks Program, 1968–1976." PhD diss., George Mason University, 2018.

Gassan, Richard H. *The Birth of American Tourism: New York, the Hudson Valley, and American Culture, 1790–1835*. Amherst: University of Massachusetts Press, 2008.

Geary, Michael M. *A Quick History of Grand Lake: Including Rocky Mountain National Park and the Grand Lake Lodge*. Ouray, CO: Western Reflections, 1999.

Gillett, Bernard. *Rocky Mountain National Park: The Climber's Guide, Estes Park Valley*. Chapel Hill, NC: Earthbound Sports, 2001.

———. *Rocky Mountain National Park: The Climber's Guide, High Peaks*. Chapel Hill, NC: Earthbound Sports, 2001.

Glassberg, David. "Reflections on the Past, Present, and Future of Civic Engagement in National Parks," In *Connections across People, Place, and Time: Proceedings of the 2017 George Wright Society Conference on Parks, Protected Areas, and Cultural Sites*, edited by Samantha Weber, 66–71. Hancock, MI: George Wright Society, 2017.

Goetzman, William H. *Exploration and Empire: The Explorer and the Scientist in the Winning of the American West*. New York: W. W. Norton, 1966.

Goldberg, Robert Alan. *Hooded Empire: The Ku Klux Klan in Colorado*. Chicago: University of Illinois Press, 1981.

Goldstein, Marcia Tremmel. "Breaking Down Barriers: Black and White Women's Visions of Integration; The Young Women's Christian Association in Denver and the Phyllis Wheatley Branch, 1915–1964." Master's thesis, University of Colorado Denver, 1995.

Gonzalez, Patrick, Fuyao Wang, Michael Notaro, Daniel J. Vimont, and John W. Williams. "Disproportionate Magnitude of Climate Change in United States National Parks." *Environmental Research Letters* 13, no. 10 (2018): 1–12.

Gootz, Thomas. *Transformation in Rocky Mountain National Park: The Effects of Climate Change and Human Intervention.* Estes Park, CO: Estes Park Friends and Foundation, 2014.

Gorby, John D. *The Stettner Way: The Life and Climbs of Joe and Paul Stettner.* Golden: Colorado Mountain Club Press, 2003.

Green, Victor H., ed. *The Negro Motorist Green Book.* New York: Victor H. Green, 1936–1967.

Grimshaw, Patricia, and Katherine Ellinghaus. "'A Higher Step for the Race': Caroline Nichols Churchill, the 'Queen Bee' and Women's Suffrage in Colorado, 1879–1893." *Australasian Journal of American Studies* 20, no. 2 (2001): 29–46.

Grinde, Donald A., and Bruce E. Johansen. *Exemplar of Liberty: Native America and the Evolution of Democracy.* Los Angeles: American Indian Studies Center, University of California, 1991.

Gross, Rebecca L. "'See, Experience, and Enjoy': Visuality and the Tourist Experience in the National Parks, 1864–1966." Master's thesis, Cooper-Hewitt, Smithsonian National Design Museum, and Parsons New School of Design, 2014.

Hahn, Steven. *A Nation under Our Feet: Black Political Struggles in the Rural South from Slavery to the Great Migration.* Cambridge, MA: Harvard University Press, 2003.

Hall, Jacquelyn Dowd. "The Long Civil Rights Movement and the Political Uses of the Past." *Journal of American History* 91, no. 4 (2005): 1233–63.

Hansen, Moya. "Entitled to Full and Equal Enjoyment: Leisure and Entertainment in the Denver Black Community, 1900–1930." *UCD Historical Studies Journal* 10 (July 1993): 47–77.

Hansen, Peter H. *The Summits of Modern Man: Mountaineering after the Enlightenment.* Cambridge, MA: Harvard University Press, 2013.

Harms, Cecily. "NAGPRA in Colorado: A Success Story." *University of Colorado Law Review* 83 (2012): 593–632.

Harris, Dianne, and D. Fairchild Ruggles, eds. *Sites Unseen: Landscape and Vision.* Pittsburgh, PA: University of Pittsburgh Press, 2007.

Hart, John Lathrop Jerome. *Fourteen Thousand Feet: A History of the Naming and Early Ascents of the High Colorado Peaks.* Denver: Colorado Mountain Club, 1925. Reprint, 1931.

Harvey, Mark W. T. *A Symbol of Wilderness: Echo Park and the American Conservation Movement.* Seattle: University of Washington Press, 2000.

Hawthorne, Hildegarde, and Esther Burnell Mills. *Enos Mills of the Rockies.* Boston: Houghton Mifflin, 1935.

Held, R. Burnell, Stanley Keith Brickler, and Arthur Thomas Wilcox. *A Study to Develop Practical Techniques for Determining the Carrying Capacity of Natural Areas in the National Park System: Final Report.* Fort Collins: Colorado State University, 1969.

Herron, John P. *Science and the Social Good: Nature, Culture, and Community, 1865–1965.* New York: Oxford University Press, 2010.

Hess, Karl, Jr. *Rocky Times in Rocky Mountain National Park: An Unnatural History.* Niwot: University Press of Colorado, 1993.

Hirsch, Leni. "For the Benefit and Enjoyment of Which People? African Americans and America's National Parks." *Harvard Undergraduate Research Journal* 10, no. 1 (Spring 2017): 26–41.

Hobbs, N. Thompson, Alan P. Covich, Dennis Ojima, John Loomis, Mallory McDuff, Stephan Weiler, Michael B. Coughenour, et al. *Final Report: An Integrated Assessment of the Effects of Climate Change on Rocky Mountain National Park and its Gateway Community: Interactions of Multiple Stressors.* 2003. https://cfpub.epa.gov /ncer_abstracts/index.cfm/fuseaction/display.highlight/abstract_id/286/report/F.

Holland, F. Ross. *Rocky Mountain National Park: Historical Background Data.* San Francisco: U.S. Office of History and Historic Architecture, Western Service Center, 1971.

Hoxie, Frederick E. *A Final Promise: The Campaign to Assimilate the Indians, 1880–1920.* Lincoln: University of Nebraska Press, 1984.

Hyde, Anne Farrar. *An American Vision: Far Western Landscape and National Culture, 1820–1920.* New York: New York University Press, 1990.

Ingersoll, Ernest. *Knocking round the Rockies.* Norman: University of Oklahoma Press, 1994.

Irving, R. L. G. *The Romance of Mountaineering.* New York: E. P. Dutton, 1935.

Isserman, Maurice. *Continental Divide: A History of American Mountaineering.* New York: W. W. Norton, 2016.

Isserman, Maurice, and Michael Kazin. *America Divided: The Civil War of the 1960s.* 6th ed. New York: Oxford University Press, 2020.

Jacoby, Karl. *Crimes against Nature: Squatters, Poachers, Thieves, and the Hidden History of American Conservation.* Berkeley: University of California Press, 2014.

Jakobsen, Christine Haugaard. "Evaluation of Interpretive Exhibits in Rocky Mountain National Park." 1999. ROMO Library.

Jessen, Kenneth Christian, and John Carr. *Estes Park: A Quick History, Including Rocky Mountain National Park.* Aurora, CO: First Light, 1996.

Johnson, Christopher. *This Grand and Magnificent Place: The Wilderness Heritage of the White Mountains.* Durham: University of New Hampshire Press, 2006.

Jones, Chris. *Climbing in North America.* Berkeley: University of California Press, 1976.

Joselit, Jenna Weissman, and Karen S. Mittelman, eds. *A Worthy Use of Summer: Jewish Summer Camping in America.* Philadelphia: National Museum of American Jewish History, 1993.

Kanfer, Stefan. *A Summer World: The Attempt to Build a Jewish Eden in the Catskills, from the Days of the Ghetto to the Rise and Decline of the Borscht Belt.* New York: Farrar, Straus and Giroux, 1989.

Katznelson, Ira. *Fear Itself: The New Deal and the Origins of Our Time.* New York: Liveright, 2014.

———. *When Affirmative Action Was White: An Untold History of Racial Inequality in Twentieth-Century America.* New York: W. W. Norton, 2005.

Kaufman, Ned. "Historic Places and the Diversity Deficit in Heritage Conservation." *CRM: The Journal of Heritage Stewardship* 1, no. 2 (Summer 2004): 68–85.

Kaufman, Polly Welts. *National Parks and the Woman's Voice: A History.* Albuquerque: University of New Mexico Press, 2006.

Kaye, Glen. *Trail Ridge.* Rocky Mountain National Park, CO: Rocky Mountain Nature Association, 1982.

Kearnes, Fara. *The Chapel on the Rock: A Brief History of Camp St. Malo and St. Catherine of Sienna Chapel.* Denver: Hughes Henshaw, 2001.

Keiter, Robert B. *To Conserve Unimpaired: The Evolution of the National Park Idea.* Washington, DC: Island Press, 2013.

Keller, Robert H., and Michael F. Turek. *American Indians and National Parks.* Tucson: University of Arizona Press, 1998.

Kelly, Caralyn J. *Thrilling and Marvellous Experiences: Place and Subjectivity in Canadian Climbing Narratives, 1885–1925.* Waterloo, ON: University of Waterloo, 2006.

Keplinger, L. W. *The First Ascent of Long's Peak: Made by an Expedition under Maj. J. W. Powell.* Topeka: Kansas State Historical Society, 1918.

Kingery, Hugh E., and Elinor Eppich Kingery. *The Colorado Mountain Club: The First Seventy-Five Years of a Highly Individual Corporation, 1912–1987.* Evergreen, CO: Cordillera Press, 1988.

Kizer, Kenneth W. "The Great American Outdoors Act of 2020: A Tool for Improving Urban Health and Health Equity." *Journal of Urban Health* 98 (2021): 143–45.

Knowlton, Lorna. *Weaving Mountain Memories: Recollections of the Allenspark Area.* Estes Park, CO: Estes Park Area Historical Museum, 1989.

Knudten, Cori Ann. "A Diminishing Shadow: Longs Peak and Auto Tourists in Postwar Rocky Mountain National Park." Master's thesis, Colorado State University, 2009.

Kroeber, Alfred L. *The Arapaho.* New York: Bulletin of the Museum of Natural History, 1902.

Kropp, Phoebe. "Wilderness Wives and Dishwashing Husbands: Comfort and the Domestic Arts of Camping in America, 1890–1910." *Journal of Social History* 43, no. 1 (Fall 2009): 5–30.

Labode, Modupe. "'Defend Your Manhood and Womanhood Rights': *The Birth of a Nation*, Race, and the Politics of Respectability in Early Twentieth-Century Denver, Colorado." *Pacific Historical Review* 84, no. 2 (May 2015): 163–94.

Lamb, Reverend Elkanah J. *Miscellaneous Meditations.* Denver: Press Room and Bindery, 1913.

———. *Past Memories and Future Thoughts.* Dayton, OH: Press of United Brethren, 1905.

Lawson, Steven F., ed. *Civil Rights Crossroads: Nation, Community, and the Black Freedom Struggle.* Lexington: University Press of Kentucky, 2003.

———. "Freedom Then, Freedom Now: The Historiography of the Civil Rights Movement." *American Historical Review* 96, no. 2 (April 1991): 456–71.

Lears, Jackson. *Rebirth of a Nation: The Making of Modern America, 1877–1920.* New York: Harper Perennial, 2009.

Lee, Michael A. "Forgotten Alliance: Jews, Chicanos, and the Dynamics of Class and Race in Denver, Colorado, 1967–1971." *Shofar: An Interdisciplinary Journal of Jewish Studies* 30, no. 2 (Winter 2012): 1–25.

Lee, Ronald R. *Public Use of the National Park System, 1872–2000.* Washington, DC: National Park Service, U.S. Department of the Interior, 1968.

Leonard, Stephen J. *Trials and Triumphs: A Colorado Portrait of the Great Depression.* Niwot: University Press of Colorado, 1993.

Leonard, Stephen J., and Thomas J. Noel. *Denver: From Mining Camp to Metropolis.* Niwot: University Press of Colorado, 1990.

Leopold, Aldo. *A Sand County Almanac and Sketches Here and There.* New York: Oxford University Press, 1949.

Leopold, A. Starker. *Wildlife Management in the National Parks: The Leopold Report.* Washington, DC: National Park Service, 1963.

Louie, Siri. "Peak Potentials and Performance Anxieties: Gender, Mountaineering, and Leadership in the Canadian West, 1906–40." In *Unsettled Pasts: Reconceiving the West through Women's History,* edited by Sarah Carter, 311–40. Calgary: University of Calgary Press, 2005.

Louter, David. *Windshield Wilderness: Cars, Roads, and Nature in Washington's National Parks.* Seattle: University of Washington Press, 2006.

MacDonald, Dougald. *Longs Peak: The Story of Colorado's Favorite Fourteener.* Englewood, CO: Westcliffe, 2004.

Mackintosh, Barry. *Visitor Fees in the National Park System: A Legislative and Administrative History.* Washington, DC: National Park Service, History Division, 1983.

Mackintosh, Barry, Janet A. McDonnell, and John H. Sprinkle Jr. "The National Parks: Shaping the System." *George Wright Forum* 35, no. 2 (2018): 1–132.

Mackintosh, Will B. *Selling the Sights: The Invention of the Tourist in American Culture.* New York: New York University Press, 2019.

Maher, Neil M. *Nature's New Deal: The Civilian Conservation Corps and the Roots of the American Environmental Movement.* New York: Oxford University Press, 2008.

Marcuse, Peter. "Is the National Parks Movement Anti-Urban?" *Parks and Recreation* 6 (July 1971): 16–21, 48–49.

Marilley, Suzanne M. *Woman Suffrage and the Origins of Liberal Feminism in the United States, 1820–1920.* Cambridge, MA: Harvard University Press, 1997.

Marincic, Amanda. "The National Historic Preservation Act: An Inadequate Attempt to Protect the Cultural and Religious Sites of Native Nations." *Iowa Law Review* 103, no. 4 (2018): 1777–2018.

Marion, Jeffrey L., and Scott E. Reid. "Development of the U.S. Leave No Trace Program: An Historical Perspective." In *Enjoyment and Understanding of the Natural Heritage: Papers Read at the 9th Scottish Natural Heritage Conference,* 81–92. Edinburgh, Scotland: Stationery Office, Patuxent Wildlife Research Center, 2001. Accessed December 27, 2021. https://www.fs.usda.gov/Internet/FSE_DOCUMENTS/fsbdev2_038125.pdf.

Mather, Stephen P. *Progress in the Development of the National Parks.* Washington, DC: Government Printing Office, 1916.

Mattes, Merrill J. "The Boulderfield Hotel: A Distant Summer in the Shadow of Longs Peak." *Colorado Heritage* 1 (1986): 30–41.

Matthews, Jean V. *The Rise of the New Woman: The Women's Movement in America, 1875–1930.* Chicago: Ivan R. Dee, 2003.

May, Elaine Tyler. *Homeward Bound: American Families in the Cold War Era.* Rev. ed. New York: Basic Books, 1999.

Mazel, David, ed. *Mountaineering Women: Stories by Early Climbers.* College Station: Texas A&M University Press, 1994.

———, ed. *Pioneering Ascents: The Origins of Climbing in America, 1642–1873.* Harrisburg, PA: Stackpole Books, 1991.

McBeth, Sally. *Native American Oral History and Cultural Interpretation in Rocky Mountain National Park.* Department of Anthropology Faculty Publications. Greeley: University of Northern Colorado, 2007. Accessed December 18, 2021. https://digscholarship.unco.edu/anthrofacpub/1.

McCammack, Brian. *Landscapes of Hope: Nature and the Great Migration in Chicago.* Cambridge, MA: Harvard University Press, 2017.

McClelland, Linda Flint. *Presenting Nature: The Historic Landscape Design of the National Park Service, 1916 to 1942.* Washington, DC: U.S. Department of the Interior, National Park Service, Cultural Resources, Interagency Resources Division, National Register of Historic Places, 1993.

McDonnell, Janet A. "'Far-Reaching Effects': The United States Military and the National Parks during World War II." *George Wright Forum* 32, no. 1 (2015): 89–110.

McIntosh, Marjorie K. *Latinos of Boulder County, Colorado, 1900–1980.* Vol. 2, *History and Contributions.* Palm Springs, CA: Old John, 2016.

Meeker, Joseph W. "Red, White, and Black in the National Parks." *North American Review* 258, no. 3 (Fall 1973): 1–10.

Mellor, Don. *American Rock: Region, Rock, and Culture in American Climbing.* Woodstock, VT: Countryman Press, 2001.

Metcalf, Michael D., and Kevin D. Black. *Archaeological Excavations at the Yarmony Pit House Site, Eagle County, Colorado.* Cultural Resource Series No. 31. Colorado: Bureau of Land Management, U.S. Department of the Interior, 1991.

Miller, Susan A. *Growing Girls: The Natural Origins of Girls' Organizations in America.* New Brunswick, NJ: Rutgers University Press, 2007.

Miller, Susan Cummins, ed. *A Sweet, Separate Intimacy: Women Writers of the American Frontier, 1800–1922.* Salt Lake City: University of Utah Press, 2000.

Mills, Elizabeth, and Eryn Mills, eds. *Genuine Sympathy.* Longs Peak, CO: Temporal Mechanical Press, 1999.

Mills, Enos Abijah. *The Adventures of a Nature Guide.* Garden City, NY: Doubleday, Page, 1920.

———. *Bird Memories of the Rockies.* New York: Houghton Mifflin, 1931.

———. *Cricket, a Mountain Pony.* Estes Park, CO: Temporal Mechanical Press, 2002.

———. *Early Estes Park.* 2nd ed. Estes Park, CO: Esther B. Mills, 1963.

———. *Enos Mills Correspondence from the Papers of J. Horace McFarland, dated July 12, 1910, to July 9, 1915.* Harrisburg: Pennsylvania State Museum, 2003.

———. *In Beaver World.* New York: Houghton Mifflin, 1913.

———. *The Rocky Mountain National Park.* Memorial ed. New York: Doubleday, Page, 1924.

———. *The Rocky Mountain Wonderland.* Boston: Houghton Mifflin, 1915.

———. *The Spell of the Rockies.* New York: Houghton Mifflin, 1911.

———. *The Story of Estes Park.* 3rd ed. Estes Park, CO: Enos Mills, 1914.

———. *The Story of Estes Park and a Guide Book.* Denver: Outdoor Life, 1905.

———. *The Story of Estes Park, Grand Lake and Rocky Mountain National Park.* 4th ed. Estes Park, CO: Enos Mills, 1917.

———. *The Story of a Thousand-Year Pine.* New York: Houghton Mifflin, 1914.

———. *Wild Life on the Rockies.* Boston: Houghton Mifflin, 1924.

———. *Your National Parks.* New York: Houghton Mifflin, 1917.

Mills, Enos Abijah, Esther Burnell Mills, and Arthur Chapman. *The Story of Longs Peak Inn.* Longs Peak, CO: Mrs. Enos A. Mills, 1930s.

Mills, Esther Burnell. *A Baby's Life in the Rocky Mountains.* Estes Park, CO: Temporal Mechanical Press, 1999.

Mills, Joe. *A Mountain Boyhood.* Lincoln: University of Nebraska Press, 1988.

Miner, Joshua L., and Joe Boldt. *Outward Bound U.S.A.: Learning through Experience in Adventure-Based Education.* New York: William Morrow, 1981.

Mittlefehldt, Sarah. *Tangled Roots: The Appalachian Trail and American Environmental Politics.* Seattle: University of Washington Press, 2016.

Moomaw, Jack C. *Recollections of a Rocky Mountain Ranger.* Estes Park, CO: YMCA of the Rockies, 2001.

Morath, Sarah J. "A Park for Everyone: The National Park Service in Urban America." *Natural Resources Journal* 56, no. 1 (2016): 1–21.

Mott, Emily. "Mind the Gap: How to Promote Racial Diversity among National Park Visitors." *Vermont Journal of Environmental Law* 17, no. 3 (2016): 443–69.

Murray, Alice Yang. *Historical Memories of the Japanese American Internment and the Struggle for Redress.* Stanford, CA: Stanford University Press, 2008.

Musil, Robert K. *Rachel Carson and Her Sisters: Extraordinary Women Who Have Shaped America's Environment.* New Brunswick, NJ: Rutgers University Press, 2014.

Musselman, Lloyd K. *Rocky Mountain National Park: Administrative History.* Washington, DC: U.S. Office of History and Historic Architecture, Eastern Service Center, 1971.

Nagel, William B. *Colorado Front Range High Trail Map: Mt. Evans to Longs Peak* [map]. 2nd ed. Denver: Colorado Mountain Club, 1935.

National Parks Conservation Association. *State of the Parks, a Resource Assessment: Rocky Mountain National Park.* Fort Collins, CO: National Parks Conservation Association, 2002.

Nesbit, Paul. *Longs Peak: Its Story and a Climbing Guide.* 12th ed. Revised and updated by Stan Adamson. Broomfield, CO: Grey Wolf Books, 2015. 11th ed., 2005.

Neverdon-Morton, Cynthia. *Finding History's Forgotten People: The Presence of African Americans in Colorado, c. 1534 to 1954.* Denver: Bureau of Land Management, U.S. Department of the Interior, 2008.

Newman, Louise Michele. *White Women's Rights: The Racial Origins of Feminism in the United States.* New York: Oxford University Press, 1999.

Newsum, Dani, Ming Vlasich, Zach Crandall, and Odette Edbrooke. *Lincoln Hills and Civil Rights in Colorado.* Report funded by the Institute of Museum and Library Sciences, n.d. https://www.historycolorado.org/sites/default/files/media/document/2018/lincoln_hills_primary_resource_set.pdf.

O'Brien, William E. "State Parks and Jim Crow in the Decade before *Brown v. Board of Education.*" *Geographical Review* 102, no. 2 (April 2012): 166–79.

Olmanson, Eric D. *The Future City and the Inland Sea: A History of Imaginative Geographies of Lake Superior.* Athens: University of Ohio Press, 2007.

Olmsted, Frederick Law. *The Papers of Frederick Law Olmsted.* Vol. 2, *Slavery and the South, 1852–1857.* Edited by Charles E. Beveridge, Charles Capen McLaughlin, and David Schuyler. Baltimore: Johns Hopkins University Press, 1981.

Olson, Sigurd F. "Spiritual Aspects of Wilderness." In *The Meaning of Wilderness: Essential Articles and Speeches*, edited and with an introduction by David Backes, 108–19. Minneapolis: University of Minnesota Press, 2001.

Omi, Michael, and Howard Winant. *Racial Formation in the United States.* New York: Routledge, 2014.

Oreskes, Naomi, and Erik M. Conway. *Merchants of Doubt: How a Handful of Scientists Obscured the Truth on Issues from Tobacco Smoke to Global Warming.* New York: Bloomsbury Press, 2010.

Packard, Fred Mallery. "An Ecological Study of the Bighorn Sheep in Rocky Mountain National Park, Colorado." *Journal of Mammalogy* 27, no. 1 (February 1946): 3–28.

———. "A Study of the Deer and Elk Herds of Rocky Mountain National Park, Colorado." *Journal of Mammalogy* 28, no. 1 (February 1947): 4–12.

Papadogiannaki, Eleonora, Yen Le, and Steven J. Hollenhorst. *Rocky Mountain National Park, Visitor Study: Winter 2011.* Fort Collins, CO: National Park Service, U.S. Department of the Interior, 2011.

Paris, Leslie. *Children's Nature: The Rise of the American Summer Camp.* New York: New York University Press, 2008.

Parnell, Jane. *Off Trail: Finding My Way Home in the Colorado Rockies.* Norman: University of Oklahoma Press, 2018.

Parsons, Brinkerhoff, Quade, and Douglas, Inc. *Rocky Mountain National Park Transportation Study: Summary Report.* U.S. Department of the Interior, National Park Service, Rocky Mountain National Park, August 29, 2000.

Pendersen, Henry F. *Those Castles of Wood: The Story of the Early Lodges of Rocky Mountain National Park and Pioneer Days of Estes Park, Colorado.* Estes Park, CO: H. F. Pendersen, 1993.

Perkins, Matt. "Rock Climbing Ethics: A Historical Perspective." *Northwest Mountaineering Journal*, no. 2 (2002). Accessed December 27, 2021. Part 1, http://www.alpenglow.org/nwmj/05/051_Ethics.html. Part 2, http://www.alpenglow.org/nwmj/05/051_Ethics2.html.

Perry, Phyllis J. *It Happened in Rocky Mountain National Park.* Guilford, CT: TwoDot, 2008.

Pettebone, David. "Methods to Quantify Recreation Impacts along the Glacier Gorge Trail in Rocky Mountain National Park." Master's thesis, Colorado State University, 2006.

Phillips, Sarah T. *This Land, This Nation: Conservation, Rural America, and the New Deal.* Cambridge: Cambridge University Press, 2007.

Philpott, William. *Vacationland: Tourism and Environment in the Colorado High Country.* Seattle: University of Washington Press, 2013.

Pickering, James H. *America's Switzerland: Estes Park and Rocky Mountain National Park, the Growth Years.* Boulder: University Press of Colorado, 2005.

———, ed. *Early Estes Park Narratives.* Vol. 3, *Days and Hours of Estes Park (1912–1944): The Journal of Charles Edwin Hewes.* Estes Park, CO: Alpenaire, 2004.

————. *Enos Mills' Colorado.* Boulder, CO: Johnson Books, 2005.

————. "Exploring and Mapping Wild Basin: William Skinner Cooper's 1908 Account." *Colorado Heritage* 2 (1989): 34–46.

————, ed. *Frederick Chapin's Colorado: The Peaks about Estes Park and Other Writings.* Niwot: University Press of Colorado, 1995.

————, ed. *Historical Literature of Estes Park: Early Estes Park Narratives.* Vols. 1 and 2. Estes Park, CO: Alpenaire, 2004.

————. *In the Vale of Elkanah: The Tahosa Valley World of Charles Edwin Hewes.* Estes Park, CO: Alpenaire, in cooperation with Estes Park Area Historical Museum, 2003.

————. *"This Blue Hollow": Estes Park, the Early Years, 1859–1915.* Niwot: University Press of Colorado, 1999.

————. "Tragedy on Longs Peak: Walter Kiener's Own Story." *Colorado Heritage* 1 (1990): 18–31.

————. *The Ways of the Mountains: Thornton Sampson, Agnes Vaille, and Other Tragedies in High Places.* Estes Park, CO: Alpenaire, in cooperation with Estes Park Area Historical Museum, 2003.

Pickering, James H., and Carey Stevanus. *Estes Park and Rocky Mountain National Park Then and Now.* Englewood, CO: Westcliffe, 2006.

Pillen, Cory. "See America: WPA Posters and the Mapping of a New Deal Democracy." *Journal of American Culture* 31, no. 1 (2008): 49–65.

Porter, Eliot. *In Wildness Is the Preservation of the World.* San Francisco: Sierra Club, 1962.

Prosser, Glenn. *The Saga of Black Canyon: The Story of the MacGregors of Estes Park.* Self-published, Estes Park, CO, 1971.

Putney, Clifford. *Muscular Christianity: Manhood and Sports in Protestant America, 1880–1920.* Cambridge, MA: Harvard University Press, 2001.

Quin, Richard H. *Rocky Mountain National Park Roads: Written Historical and Descriptive Data.* Historic American Engineering Record No. CO-78. Washington, DC: U.S. Department of the Interior, 1993.

Ramsey, Jane. *Early Estes Park Artists, 1870–1970.* Estes Park, CO: Alpenaire, 2005.

Randall, Glenn. *Longs Peak Tales: Adventure Tales on One of America's Greatest Mountains.* Boulder, CO: Stonehenge Books, 1981.

Raney, Patricia, and Janet Robertson. *Rocky Mountain Rustic: Historic Buildings of the Rocky Mountain National Park Area.* Estes Park, CO: Lindberg, Raney, and Robertson, 2004.

Reid, Ira De Augustine. *The Negro Population in Denver, Colorado: A Survey of Its Economic and Social Status.* Denver: Lincoln Press, 1929.

Reynolds, John J. "Whose America? Whose Idea? Making 'America's Best Idea' Reflect New American Realities." *George Wright Forum* 27, no. 2 (2010): 125–34.

Richardson, Heather Cox. *How the South Won the Civil War: Oligarchy, Democracy, and the Continuing Fight for the Soul of America.* New York: Oxford University Press, 2020.

Richmond, Gerald Martin. *Raising the Roof of the Rockies: A Geological History of the Mountains and of the Ice Age in the Rocky Mountain National Park.* Denver: Rocky Mountain Nature Association, 1974.

Roach, Gerry. *Colorado's Fourteeners: From Hikes to Climbs.* 2nd ed. Golden, CO: Fulcrum, 1999.

Roberts, Nina. "Ethnic Minority Visitors and Non-Visitors: An Examination of Constraints Regarding Outdoor Recreation Participation in Rocky Mountain National Park." PhD diss., Colorado State University, 2003.

Robertson, Janet. *The Magnificent Mountain Women: Adventures in the Colorado Rockies.* Lincoln: University of Nebraska Press, 1990.

Robertson, Janet Neuhoff, James E. Fell Jr., David Hite, Christopher J. Case, and Walter R. Borneman. *100 Years Up High: Colorado Mountains and Mountaineers.* Golden: Colorado Mountain Club Press, 2012.

Rodnitzky, Jerome L. "Recapturing the West: The Dude Ranch in American Life." *Arizona and the West / Journal of the Southwest* 10, no. 2 (Summer 1968): 111–26.

Rome, Adam. *The Bulldozer in the Countryside: Suburban Sprawl and the Rise of American Environmentalism.* New York: Cambridge University Press, 2001.

Ross-Bryant, Lynn. *Pilgrimage to the National Parks: Religion and Nature in the United States.* New York: Routledge, 2013.

Rossiter, Richard. *Rocky Mountain National Park: A Comprehensive Guide to Scrambles, Rock Routes, and Ice/Mixed Climbs on the High Peaks.* Boulder, CO: Fixed Pin, 2015.

Rothman, Hal. *Devil's Bargains: Tourism in the Twentieth-Century American West.* Lawrence: University Press of Kansas, 1998.

Rothstein, Richard. *The Color of Law: A Forgotten History of How Our Government Segregated America.* New York: Liveright, 2017.

Rugh, Susan Sessions. *Are We There Yet? The Golden Age of American Family Vacations.* Lawrence: University Press of Kansas, 2008.

Runte, Alfred. *National Parks: The American Experience.* 4th ed. Lanham, MD: Taylor Trade Publishing, 2010.

Sale, Kirkpatrick. *The Green Revolution: The American Environmental Movement, 1962–1992.* New York: Hill and Wang, 1993.

Sanchez, George J. "Face the Nation: Race, Immigration, and the Rise of Nativism in Late Twentieth Century America." *International Migration Review* 31, no. 4 (1997): 1009–30.

Sargent, Shirley. *Pioneers in Petticoats: Yosemite's Early Women, 1856–1900.* Los Angeles: Trans-Anglo Books, 1996.

Sauvajot, Raymond M. "National Parks and the Scaling Up Imperative." *George Wright Forum* 33, no. 2 (2016): 145–48.

Sayre, Gordon. "Urban Climbers in the Wilderness: Mounts Hood, Rainier, and Shasta and the History of Popular Mountaineering." In *Imagining the Big Open: Nature, Identity, and Play in the New West*, edited by Liza Nicholas, Elaine M. Bapis, and Thomas J. Harvey, 92–110. Salt Lake City: University of Utah Press, 2003.

Scharff, Virginia J. *Seeing Nature through Gender.* Lawrence: University Press of Kansas, 2003.

Schrepfer, Susan R. *Nature's Altars: Mountains, Gender, and American Environmentalism.* Lawrence: University Press of Kansas, 2005.

Schulte, Steven C. *Wayne Aspinall and the Shaping of the American West.* Boulder: University Press of Colorado, 2002.

Schultz, Courtney L., Jason N. Bocarro, KangJae Jerry Lee, Aby Sene-Harper, Mickey Fearn, and Myron F. Floyd. "Whose National Park Service? An Examination of Relevancy, Diversity, and Inclusion Programs from 2005–2016." *Journal of Park and Recreation Administration* 37, no. 4 (Winter 2019): 51–69.

Schuster, Elke, S. Shea Johnson, and Jonathan G. Taylor. *Wilderness Experience in Rocky Mountain National Park 2002: Report to Respondents.* Fort Collins, CO: Fort Collins Science Center, U.S. Geological Survey, 2003.

Scott, David, and KangJae Jerry Lee. "People of Color and Their Constraints to National Parks Visitation." *George Wright Forum* 35, no. 1 (2018): 73–82.

Sears, John F. *Sacred Places: American Tourist Attractions in the Nineteenth Century.* New York: Oxford University Press, 1989.

Seiler, Cotten. "'So That We as a Race Might Have Something Authentic to Travel By': African American Automobility and Cold-War Liberalism." *American Quarterly* 58, no. 4 (December 2006): 1091–117.

Sellars, Richard W. *Preserving Nature in the National Parks: A History.* 2nd ed. New Haven, CT: Yale University Press, 2009.

Shafer, Craig L. "Conservation Biology Trailblazers: George Wright, Ben Thompson, and Joseph Dixon." *Conservation Biology* 15, no. 2 (April 2001): 332–44.

———. "The Rise, Fall, and Legacy of Part Two of the National Park System Plan: Natural History." *George Wright Forum* 33, no. 1 (2016): 29–46.

Shaffer, Marguerite S. *See America First: Tourism and National Identity, 1880–1940.* Washington, DC: Smithsonian Institution Press, 2001.

Shellenbarger, Melanie. *High Country Summers: The Early Second Homes of Colorado, 1880–1940.* Tucson: University of Arizona Press, 2012.

Shoemaker, John. "The Mountains Are Calling, but Who's Picking Up? Exploring Diversity in Rocky Mountain National Park." 2019. Regis University Student Publications, 934. https://epublications.regis.edu/theses/934.

Simmons, Thomas H., and R. Laurie Simmons. "Wink's Panorama." National Historic Landmark nomination. National Park Service, 2021.

Simon, Gregory L., and Peter S. Alagona. "Beyond Leave No Trace Ethics." *Place and Environment* 12, no. 1 (2009): 17–34.

Sitkoff, Harvard. *The Struggle for Black Equality.* Rev. ed. New York: Hill and Wang, 2008.

Slotkin, Richard. *Gunfighter Nation: The Myth of the Frontier in Twentieth-Century America.* New York: Atheneum, 1992.

Smith, Cyndi. *Off the Beaten Track: Women Adventurers and Mountaineers in Western Canada.* Jasper, AB: Coyote Books, 1989.

Smith, Rogers M. *Civic Ideals: Conflicting Visions of Citizenship in U.S. History.* New Haven, CT: Yale University Press, 1997.

Sorin, Gretchen Sullivan. *Driving while Black: African American Travel and the Road to Civil Rights.* New York: Liveright, 2020.

Spears, Betty. *Added* "Mary, Mary, Quite Contrary, Why Do Women Play?" *Canadian Journal of History of Sport* 1 (1987): 1867–75.

Spence, Mark David. *Dispossessing the Wilderness: Indian Removal and the Making of the National Parks.* New York: Oxford University Press, 1999.

Sprague, Abner. *My Pioneer Life: The Memoirs of Abner E. Sprague.* Estes Park, CO: Rocky Mountain Nature Association, 1999.

Standish, Sierra. "East Longs Peak Trail." National Register of Historic Places registration form. Washington, DC: U.S. Department of the Interior, National Park Service, 2007.

Stanfield McCown, Rebecca. "Evaluation of National Park Service 21st Century Relevancy Initiatives: Case Studies Addressing Racial and Ethnic Diversity in the National Park Service." PhD diss., University of Vermont, 2011.

Stauffer, Ruth. *Historical Vignettes of Early Days in Estes Park.* Estes Park, CO: Estes Park Area Historical Museum, 1976.

Stern, Arthur C. "History of Air Pollution Legislation in the United States." *Journal of the Air Pollution Control Association* 32, no. 1 (January 1982): 44–61.

Sterngrass, Jon. *First Resorts: Pursuing Pleasure at Saratoga Springs, Newport, and Coney Island.* Baltimore: Johns Hopkins University Press, 2001.

Stevens, Stan, ed. *Indigenous Peoples, National Parks, and Protected Areas: A New Paradigm Linking Culture, Conservation, and Rights.* Tucson: University of Arizona Press, 2014.

Stewart, Mart A. *"What Nature Suffers to Groe": Life, Labor, and Landscape on the Georgia Coast.* Athens: University of Georgia Press, 2002.

Stodolska, Monika, Kimberly J. Shinew, Myron F. Floyd, and Gordon J. Walker, eds. *Race, Ethnicity, and Leisure: Perspectives on Research, Theory, and Practice.* Champaign, IL: Human Kinetics, 2014.

Stradling, David. *Making Mountains: New York City and the Catskills.* Seattle: University of Washington Press, 2007.

Sutter, Paul S. *Driven Wild: How the Fight against Automobiles Launched the Modern Wilderness Movement.* Seattle: University of Washington Press, 2002.

Svonkin, Stuart. *Jews against Prejudice: American Jews and the Fight for Civil Liberties.* New York: Columbia University Press, 1997.

Swain, Donald C. "The National Park Service and the New Deal, 1933–1940." *Pacific Historical Review* 41, no. 3 (August 1972): 312–32.

Taylor, Candacy. *Overground Railroad: The Green Book and the Roots of Black Travel in America.* New York: Abrams Press, 2020.

Taylor, Joseph E., III. *Pilgrims of the Vertical: Yosemite Rock Climbers and Nature at Risk.* Cambridge, MA: Harvard University Press, 2010.

Taylor, Patricia, and Burke Grandjean. "Visitor Satisfaction along the Highway 7 Corridor to Rocky Mountain National Park." Unpublished technical report, 2006. https://irma.nps.gov/Datastore/Reference/Profile/2181952.

Taylor, Patricia, Burke D. Grandjean, and James H. Gramann. *National Park Service Comprehensive Survey of the American Public, 2008–2009: Racial and Ethnic Diversity of National Park System Visitors and Non-Visitors.* Natural Resource Report. NPS/NRSS/SSD/NRR—2011/432. Fort Collins, CO: National Park Service, 2011.

Taylor, Quintard. *In Search of the Racial Frontier: African Americans in the American West, 1528–1990.* New York: Norton, 1998.

Thakar, Nidhi, Claire Moser, and Laura E. Durso. "Building a More Inclusive National Park System for All Americans." Center for American Progress, June 24, 2015. Accessed December 18, 2021. https://cdn.americanprogress.org/wp-content/uploads/2015/06/DiversityNPS-brief1.pdf.

Theoharis, Jeanne, and Komozi Woodard, eds. *Freedom North: Black Freedom Struggles Outside the South, 1940–1980*. New York: Palgrave Macmillan, 2003.

Tice, John H. *Over the Plains and on the Mountains, or Kansas and Colorado Agriculturally, Mineralogically and Aesthetically*. Chicago: Westerns News, 1872.

Toll, Oliver W. *Arapaho Names and Trails: A Report of a 1914 Pack Trip*. Estes Park, CO: Rocky Mountain Nature Association, 2003.

Toll, Roger W., comp., and Robert Sterling Yard, ed. *Mountaineering in the Rocky Mountain National Park*. Washington, DC: National Park Service, U.S. Department of the Interior, Government Printing Office, 1919.

———. *The Mountain Peaks of Colorado, Containing a List of Named Points of Elevation in the State of Colorado with Elevations and Topographic Details*. Denver: Colorado Mountain Club, 1923.

Trahan, Richard G. "Day-Use Limitation in National Parks: Visitor and Park Personnel Attitudes toward Day-Use Limitation Systems for Rocky Mountain National Park." University of Northern Colorado, 1977. ROMO Library.

———. "Social Science Research: Rocky Mountain National Park." University of Northern Colorado, 1978. ROMO Library.

Trahan, Richard G., and Karen M. Jennison. "Perceptions of Day Hikers toward the National Park Environment." University of Northern Colorado, 1976. ROMO Library.

Trimble, Stephen. *Longs Peak: A Rocky Mountain Chronicle*. Estes Park, CO: Rocky Mountain Nature Association, 1984.

Tuler, Seth, and Dominic Golding. *A Comprehensive Study of Visitor Safety in the National Park System: Final Report*. Worcester, MA: George Perkins Marsh Institute, Clark University, 2002.

Turner, James Morton. "From Woodcraft to 'Leave no Trace': Wilderness, Consumerism, and Environmentalism in Twentieth Century America." *Journal of Environmental History* 7, no. 3 (July 2002): 462–84.

———. "'The Specter of Environmentalism': Wilderness, Environmental Politics, and the Evolution of the New Right." *Journal of American History* 96, no. 1 (2009): 123–48.

Ullman, James Ramsey. *The Age of Mountaineering*. Philadelphia: J. B. Lippincott, 1954.

Union Pacific System. *Colorado Mountain Playgrounds*. Omaha, NE: W. H. Murray, 1925.

Unrau, Harlan D., and G. Frank Williss. *Expansion of the National Park Service in the 1930s: An Administrative History*. Denver: National Park Service, Denver Service Center, 1983.

URS Co. *Rocky Mountain National Park Transportation Study: Phase II Draft Report*. 1975. ROMO Library.

Valandra, Edward Charles. *Not without Our Consent: Lakota Resistance to Termination, 1950–1959*. Champaign: University of Illinois Press, 2006.

Vandersall, Ray. "Building the View: Trail Ridge Road in Rocky Mountain National Park." Master's thesis, University of Wyoming, 2004.

Vargas, Zaragosa. *Crucible of Struggle: A History of Mexican Americans from Colonial Times to the Present Era*. New York: Oxford University Press, 2011.

Vaske, Jerry J., and Katie M. Lyon. *Linking the 2010 Census to National Park Visitors.* Natural Resource Technical Report NPS/WASO/NRTR—2014/880. Fort Collins, CO: National Park Service, 2014.

Wall, Sharon. *The Nurture of Nature: Childhood, Antimodernism, and Ontario Summer Camps, 1920–1955.* Vancouver: University of British Columbia Press, 2009.

Ward, Colin, and Dennis Hardy. *Goodnight Campers! The History of the British Holiday Camp.* London: Mansell, 1986.

Warren, Louis S. *The Hunter's Game: Poachers and Conservationists in Twentieth Century America.* New Haven, CT: Yale University Press, 1997.

Wasinger, Holly. "From Five Points to Struggle Hill: The Race Line and Segregation in Denver." *Colorado Heritage,* Autumn 2005, 28–39.

Weber, Joe, and Selima Sultana. "Why Do So Few Minority People Visit National Parks? Visitation and the Accessibility of 'America's Best Idea.'" *Annals of the Association of American Geographers* 103, no. 3 (2013): 437–64.

Weinbaum, Alexandra, Lynn Gregory, Alex Wilkie, Lesley Hirsch, and Cheri Fancsali. *Expeditionary Learning Outward Bound, Summary Report.* New York: Academy for Educational Development, 1996.

Weiss, Jessica. *To Have and to Hold: Marriage, the Baby Boom, and Social Change.* Chicago: University of Chicago Press, 2000.

Wells, Christopher. *Car Country: An Environmental History.* Seattle: University of Washington Press, 2014.

West, Elliott. *The Contested Plains: Indians, Goldseekers, and the Rush to Colorado.* Lawrence: University Press of Kansas, 1998.

Wexler, Arnold. "The Theory of Belaying." *American Alpine Journal* 7, no. 4 (1950): 380–404.

Whitaker, Matthew C. *Race Work: The Rise of Civil Rights in the Urban West.* Lincoln: University of Nebraska Press, 2005.

Whiteley, Lee, and Jane Whiteley. *The Playground Trail: The National Park to Park Highway; To and through the National Parks of the West in 1920.* Boulder, CO: Johnson, 2003.

Willard, Beatrice E., David J. Cooper, and Bruce C. Forbes. "Natural Regeneration of Alpine Tundra Vegetation after Human Trampling: A 42-Year Data Set from Rocky Mountain National Park, Colorado, U.S.A." *Arctic, Antarctic, and Alpine Research* 39, no. 1 (2007): 177–83.

Willard, James F. "Evans and the Saint Louis Western Colony." *Trail* 11, no. 10 (March 1919): 5–11.

Williams, Chad L. *Torchbearers of Democracy: African American Soldiers in the World War I Era.* Chapel Hill: University of North Carolina Press, 2010.

Williams, Chris. "'That Boundless Ocean of Mountains': British Alpinists and the Appeal of the Canadian Rockies, 1885–1920." *International Journal of the History of Sport* 22, no. 1 (2005): 70–87.

Williams, Cicely D. *Women on the Rope: The Feminine Share in Mountain Adventure.* London: George Allen and Unwin, 1973.

Wirth, Conrad L. "National Parks." In *First World Conference on National Parks, Proceedings,* edited by Alexander B. Adams, 13–21. Washington, DC: National Park Service, U.S. Department of the Interior, 1962.

Wolcott, Victoria W. *Race, Riots, and Rollercoasters: The Struggle over Segregated Recreation in America.* Philadelphia: University of Pennsylvania Press, 2012.

Worster, Donald. *A Passion for Nature: The Life of John Muir.* New York: Oxford University Press, 2008.

Wray, Jacilee, Alexa Roberts, Allison Peña, and Shirley J. Fiske. "Creating Policy for the National Park Service: Addressing Native Americans and Other Traditionally Associated Peoples." *George Wright Forum* 26, no. 3 (2009): 43–50.

Wright, George M., Joseph S. Dixon, and Ben H. Thompson. *Fauna of the National Parks of the United States: A Preliminary Survey of Faunal Relations in National Parks.* Fauna Series No. 1. Washington, DC: U.S. Government Printing Office, 1933.

———. *Fauna of the National Parks of the United States: Wildlife Management in the National Parks.* Fauna Series No. 2. Washington, DC: U.S. Government Printing Office, 1935.

Wynn, Neil. *The African American Experience during World War II.* Lanham, MD: Rowman and Littlefield, 2010.

Young, Terence. "'A Contradiction in Democratic Government': W. J. Trent, Jr., and the Struggle to Desegregate National Park Campgrounds." *Environmental History* 14, no. 4 (October 2009): 651–82.

———. *Heading Out: A History of American Camping.* Ithaca, NY: Cornell University Press, 2017.

Zheng, Christopher. "31 Years of NAGPRA: Evaluating the Restitution of Native American Ancestral Remains and Belongings." Center for Art Law, May 15, 2018. Accessed January 23, 2022. https://itsartlaw.org/2021/05/18/31-years-of-nagpra/.

Zietkiewicz, Susan Q. "Nature's Playground: An Environmental History of Early Estes Park." Master's thesis, Colorado State University, 2001.

GOVERNMENT AND ADVISORY BOARD PUBLICATIONS

NPS (National Park Service, U.S. Department of the Interior). *America's Great Outdoors: A Promise to Future Generations.* 2011.

———. *Board of Review Report for the Ouzel Fire, Rocky Mountain National Park.* Denver: National Park Service, Rocky Mountain Region, 1979.

———. *A Call to Action: Preparing for a Second Century of Stewardship and Engagement.* Washington, DC: National Park Service, 2015.

———. *Circular of General Information Regarding Rocky Mountain National Park, Colorado.* Washington, DC: U.S. Government Printing Office, 1931.

———. *Climate Change Response Strategy, September 2010.* Washington, DC: National Park Service, 2010.

———. Director's Orders. "Director's Orders and Related Documents." Accessed February 17, 2022. https://www.nps.gov/policy/DOrders.cfm/.

———. *Economic Feasibility Study Concessions Operation: Ski Estes Park, Hidden Valley, Rocky Mountain National Park, Estes Park, Colorado.* Denver: National Park Service, Denver Service Center, Professional Support Division, Concessions Branch, 1989.

———. *Foundation Document: Rocky Mountain National Park, Colorado.* Washington, DC: U.S. Government Printing Office, May 2013.

―――. *The Future of America's National Parks: National Park Service Centennial Initiative 2008 Progress Report*. Washington, DC: U.S. Government Printing Office, 2009.

―――. *General Information Regarding Rocky Mountain National Park, Season of 1918*. Washington, DC: General Printing Office, 1918.

―――. *Management Policies 2006*. Washington, DC: U.S. Government Printing Office, 2006. https://www.nps.gov/subjects/policy/upload/MP_2006.pdf.

―――. "Mission 66 for the National Park System." Typescript report, February 1, 1956. Accessed January 17, 2022. http://npshistory.com/publications/mission66 /park-system.pdf.

―――. *Mission 66: Our Heritage: A Plan for Its Protection and Use*. Washington, DC: U.S. Government Printing Office, 1956.

―――. *Motorists Guide: Rocky Mountain National Park, 1938*. U.S. Geological Survey, 1938.

―――. *Planning for a Changing Climate: Climate-Smart Planning and Management in the National Park Service*. Fort Collins, CO: NPS Climate Change Response Program, 2021. https://irma.nps.gov/DataStore/Reference/Profile/2279647.

―――. *Rocky Mountain National Park Backcountry Management Plan*. Estes Park, CO, 1984.

―――. *Rocky Mountain National Park, Colorado*. Washington, DC: U.S. Government Printing Office, 1937.

―――. *Rocky Mountain National Park, Colorado*. Revised. Washington, DC, 1963.

―――. *Rocky Mountain National Park: Final Master Plan*. Denver: Denver Service Center, 1976.

―――. *Rules and Regulations, Rocky Mountain National Park, 1920*. Washington, DC: U.S. Government Printing Office, 1920. [Most ROMO brochures may be viewed at http://www.npshistory.com/publications/romo/index.htm#brochures.]

―――. *Statement for Management*. Estes Park, CO, June 1992.

―――. *A Study of the Park and Recreation Problem of the United States*. Washington, DC: U.S. Government Printing Office, 1941.

―――. *Trails Plan: Rocky Mountain National Park*. Denver: Denver Service Center, 1982.

―――. *Urban Agenda: Call to Action Initiative*. Washington, DC: National Park Service, 2015. https://www.nps.gov/subjects/urban/upload/UrbanAgenda_web .pdf.

―――. *VERP: The Visitor Experience and Resource Protection (VERP) Framework: A Handbook for Planners and Managers*. Denver: Denver Service Center, 1997.

NPS Advisory Board. *Rethinking the National Parks for the 21st Century: A Report of the National Park System Advisory Board, July 2001*. Washington, DC: National Park Service, 2001.

NPS Advisory Board Science Committee. *Revisiting Leopold: Resource Stewardship in the National Parks*. Washington, DC: National Park System Advisory Board, 2012.

NPS, National Parks Second Century Commission. *Advancing the National Park Idea*. Washington, DC: National Parks Conservation Association, 2009.

NPS, Resource Systems Group, and Wyoming Survey and Analysis Center. *National Park Service Comprehensive Survey of the American Public: 2018—Racial and*

Ethnic Diversity of National Park System Visitors and Non-Visitors. Natural Resource Report NPS/NRSS/EQD/NRR—2019/2042. Fort Collins, CO: National Park Service, 2019.

NPS, Rocky Mountain Region. "Draft Environmental Assessment Management/ Development Concept Plan: Longs Peak/Wild Basin/Lily Lake." July 1994.

NPS, Wilderness Character Integration Team. *Wilderness Stewardship Plan Handbook, 2014.* Washington, DC: Wilderness Stewardship Program, 2014.

U.S. Congress. *Hearing Before the Committee on the Public Lands on S. 6309, a Bill to Establish the Rocky Mountain National Park in the State of Colorado,* December 23, 30, 1914, and January 9, 1915. House of Representatives, 63rd Cong., 3rd Sess. Washington, DC: U.S. Government Printing Office, 1915.

U.S. Department of the Interior. *The Rocky Mountain National Park.* New York: Charles Scribner's Sons, 1916.

U.S. Geological Survey (U.S. Department of the Interior) and Natural Resources Ecology Lab, Colorado State University. *Ecological Evaluation of the Abundance and Effect of Elk Herbivory in Rocky Mountain National Park, Colorado, 1994–1999.* Open File Report 02–208. https://pubs.usgs.gov/of/2002/0208/report.pdf.

U.S. Railroad Administration (U.S. Department of the Interior). *Rocky Mountain National Park, Colorado.* Washington, DC: General Printing Office, National Park Series, 1919.

ORAL HISTORIES AND RECORDED PRESENTATIONS

Beard, Don. Transcript of Public Affairs Presentation to Superintendents Meeting, 1962. Museum Catalog no. ROMO-21369.

Borneman, Walt, and Marlene Borneman. Interview by Ruth Alexander, November 11, 2016. ROMO-01851, Longs Peak Oral Histories

Braly, Guy, and Glen Tallman. "Trail Ridge Road 50th Anniversary: Oral Interviews with Guy Braly and Glen Tallman on Construction Memories," 1982. Estes Park Area Historical Museum.

Caldwell, Mike. Interview by Ruth Alexander, August 12, 2009. ROMO-01851, Longs Peak Oral Histories.

Caldwell, Tommy. Interview by Ruth Alexander, August 12, 2009. ROMO-01851, Longs Peak Oral Histories.

Casey, Tom. Interview by Jim Lindberg, Joe Arnold, and Cheri Yost, April 14, 2004. Museum Catalog, ROMO Archives.

Cheri, Kevin. Interview by Lu Ann Jones, 2018. https://www.nps.gov/subjects /oralhistory/podcasts-episode-8.htm.

Collier, Robert, Jr. Interview by Merrill Mattes and Chet Harris, November 21, 1961. Transcript, Museum Catalog no. ROMO-21370.

Detterline, Jim. Interview by Bryon Hoerner, November 12, 2013. Estes Park Museum. https://ia601202.us.archive.org/15/items/JimDetterlineOhTranscript/jim %20detterline%20oh%20transcript.pdf.

Gordon, Jane. Interview by Ruth Alexander, July 30, 2009. ROMO-01851, Longs Peak Oral Histories.

Griffith, Dan. Interview by Ferrel Atkins, 1966. Estes Park Public Library.

Hartzog, George. Interview by Dorothy Collier, Radio KCOL, January 26, 1957. Transcript, ROMO Library.

Hornbein, Thomas. Interview by Ruth Alexander, October 28, 2016. ROMO-01851, Longs Peak Oral Histories.

Kamps, Bonnie. Interview by Ruth Alexander, August 26, 2009. ROMO-01851, Longs Peak Oral Histories,.

Longs Peak Reunion. Transcript of video recordings, 1991. Estes Park Museum.

Longs Peaks Reunion. Typescript of program, 1993. Estes Park Museum.

MacCracken, Richard. Oral history interview, 1959. Transcript, Estes Park Public Library.

Magnuson, Mark. Interview by Ruth Alexander, June 11, 2009. ROMO-01851, Longs Peak Oral Histories.

McLaren, Fred. Interview by Ferrel Atkins and Jim Larson, 1985. Estes Park Public Library.

Moomaw, Jack. Interview by William Ramaley, 1966. ROMO Library.

Peck, George, Jr. "Winter Sports in the Estes Park Area," 1984. Audiotape, Estes Park Public Library.

Rearick, Dave. Interview by Ruth Alexander, June 9, 2009. ROMO-01851, Longs Peak Oral Histories.

Reveley, Chris. Interview by Ruth Alexander, October 15, 2016. ROMO-01851, Longs Peak Oral Histories.

Robertson, Dave. Interview by Ruth Alexander, October 18, 2016. ROMO-01851, Longs Peak Oral Histories.

Robertson, Janet. "A Feminist's View of Long's Peak: Women's History Month Program," 1987. Sound recording, Estes Park Area Historical Museum.

———. Interview by Ruth Alexander, October 18, 2016. ROMO-01851, Longs Peak Oral Histories.

Seidel, Jacob. Interview by Ruth Alexander, August 13, 2021. Parks as Portals to Learning Oral Histories, ROMO.

Stanton, Robert G. Interview by Janet A. McDonnell, 2004. https://www.nps.gov/parkhistory/online_books/director/stanton.pdf.

Sturmer, Kevin. Interview by Ruth Alexander, October 18, 2016. ROMO-01851, Longs Peak Oral Histories.

INDEX

Italicized references indicate illustrations.

Armstrong, Cheryl, 204
Army, U.S. *See* U.S. Army
ascender devices, 158
aspen health, 200; elk and, 78, 82, 169, 200
Atlas of Colorado (1877), 19
Atwood, Stephanie, 182
Aubuchon, Gregory, 53
Austill, Anne Pfifer. *See* Pfifer, Anne and Isabel
automobile accidents, 79
automobile touring, 69; African Americans, 86, 143; early years, 30–31, 33, 34–35; Rocky Mountain NP, 192; statistics, 72; post–World War II, 123, 126–27, 133, 138, 141, 199

Bachar, Don, 183
Bachman, Don, 161–62
Baldwin, Ben, 226
Barnard, Emma, 39
Beard, Dan, 164
Bear Lake, 35, 133, 154, 221; ranger station, 244–45n66; shuttle to, 199
Bear Lake Road, 36, 46, 138; on map, *xx*
Bear Lake Trail School, 59
Bear Lodge (Wyo.), 211
Bears Ears National Monument, 211
Beaver Meadows, 78, 82, 133; visitor center, *116*, 133
Beckwourth Mountain Club. *See* James P. Beckwourth Mountain Club (BMC)
Bedayn, Raffi, 129
belaying, 51, 129, 151, 197, 210; failure, 65; Stettners, 61, 75
Bell, John, 16
Bendixon, Joan, 153
Beyer, Jim, 182
biosphere reserves, 180
Bird, Isabella, 20 21
bivouacs and bivouacking, 153, 193, 194, 197, 259n31; Broadway (ledge), 150–51, 181, 187, 194
Black Americans. *See* African Americans
Black Canyon of the Gunnison, 78, 183
Blaurock, Carl, 51, 52, 54, 62
blazes, 37
BMC. *See* James P. Beckwourth Mountain Club

bolts and bolting, 129–32, 151, 167–68, 183–87, 195, 196, 215–17, 258n16; *Cable* route, 56; hand-drilling, *120*; power drill use, 184, 195, 196
Borneman, Walter, *A Climbing Guide to Colorado's Fourteeners*, 184
Bosetti, Joseph, 63, 84
Bossier, Floyd "Tex," 157
Boucher, Bob, 157
Boulder, Colo., 144, 168, 174; climbers from, 153–54, 184; Colorado Guide Service, 157. *See also* University of Colorado
Boulder Climbing Community, 215
Boulderfield, 20, 22–23, *98*, *110*, 134; trails, 23, 56, 57, 73, 238n21
Boulderfield Shelter Cabin, 50–51, 57–61, 65–68, 73, 74, 81, *105*, 240n52; demolition, 83; guides, 58, 60, 68, 74, 76, 83; initial price of stay, 241n12; on map, *32*; telephone, 56, 57, 61, 134, 238n23
Bowles, Samuel, 18, 21
boys' summer camps. *See* summer camps, boys'
Brainard Lake, 74, 175
Briggs, Bill, 178, 184
Briggs, Roger, 157, 183, 187, 215
Broadway (ledge), 51, *101*, *118*, *122*; bivouacs, 150–51, 181, 187, 194; naming, 52
Brower, David, 140, 163, 164
Brown Girls Climb, 211–12
Brown v. Board of Education, 144–45
Brunswig, Robert, 223–24
Buhl, Clara, 52
Buhl, Hermann, 52, 57
Burnell, Elizabeth, 43–44
Burnell, Esther. *See* Mills, Esther Burnell
Butler, William, 57
Butts, David, 167
Byers, William N., 19–20

cabin shelters. *See* shelter cabins and emergency shelters
Cable route, 49, 50, 56–64, *104*, *107*, *117*, 131, 161–62; cable removal (1973), 187–88; cable removal recommendation (1967), 162, 176, 254n49; cable

154; founding, 234n13; fourteener supplement, 62; "hints for beginners," 91; memorial for Agnes Vaille, 55; Nold, 175; Reed, 159

trailhead register statistics, 189

trail markers, 37

Trail Ridge Road, 36, 46, 69, 71–72, 82, 192, 199; congestion, 127; environmental aspects, 139; on map, *xx*; Mission 66, 133–34; Rock Cut, *112*, 139; wayside parking construction, 76

trails, 37, 196; channeling of visitors, 192–93; maintenance and improvement, 33, 37, 56–57, 58, 59, 193; in park visitor guides, 72; user-created, 194. *See also* East Longs Peak Trail; North Longs Peak Trail

transmountain water tunnel, 79

transportation, 23, 24, 35. *See also* motor vehicles; roads

trash, 187, 188, 191, 193, 194

travel guides, African American, 86, 87, 144

Trough. See *Keyhole* route: Trough

Trowbridge, C. R., 36

Trump, Donald, 218, 219–20

Turner, James Morton, 10, 191

Twin Sisters Peak, *103*, *121*

Udall, Stewart, 171

UNESCO biosphere reserves. *See* biosphere reserves

University of Colorado, 174, 224; Rearick, 154

Urban Agenda (NPS), 226

urban youth, 173–74, 175, 203, 204

U.S. Army: Indian removals, 18; post–Civil War western expeditions, 19; World War II mountaineering, 89, 128

U.S. Forest Service, 26, 29, 139, 140, 169, 191, 217

U.S. Geological Survey, 220

Utes, 14, 17, 18, 87, 145, 206, 224

Vaille, Agnes Wolcott, 49, 52, 53–55, 58, *102*; peak bagging, 62

Vaille, Harriet, 27

Vaille Shelter. *See* Agnes Vaille Shelter

vandalism, 91

Van Diver, Brad, *111*, 129

visitor brochures, 69, 72, 126, 127, 157, 185

visitor centers, *116*, 133, 141, 223

visual intrusions, 196

Wagar, John V. K., 87–89

Walker, Kris, 182

War on Poverty, 148, 172, 176

waste, 187, 191, 196; collection and treatment, 76, *119*, 167, 193; disposal, 66, 83, 166, 193, 214; water contamination, 194, 196. *See also* toilets; trash

Waterhole #3 route, 182

water tunnel, transmountain, 79

Watson, Edwin, 76, 79–80

Way, L. Claude, 36, 37

weddings on Longs Peak, 59

Weidner, Chris, 209

Wentzel, Helene, 73–74

Westbay, Billy, 183

Westbrook, J. H. P., 64

Wharton, John, 154, 155

wilderness, 164–65, 185–97, 219

Wilderness Act, 159, 165, 167, 179, 185–86, 188, 217, 258–59n26

Wilderness Society, 191, 212

wildfires, 200, 228; CCC firefighting, 76; fire lookouts, *103*; suppression of, 47, 78, 139, 169, 180, 199–200

wildflowers, 45, 190

wildlife, 30, 77–79, 83, 91, 138–39, 196; habitat disturbance, 47; predator eradication and loss, 46, 70, 78, 85, 218–19; restoration, 199; studies and reports (1970–2000), 198, 199, 219. *See also* elk; raptors

Wildlife Management in the National Parks: The Leopold Report (Leopold), 198, 219

Willard, Beatrice, 139, 166

Willmon, Prince, 153

willows, 169, 200, 221

Window route, *122*, 129

Wind River Reservation, 18, 27, *97*

winter climbing, 52–53, 57, *102*, 157

winter recreation, 79, 82, 139. *See also* skiing

Wirth, Conrad L., 124, 132, 139, 171